McDougal Littell

Geometry

Larson Boswell Kanold Stiff

Notetaking Guide

The Notetaking Guide contains a lesson-by-lesson framework that allows students to take notes on and review the main concepts of each lesson in the textbook. Each Notetaking Guide lesson features worked-out examples and Checkpoint exercises. Each example has a number of write-on lines for students to complete, either in class as the example is discussed or at home as part of a review of the lesson. Each chapter concludes with a review of the main vocabulary of the chapter. Upon completion, each chapter of the Notetaking Guide can be used by students to help review for the test on that particular chapter.

McDougal Littell
A DIVISION OF HOUGHTON MIFFLIN COMPANY
Evanston, Illinois • Boston • Dallas

Printed in the U.S.A

ISBN 13: 978-0-618-73692-8
ISBN 10: 0-618-73692-1

10 11 12 13 14-1417-18 17 16 15 14 13 12 11 10
4500246088

Contents

Geometry Notetaking Guide

4 Congruent Triangles

5 Relationships within Triangles

6 Similarity

Identify Points, Lines, and Planes

• Name and sketch geometric figures.

Your Notes

VOCABULARY

Undefined term

Point

Line

Plane

Collinear points

Coplanar points

Defined Terms

Line segment, endpoints

Ray

Opposite rays

Intersection

Your Notes

UNDEFINED TERMS

Point A **point** has _____ dimension. It is represented by a _____.

point A

Line A **line** has _____ dimension. It is represented by a _____ with two arrowheads, but it extends without end.

Through any _____ points, there is exactly _____ line. You can use any _____ points on a line to name it.

line ℓ, line AB ($\overleftrightarrow{AB}$), or line BA ($\overleftrightarrow{BA}$)

Plane A **plane** has _____ dimensions. It is represented by a shape that looks like a floor or wall, but it extends without end.

plane M or plane ABC

Through any _____ points not on the same line, there is exactly _____ plane. You can use _____ points that are not all on the same line to name a plane.

There is a line through points L and Q that is not shown in the diagram. Try to imagine what plane LMQ would look like if it were shown.

Example 1 *Name points, lines, and planes*

a. Give two other names for $\overleftrightarrow{LN}$. Give another name for plane Z.

b. Name three points that are collinear. Name four points that are coplanar.

a. Other names for $\overleftrightarrow{LN}$ are _____ and _____. Other names for plane Z are plane _____ and _____.

b. Points _____ lie on the same line, so they are collinear. Points _____ lie on the same plane, so they are coplanar.

Checkpoint **Use the diagram in Example 1.**

1. Give two other names for $\overleftrightarrow{MQ}$. Name a point that is not coplanar with points L, N, and P.

Your Notes

DEFINED TERMS: SEGMENTS AND RAYS

Line *AB* (written as _____) and points *A* and *B* are used here to define the terms below.

line

A B

Segment The **line segment** *AB*, or segment *AB*, (written as _____) consists of the endpoints *A* and *B* and all points on $\overleftrightarrow{AB}$ that are __________ *A* and *B*.

Note that $\overline{AB}$ can also be named _____.

segment

endpoint endpoint

A B

Ray The **ray** *AB* (written as _____) consists of the endpoint *A* and all points on $\overleftrightarrow{AB}$ that lie on the same side of ____ as ____.

Note that $\overrightarrow{AB}$ and $\overrightarrow{BA}$ are __________ rays.

ray

endpoint

A B

endpoint

A B

Example 2 *Name segments, rays, and opposite rays*

In Example 2, $\overrightarrow{WY}$ and $\overrightarrow{WX}$ have a common __________, but are *not* __________. So they are not opposite rays.

a. Give another name for $\overline{VX}$.

b. Name all rays with endpoints *W*. Which of these rays are opposite rays?

Y X W V Z

a. Another name for $\overline{VX}$ is _____.

b. The rays with endpoint *W* are __________.

The opposite rays with endpoint *W* are __________, and __________.

Checkpoint Use the diagram in Example 2.

2. Give another name for $\overline{YW}$.

3. Are $\overrightarrow{VX}$ and $\overrightarrow{XV}$ the same ray? Are $\overrightarrow{VW}$ and $\overrightarrow{VX}$ the same ray? *Explain.*

Your Notes

Example 3 ***Sketch intersections of lines and planes***

a. Sketch a plane and a line that intersects the plane at more than one point.

b. Sketch a plane and a line that is in the plane. Sketch another line that intersects the line and plane at a point.

a. **b.**

Example 4 ***Sketch intersections of planes***

Sketch two planes that intersect in a line.

Step 1 Draw one plane as if you are facing it.

Step 2 Draw a second plane that is ________. Use dashed lines to show where one plane is hidden.

Step 3 Draw the line of ________.

Checkpoint **Complete the following exercises.**

4. Sketch two different lines that intersect a plane at different points.

5. Name the intersection of $\overleftrightarrow{MX}$ and line a.

6. Name the intersection of plane C and plane D.

C
Y
a
M
D
X

Homework

1.2 Use Segments and Congruence

Goal • Use segment postulates to identify congruent segments.

Your Notes

VOCABULARY

Postulate, axiom

Theorem

Coordinate

Distance

Between

Congruent segments

POSTULATE 1 RULER POSTULATE

The points on a line can be matched one to one with real numbers. The real number that corresponds to a point is the ________ of the point.

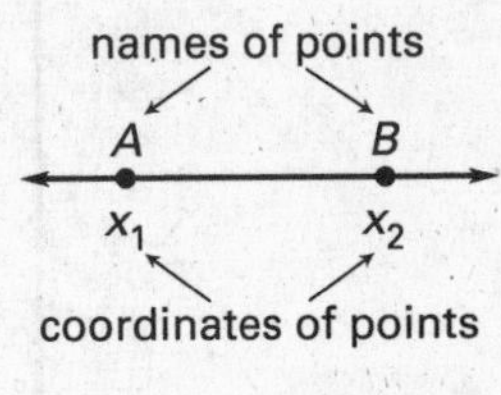

The ________ between points A and B, written as AB, is the absolute value of the difference of the coordinates of A and B.

A B

x_1 x_2

$AB = |x_2 - x_1|$

Your Notes

Example 1 ***Apply the Ruler Postulate***

Measure the length of $\overline{CD}$ to the nearest tenth of a centimeter.

Solution

Align one mark of a metric ruler with *C*. Then estimate the coordinate of *D*. For example, if you align *C* with 1, *D* appears to align with _____.

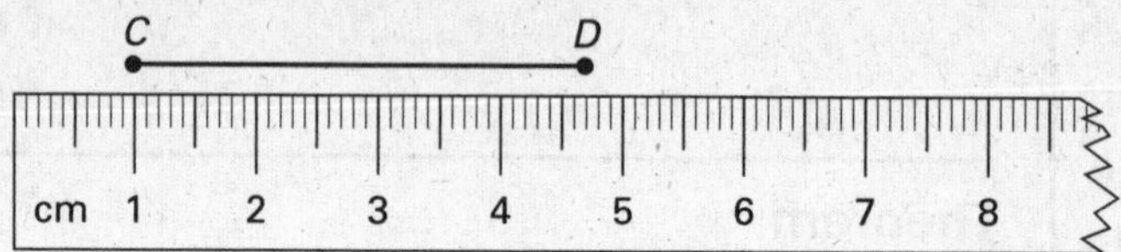

$CD = |\_\_\_\_ - \_\_\_\_| = \_\_\_\_$ **Ruler postulate**

The length of $\overline{CD}$ is about _____ centimeters.

POSTULATE 2 SEGMENT ADDITION POSTULATE

If *B* is between *A* and *C*, then $AB + BC = AC$.

If $AB + BC = AC$, then *B* is between *A* and *C*.

Example 2 ***Apply the Segment Addition Postulate***

Road Trip The locations shown lie in a straight line. Find the distance from the starting point to the destination.

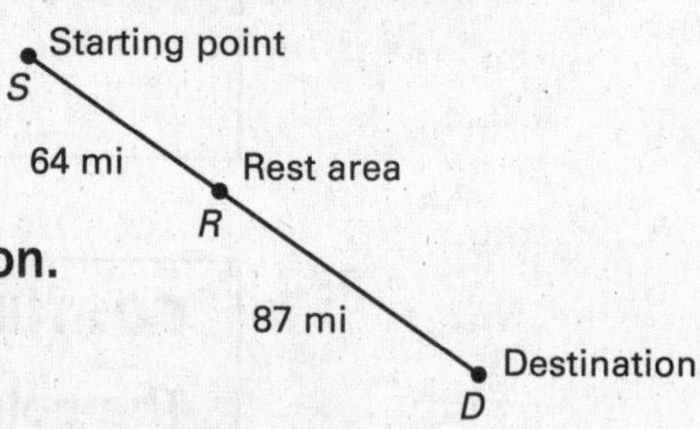

Solution

The rest area lies between the starting point and the destination, so you can apply the Segment Addition Postulate.

$SD = \_\_\_\_ + \_\_\_\_$ **Segment Addition Postulate**

$= \_\_\_\_ + \_\_\_\_$ **Substitute for _____ and _____.**

$= \_\_\_\_$ **Add.**

The distance from the starting point to the destination is _____ miles.

Your Notes

Example 3 ***Find a length***

Use the diagram to find *KL*.

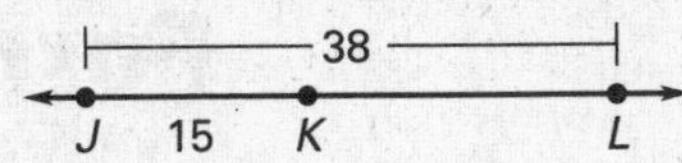

Use the Segment Addition Postulate to write an equation. Then solve the equation to find *KL*.

____ = ____ + *KL* **Segment Addition Postulate**

____ = ____ + *KL* **Substitute for ____ and ____.**

____ = *KL* **Subtract ____ from each side.**

Example 4 ***Compare segments for congruence***

Plot *F*(4, 5), *G*(−1, 5), *H*(3, 3), and *J*(3, −2) in a coordinate plane. Then determine whether $\overline{FG}$ and $\overline{HJ}$ are congruent.

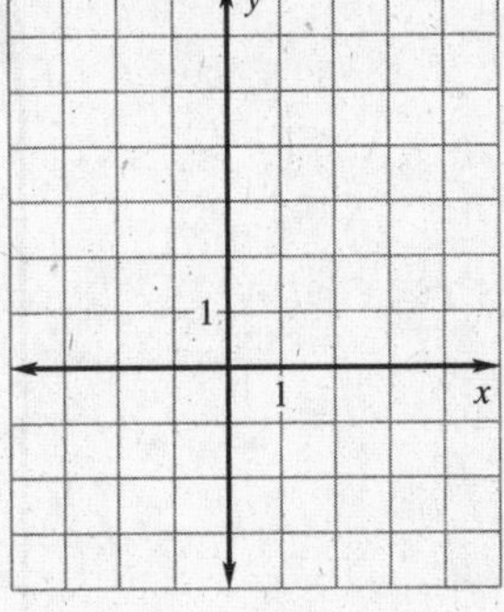

Horizontal segment: Subtract the ________ of the endpoints.

FG = |________| = ____

Vertical segment: Subtract the ________ of the endpoints.

HJ = |________| = ____

$\overline{FG}$ and $\overline{HJ}$ have the ______ length. So $\overline{FG}$ ____ $\overline{HJ}$.

✔ ***Checkpoint*** **Complete the following exercises.**

1. Find the length of $\overline{AB}$ to the nearest $\frac{1}{8}$ inch.

A B

2. Find *QS* and *PQ*.

55
P Q 31 R 30 S

3. Consider the points *A*(−2, −1), *B*(4, −1), *C*(3, 0), and *D*(3, 5). Are $\overline{AB}$ and $\overline{CD}$ congruent?

Homework

1.3 Use Midpoint and Distance Formulas

Goal • Find lengths of segments in the coordinate plane.

Your Notes

VOCABULARY

Midpoint

Segment bisector

Example 1 *Find segments lengths*

Find *RS*.

R — 21.7 — T — S; V, W

Solution

Point ___ is the midpoint of $\overline{RS}$. So, RT = ___ = 21.7.

RS = ___ + ___ **Segment Addition Postulate**

= ___ + ___ **Substitute.**

= ___ **Add.**

The length of $\overline{RS}$ is ___.

Checkpoint Complete the following exercise.

1. Find *AB*.

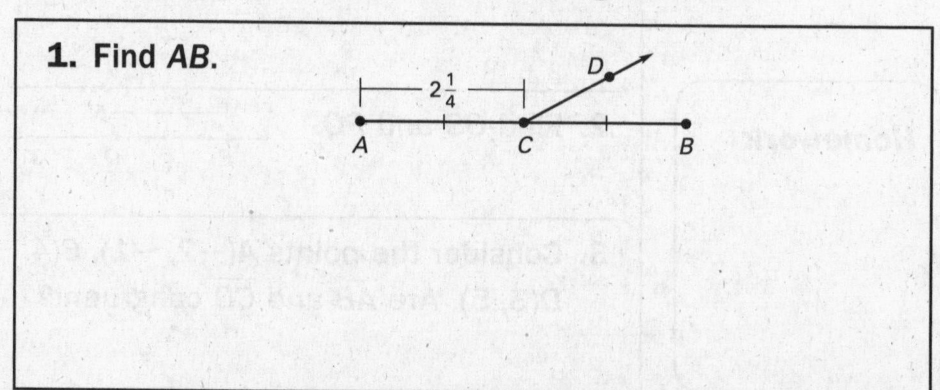

Your Notes

Example 2 ***Use algebra with segment lengths***

Point C is the midpoint of $\overline{BD}$. Find the length of $\overline{BC}$.

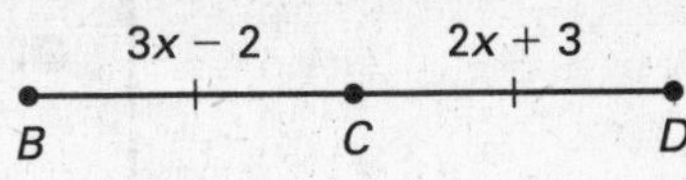

Solution

Step 1 Write and solve an equation.

$BC = CD$		**Write equation.**
______ = ______		**Substitute.**
______ = ____		**Subtract ____ from each side.**
$x =$ ____		**Add ____ to each side.**

Step 2 Evaluate the expression for BC when $x =$ ____.

$BC =$ ________ $=$ __________ $=$ ____

So, the length of $\overline{BC}$ is ____.

Checkpoint Complete the following exercise.

2. Point K is the midpoint of $\overline{JL}$. Find the length of $\overline{KL}$.

8 − 3x   2x + 5

J   K   L

THE MIDPOINT FORMULA

The coordinates of the midpoint of a segment are the averages of the x-coordinates and of the y-coordinates of the endpoints.

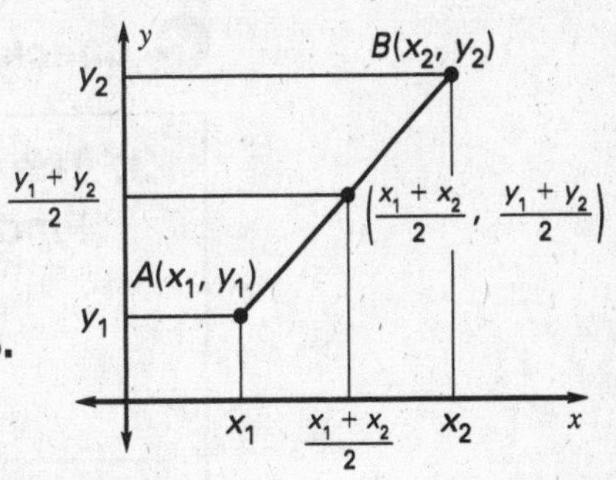

If $A(x_1, y_1)$ and $B(x_2, y_2)$ are points in a coordinate plane, then the midpoint M of $\overline{AB}$ has coordinates $\left(\frac{x_1 + x_2}{2}, \frac{y_1 + y_2}{2}\right)$.

Your Notes

Example 3 *Use the Midpoint Formula*

a. Find Midpoint The endpoints of $\overline{PR}$ are $P(-2, 5)$ and $R(4, 3)$. Find the coordinates of the midpoint M.

b. Find Endpoint The midpoint of $\overline{AC}$ is $M(3, 4)$. One endpoint is $A(1, 6)$. Find the coordinates of endpoint C.

Solution

a. Use the Midpoint Formula.

$$M\left(\frac{\square + \square}{\square}, \frac{\square + \square}{\square}\right)$$

$= M(\_\_\_, \_\_\_)$

The coordinates of the midpoint of $\overline{PR}$ are ________.

Multiply each side of the equation by the denominator to clear the fraction.

b. Let (x, y) be the coordinates of endpoint C. Use the Midpoint Formula to find x and y.

Step 1 Find x. **Step 2 Find** y.

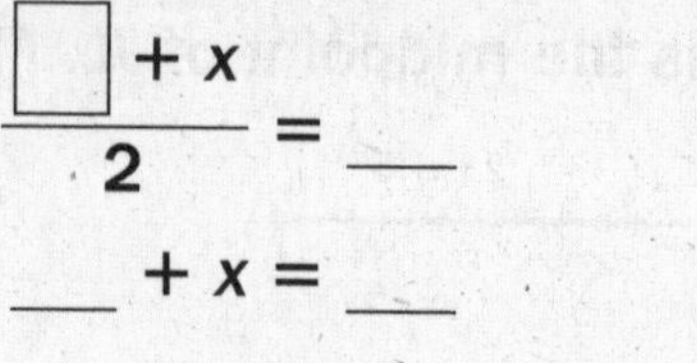

$\frac{\square + x}{2} = \_\_\_$ $\frac{\square + y}{2} = \_\_\_$

$\_\_\_ + x = \_\_\_$ $\_\_\_ + y = \_\_\_$

$x = \_\_\_$ $y = \_\_\_$

The coordinates of endpoint C are ________.

Checkpoint Complete the following exercises.

3. The endpoints of $\overline{CD}$ are $C(-8, -1)$ and $D(2, 4)$. Find the coordinates of the midpoint M.

4. The midpoint of $\overline{XZ}$ is $M(5, -6)$. One endpoint is $X(-3, 7)$. Find the coordinates of endpoint Z.

Your Notes

THE DISTANCE FORMULA

If $A(x_1, y_1)$ and $B(x_2, y_2)$ are points in a coordinate plane, then the distance between A and B is

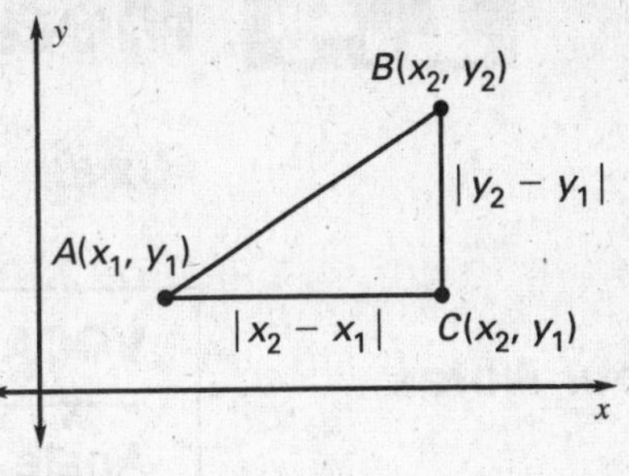

$AB = \sqrt{(\_\_\_\_\_\_)^2 + (\_\_\_\_\_\_)^2}$

Example 4 ***Use the Distance Formula***

What is the approximate length of $\overline{RT}$, with endpoints $R(3, 2)$ and $T(-4, 3)$?

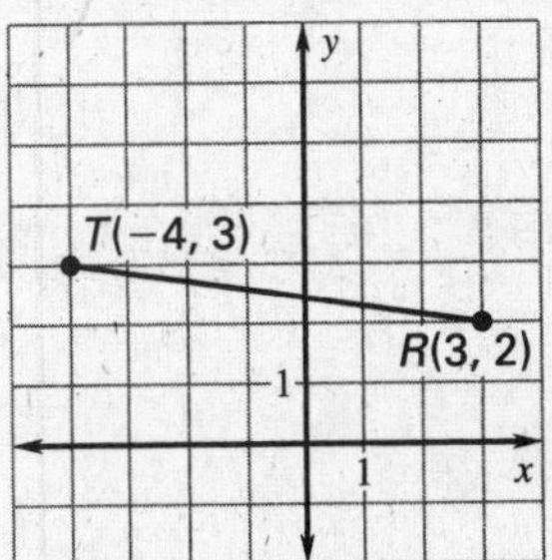

Solution

Use the Distance Formula.

$RT = \sqrt{(\_\_\_\_\_\_)^2 + (\_\_\_\_\_\_)^2}$ **Distance Formula**

$= \sqrt{(\_\_\_\_ - 3)^2 + (\_\_\_ - \_\_\_)^2}$ **Substitute.**

$= \sqrt{(\_\_\_\_)^2 + (\_\_\_)^2}$ **Subtract.**

$= \sqrt{\_\_\_\_ + \_\_\_\_}$ **Evaluate powers.**

$= \sqrt{\_\_\_\_}$ **Add.**

$\approx \_\_\_\_\_\_$ **Use a calculator.**

The symbol $\approx$ means "is approximately equal to."

The length of $\overline{RT}$ is about ______.

✔ ***Checkpoint*** **Complete the following exercise.**

Homework

5. What is the approximate length of $\overline{GH}$, with endpoints $G(5, -1)$ and $H(-3, 6)$?

Measure and Classify Angles

Goal • Name, measure, and classify angles.

Your Notes

VOCABULARY

Angle

Sides of an angle

Vertex of an angle

Measure of an angle

Acute angle

Right angle

Obtuse angle

Straight angle

Congruent angles

Angle bisector

Example 1 ***Name angles***

Name the three angles in the diagram.

________, or ________

________, or ________

________, or ________

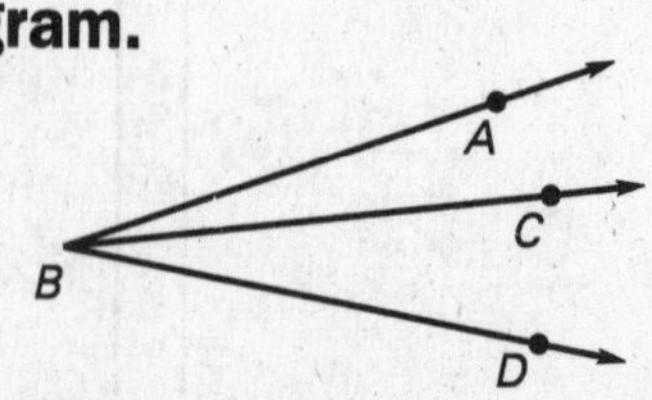

A
C
B
D

You should not name any of these angles *B* because all three angles have *B* as their ________.

Your Notes

POSTULATE 3: PROTRACTOR POSTULATE

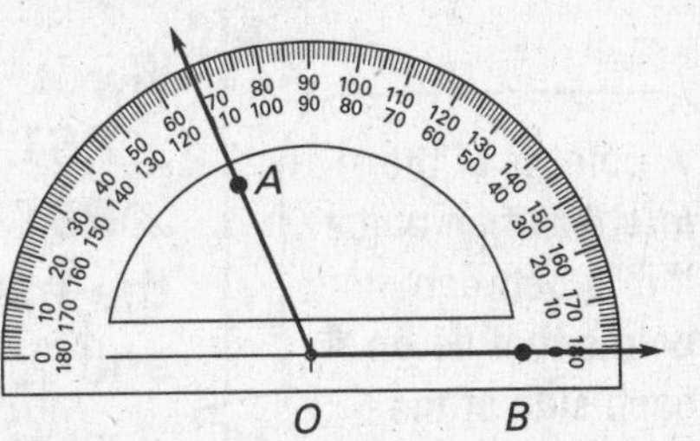

Consider $\overrightarrow{OB}$ and point A on one side of $\overrightarrow{OB}$. The rays of the form $\overrightarrow{OA}$ can be matched one to one with the real numbers from 0 to ______.

The measure of ________ is equal to ________ between the real numbers ________ for $\overrightarrow{OA}$ and $\overrightarrow{OB}$.

Example 2 ***Measure and classify angles***

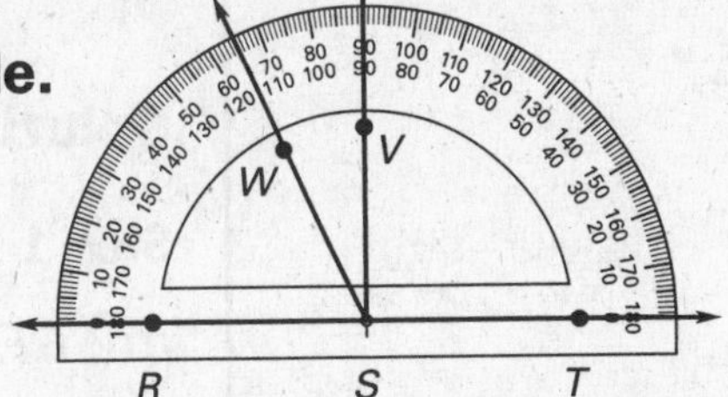

Use the diagram to find the measure of the indicated angle. Then classify the angle.

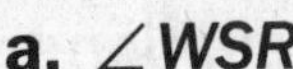

a. $\angle WSR$ **b.** $\angle TSW$

c. $\angle RST$ **d.** $\angle VST$

a. $\overrightarrow{SR}$ is lined up with the 0° on the ______ scale of the protractor. $\overrightarrow{SW}$ passes through ____ on the ______ scale. So, $m\angle WSR =$ ____. It is ________ angle.

b. $\overrightarrow{ST}$ is lined up with the 0° on the ______ scale of the protractor. $\overrightarrow{SW}$ passes through ____ on the ______ scale. So, $m\angle TSW =$ ____. It is ________ angle.

c. $m\angle RST =$ ______. It is ________ angle.

d. $m\angle VST =$ ______. It is ________ angle.

✔ ***Checkpoint*** **Complete the following exercises.**

1. Name all the angles in the diagram at the right.

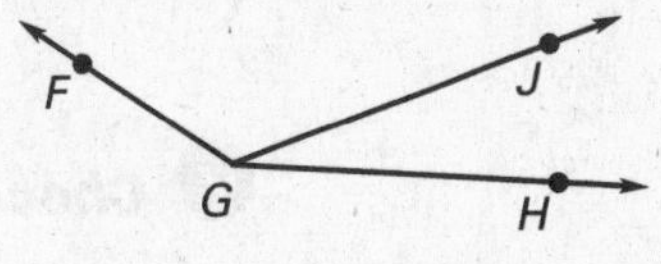

2. What type of angles do the x-axis and y-axis form in a coordinate plane?

Your Notes

A point is in the *interior* of an angle if it is between points that lie on each side of the angle.

POSTULATE 4: ANGLE ADDITION POSTULATE

Words If P is in the interior of $\angle RST$, then the measure of $\angle RST$ is equal to the sum of the measures of $\angle$_____ and $\angle$_____.

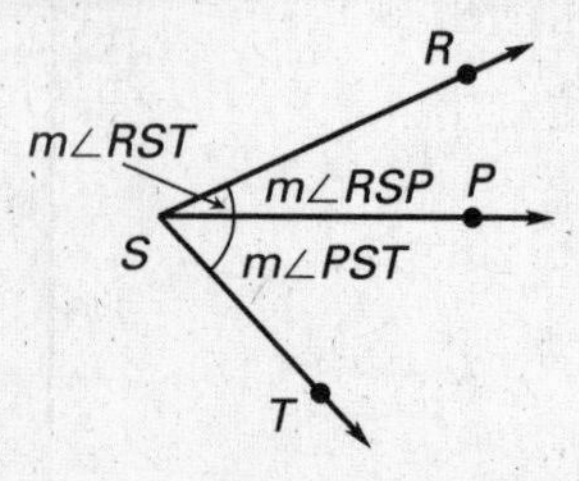

Symbols If P is in the interior of $\angle RST$, then $m\angle RST = m\angle$_____ $+ m\angle$_____.

Example 3 ***Find angle measures***

Given that $m\angle GFJ = 155°$, find $m\angle GFH$ and $m\angle HFJ$.

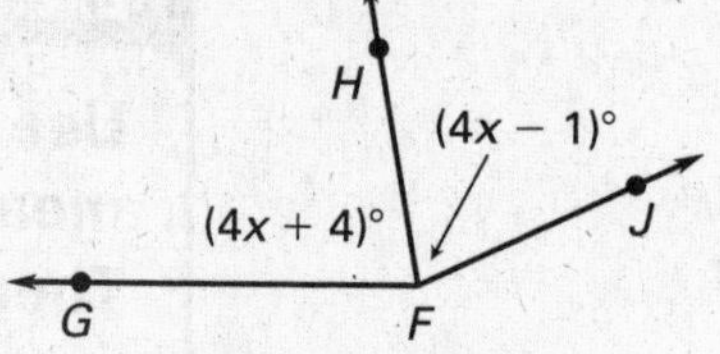

Solution

Step 1 Write and solve an equation to find the value of x.

$m\angle GFJ = m\angle$_____ $+ m\angle$_____	**Angle Addition Postulate**
_____ = (_____)° + (_____)°	**Substitute.**
_____ = _____	**Combine like terms.**
_____ = _____	**Subtract ___ from each side.**
_____ $= x$	**Divide each side by ___.**

Step 2 Evaluate the given expressions when $x =$ _____.

$m\angle GFH =$ (_____)° = (_____)° = _____.

$m\angle HFJ =$ (_____)° = (_____)° = _____.

So, $m\angle GFH =$ _____ and $m\angle HFJ =$ _____.

Checkpoint **Complete the following exercise.**

3. Given that $\angle VRS$ is a right angle, find $m\angle VRT$ and $\angle TRS$.

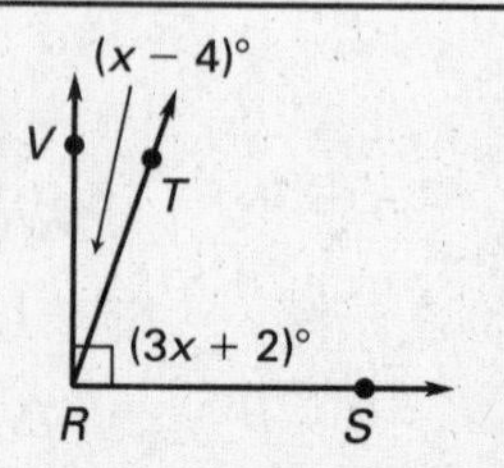

Your Notes

Example 4 ***Identify congruent angles***

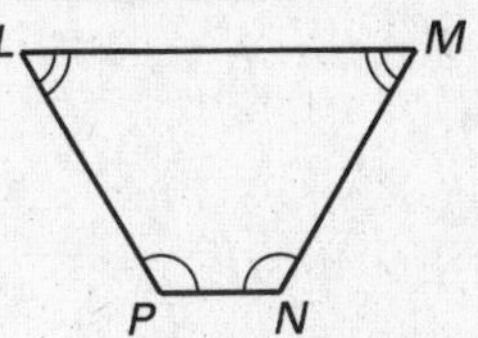

Identify all pairs of congruent angles in the diagram. If $m\angle P = 120°$, what is $m\angle N$?

Solution

There are two pairs of congruent angles:

$\angle P \cong$ ______ and $\angle L \cong$ ______

Because $\angle P \cong$ ______, $m\angle P =$ ______.
So, $m\angle N =$ ______.

Example 5 ***Double an angle measure***

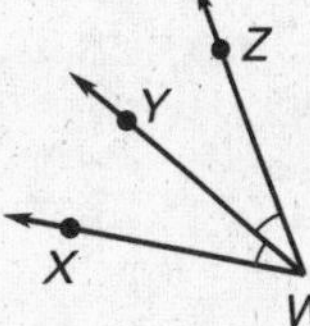

In the diagram at the right, $\overrightarrow{WY}$ bisects $\angle XWZ$, and $m\angle XWY = 29°$. Find $m\angle XWZ$.

Solution

By the Angle Addition Postulate,
$m\angle XWZ =$ ________ + ________.

Because $\overrightarrow{WY}$ bisects $\angle XWZ$, you know
________ $\cong$ ________.

So, ________ = ________, and you can write
$m\angle XWZ =$ ________ + ________
= ____ + ____ = ____.

Checkpoint **Complete the following exercises.**

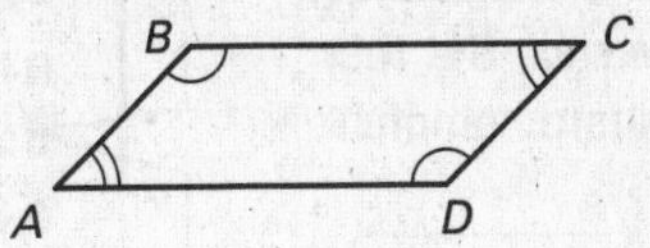

4. Identify all pairs of congruent angles in the diagram. If $m\angle B = 135°$, what is $m\angle D$?

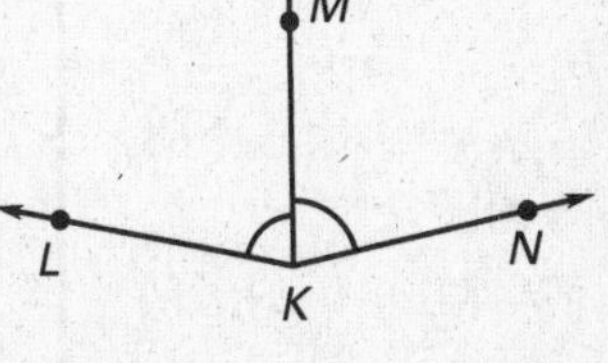

5. In the diagram below, $\overrightarrow{KM}$ bisects $\angle LKN$ and $m\angle LKM = 78°$. Find $m\angle LKN$.

Homework

1.5 Describe Angle Pair Relationships

Goal • Use special angle relationships to find angle measures.

Your Notes

VOCABULARY

Complementary angles

Supplementary angles

Adjacent angles

Linear pair

Vertical angles

Example 1 ***Identify complements and supplements***

In the figure, name a pair of complementary angles, a pair of supplementary angles, and a pair of adjacent angles.

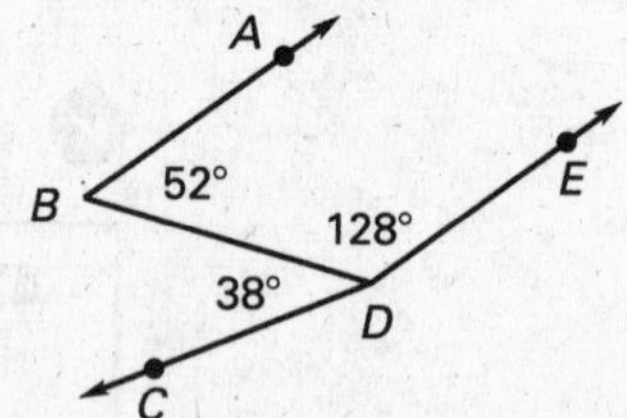

In Example 1, $\angle BDE$ and $\angle CDE$ share a common vertex. But they share common _______ points, so they are *not* adjacent angles.

Solution

Because _____ + _____ = 90°, _______ and _______ are _______________ angles.

Because _____ + _____ = 180°, _______ and _______ are _______________ angles.

Because _______ and _______ share a common vertex and side, they are _________ angles.

Your Notes

Angles are sometimes named with numbers. An angle measure in a diagram has a degree symbol. An angle name does not.

Example 2 *Find measures of complements and supplements*

a. Given that $\angle 1$ is a complement of $\angle 2$ and $m\angle 2 = 57°$, find $m\angle 1$.

b. Given that $\angle 3$ is a supplement of $\angle 4$ and $m\angle 4 = 41°$, find $m\angle 3$.

Solution

a. You can draw a diagram with complementary adjacent angles to illustrate the relationship.

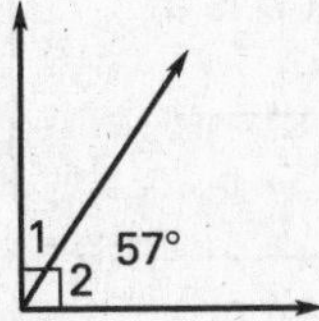

$m\angle 1 =$ _____ $-$ _____ $=$ _____ $-$ _____ $=$ _____

b. You can draw a diagram with supplementary adjacent angles to illustrate the relationship.

3 4 41°

$m\angle 3 =$ _____ $-$ _____ $=$ _____ $-$ _____ $=$ _____

Checkpoint **Complete the following exercises.**

1. In the figure, name a pair of complementary angles, a pair of supplementary angles, and a pair of adjacent angles.

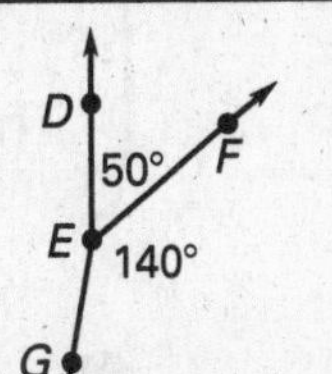

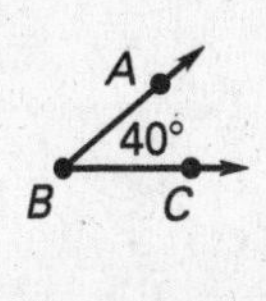

2. Given that $\angle 1$ is a complement of $\angle 2$ and $m\angle 1 = 73°$, find $m\angle 2$.

3. Given that $\angle 3$ is a supplement of $\angle 4$ and $m\angle 4 = 37°$, find $m\angle 3$.

Your Notes

In a diagram, you can assume that a line that looks straight *is* straight. In Example 3, *B*, *C*, and *D* lie on $\overleftrightarrow{BD}$. So, $\angle BCD$ is a ________ angle.

Example 3 *Find angle measures*

Basketball The basketball pole forms a pair of supplementary angles with the ground. Find $m\angle BCA$ and $m\angle DCA$.

A
$(3x + 8)°$ $(4x - 3)°$
B C D

Solution

Step 1 Use the fact that ______ is the sum of the measures of supplementary angles.

$m\angle BCA + m\angle DCA =$ ______	**Write equation.**
(______)° + (______)° = ______	**Substitute.**
______ = ______	**Combine like terms.**
____ = ______	**Subtract.**
____ = ______	**Divide.**

Step 2 Evaluate the original expressions when $x =$ ____.

$m\angle BCA =$ (______)° = (__________)° = ______.

$m\angle DCA =$ (______)° = (__________)° = ______.

The angle measures are ______ and ______.

Checkpoint Complete the following exercise.

4. In Example 3, suppose the angle measures are $(5x + 1)°$ and $(6x + 3)°$. Find $m\angle BCA$ and $m\angle DCA$.

Your Notes

In the diagram, one side of $\angle 1$ and one side of $\angle 4$ are opposite rays. But the angles are not a linear pair because they are not __________.

Example 4 *Identify angle pairs*

Identify all of the linear pairs and all of the vertical angles in the figure at the right.

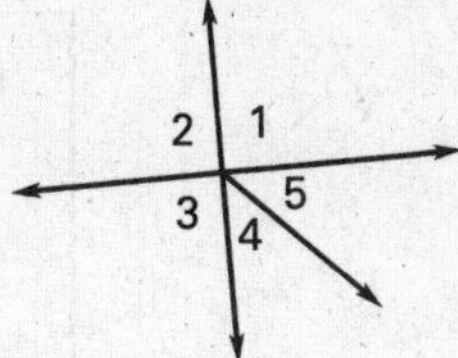

Solution

To find vertical angles, look for angles formed by ______________.

_____ and _____ are vertical angles.

To find linear pairs, look for adjacent angles whose noncommon sides are ______________.

_____ and _____ are a linear pair. _____ and _____ are a linear pair.

Checkpoint Complete the following exercise.

5. Identify all of the linear pairs and all of the vertical angles in the figure.

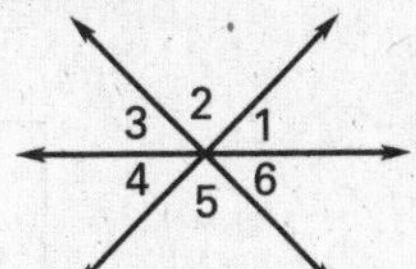

You may find it useful to draw a diagram to represent a word problem like the one in Example 5.

Example 5 *Find angle measures in a linear pair*

Two angles form a linear pair. The measure of one angle is 4 times the measure of the other. Find the measure of each angle.

Solution

Let $x°$ be the measure of one angle. The measure of the other angle is _____. Then use the fact that the angles of a linear pair are ______________ to write an equation.

___ + _____ = _____ **Write an equation.**

_____ = _____ **Combine like terms.**

_____ = _____ **Divide each side by ___.**

The measures of the angles are _____ and _______ = _____.

Your Notes

Checkpoint Complete the following exercise.

6. Two angles form a linear pair. The measure of one angle is 3 times the measure of the other. Find the meaure of each angle.

Homework

CONCEPT SUMMARY: INTERPRETING A DIAGRAM

There are some things you can conclude from a diagram, and some you cannot. For example, here are some things that you can conclude from the diagram at the right.

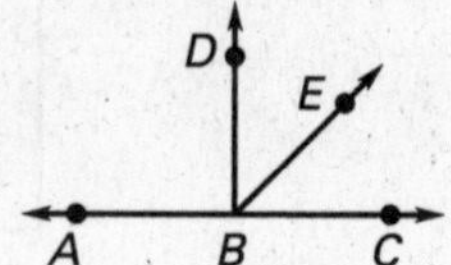

- All points shown are ________.
- Points *A*, *B*, and *C* are ________, and *B* is between *A* and *C*.
- $\overleftrightarrow{AC}$, $\overrightarrow{BD}$, and $\overrightarrow{BE}$ ________ at point *B*.
- $\angle DBE$ and $\angle EBC$ are ________ angles, and $\angle ABC$ is a ________.
- Point *E* lies in the ________ of $\angle DBC$.

In the diagram above, you cannot conclude that $\overline{AB} \cong \overline{BC}$, that $\angle DBE \cong \angle EBC$, or that $\angle ABD$ is a right angle. This information must be indicated, as shown at the right.

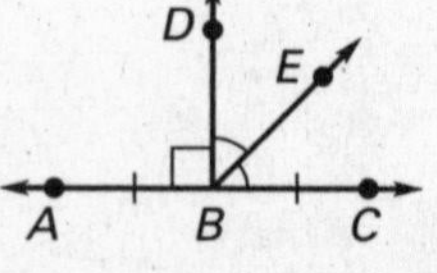

1.6 Classify Polygons

 • Classify polygons.

Your Notes

VOCABULARY

Polygon

Sides

Vertex

Convex

Concave

***n*-gon**

Equilateral

Equiangular

Regular

Your Notes

IDENTIFYING POLYGONS

In geometry, a figure that lies in a plane is called a *plane figure*. A __________ is a closed plane figure with the following properties.

1. It is formed by three or more line segments called _______.
2. Each side intersects exactly ______ sides, one at each endpoint, so that no two sides with a common endpoint are __________.

Each endpoint of a side is a ________ of the polygon. The plural of vertex is *vertices*. A polygon can be named by listing the vertices in consecutive order. For example, *ABCDE* and *CDEAB* are both correct names for the polygon at the right.

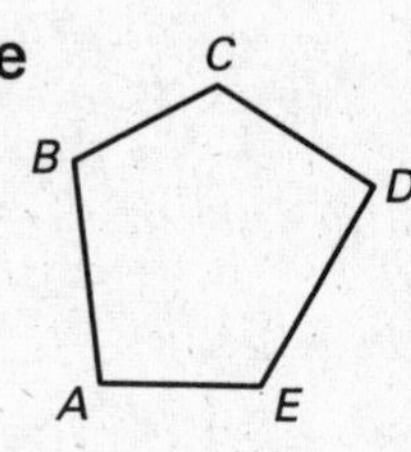

Example 1 ***Identify polygons***

Tell whether the figure is a polygon and whether it is *convex* or *concave*.

A *plane figure* is two-dimensional. Later, you will study three-dimensional *space figures* such as prisms and cylinders.

a. 

b. 

c. 

Solution

a. Some segments intersect more than two segments, so it is _______________.

b. The figure is ___________________.

c. The figure is ___________________.

Checkpoint **Tell whether the figure is a polygon and whether it is *convex* or *concave*.**

1. 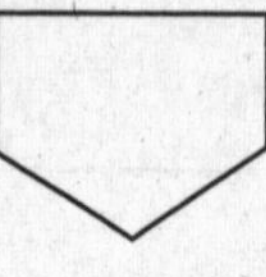	**2.** 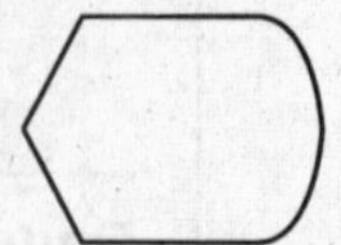

Your Notes

Example 2 *Classify polygons*

Classify the polygon by the number of sides. Tell whether the polygon is *equilateral*, *equiangular*, or *regular*.

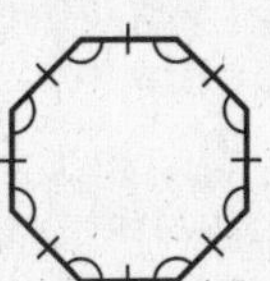

Solution

The polygon has ___ sides. It is equilateral and equiangular, so it is a ______________.

Example 3 *Find side lengths*

The head of a bolt is shaped like a regular hexagon. The expressions shown represent side lengths of the hexagonal bolt. Find the length of a side.

$(4x + 3)$ mm

$(5x - 1)$ mm

> *Hexagonal* means "shaped like a hexagon."

Solution

First, write and solve an equation to find the value of x. Use the fact that the sides of a regular hexagon are __________.

_______ = _______ **Write an equation.**

___ = ___ **Simplify.**

Then evaluate one of the expressions to find a side length when x = ___. $4x + 3 = 4($ ___ $) + 3 =$ ___

The length of a side is ___ millimeters.

✔ ***Checkpoint*** **Complete the following exercises.**

3. Classify the polygon by the number of sides. Tell whether the polygon is *equilateral*, *equiangular*, or *regular*.

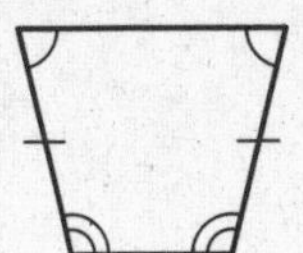

4. The expressions $(4x + 8)°$ and $(5x - 5)°$ represent the measures of two of the congruent angles in Example 3. Find the measure of an angle.

Homework

1.7 Find Perimeter, Circumference, and Area

Goal • Find dimensions of polygons.

Your Notes

FORMULAS FOR PERIMETER P, AREA A, AND CIRCUMFERENCE C

Square side length s $P =$ ______ $A =$ ______	**Rectangle** length ℓ and width w $P =$ ______ $A =$ ______
Triangle side lengths a, b, and c, base b, and height h. $P =$ ______ $A =$ ______	**Circle** radius r $C =$ ______ $A =$ ______ Pi (π) is the ratio of a circle's circumference to its diameter.

Example 1 ***Find the perimeter and area of a rectangle***

Tennis The in-bounds portion of a singles tennis court is shown. Find its perimeter and area.

78 ft

27 ft

Perimeter

$P = 2\ell + 2w$

$= 2(\_\_\_\_) + 2(\_\_\_\_)$

$=$ ______

Area

$A = \ell w$

$=$ ____(____)

$=$ ______

The perimeter is ____ ft and the area is ______ ft^2.

Checkpoint Complete the following exercise.

1. In Example 1, the width of the in-bounds rectangle increases to 36 feet for doubles play. Find the perimeter and area of the in-bounds rectangle.

Your Notes

> The approximations 3.14 and $\frac{22}{7}$ are commonly used as approximations for the irrational number π. Unless told otherwise, use 3.14 for π.

Example 2 *Find the circumference and area of a circle*

Archery The smallest circle on an Olympic target is 12 centimeters in diameter. Find the approximate circumference and area of the smallest circle.

Solution

First find the radius. The diameter is 12 centimeters, so the radius is $\frac{1}{2}$(_____) = ___ centimeters.

Then find the circumference and area. Use 3.14 for π.

$P = 2\pi r \approx 2(\_\_\_)(\_\_\_) = \_\_\_\_\_\_$

$A = \pi r^2 \approx \_\_\_\_(\_\_)^2 = \_\_\_\_\_\_$

✔ ***Checkpoint*** **Find the approximate circumference and area of the circle.**

2. 8 m

Example 3 *Using a coordinate plane*

Triangle *JKL* has vertices *J*(1, 6), *K*(6, 6), and *L*(3, 2). Find the approximate perimeter of triangle *JKL*.

Solution

First draw triangle *JKL* in a coordinate plane. Then find the side lengths. Because $\overline{JK}$ is horizontal, use the ____________ to find *JK*. Use the ____________ to find *JL* and *LK*.

> Write down your calculations to make sure you do not make a mistake substituting values in the Distance Formula.

$JK = |\_\_\_ - \_\_\_| = \_\_\_$ units

$JL = \sqrt{(\_\_\_ - 1)^2 + (2 - \_\_\_)^2} = \sqrt{\_\_\_} \approx \_\_\_\_$ units

$LK = \sqrt{(\_\_\_ - 3)^2 + (\_\_\_ - 2)^2} = \sqrt{\_\_\_} = \_\_\_$ units

Then find the perimeter.

$P = JK + JL + LK \approx \_\_\_ + \_\_\_ + \_\_\_ = \_\_\_\_$ units.

Your Notes

Example 4 *Solve a multi-step problem*

Lawn care You are using a roller to smooth a lawn. You can roll about 125 square yards in one minute. About how many minutes does it take to roll a lawn that is 120 feet long and 75 feet wide?

Solution

You can roll the lawn at a rate of 125 square yards per minute. So, the amount of time it takes you to roll the lawn depends on its _____.

Step 1 **Find** the area of the rectangular lawn.

Area = ℓw = _____(____) = ______ ft^2

The rolling rate is in square yards per minute. Rewrite the area of the lawn in square yards. There are ___ feet in 1 yard, and $\_\_\_^2$ = ___ square feet in one square yard.

$$9000\ \cancel{\text{ft}^2} \cdot \frac{1\ \text{yd}^2}{\square\ \cancel{\text{ft}^2}} = \_\_\_\_\_\_\ \text{yd}^2$$ **Use unit analysis.**

Step 2 **Write** a verbal model to represent the situation. Then write and solve an equation based on the verbal model.

Let t represent the total time (in minutes) needed to roll the lawn.

Area of lawn (yd^2)	=	Rolling rate (yd^2 per min)	×	Total time (min)

_______ = _____ • t **Substitute.**

___ = t **Divide each side by _____.**

It takes about ___ minutes to roll the lawn.

Your Notes

Example 5 *Find unknown length*

The base of a triangle is 24 feet. Its area is 216 square feet. Find the height of the triangle.

Solution

$A =$ ______ **Area of a triangle**

______ $=$ ________ **Substitute.**

______ $=$ ______ **Multiply.**

______ $= h$ **Solve for h.**

The height is ____ feet.

Checkpoint **Complete the following exercises.**

3. Find the perimeter of the triangle shown at the right.

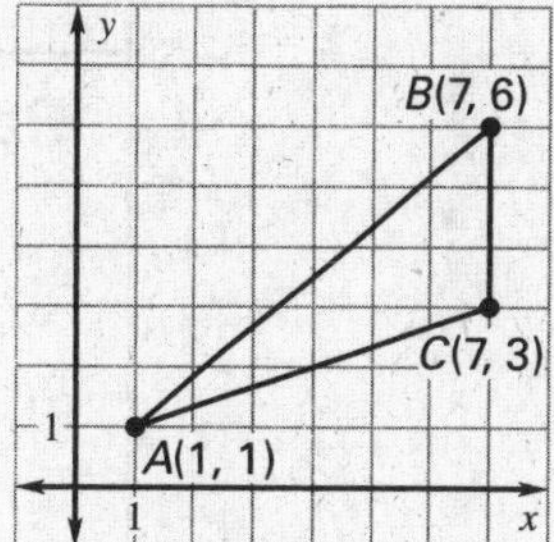

4. Suppose a lawn is half as long and half as wide as the lawn in Example 4. Will it take half the time to roll the lawn? *Explain.*

5. The area of a triangle is 96 square inches, and its height is 8 inches. Find the length of its base.

Homework

Words to Review

Give an example of the vocabulary word.

Point, line, plane	Collinear points
Coplanar points	Line segment, endpoints
Ray	Opposite rays
Intersection	Postulate, axiom
Coordinate	Distance

Between	Congruent segments
Midpoint	Segment bisector
Angle, sides, vertex	Measure of an angle
Acute angle	Right angle
Obtuse angle	Straight angle

Angle bisector, congruent angles	Supplementary angles, linear pair
Complementary angles, adjacent angles	Vertical angles
Polygon, side, vertex	Concave, convex
n-gon	Equilateral, equiangular, regular

Review your notes and Chapter 1 by using the Chapter Review on pages 60–63 of your textbook.

2.1 Use Inductive Reasoning

Goal • Describe patterns and use inductive reasoning.

Your Notes

VOCABULARY

Conjecture

Inductive Reasoning

Counterexample

Example 1 ***Describe a visual pattern***

Describe how to sketch the fourth figure in the pattern. Then sketch the fourth figure.

Figure 1 Figure 2 Figure 3

Solution

Each rectangle is divided into ______ as many equal regions as the figure number. Sketch the fourth figure by dividing the rectangle into ______. Shade the section just ______ the horizontal segment at the ______.

______
Figure 4

Checkpoint Complete the following exercise.

1. Sketch the fifth figure in the pattern in Example 1.

Your Notes

Three dots (. . .) tell you that the pattern continues.

Example 2 ***Describe the number pattern***

Describe the pattern in the numbers −1, −4, −16, −64, ... Write the next three numbers in the pattern.

Notice that each number in the pattern is ______ times the previous number.

−1, −4, −16, −64, . . .

× ___ × ___ × ___ × ___

The next three numbers are ____________________.

Example 3 ***Make a conjecture***

Given five noncollinear points, make a conjecture about the number of ways to connect different pairs of the points.

Make a table and look for a pattern. Notice the pattern in how the number of connections ____________. You can use the pattern to make a conjecture.

Number of points	1	2	3	4	5
Picture					
Number of connections	___	___	___	___	?

+ ___ + ___ + ___ + ?

Conjecture You can connect five noncollinear points ______, or ______ different ways.

Checkpoint **Complete the following exercises.**

2. Describe the pattern in the numbers 1, 2.5, 4, 5.5, . . . and write the next three numbers in the pattern.

3. Rework Example 3 if you are given six noncollinear points.

Your Notes

Example 4 *Make and test a conjecture*

Numbers such as 1, 3, and 5 are called consecutive odd numbers. Make and test a conjecture about the sum of any three consecutive odd numbers.

Step 1 Find a pattern using groups of small numbers.

$1 + 3 + 5 =$ ____
$= 3 \cdot 3$

$3 + 5 + 7 =$ ____
$=$ ____ $\cdot 3$

$5 + 7 + 9 =$ ____
$=$ ____ $\cdot 3$

$7 + 9 + 11 =$ ____
$=$ ____ $\cdot 3$

Conjecture The sum of any three consecutive odd numbers is three times ________________.

Step 2 Test your conjecture using other numbers.

$-1 + 1 + 3 =$ ____ $=$ ____ $\cdot 3$ ✓

$103 + 105 + 107 =$ ____ $=$ ____ $\cdot 3$ ✓

✔ ***Checkpoint*** **Complete the following exercise.**

4. Make and test a conjecture about the sign of the product of any four negative numbers.

Example 5 *Find a counterexample*

A student makes the following conjecture about the difference of two numbers. Find a counterexample to disprove the student's conjecture.

Conjecture The difference of any two numbers is always smaller than the larger number.

To find a counterexample, you need to find a difference that is ________ than the ________ number.

$8 - (-4) =$ ____

Because ____ $\nless$ ____, a counterexample exists. The conjecture is false.

Your Notes

Example 6 *Making conjectures from data displays*

The scatter plot shows the average salary of players in the National Football League (NFL) since 1999. Make a conjecture based on the graph.

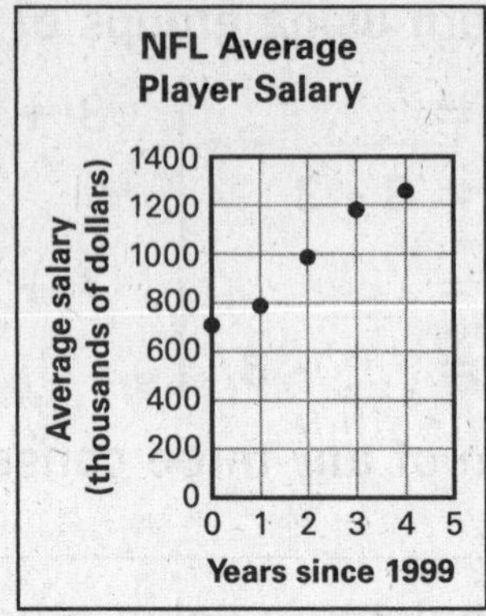

Solution

The scatter plot shows that the values _______ each year. So, one possible conjecture is that the average player in the NFL is earning _______ money today than in 1999.

Checkpoint **Complete the following exercises.**

5. Find a counterexample to show that the following conjecture is false.

   Conjecture The quotient of two numbers is always smaller than the dividend.

6. Use the graph in Example 6 to make a conjecture that *could* be true. Give an explanation that supports your reasoning.

Homework

2.2 Analyze Conditional Statements

Goal • Write definitions as conditional statements.

Your Notes

VOCABULARY

Conditional statement

If-then form

Hypothesis

Conclusion

Negation

Converse

Inverse

Contrapositive

Equivalent statements

Perpendicular lines

Biconditional statement

Your Notes

Example 1 ***Rewrite a statement in if-then form***

Rewrite the conditional statement in if-then form.

All vertebrates have a backbone.

Solution

First, identify the hypothesis and the conclusion. When you rewrite the statement in if-then form, you may need to reword the hypothesis or conclusion.

All vertebrates have a backbone.

If ______________________, then ________ __________.

Checkpoint **Write the conditional statement in if-then form.**

1. All triangles have 3 sides.	**2.** When $x = 2$, $x^2 = 4$.

Example 2 ***Write four related conditional statements***

Write the if-then form, the converse, the inverse, and the contrapositive of the conditional statement "Olympians are athletes." Decide whether each statement is *true* or *false*.

Solution

If-then form ______________________________

Converse ______________________________

Inverse ______________________________

Contrapositive ______________________________

Your Notes

PERPENDICULAR LINES

Definition If two lines intersect to form a ______ angle, then they are perpendicular lines.

The definition can also be written using the converse: If any two lines are perpendicular lines, then they intersect to form a ______ angle.

You can write "line ℓ is perpendicular to line m" as $\ell \perp m$.

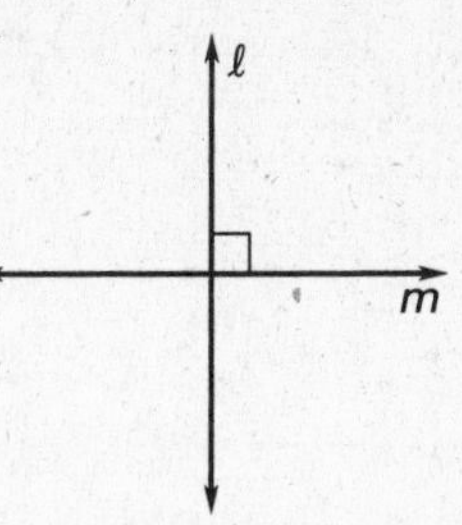

Example 3 *Use definitions*

Decide whether each statement about the diagram is true. *Explain* your answer using the definitions you have learned.

a. $\overleftrightarrow{AC} \perp \overleftrightarrow{BD}$

b. $\angle AED$ and $\angle BEC$ are a linear pair.

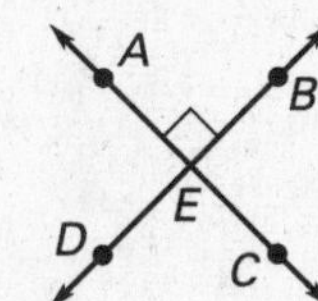

Solution

a. The statement is ______. The right angle symbol indicates that the lines intersect to form a ______ angle. So you can say the lines are ______________.

b. The statement is ______. Because $\angle AED$ and $\angle BEC$ are not __________ angles, $\angle AED$ and $\angle BEC$ are not a __________.

Example 4 *Write a biconditional*

Write the definition of parallel lines as a biconditional.

Definition: If two lines lie in the same plane and do not intersect, then they are parallel.

Solution

Converse: ____

____

Biconditional: ____________________________________

____

Your Notes

✔ *Checkpoint* Complete the following exercises.

3. Write the if-then form, the converse, the inverse, and the contrapositive of the conditional statement "Squares are rectangles." Decide whether each statement is *true* or *false*.

4. Decide whether each statement about the diagram is true. *Explain* your answer using the definitions you have learned.

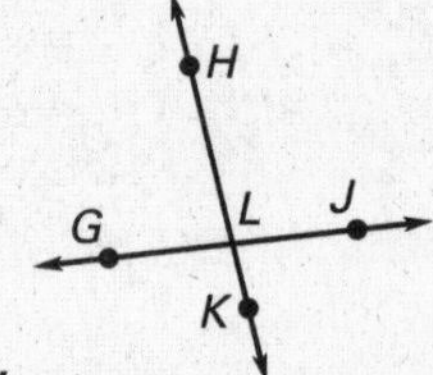

a. $\angle GLK$ and $\angle JLK$ are supplementary.

b. $\overleftrightarrow{GJ} \perp \overleftrightarrow{HK}$

5. Write the statement below as a biconditional.

Statement: If a student is a boy, he will be in group A. If a student is in group A, the student must be a boy.

Homework

2.3 Apply Deductive Reasoning

Goal • Form logical arguments using deductive reasoning.

Your Notes

VOCABULARY

Deductive Reasoning

LAWS OF LOGIC

The Law of Detachment is also called a *direct argument*. The Law of Syllogism is sometimes called the *chain rule*.

Law of Detachment If the hypothesis of a true conditional statement is true, then the ________ is also true.

Law of Syllogism

If hypothesis *p*, then conclusion *q*.
If hypothesis *q*, then conclusion *r*.
If these statements are true,

If hypothesis *p*, then conclusion *r*.
then this statement is true.

Example 1 ***Use the Law of Detachment***

Use the Law of Detachment to make a valid conclusion in the true situation.

a. If two angles have the same measure, then they are congruent. You know that $m\angle A = m\angle B$.

b. Jesse goes to the gym every weekday. Today is Monday.

Solution

a. Because $m\angle A = m\angle B$ satisfies the hypothesis of a true conditional statement, the conclusion is also true. So, ________.

b. First, identify the hypothesis and the conclusion of the first statement. The hypothesis is "________," and the conclusion is "________."

"Today is Monday" satisfies the hypothesis of the conditional statement, so you can conclude that ________________.

Your Notes

Example 2 ***Use the Law of Syllogism***

If possible, use the Law of Syllogism to write the conditional statement that follows from the pair of true statements.

a. If Ron eats lunch today, then he will eat a sandwich. If Ron eats a sandwich, then he will drink a glass of milk.

b. If $x^2 > 36$, then $x^2 > 30$. If $x > 6$, then $x^2 > 36$.

c. If a triangle is equilateral, then all of its sides are congruent. If a triangle is equilateral, then all angles in the interior of the triangle are congruent.

Solution

The order in which the statements are given does not affect whether you can use the Law of Syllogism.

a. The conclusion of the first statement is the hypothesis of the second statement, so you can write the following.

If Ron eats lunch today, then ______________________.

b. Notice that the conclusion of the second statement is the hypothesis of the first statement, so you can write the following.

If $x > 6$, then __________.

c. Neither statement's conclusion is the same as the other statement's ____________. You cannot use the Law of Syllogism to write a new conditional statement.

✓ *Checkpoint* Complete the following exercises.

1. If $0° < m\angle A < 90°$, then A is acute. The measure of $\angle A$ is 38°. Using the Law of Detachment, what statement can you make?

2. State the law of logic that is illustrated below.

If you do your homework, then you can watch TV. If you watch TV, then you can watch your favorite show.

If you do your homework, then you can watch your favorite show.

Your Notes

Example 3 ***Use inductive and deductive reasoning***

What conclusion can you make about the sum of an odd integer and an odd integer?

Solution

Step 1 **Look** for a pattern in several examples. Use inductive reasoning to make a conjecture.

$-3 + 5 =$ ___, $-1 + 5 =$ ___, $3 + 5 =$ ___

$-3 + (-5) =$ ____, $1 + (-5) =$ ____,
$3 + (-5) =$ ____

Conjecture: Odd integer + Odd integer = _____ integer

Step 2 **Let** n and m each be any integer. Use deductive reasoning to show the conjecture is true.

$2n$ and $2m$ are _____ integers because any integer multiplied by 2 is _____.

$2n -$ ___ and $2m +$ ___ are _____ integers because $2n$ and $2m$ are _____ integers.

$(2n -$ ___$) + (2m +$ ___$)$ represents the sum of an _____ integer $2n -$ ___ and an _____ integer $2m +$ ___.

$(2n -$ ___$) + (2m +$ ___$) =$ ___$(n + m)$

The result is the product of ___ and an integer $n + m$. So, ___$(n + m)$ is an _____ integer.

The sum of an odd integer and an odd integer is an _____ integer.

✓ ***Checkpoint*** **Complete the following exercise.**

3. Use inductive reasoning to make a conjecture about the sum of a negative integer and itself. Then use deductive reasoning to show the conjecture is true.

Your Notes

Example 4 *Reasoning from a graph*

Tell whether the statement is the result of *inductive reasoning* or *deductive reasoning*. *Explain* your choice.

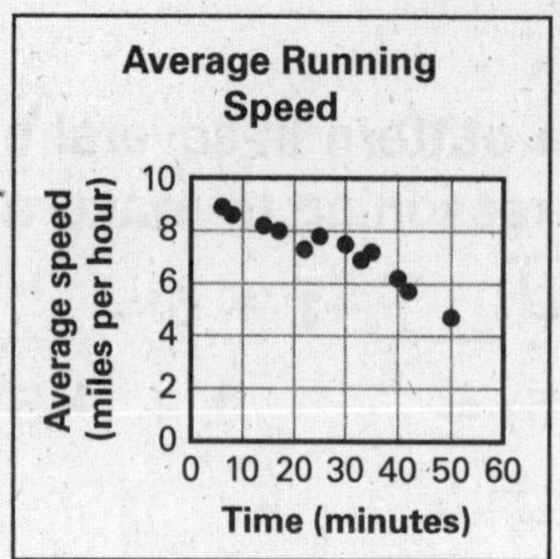

a. The runner's average speed decreases as time spent running increases.

b. The runner's average speed is slower when running for 40 minutes than when running for 10 minutes.

Solution

a. ________ reasoning, because it is based on a pattern in the data

b. ________ reasoning, because you are comparing values that are given on the graph

Checkpoint **Complete the following exercises.**

4. Use inductive reasoning to write another statement about the graph in Example 4.

5. Use deductive reasoning to write another statement about the graph in Example 4.

Homework

2.4 Use Postulates and Diagrams

Goal • Use postulates involving points, lines, and planes.

Your Notes

VOCABULARY

Line perpendicular to a plane

POINT, LINE, AND PLANE POSTULATES

Postulate 5 Through any two points there exists exactly one ______.

Postulate 6 A line contains at least two ________.

Postulate 7 If two lines intersect, then their intersection is exactly ___________.

Postulate 8 Through any three ______________ points there exists exactly one plane.

Postulate 9 A plane contains at least three ______________ points.

Postulate 10 If two points lie in a plane, then the line containing them _________________.

Postulate 11 If two planes intersect, then their intersection is a ______.

Example 1 ***Identify a postulate illustrated by a diagram***

State the postulate illustrated by the diagram.

Solution

Postulate ___ Through any three ______________ points there exists exactly one plane.

Your Notes

Example 2 ***Identify postulates from a diagram***

Use the diagram to write examples of Postulates 9 and 11.

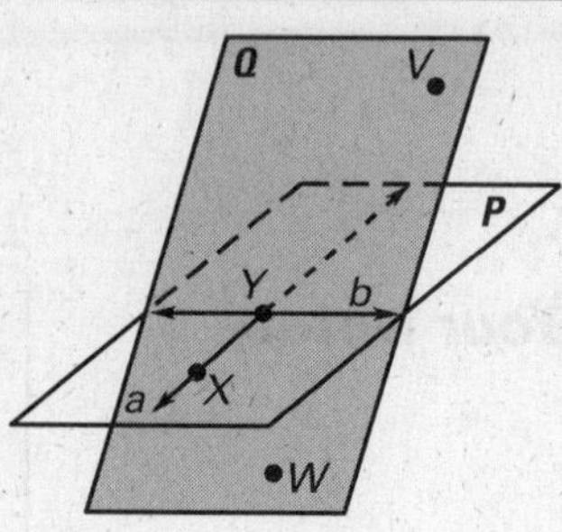

Postulate 9 Plane ____ contains at least three noncollinear points, ____________.

Postulate 11 The intersection of plane *P* and plane *Q* is ________.

✔ ***Checkpoint*** **Use the diagram in Example 2 to complete the following exercises.**

1. Which postulate allows you to say that the intersection of line *a* and line *b* is a point?

____

2. Write examples of Postulates 5 and 6.

CONCEPT SUMMARY: INTERPRETING A DIAGRAM

When you interpret a diagram, you can only assume information about size or measure if it is marked.

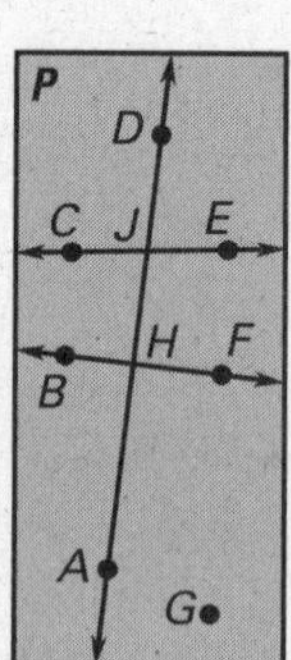

YOU CAN ASSUME

All points shown are ____________.

∠*AHB* and ________ are a linear pair.

∠*AHF* and ________ are vertical angles.

A, *H*, *J*, and *D* are .

$\overleftrightarrow{AD}$ and $\overleftrightarrow{BF}$ intersect at ____.

YOU CANNOT ASSUME

G, *F*, and *E* are collinear.

$\overleftrightarrow{BF}$ and $\overleftrightarrow{CE}$ intersect.

$\overleftrightarrow{BF}$ and $\overleftrightarrow{CE}$ do not intersect.

$\angle BHA \cong \angle CJA$

$\overleftrightarrow{AD} \perp \overleftrightarrow{BF}$ or $m\angle AHB = 90°$

Your Notes

Example 3 *Use given information to sketch a diagram*

Sketch a diagram showing $\overline{RS}$ perpendicular to $\overleftrightarrow{TV}$, intersecting at point X.

Notice that the picture was drawn so that X does not look like a midpoint of $\overline{RS}$.

Solution

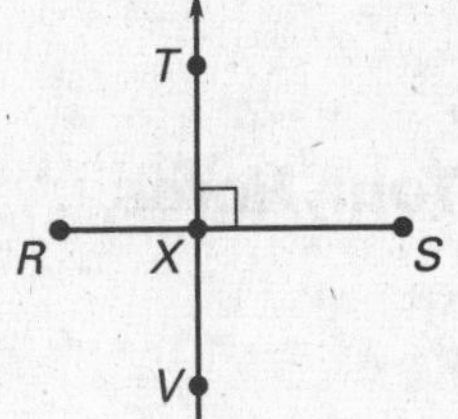

Step 1 Draw $\overline{RS}$ and label points R and S.

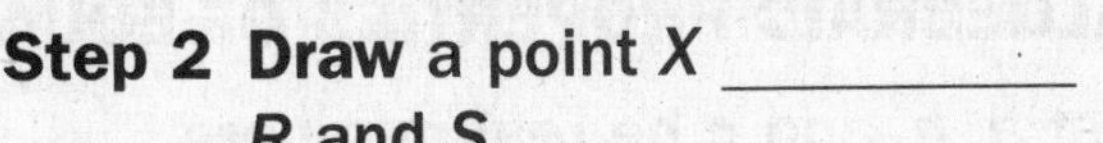

Step 2 Draw a point X ________ R and S.

Step 3 Draw $\overleftrightarrow{TV}$ through X so that it is ________ to $\overline{RS}$.

Example 4 *Interpret a diagram in three dimensions*

Which of the following statements *cannot* be assumed from the diagram?

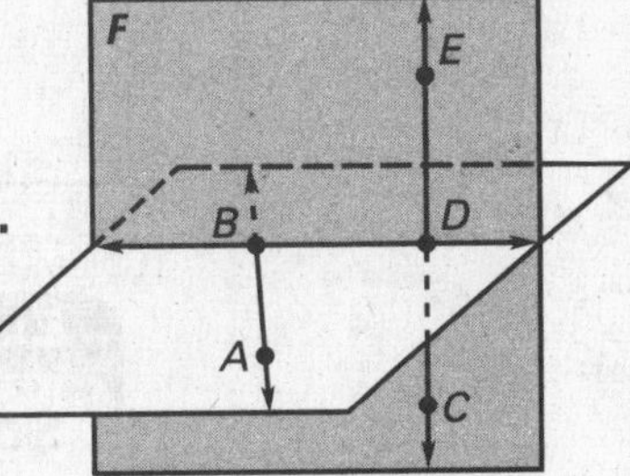

E, D, and C are collinear.

The intersection of $\overleftrightarrow{BD}$ and $\overleftrightarrow{EC}$ is D.

$\overleftrightarrow{BD} \perp \overleftrightarrow{EC}$

$\overleftrightarrow{EC} \perp$ plane G

Solution

With no right angles marked, you cannot assume that ________ or ________.

✔ ***Checkpoint*** **Complete the following exercises.**

3. In Example 3, if the given information indicated that $\overline{RX}$ and $\overline{XS}$ are congruent, how would the diagram change?

4. In the diagram for Example 4, can you assume that $\overleftrightarrow{BD}$ is the intersection of plane F and plane G?

Homework

2.5 Reason Using Properties from Algebra

Goal • Use algebraic properties in logical arguments.

Your Notes

ALGEBRAIC PROPERTIES OF EQUALITY

Let a, b, and c be real numbers.

Addition Property If $a = b$, then ________.

Subtraction Property If $a = b$, then ________.

Multiplication Property If $a = b$, then ________.

Division Property If $a = b$ and $c \neq 0$, then ________.

Substitution Property If $a = b$, then ________ ________ ________.

Example 1 ***Write reasons for each step***

Solve $2x + 3 = 9 - x$. Write a reason for each step.

Equation	Explanation	Reason
$2x + 3 = 9 - x$	Write original equation.	Given
$2x + 3 +$ ___ $= 9 - x +$ ___	Add ___ to each side.	________
___ $+ 3 =$ ___	Combine like terms.	________
___ $=$ ___	Subtract ___ from each side.	________
$x =$ ___	Divide each side by ___.	________

The value of x is ___.

Your Notes

DISTRIBUTIVE PROPERTY

$a(b + c) =$ ________, where a, b, and c are real numbers.

Example 2 ***Use the Distributive Property***

Solve $-4(6x + 2) = 64$. Write a reason for each step.

Solution

Equation	Explanation	Reason
$-4(6x + 2) = 64$	Write original equation.	Given
________ $= 64$	Multiply.	________ ________
______ $=$ ____	Add ____ to each side.	________ Property of Equality
____ $=$ ____	Divide each side by ______.	________ Property of Equality

Checkpoint Complete the following exercises.

1. Solve $x - 5 = 7 + 2x$. Write a reason for each step.

2. Solve $4(5 - x) = -2x$. Write a reason for each step.

Your Notes

Example 3 *Use properties in the real world*

Speed A motorist travels 5 miles per hour slower than the speed limit s for 3.5 hours. The distance traveled d can be determined by the formula $d = 3.5(s - 5)$. Solve for s.

Equation	Explanation	Reason
$d = 3.5(s - 5)$	Write original equation.	Given
$d =$ ________	Multiply.	________
$d +$ ____ $=$ ____	Add ____ to each side.	________ Property of Equality
$\frac{d + \square}{\square} = s$	Divide each side by ____.	________ Property of Equality

REFLEXIVE PROPERTY OF EQUALITY

Real Numbers For any real number a, ________.

Segment Length For any segment AB, ________.

Angle Measure For any angle A, ________.

SYMMETRIC PROPERTY OF EQUALITY

Real Numbers For any real numbers a and b, if $a = b$, then ________.

Segment Length For any segments AB and CD, if $AB = CD$, then ________.

Angle Measure For any angles A and B, if $m\angle A = m\angle B$, then ________.

TRANSITIVE PROPERTY OF EQUALITY

Real Numbers For any real numbers a, b, and c, if $a = b$ and $b = c$, then ________.

Segment Length For any segments AB, CD, and EF, if $AB = CD$ and $CD = EF$, then ________.

Angle Measure For any angles A, B, and C, if $m\angle A = m\angle B$ and $m\angle B = m\angle C$, then ________.

Your Notes

Example 4 ***Use properties of equality***

Show that $CF = AD$.

Equation	Reason
$AB =$ ____	Given
$BC =$ ____	Given
$AC = AB + BC$	____________
____	
$DF =$ ____ + ____	Segment Addition Postulate
$DF = BC + AB$	________ Property of Equality
$DF =$ ____	________ Property of Equality
$DF + CD =$ ____ $+ CD$	________ Property of Equality
____ = ____	Substitution Property of Equality

✓ *Checkpoint* Complete the following exercises. In Exercises 4–6, name the property of equality that the statement illustrates.

3. Suppose the equation in Example 3 is $d = 5(s + 3)$. Solve for s. Write a reason for each step.

4. If $GH = JK$, then $JK = GH$.

5. If $r = s$, and $s = 44$, then $r = 44$.

6. $m\angle N = m\angle N$

Homework

2.6 Prove Statements about Segments and Angles

Goal • Write proofs using geometric theorems.

Your Notes

VOCABULARY

Proof

Two-column proof

Theorem

Example 1 ***Write a two-column proof***

Use the diagram to prove $m\angle 1 = m\angle 4$.

Given $m\angle 2 = m\angle 3$, $m\angle AXD = m\angle AXC$

Prove $m\angle 1 = m\angle 4$

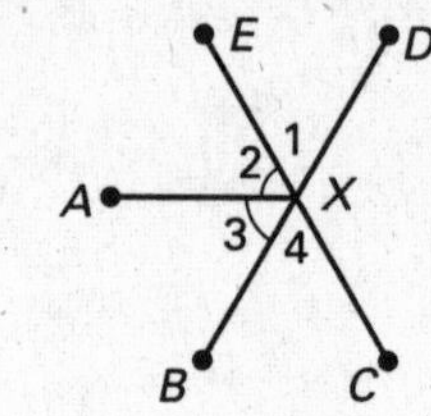

Writing a two-column proof is a formal way of organizing your reasons to show a statement is true.

Statements	Reasons
1. $m\angle AXC = m\angle AXD$	1. ______
2. $m\angle AXD = m\angle$ ___ $+ m\angle$ ___	2. Angle Addition Postulate
3. $m\angle AXC = m\angle$ ___ $+ m\angle$ ___	3. Angle Addition Postulate
4. $m\angle 1 + m\angle 2 = m\angle 3 + m\angle 4$	4. ______
5. $m\angle 2 = m\angle 3$	5. ______
6. $m\angle 1 + m\angle$ ___ $= m\angle 3 + m\angle 4$	6. Substitution Property of Equality
7. $m\angle 1 = m\angle 4$	7. ______

Your Notes

THEOREM 2.1 CONGRUENCE OF SEGMENTS

Segment congruence is reflexive, symmetric, and transitive.

Reflexive For any segment AB, __________.

Symmetric If $\overline{AB} \cong \overline{CD}$, then __________.

Transitive If $\overline{AB} \cong \overline{CD}$ and $\overline{CD} \cong \overline{EF}$, then __________.

THEOREM 2.2 CONGRUENCE OF ANGLES

Angle congruence is reflexive, symmetric, and transitive.

Reflexive For any angle A, __________.

Symmetric If $\angle A \cong \angle B$, then __________.

Transitive If $\angle A \cong \angle B$ and $\angle B \cong \angle C$, then __________.

Example 2 ***Name the property shown***

Name the property illustrated by the statement.

If $\angle 5 \cong \angle 3$, then $\angle 3 \cong \angle 5$.

____

Checkpoint **Complete the following exercises.**

1. Three steps of a proof are shown. Give the reasons for the last two steps.

Given $BC = AB$

Prove $AC = AB + AB$

A B C

Statements	Reasons
1. $BC = AB$	1. Given
2. $AC = AB + BC$	2. __________
3. $AC = AB + AB$	3. __________

2. Name the property illustrated by the statement.
If $\angle H \cong \angle T$ and $\angle T \cong \angle B$, then $\angle H \cong \angle B$.

Your Notes

Before writing a proof, organize your reasoning by copying or drawing a diagram for the situation described. Then identify the GIVEN and PROVE statements.

Example 3 *Use properties of equality*

If you know that $\overrightarrow{BD}$ bisects $\angle ABC$, prove that $m\angle ABC$ is two times $m\angle 1$.

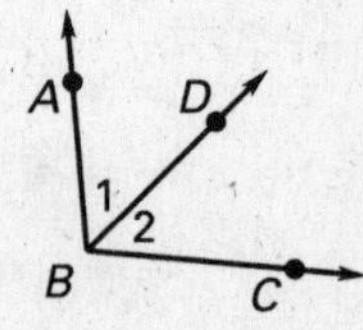

Given $\overrightarrow{BD}$ bisects $\angle ABC$.

Prove $m\angle ABC = 2 \cdot m\angle 1$

Statements	Reasons
1. $\overrightarrow{BD}$ bisects $\angle ABC$.	1. ________
2. ________	2. Definition of angle bisector
3. ________	3. Definition of congruent angles
4. $m\angle 1 + m\angle 2 = m\angle ABC$	4. ________
5. $m\angle 1 + m\angle$ ___ $= m\angle ABC$	5. Substitution Property of Equality
6. ________	6. Distributive Property

CONCEPT SUMMARY: WRITING A TWO-COLUMN PROOF

Proof of the Symmetric Property of Segment Congruence

Given $\overline{AB} \cong \overline{CD}$

Prove $\overline{CD} \cong \overline{AB}$

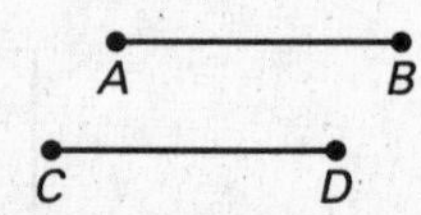

Copy or draw diagrams and label information to help develop proofs.

Statements	Reasons
1. $\overline{AB} \cong \overline{CD}$	1. ________
2. ________	2. Definition of congruent segments
3. ________	3. Symmetric Property of Equality
4. $\overline{CD} \cong \overline{AB}$	4. Definition of congruent segments

Statements based on facts that you know or conclusions from deductive reasoning

The number of statements will vary.

Remember to give a reason for the last statement.

Definitions, postulates, or proven theorems that allow you to state the corresponding statement.

Your Notes

Example 4 ***Solve a multi-step problem***

Interstate There are two exits between rest areas on a stretch of interstate. The Rice exit is halfway between rest area A and the Mason exit. The distance between rest area B and the Mason exit is the same as the distance between rest area A and the Rice exit. Prove that the Mason exit is halfway between the Rice exit and rest area B.

Solution

Step 1 Draw a diagram.

Step 2 Draw diagrams showing relationships.

Step 3 Write a proof.

Given *R* is the midpoint of $\overline{AM}$, $MB = AR$.

Prove *M* is the midpoint of $\overline{RB}$.

Statements	Reasons
1. *R* is the midpoint of $\overline{AM}$, $MB = AR$.	1. ________
2. ________	2. Definition of midpoint
3. ________	3. Definition of congruent segments
4. $MB = RM$	4. ________
5. ________	5. Definition of congruent segments
6. *M* is the midpoint of $\overline{RB}$.	6. ________

Homework

✔ ***Checkpoint*** **Complete the following exercise.**

3. In Example 4, there are rumble strips halfway between the Rice and Mason exits. What other two places are the same distance from the rumble strips?

2.7 Prove Angle Pair Relationships

Goal • Use properties of special pairs of angles.

Your Notes

THEOREM 2.3 RIGHT ANGLES CONGRUENCE THEOREM

All right angles are ________.

Example 1 ***Use right angle congruence***

The given information in Example 1 is about perpendicular lines. You must then use deductive reasoning to show that the angles are right angles.

Write a proof.

Given $\overline{JK} \perp \overline{KL}$, $\overline{ML} \perp \overline{KL}$

Prove $\angle K \cong \angle L$

Statements	Reasons
1. $\overline{JK} \perp \overline{KL}$, $\overline{ML} \perp \overline{KL}$	1. ________
2. ________	2. Definition of perpendicular lines
3. $\angle K \cong \angle L$	3. ________

THEOREM 2.4 CONGRUENT SUPPLEMENTS THEOREM

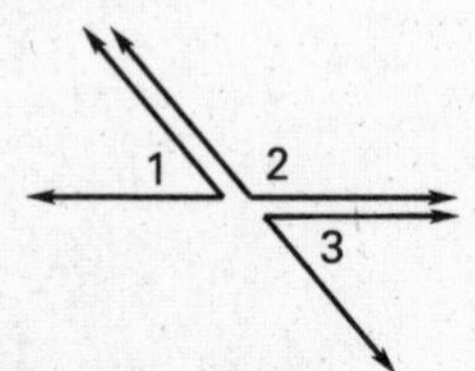

If two angles are supplementary to the same angle (or to congruent angles), then they are ________.

If $\angle 1$ and $\angle 2$ are supplementary and $\angle 3$ and $\angle 2$ are supplementary, then ________.

THEOREM 2.5 CONGRUENT COMPLEMENTS THEOREM

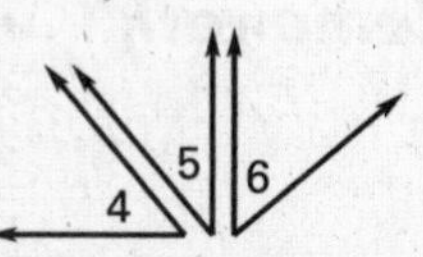

If two angles are complementary to the same angle (or to congruent angles), then they are ________.

If $\angle 4$ and $\angle 5$ are complementary and $\angle 6$ and $\angle 5$ are complementary, then ________.

Your Notes

Example 2 Use the Congruent Supplements Theorem

Write a proof.

Given $\angle 1$ and $\angle 2$ are supplements.
$\angle 1$ and $\angle 4$ are supplements.
$m\angle 2 = 45°$

Prove $m\angle 4 = 45°$

Statements	Reasons
1. $\angle 1$ and $\angle 2$ are supplements. $\angle 1$ and $\angle 4$ are supplements.	1. ______
2. ______	2. Congruent Supplements Theorem
3. $m\angle 2 = m\angle 4$	3. ______
4. $m\angle 2 = 45°$	4. ______
5. ______	5. Substitution Property of Equality

Checkpoint Complete the following exercises.

1. In Example 1, suppose you are given that $\angle K \cong \angle L$. Can you use the Right Angles Congruence Theorem to prove that $\angle K$ and $\angle L$ are right angles? *Explain.*

2. Suppose $\angle A$ and $\angle B$ are complements, and $\angle A$ and $\angle C$ are complements. Can $\angle B$ and $\angle C$ be supplements? *Explain.*

Your Notes

POSTULATE 12 LINEAR PAIR POSTULATE

If two angles form a linear pair, then they are ________.

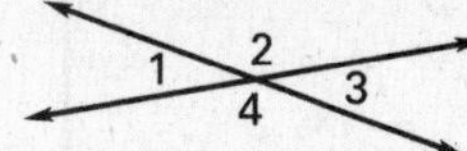

$\angle 1$ and $\angle 2$ form a linear pair, so $\angle 1$ and $\angle 2$ are supplementary and $m\angle 1 + m\angle 2 =$ ____.

THEOREM 2.6 VERTICAL ANGLES CONGRUENCE THEOREM

Vertical angles are ________.

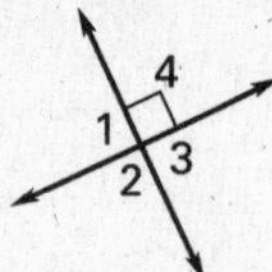

Example 3 ***Use the Vertical Angles Congruence Theorem***

You can use information labeled in a diagram in your proof.

Write a proof.

Given $\angle 4$ is a right angle.

Prove $\angle 2$ and $\angle 4$ are supplementary.

Statements	Reasons
1. $\angle 4$ is a right angle.	1. ________
2. ________	2. Definition of a right angle
3. $\angle 2 \cong \angle 4$	3. ________
4. ________	4. Definition of congruent angles
5. $m\angle 2 = 90°$	5. ________
6. ________	6. $m\angle 2 + m\angle 4 = 180°$

Checkpoint In Exercises 3 and 4, use the diagram.

3. If $m\angle 4 = 63°$, find $m\angle 1$ and $m\angle 2$.

____

4. If $m\angle 3 = 121°$, find $m\angle 1$, $m\angle 2$, and $m\angle 4$.

Your Notes

Example 4 *Find angle measures*

Write and solve an equation to find x. Use x to find $m\angle FKG$.

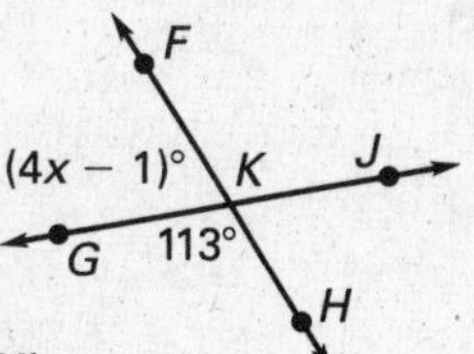

Solution

Because $m\angle FKG$ and $m\angle GKH$ form a linear pair, the sum of their measures is ______.

$(4x - 1)° + 113° =$ ______	**Write equation.**
$4x +$ ______ $=$ ______	**Simplify.**
$4x =$ ____	**Subtract ______ from each side.**
$x =$ ____	**Divide each side by 4.**

Use $x =$ ____ to find $m\angle FKG$.

$m\angle FKG = (4x - 1)°$	**Write equation.**
$= [4(\_\_\_\_) - 1]°$	**Substitute ____ for x.**
$= [\_\_\_\_ - 1]°$	**Multiply.**
$=$ ______	**Simplify.**

The measure of $\angle FKG$ is ____.

✔ ***Checkpoint*** **Complete the following exercise.**

5. Find $m\angle AEB$.

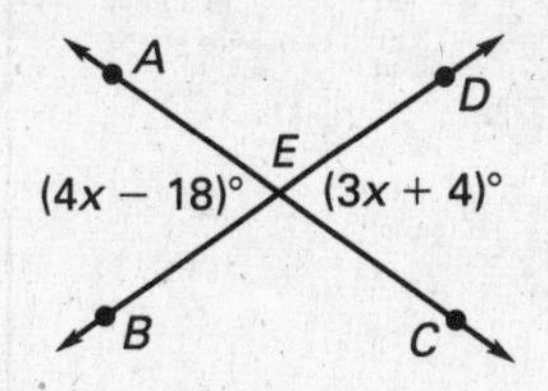

Homework

Words to Review

Give an example of the vocabulary word.

Conjecture	Inductive reasoning
Counterexample	Conditional statement
If-then form	Hypothesis
Conclusion	Negation
Converse	Inverse

Contrapositive	Equivalent statements
Perpendicular lines	Biconditional statement
Deductive reasoning	Line perpendicular to a plane
Proof	Theorem
Two-column proof	

Review your notes and Chapter 2 by using the Chapter Review on pages 134–137 of your textbook.

3.1 Identify Pairs of Lines and Angles

Goal • Identify angle pairs formed by three intersecting lines.

Your Notes

VOCABULARY

Parallel lines

Skew lines

Parallel planes

Transversal

Corresponding angles

Alternate interior angles

Alternate exterior angles

Consecutive interior angles

Your Notes

Example 1 *Identify relationships in space*

Think of each segment in the figure as part of a line. Which line(s) or plane(s) in the figure appear to fit the description?

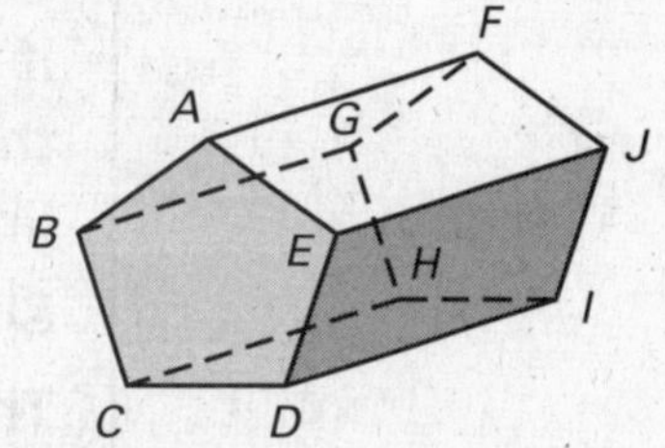

a. Line(s) parallel to $\overleftrightarrow{AF}$ and containing point E

b. Line(s) skew to $\overleftrightarrow{AF}$ and containing point E

c. Line(s) perpendicular to $\overleftrightarrow{AF}$ and containing point E

d. Plane(s) parallel to plane FGH and containing point E

Solution

a. _______________ all appear parallel to $\overleftrightarrow{AF}$, but only _____ contains point E.

b. _______________ all appear skew to $\overleftrightarrow{AF}$, but only _____ contains point E.

c. _______________ all appear perpendicular to $\overleftrightarrow{AF}$, but only _____ contains point E.

d. Plane _____ appears parallel to plane FGH and contains point E.

Checkpoint Think of each segment in the figure as part of a line. Which line(s) or plane(s) in the figure appear to fit the description?

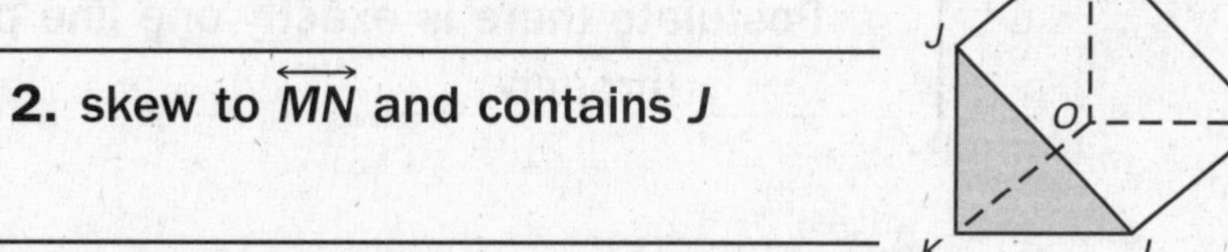

1. parallel to $\overleftrightarrow{MN}$ and contains J

____

2. skew to $\overleftrightarrow{MN}$ and contains J

____

3. perpendicular to $\overleftrightarrow{MN}$ and contains J

____

4. Name the plane that contains J and appears to be parallel to plane MNO.

Your Notes

POSTULATE 13 PARALLEL POSTULATE

If there is a line and a point not on the line, then there is ________ line through the point parallel to the given line.

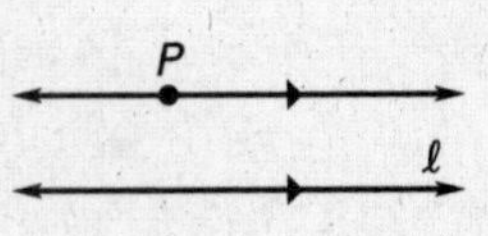

There is exactly one line through P parallel to ℓ.

POSTULATE 14 PERPENDICULAR POSTULATE

If there is a line and a point not on the line, then there is ________ line through the point perpendicular to the given line.

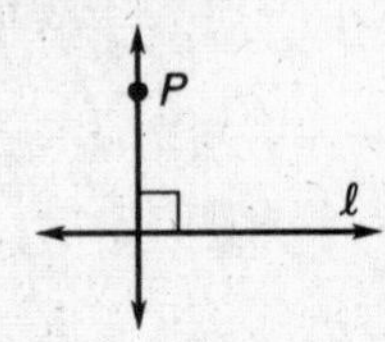

There is exactly one line through P perpendicular to ℓ.

Example 2 *Identify parallel and perpendicular lines*

Use the diagram at the right to answer each question.

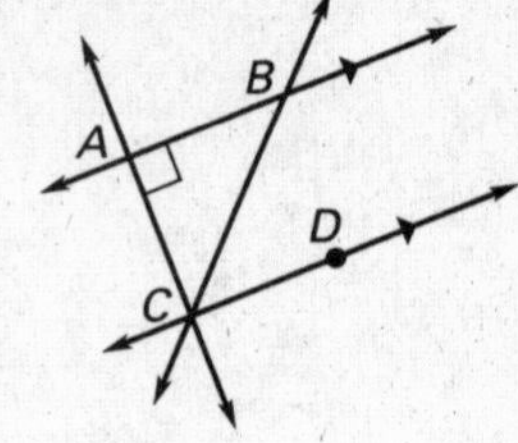

a. Name a pair of parallel lines.

b. Name a pair of perpendicular lines.

c. Is $\overleftrightarrow{AB} \perp \overleftrightarrow{BC}$? *Explain.*

Solution

a.

b.

c. $\overleftrightarrow{AB}$ ________ perpendicular to $\overleftrightarrow{BC}$, because $\overleftrightarrow{AB}$ is perpendicular to $\overleftrightarrow{AC}$ and by the ________ Postulate there is exactly one line perpendicular to ____ through ____.

Checkpoint Complete the following exercise.

5. In Example 2, can you use the Perpendicular Postulate to show that $\overleftrightarrow{AC} \perp \overleftrightarrow{CD}$? *Explain.*

Your Notes

ANGLES FORMED BY TRANSVERSALS

Two angles are ______________ angles if they have corresponding positions. For example, ∠2 and ∠6 are above the lines and to the right of the transversal *t*.

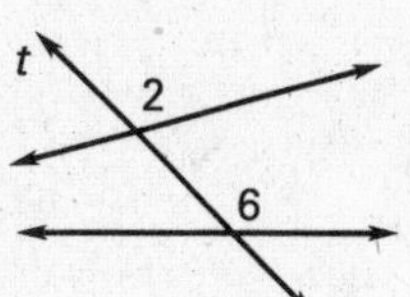

Two angles are ______________ angles if they lie between the two lines and on opposite sides of the transversal.

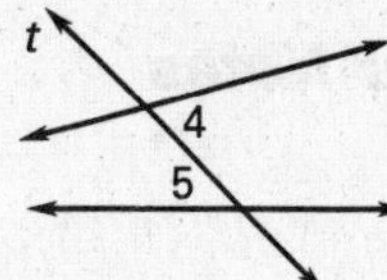

Two angles are ______________ angles if they lie outside the two lines and on opposite sides of the transversal.

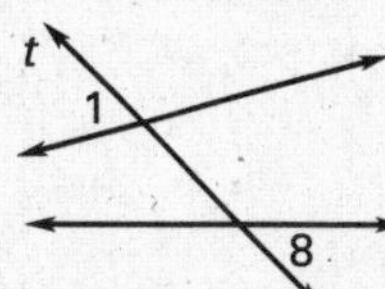

Another name for consecutive interior angles is

____

Two angles are ______________ angles if they lie between the two lines and on the same side of the transversal.

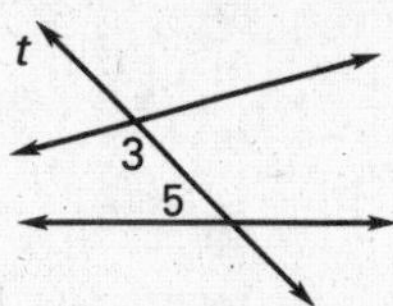

Example 3 ***Identify angle relationships***

Identify all pairs of (a) corresponding angles, (b) alternate interior angles, (c) alternate exterior angles, and (d) consecutive interior angles.

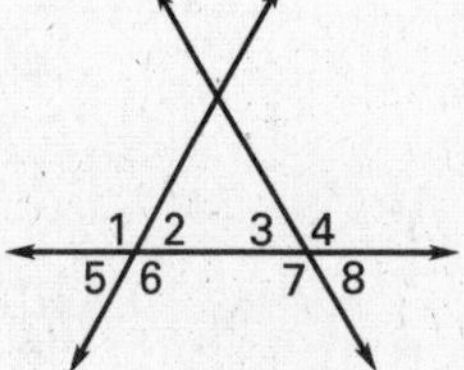

a. ∠1 and _____, ∠2 and _____, ∠5 and _____, _____ and _____

b. ∠2 and _____, _____ and _____

c. ∠5 and _____, _____ and _____

d. ∠2 and _____, _____ and _____

✔ ***Checkpoint*** **Classify the pair of numbered angles.**

6.	7.
3, 4	1, 2

Homework

3.2 Use Parallel Lines and Transversals

Goal • Use angles formed by parallel lines and transversals.

Your Notes

POSTULATE 15 CORRESPONDING ANGLES POSTULATE

If two parallel lines are cut by a transversal, then the pairs of corresponding angles are ________.

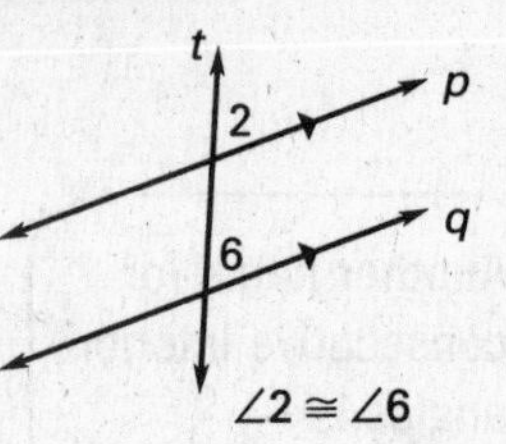

Example 1 ***Identify congruent angles***

The measure of three of the numbered angles is 125°. Identify the angles. *Explain* your reasoning.

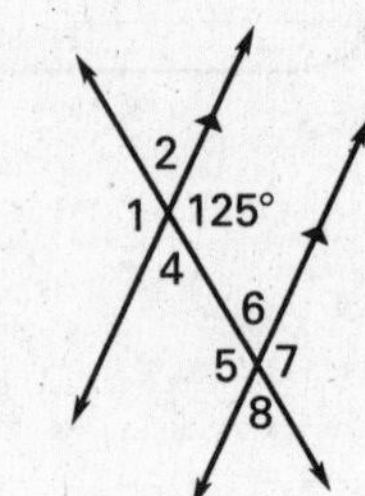

Solution

By the Corresponding Angles Postulate, ________ = 125°.

Using the Vertical Angles Congruence Theorem, ________ = 125°.

Because ∠1 and ∠5 are corresponding angles, by the ________________________, you know that ________ = 125°.

✔ ***Checkpoint*** **Complete the following exercise using the diagram shown.**

1. If $m\angle 7 = 75°$, find $m\angle 1$, $m\angle 3$, and $m\angle 5$. Tell which postulate or theorem you use in each case.

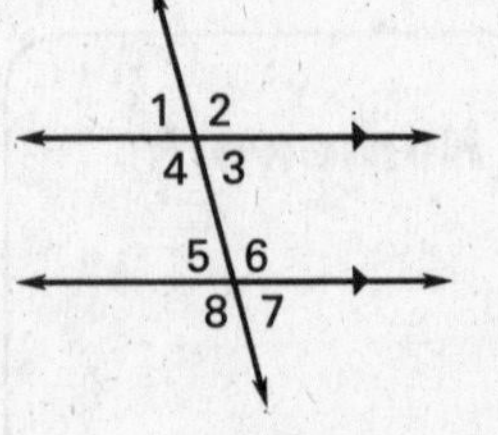

Your Notes

THEOREM 3.1 ALTERNATE INTERIOR ANGLES THEOREM

If two parallel lines are cut by a transversal, then the pairs of alternate interior angles are ____________.

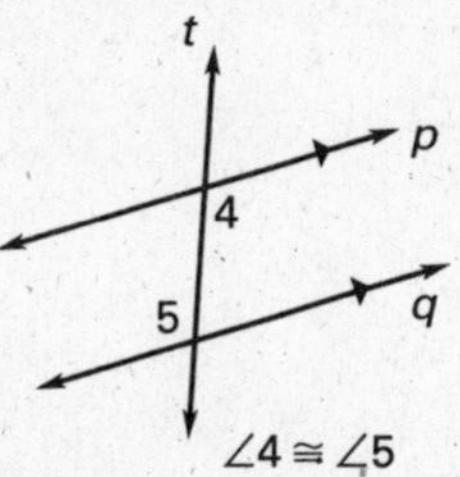

THEOREM 3.2 ALTERNATE EXTERIOR ANGLES THEOREM

If two parallel lines are cut by a transversal, then the pairs of alternate exterior angles are ____________.

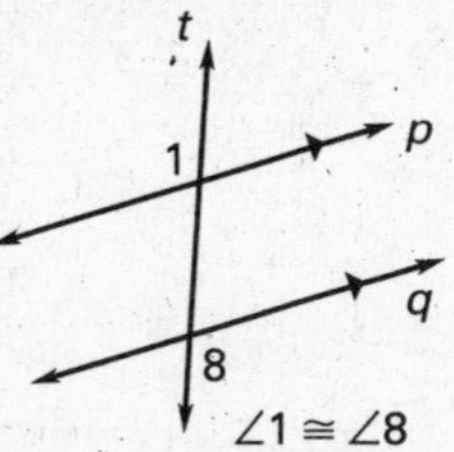

THEOREM 3.3 CONSECUTIVE INTERIOR ANGLES THEOREM

If two parallel lines are cut by a transversal, then the pairs of consecutive interior angles are ____________.

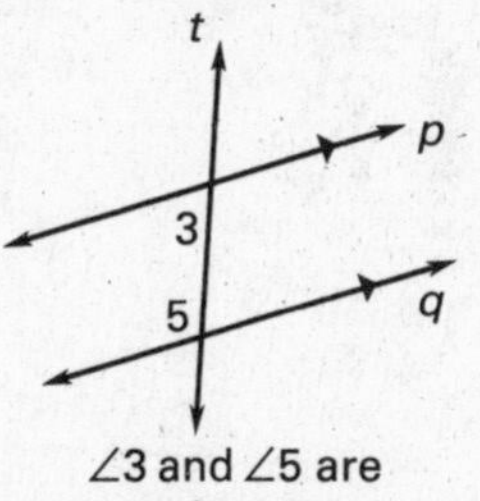

Example 2 *Use properties of parallel lines*

Find the value of *x*.

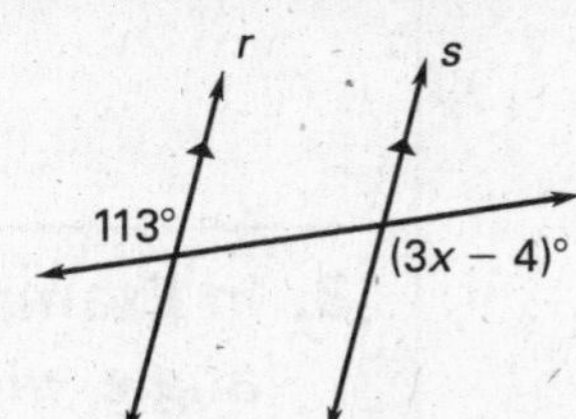

Solution

Lines *r* and *s* are __________, so you can use the theorems about parallel lines.

______ $= (3x - 4)°$ ______________________________

______ $= 3x$ **Add ___ to each side.**

______ $= x$ **Divide each side by ___.**

The value of x is ____.

Your Notes

Example 3 ***Solve a real-world problem***

Runways A taxiway is being constructed that intersects two parallel runways at an airport. You know that $m\angle 2 = 98°$. What is $m\angle 1$? How do you know?

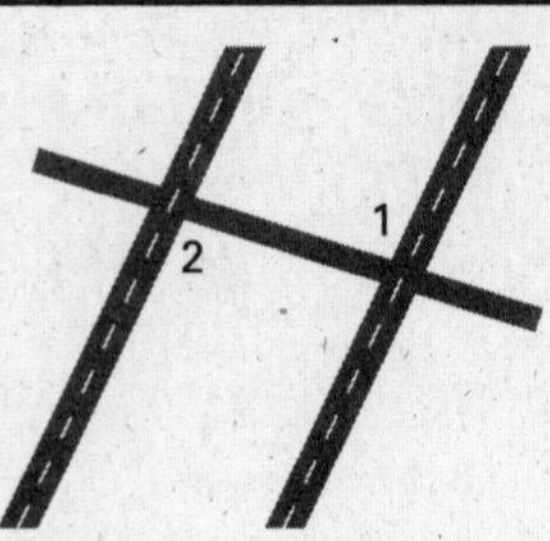

Solution

Because the runways are parallel, $\angle 1$ and $\angle 2$ are ________________. By the Alternate Interior Angles Theorem, $\angle 1 \cong$ ____. By the definition of congruent angles, $m\angle 1 =$ ____ $=$ ____.

Checkpoint Complete the following exercises.

2. Find the value of x.

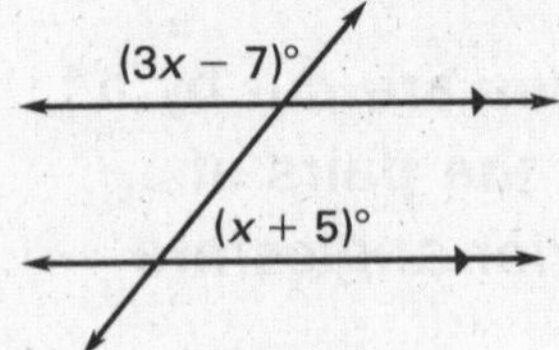

3. In Example 3, suppose $\angle 3$ is the consecutive interior angle with $\angle 2$. What is $m\angle 3$?

Homework

3.3 Prove Lines are Parallel

Goal • Use angle relationships to prove that lines are parallel.

Your Notes

VOCABULARY

Paragraph proof

POSTULATE 16 CORRESPONDING ANGLES CONVERSE

If two lines are cut by a transversal so the corresponding angles are congruent, then the lines are ________.

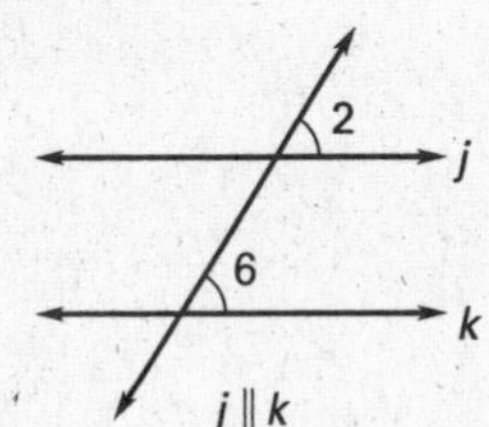

Example 1 ***Apply the Corresponding Angles Converse***

Find the value of x that makes $m \parallel n$.

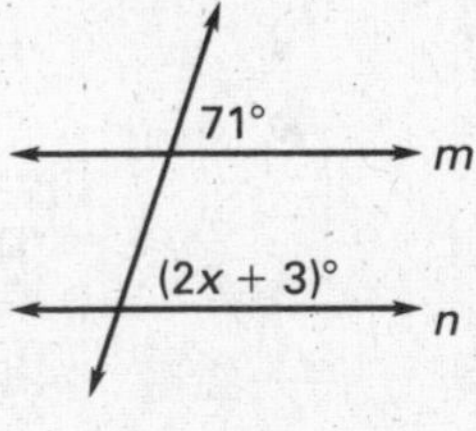

Solution

Lines m and n are parallel if the marked corresponding angles are congruent.

$(2x + 3)° =$ _____ **Use Postulate 16 to write an equation.**

$2x =$ _____ **Subtract ___ from each side.**

$x =$ _____ **Divide each side by ___.**

The lines m and n are parallel when $x =$ _____.

✔ ***Checkpoint*** **Find the value of x that makes $a \parallel b$.**

1.

Your Notes

THEOREM 3.4 ALTERNATE INTERIOR ANGLES CONVERSE

If two lines are cut by a transversal so the alternate interior angles are congruent, then the lines are __________.

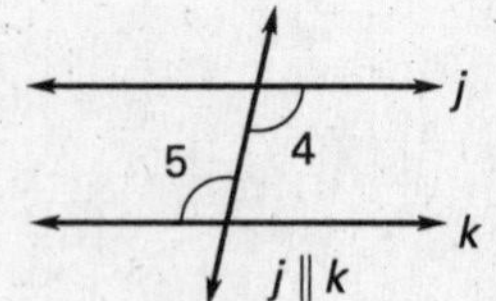

THEOREM 3.5 ALTERNATE EXTERIOR ANGLES CONVERSE

If two lines are cut by a transversal so the alternate exterior angles are congruent, then the lines are __________.

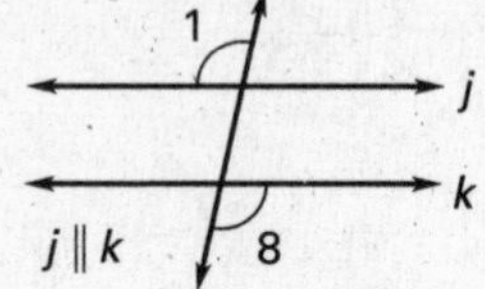

THEOREM 3.6 CONSECUTIVE INTERIOR ANGLES CONVERSE

If two lines are cut by a transversal so the consecutive interior angles are supplementary, then the lines are __________.

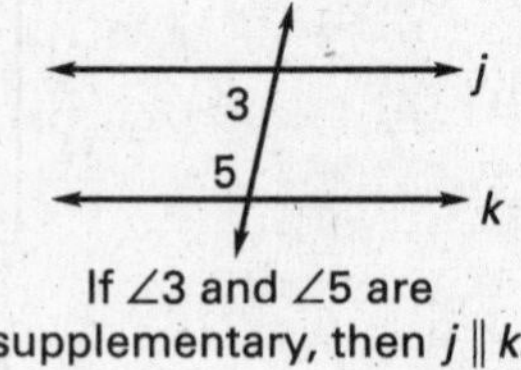

If ∠3 and ∠5 are supplementary, then $j \parallel k$.

Example 2 ***Solve a real-world problem***

Flags How can you tell whether the sides of the flag of Nepal are parallel?

Solution

Because the ____________________ are congruent, you know that the sides of the flag are __________.

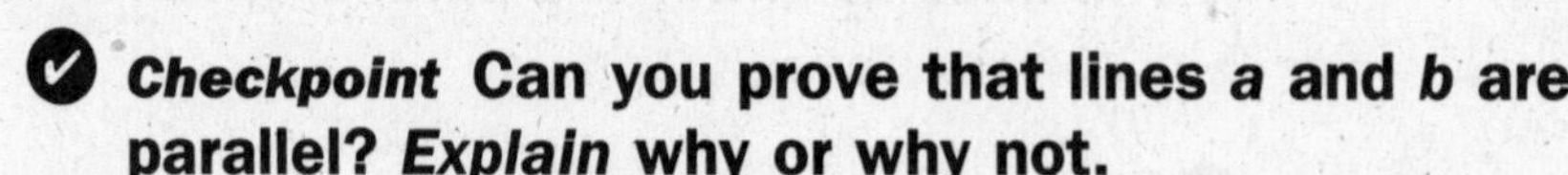

Checkpoint **Can you prove that lines *a* and *b* are parallel? *Explain* why or why not.**

2. $m\angle 1 + m\angle 2 = 180°$

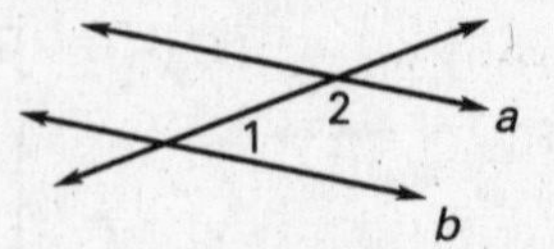

Your Notes

Example 3 ***Write a paragraph proof***

In the figure, $a \parallel b$ and $\angle 1$ is congruent to $\angle 3$. Prove $x \parallel y$.

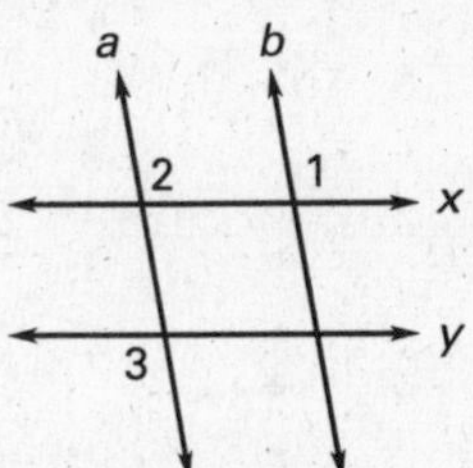

Solution

Look at the diagram to make a plan. The diagram suggests that you look at angles 1, 2, and 3. Also, you may find it helpful to focus on one pair of lines and one transversal at a time.

Plan for Proof

a. Look at $\angle 1$ and $\angle 2$.

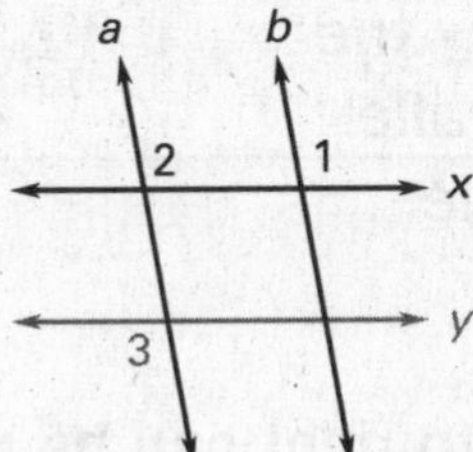

________________ because $a \parallel b$.

b. Look at $\angle 2$ and $\angle 3$.

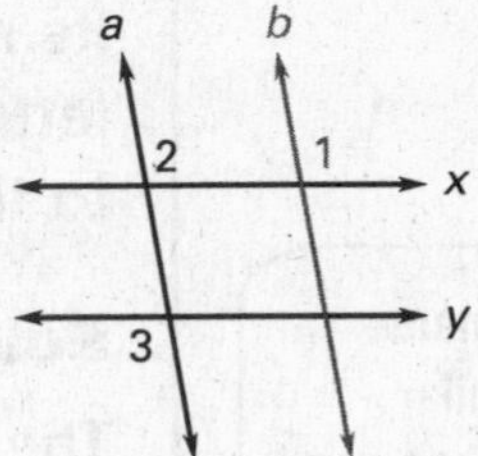

If $\angle 2 \cong \angle 3$ then ________.

In paragraph proofs, transitional words such as *so*, *then*, and *therefore* help to make the logic clear.

Plan in Action

a. It is given that $a \parallel b$, so by the ________________, $\angle 1 \cong \angle 2$.

b. It is also given that $\angle 1 \cong \angle 3$. Then __________ by the Transitive Property of Congruence for angles. Therefore, by the ________________________, $x \parallel y$.

✔ ***Checkpoint*** **Complete the following exercise.**

3. In Example 3, suppose it is given that $\angle 1 \cong \angle 3$ and $x \parallel y$. Complete the following paragraph proof showing that $a \parallel b$.

It is given that $x \parallel y$. By the Exterior Angles Postulate, __________.

It is also given that $\angle 1 \cong \angle 3$. Then __________ by the Transitive Property of Congruence for angles. Therefore, by the ____________________ __________, $a \parallel b$.

Your Notes

THEOREM 3.7 TRANSITIVE PROPERTY OF PARALLEL LINES

If two lines are parallel to the same line, then they are ________ to each other.

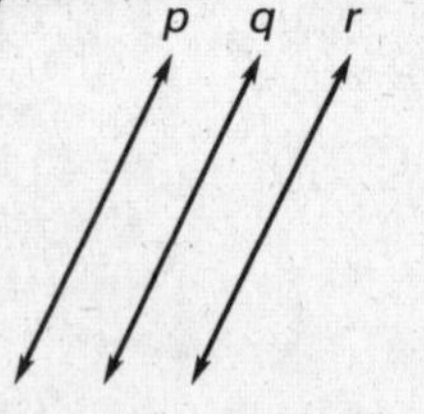

If $p \parallel q$ and $q \parallel r$, then $p \parallel r$.

Example 4 ***Use the Transitive Property of Parallel Lines***

Utility poles Each utility pole shown is parallel to the pole immediately to its right. *Explain* why the leftmost pole is parallel to the rightmost pole.

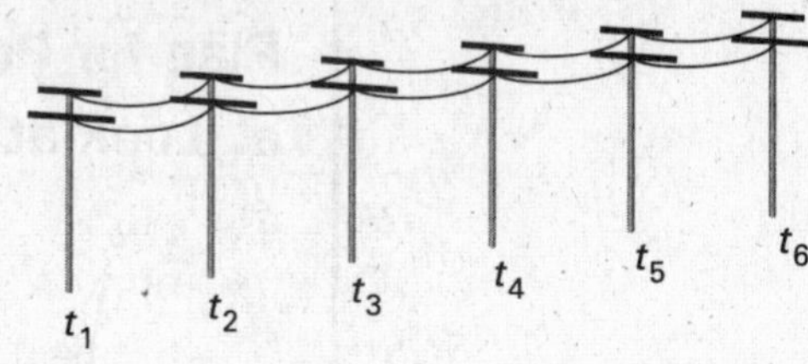

When you name several similar items, you can use one variable with subscripts to keep track of the items.

Solution

The poles from left to right can be named $t_1, t_2, t_3, \ldots, t_6$. Each pole is parallel to the one to its right, so $t_1 \parallel$ ____, $t_2 \parallel$ ____, and so on. Then $t_1 \parallel t_3$ by the ________________. Similarly, because $t_3 \parallel t_4$, it follows that $t_1 \parallel$ ____. By continuing this reasoning, $t_1 \parallel$ ____. So, the leftmost pole is parallel to the rightmost pole.

✔ ***Checkpoint*** **Complete the following exercise.**

4. Each horizontal piece of the window blinds shown is called a slat. Each slat is parallel to the slat immediately below it. *Explain* why the top slat is parallel to the bottom slat.

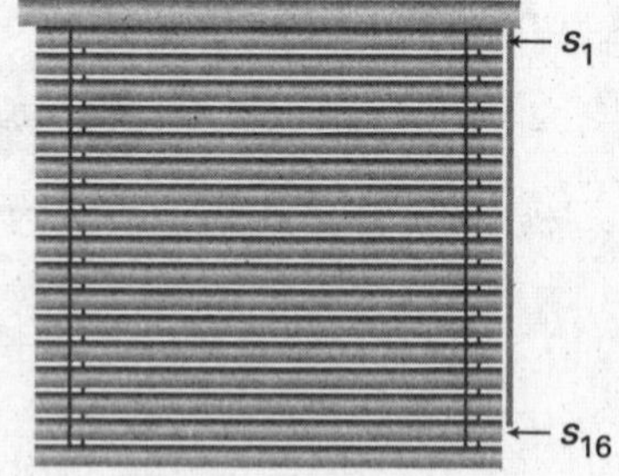

Homework

3.4 Find and Use Slopes of Lines

Goal • Find and compare slopes of lines.

Your Notes

VOCABULARY

Slope

SLOPE OF LINES IN THE COORDINATE PLANE

Negative slope: ______ from left to right, as in line *j*

Positive slope: ______ from left to right, as in line *k*

Undefined slope: ______, as in line *n*

Zero slope (slope of 0): ______, as in line ℓ

Example 1 ***Find slopes of lines in a coordinate plane***

Slope

$m = \frac{\text{rise}}{\text{run}}$

$= \frac{y_2 - y_1}{x_2 - x_1}$

Find the slope of line *a* and line *c*.

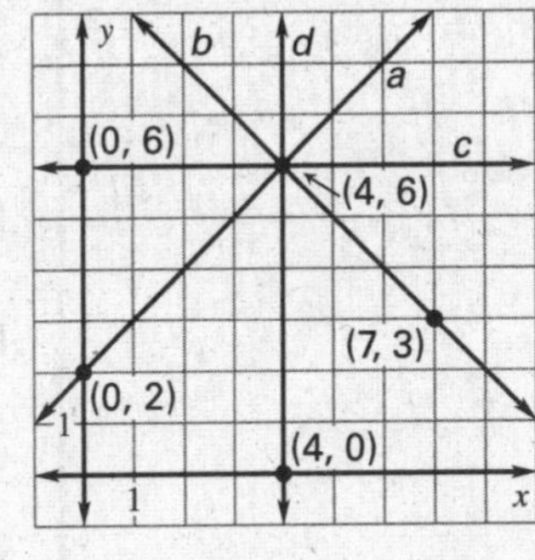

Slope of line *a*:

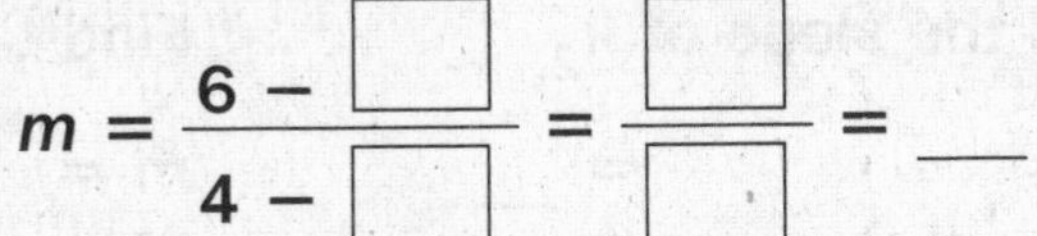

$m = \frac{6 - \square}{4 - \square} = \frac{\square}{\square} = \_\_\_$

Slope of line *c*:

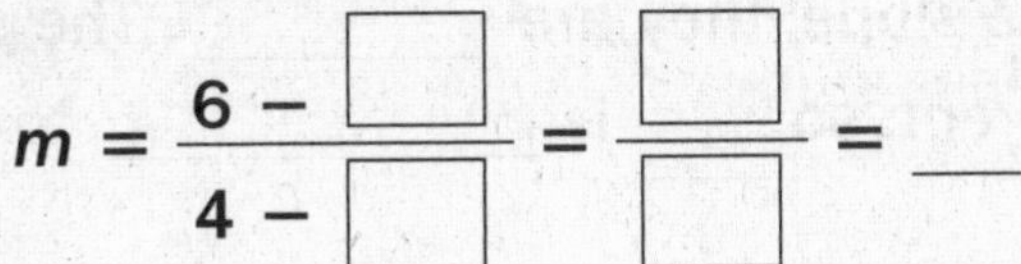

$m = \frac{6 - \square}{4 - \square} = \frac{\square}{\square} = \_\_\_$

Checkpoint **Use the graph in Example 1. Find the slope of the line.**

1. line *b*	**2.** line *d*

Your Notes

POSTULATE 17 SLOPES OF PARALLEL LINES

In a coordinate plane, two nonvertical lines are parallel if and only if they have the same ________.

Any two ________ lines are parallel.

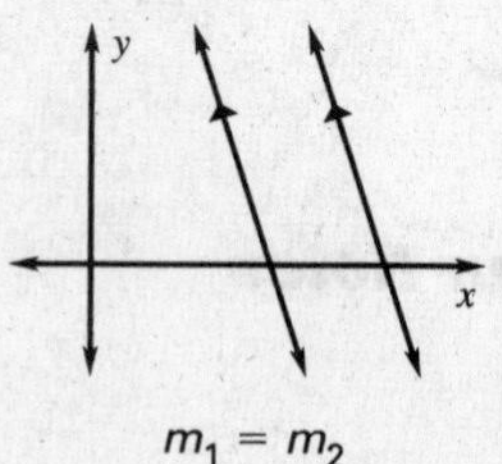

POSTULATE 18 SLOPES OF PERPENDICULAR LINES

If the product of two numbers is -1, then the numbers are called *negative reciprocals*.

In a coordinate plane, two nonvertical lines are perpendicular if and only if the product of their slopes is ____.

Horizontal lines are ________ to vertical lines.

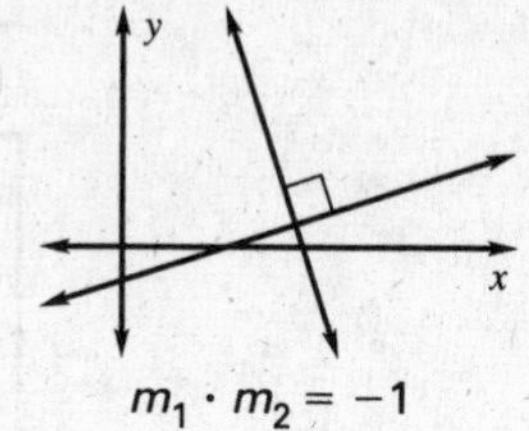

Example 2 ***Identify parallel lines***

Find the slope of each line. Which lines are parallel?

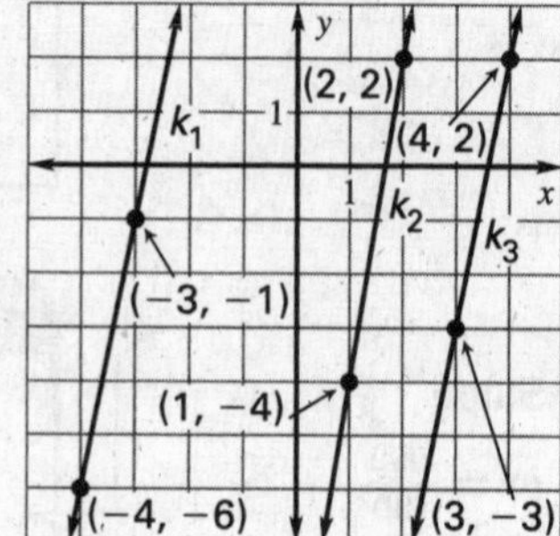

Solution

Find the slope of k_1.

$m = \frac{\_\_\_\_}{\_\_\_\_} = \frac{\_\_}{\_\_} = \_\_$

Find the slope of k_2.

$m = \frac{\_\_\_\_}{\_\_\_\_} = \_\_$

Find the slope of k_3.

$m = \frac{\_\_\_\_}{\_\_\_\_} = \_\_$

Compare the slopes. Because ___ and ___ have the same slope, they are ________. The slope of ___ is different, so ___ is ________ to the other lines.

Checkpoint **Complete the following exercise.**

3. Line *c* passes through (2, −2) and (5, 7). Line *d* passes through (−3, 4) and (1, −8). Are the two lines parallel? *Explain* how you know.

Your Notes

Example 3 *Draw a perpendicular line*

Line h passes through $(1, -2)$ and $(5, 6)$. Graph the line perpendicular to h that passes through the point $(2, 5)$.

Step 1 Find the slope m_1 of h through $(1, -2)$ and $(5, 6)$.

$m_1 = \frac{\_\_\_\_\_\_}{\_\_\_\_\_\_} = \frac{\_\_\_}{\_\_\_} = \_\_\_$

Step 2 Find the slope m_2 of a line perpendicular to h.

$\_\_\_ \cdot m_2 = -1$

$m_2 = \_\_\_$

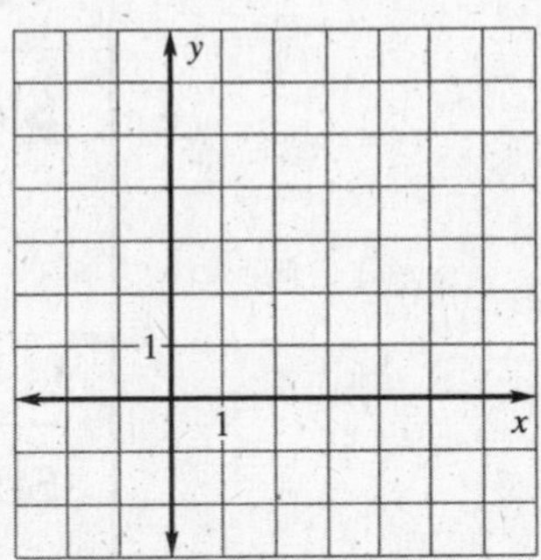

Step 3 Use the rise and run to graph the line.

Given a point on a line and the line's slope, you can use the rise and run to find a second point and draw the line.

Example 4 *Analyze graphs*

Delivery A trucker made three deliveries. The graph shows the trucker's distance to the destination from the starting time to the arrival time for each delivery. Use slopes to make a statement about the deliveries.

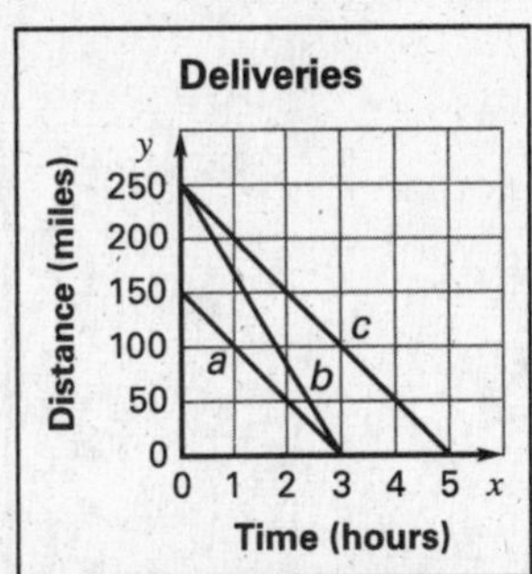

The rate at which the trucker drives is represented by the ______ of the segments. Segments ___ and ___ have the same slope, so deliveries a and c were driven at the same ______.

✓ ***Checkpoint*** **Complete the following exercises.**

4. Line n passes through $(1, 6)$ and $(8, 4)$. Line m passes through $(0, 5)$ and $(2, 12)$. Is $n \perp m$? *Explain.*

5. In Example 4, which delivery included the fastest rate of travel?

Homework

3.5 Write and Graph Equations of Lines

Goal • Find equations of lines.

Your Notes

VOCABULARY

Slope-intercept form

Standard form

Example 1 ***Write an equation of a line from a graph***

Write an equation of the line in slope-intercept form.

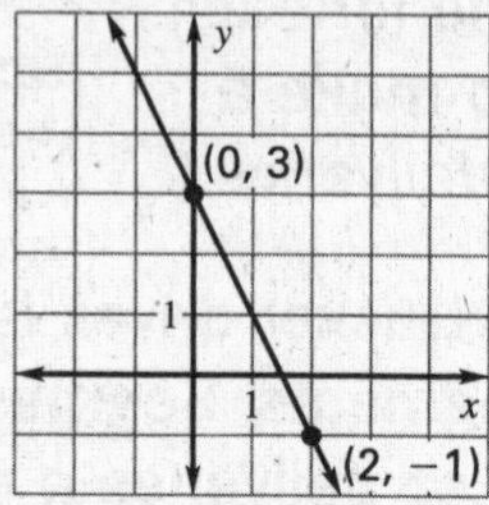

Solution

Step 1 **Find** the slope. Choose two points on the graph of the line, (0, 3) and (2, −1).

$m = \_\_\_\_\_\_ = \_\_\_\_\_\_ = \_\_\_\_$

Step 2 **Find** the y-intercept. The line intersects the y-axis at the point ______, so the y-intercept is ____.

Step 3 **Write** the equation.

$y = mx + b$ **Use slope-intercept form.**

$y = \_\_\_\_\_\_$ **Substitute _____ for *m* and ____ for *b*.**

Your Notes

The graph of a linear equation represents all the solutions of the equation. So, the given point must be a solution of the equation.

Example 2 *Write an equation of a parallel line*

Write an equation of the line passing through the point (1, −1) that is parallel to the line with the equation $y = 2x - 1$.

Solution

Step 1 **Find** the slope m. The slope of a line parallel to $y = 2x - 1$ is the same as the given line, so the slope is ___.

Step 2 **Find** the y-intercept b by using $m =$ ___ and $(x, y) =$ ________.

$y = mx + b$	**Use slope-intercept form.**
____ $=$ ___(___) $+ b$	**Substitute for x, y, and m.**
____ $= b$	**Solve for b.**

Because $m =$ ___ and $b =$ _____, an equation of the line is $y =$ ________.

✔ ***Checkpoint*** **Complete the following exercises.**

1. Write an equation of the line in the graph at the right.

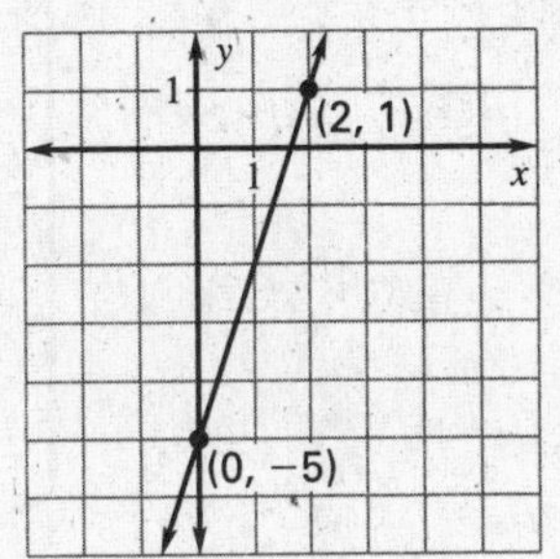

2. Write an equation of the line that passes through the point (−2, 5) and is parallel to the line with the equation $y = -2x + 3$.

Your Notes

Example 3 ***Write an equation of a perpendicular line***

Write an equation of the line j passing through the point (3, 2) that is perpendicular to the line k with the equation $y = -3x + 1$.

Solution

Step 1 **Find** the slope m of line j. The slope of k is ____.

____ $\cdot\, m =$ ____ **The product of the slopes of perpendicular lines is ____.**

$m = \frac{\quad}{\quad}$ **Divide each side by ____.**

Step 2 **Find** the y-intercept b by using $m = \frac{\quad}{\quad}$ and $(x, y) =$ ____.

$y = mx + b$ **Use slope-intercept form.**

____ $=$ $\frac{\quad}{\quad}$(____) $+ b$ **Substitute for x, y, and m.**

____ $= b$ **Solve for b.**

Because $m = \frac{\quad}{\quad}$ and $b =$ ____, an equation of line j is $y =$ ____.

You can check that the lines j and k are perpendicular by graphing, then using a protractor to measure one of the angles formed by the lines.

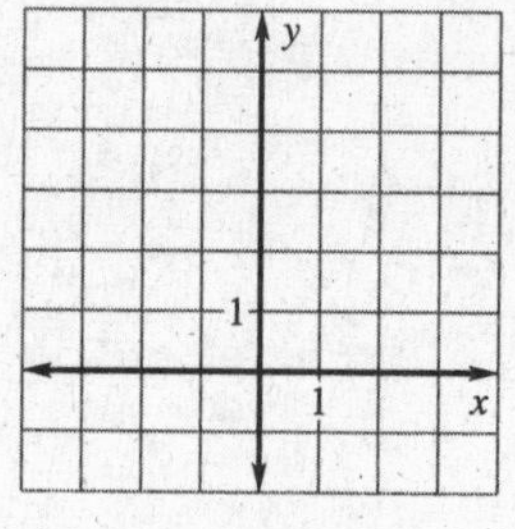

Checkpoint **Complete the following exercise.**

3. Write an equation of the line passing through the point (−8, −2) that is perpendicular to the line with the equation $y = 4x - 3$.

Your Notes

Example 4 *Write an equation of a line from a graph*

Rent The graph models the total cost of renting an apartment. Write an equation of the line. *Explain* the meaning of the slope and the *y*-intercept of the line.

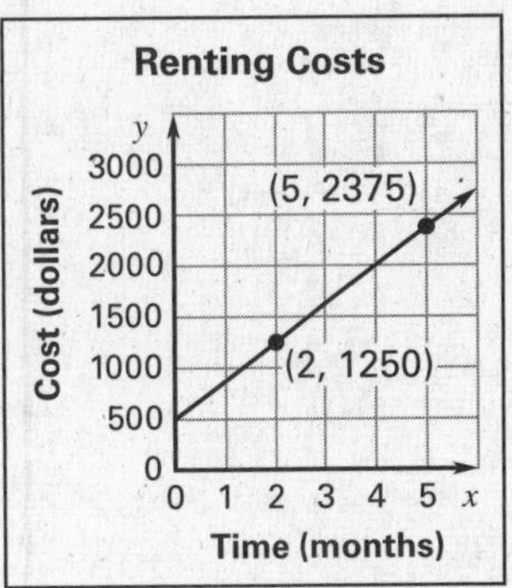

Step 1 Find the slope.

$m =$ ______

$=$ ______ $=$ ______

Step 2 Find the *y*-intercept. Use a point on the graph.

$y = mx + b$ **Use slope-intercept form.**

______ $=$ ______ $\cdot$ ______ $+ b$ **Substitute.**

______ $= b$ **Simplify.**

Step 3 Write the equation. Because $m =$ ______ and $b =$ ______, an equation is $y =$ ______.

The equation $y =$ ______ models the cost. The slope is the ______, and the ______ is the initial cost to rent the apartment.

Example 5 *Graph a line with equation in standard form*

Graph $2x + 3y = 6$.

The equation is in standard form, so use the ______.

Step 1 Find the intercepts.

To find the *x*-intercept, let $y =$ ___.

$2x + 3y = 6$

$2x + 3(\_\_\_) = 6$

$x =$ ___

To find the *y*-intercept, let $x =$ ___.

$2x + 3y = 6$

$2(\_\_\_) + 3y = 6$

$y =$ ___

Step 2 Graph the line.

The line intersects the axes at ______ and ______. Graph these points, then draw a line through the points.

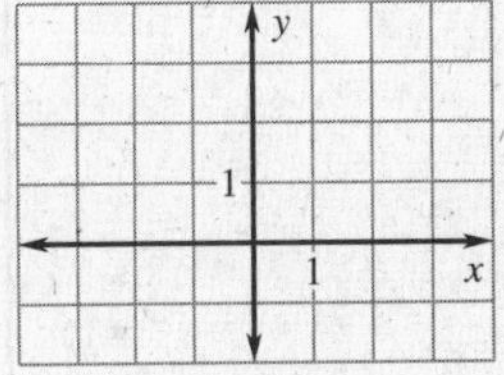

Your Notes

Example 6 ***Solve a real-world problem***

Subscriptions You can buy a magazine at a store for \$3. You can subscribe yearly to the magazine for a flat fee of \$18. After how many magazines is the subscription a better buy?

Solution

Step 1 Model each purchase with an equation.

Cost of yearly subscription: $y =$ _____

Cost of one magazine: $y =$ ___x, where x represents the number of magazines

Step 2 Graph each equation.

The point of intersection is ________. Using the graph, you can see that it is cheaper to buy magazines individually if you buy less than ___ magazines per year. If you buy more than ___ magazines per year, it is cheaper to buy a subscription.

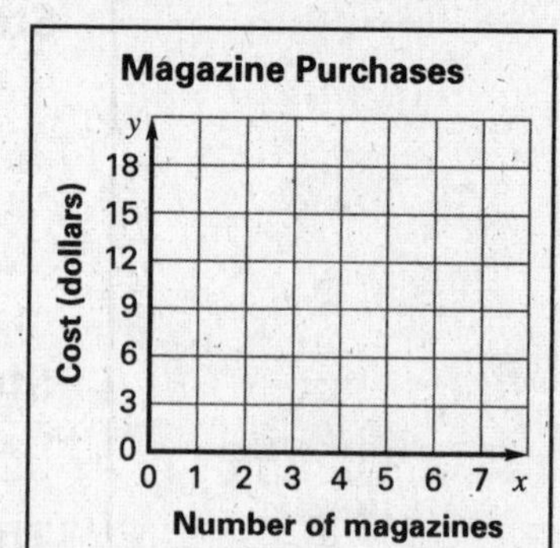

The point at which the costs are the same is sometimes called the *break-even point*.

Checkpoint Complete the following exercises.

4. The equation $y = 650x + 425$ models the total cost of joining a health club for x years. What are the meaning of the slope and y-intercept of the line?

5. Graph $y = 3$ and $x = 3$.

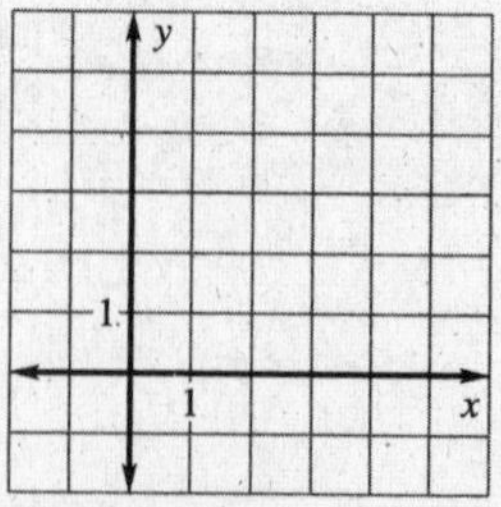

6. In Example 6, suppose you can buy the magazine at a different store for \$2.50. After how many magazines is the subscription the better buy?

Homework

3.6 Prove Theorems About Perpendicular Lines

Goal • Find the distance between a point and a line.

Your Notes

VOCABULARY

Distance from a point to a line

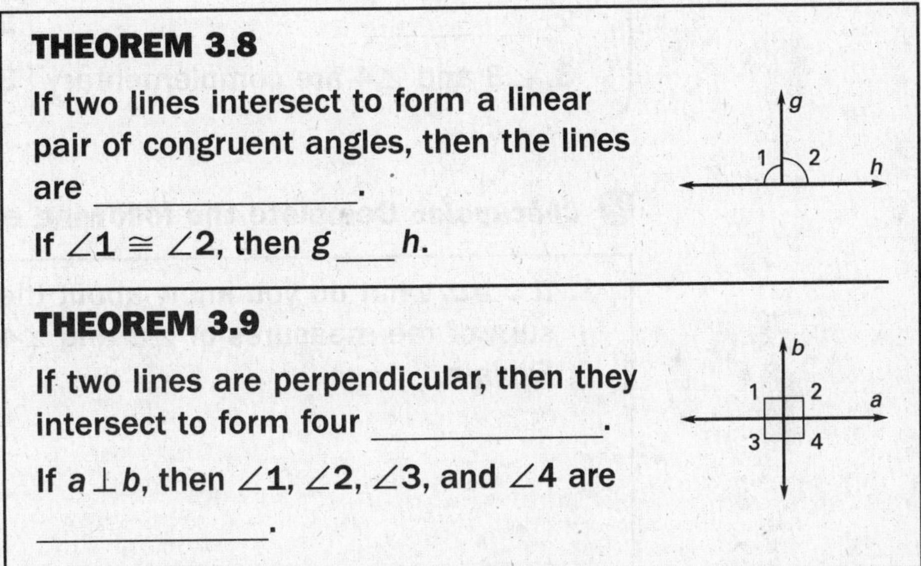

THEOREM 3.8

If two lines intersect to form a linear pair of congruent angles, then the lines are __________.

If $\angle 1 \cong \angle 2$, then g ___ *h*.

THEOREM 3.9

If two lines are perpendicular, then they intersect to form four __________.

If $a \perp b$, then $\angle 1$, $\angle 2$, $\angle 3$, and $\angle 4$ are __________.

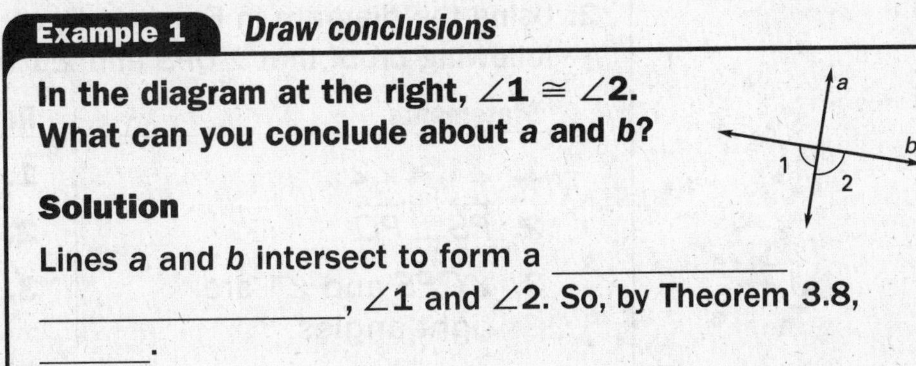

Example 1 ***Draw conclusions***

In the diagram at the right, $\angle 1 \cong \angle 2$. What can you conclude about *a* and *b*?

Solution

Lines *a* and *b* intersect to form a __________ __________, $\angle 1$ and $\angle 2$. So, by Theorem 3.8, ______.

Your Notes

THEOREM 3.10

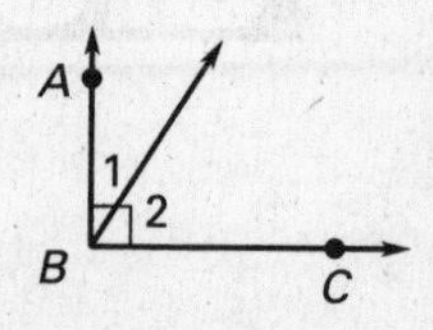

If two sides of two adjacent acute angles are perpendicular, then the angles are ________________.

If $\overrightarrow{BA} \perp \overrightarrow{BC}$, then $\angle 1$ and $\angle 2$ are ________________.

Example 2 ***Write a proof***

In the diagram at the right, $\angle 1 \cong \angle 2$. Prove that $\angle 3$ and $\angle 4$ are complementary.

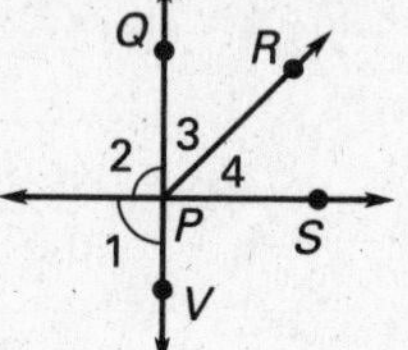

Given $\angle 1 \cong \angle 2$

Prove $\angle 3$ and $\angle 4$ are complementary.

Statements	Reasons
1. $\angle 1 \cong \angle 2$	1. __________
2. __________	2. Theorem 3.8
3. $\angle 3$ and $\angle 4$ are complementary.	3. __________

Checkpoint **Complete the following exercises.**

1. If $c \perp d$, what do you know about the sum of the measures of $\angle 3$ and $\angle 4$? *Explain.*

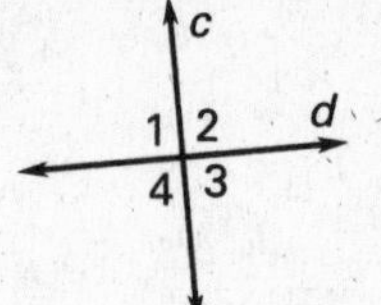

2. Using the diagram in Example 2, complete the following proof that $\angle QPS$ and $\angle 1$ are right angles.

Statements	Reasons
1. $\angle 1 \cong \angle 2$	1. __________
2. $\overleftrightarrow{PS} \perp \overleftrightarrow{PQ}$	2. __________
3. $\angle QPS$ and $\angle 1$ are right angles.	3. __________

Your Notes

THEOREM 3.11 PERPENDICULAR TRANSVERSAL THEOREM

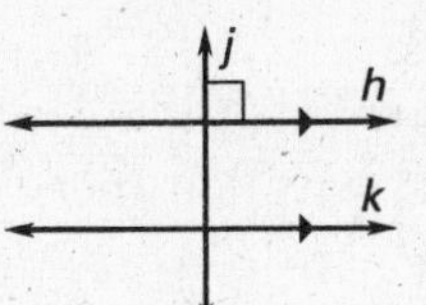

If a transversal is perpendicular to one of two parallel lines, then it is ________ to the other.

If $h \parallel k$ and $j \perp h$, then j ___ k.

THEOREM 3.12 LINES PERPENDICULAR TO A TRANSVERSAL THEOREM

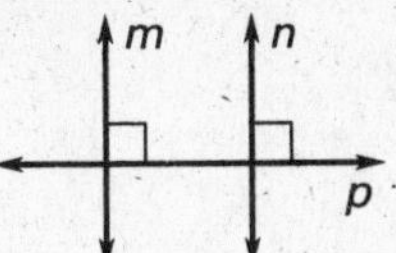

In a plane, if two lines are perpendicular to the same line, then they are ________ to each other.

If $m \perp p$ and $n \perp p$, then m ___ n.

Example 3 ***Draw conclusions***

Determine which lines, if any, must be parallel in the diagram. *Explain* your reasoning.

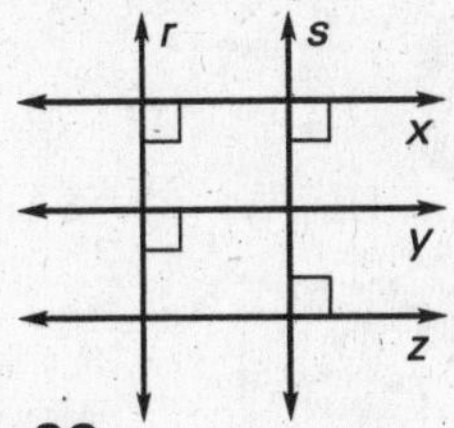

Solution

Lines *r* and *s* are both perpendicular to ___, so by Theorem 3.12, ______. Similarly, lines *x* and *y* are both perpendicular to *r*, so ______. Also, lines ___ and ___ are both perpendicular to *s*, so ______. Finally, because *y* and *z* are both parallel to ___, you know that ______ by the Transitive Property of Parallel Lines.

✔ ***Checkpoint*** **Use the diagram to complete the following exercises.**

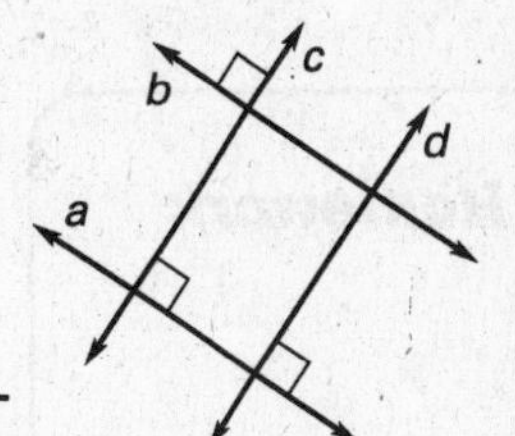

3. Is $c \parallel d$? *Explain.*

4. Is $b \perp d$? *Explain.*

Your Notes

Example 4 ***Find the distance between two parallel lines***

Railroads The section of broad gauge railroad track at the right are drawn on a graph where units are measured in inches. What is the width of the track?

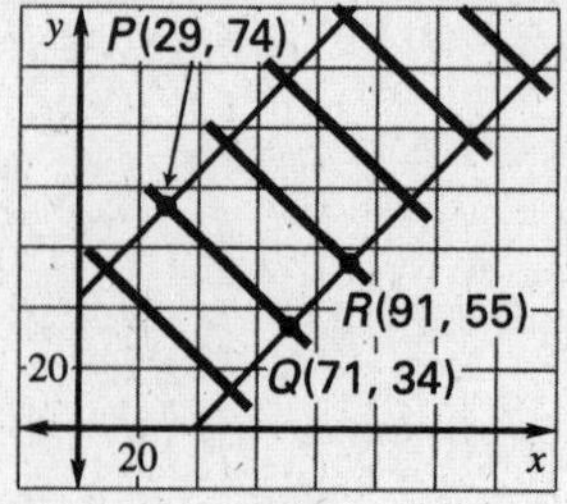

Solution

You need to find the length of a perpendicular segment from one side of the track to the other.

Using $Q(71, 34)$ and $R(91, 55)$, the slope of each rail is

$$\frac{55 - \square}{91 - \square} = \_\_\_\_$$

The segment PQ has a slope of

$$\frac{74 - \square}{29 - \square} = \_\_\_\_ = \_\_\_\_$$

The segment PQ is perpendicular to the rail so PQ is

$d = \sqrt{(\_\_\_\_\_\_)^2 + (\_\_\_\_\_\_)^2} = \_\_\_\_.$

The width of the track is _____.

✔ ***Checkpoint*** **Complete the following exercise.**

5. What is the approximate distance from line m to line n?

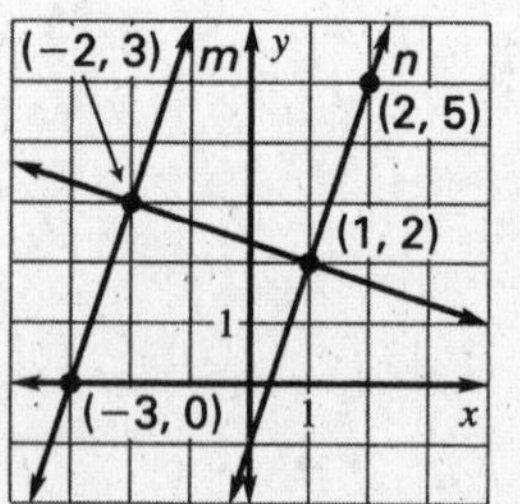

Homework

Words to Review

Give an example of the vocabulary word.

Parallel lines	Skew lines
Parallel planes	Transversal
Corresponding angles	Alternate interior angles
Alternate exterior angles	Consecutive interior angles

Paragraph proof	Slope
Slope-intercept form	**Standard form**
Distance from a point to a line.	

Review your notes and Chapter 3 by using the Chapter Review on pages 202–205 of your textbook.

4.1 Apply Triangle Sum Properties

Goal • Classsify triangles and find measures of their angles.

Your Notes

VOCABULARY

Triangle

Interior angles

Exterior angles

Corollary to a theorem

CLASSIFYING TRIANGLES BY SIDES

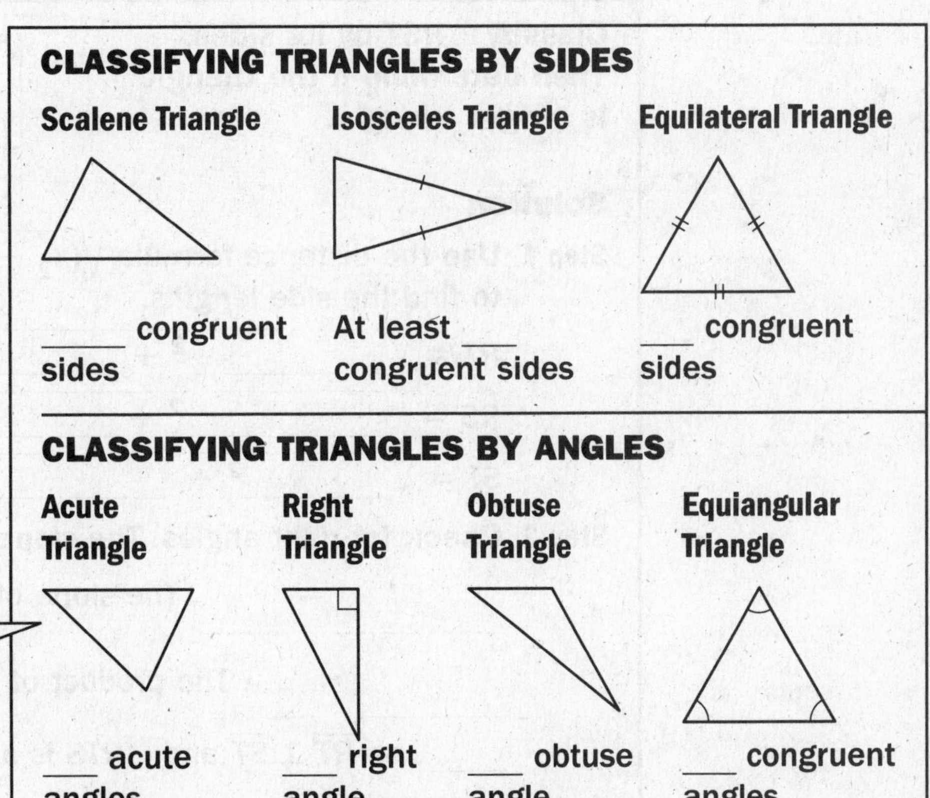

Notice that an equilateral triangle is also isosceles. An equiangular triangle is also acute.

Your Notes

Example 1 ***Classify triangles by sides and by angles***

Shuffleboard Classify the triangular shape of the shuffleboard scoring area in the diagram by its sides and by measuring its angles.

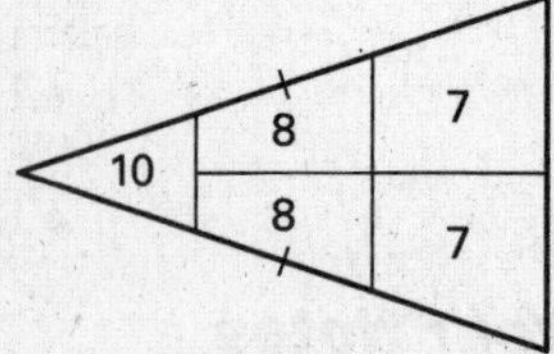

Solution

The triangle has a pair of congruent sides, so it is __________. By measuring, the angles are about _______________. It is an ______________ triangle.

✓ ***Checkpoint*** **Complete the folowing exercise.**

1. Draw an isosceles right triangle and an obtuse scalene triangle.

Example 2 ***Classify a triangle in a coordinate plane***

Classify $\triangle RST$ by its sides. Then determine if the triangle is a right triangle.

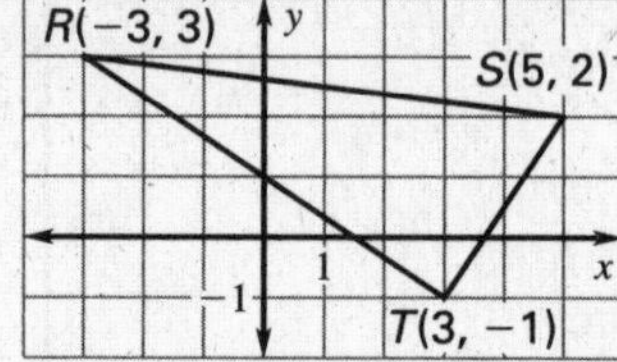

Solution

Step 1 Use the distance formula $\sqrt{(x_2 - x_1)^2 + (y_2 - y_1)^2}$ to find the side lengths.

$RT = \sqrt{\underline{\qquad\qquad}^2 + \underline{\qquad\qquad}^2} = \underline{\qquad}$

$RS = \sqrt{\underline{\qquad\qquad}^2 + \underline{\qquad\qquad}^2} = \underline{\qquad}$

$ST = \sqrt{\underline{\qquad\qquad}^2 + \underline{\qquad\qquad}^2} = \underline{\qquad}$

Step 2 Check for right angles. The slope of $\overline{RT}$ is $\frac{\qquad}{\qquad} = \frac{\qquad}{\qquad}$. The slope of $\overline{ST}$ is $\frac{\qquad}{\qquad} = \frac{\qquad}{\qquad}$. The product of the slopes is ______, so $\overline{RT} \perp \overline{ST}$ and $\angle RTS$ is a ________ angle.

Therefore, $\triangle RST$ is a ______________ triangle.

Your Notes

THEOREM 4.1: TRIANGLE SUM THEOREM

The sum of the measures of the interior angles of a triangle is ______.

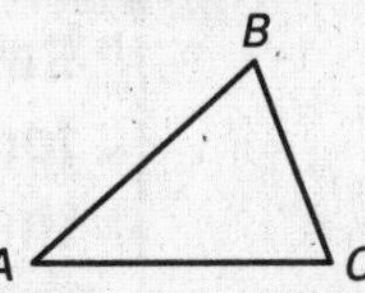

$m\angle A + m\angle B + m\angle C =$ ______

THEOREM 4.2: EXTERIOR ANGLE THEOREM

The measure of an exterior angle of a triangle is equal to the sum of the measures of the two ______ angles.

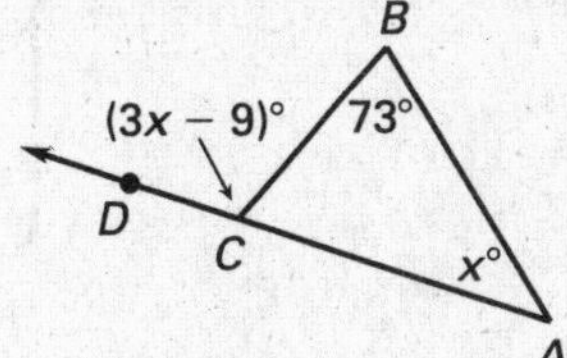

$m\angle 1 = m\angle$ ___ $+ m\angle$ ___

Example 3 ***Find angle measure***

Use the diagram at the right to find the measure of $\angle DCB$.

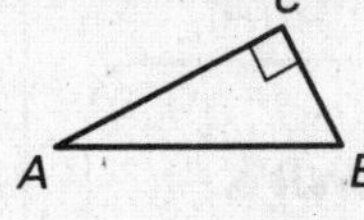

Solution

Step 1 **Write** and solve an equation to find the value of x.

$(3x - 9)° =$ ______ — **Exterior Angle Theorem**

$x =$ ______ — **Solve for x.**

Step 2 **Substitute** ____ for x in $3x - 9$ to find $m\angle DCB$.

$3x - 9 = 3 \cdot$ ____ $- 9 =$ ____

The measure of $\angle DCB$ is ______.

COROLLARY TO THE TRIANGLE SUM THEOREM

The acute angles of a right triangle are ______.

$m\angle A + m\angle B =$ ______

Your Notes

Example 4 ***Find angle measures from a verbal description***

Ramps The front face of the wheelchair ramp shown forms a right triangle. The measure of one acute angle in the triangle is eight times the measure of the other. Find the measure of each acute angle.

Solution

First, sketch a diagram of the situation. Let the measure of the smaller acute angle be $x°$. Then the measure of the larger acute angle is _____.

Use the Corollary to the Triangle Sum Theorem to set up and solve an equation.

$x° +$ _____ $=$ _____ **Corollary to the Triangle Sum Theorem**

$x =$ _____ **Solve for *x*.**

So, the measures of the acute angles are _____ and _____.

Checkpoint Complete the following exercises.

2. Triangle *JKL* has vertices $J(-2, -1)$, $K(1, 3)$, and $L(5, 0)$. Classify it by its sides. Then determine if it is a right triangle.

3. Find the measure of $\angle 1$ in the diagram shown.

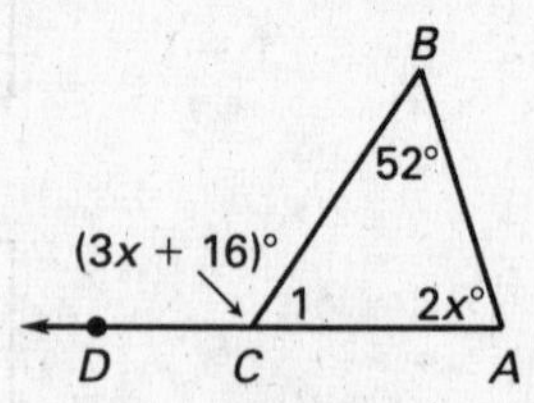

4. In Example 4, what is the measure of the obtuse angle formed between the ramp and a segment extending from the horizontal leg?

Homework

4.2 Apply Congruence and Triangles

Goal • Identify congruent figures.

Your Notes

VOCABULARY

Congruent figures

Corresponding parts

Example 1 *Identify congruent parts*

Write a congruence statement for the triangles. Identify all pairs of congruent corresponding parts.

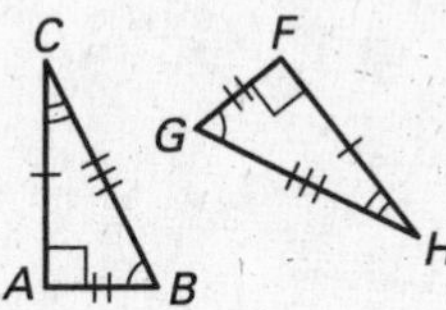

To help you identify corresponding parts, turn $\triangle FGH$.

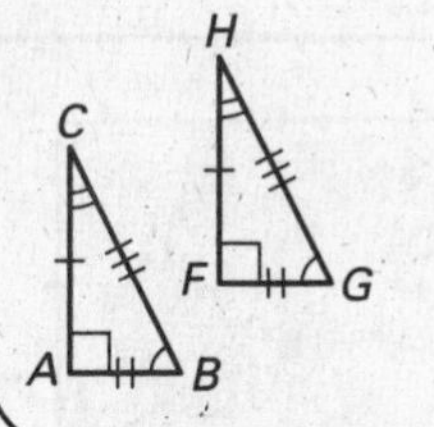

Solution

The diagram indicates that $\triangle ABC \cong \triangle$ ______.

Corresponding angles $\angle A \cong$ ______, $\angle B \cong$ ______, $\angle C \cong$ ______

Corresponding sides $\overline{AB} \cong$ ______, $\overline{BC} \cong$ ______, $\overline{CA} \cong$ ______

Example 2 *Use properties of congruent figures*

In the diagram, $QRST \cong WXYZ$.

a. Find the value of x.

b. Find the value of y.

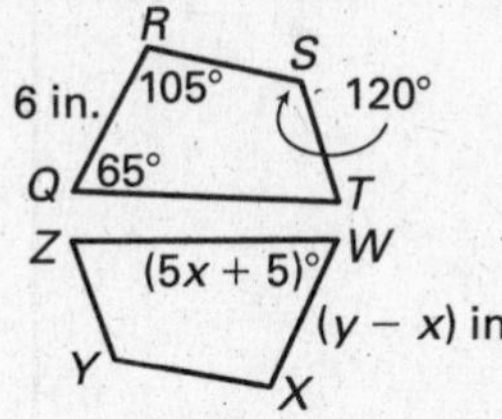

Solution

a. You know $\angle Q \cong \angle W$.

$m\angle Q =$ ______

$65° =$ ______

______ $=$ ______

______ $= x$

b. You know $\overline{QR} \cong \overline{WX}$.

$QR =$ ______

$6 =$ ______

$6 =$ ______

______ $= y$

Your Notes

✔ ***Checkpoint*** **In Exercises 1 and 2, use the diagram shown in which *FGHJ* ≅ *STUV*.**

1. Identify all pairs of congruent corresponding parts.

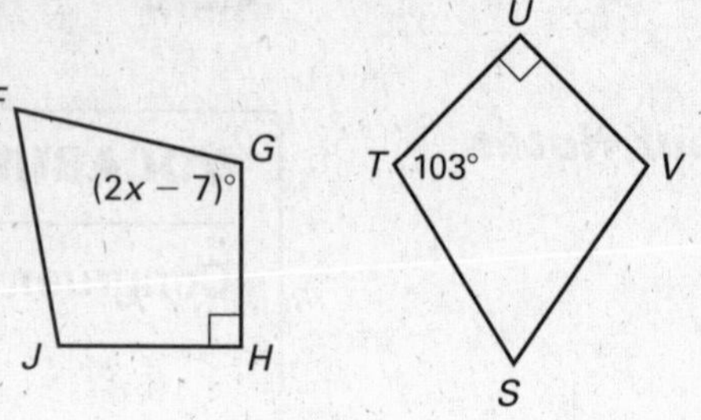

2. Find the value of x and find $m\angle G$.

Example 3 ***Show that figures are congruent***

Maps If you cut the rectangular map in half along $\overline{PR}$, will the sections of the map be the same size and shape? *Explain.*

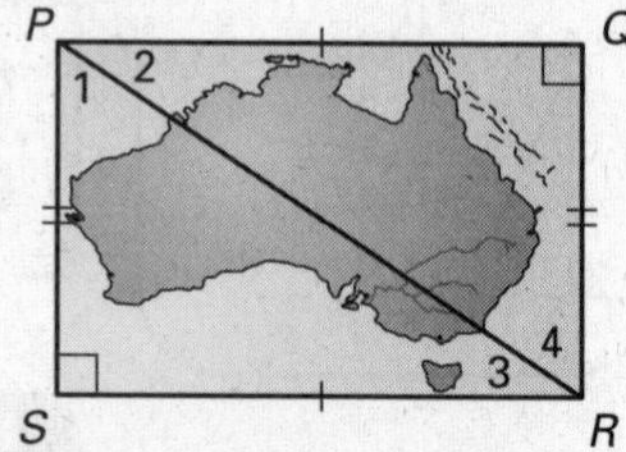

Solution

From the diagram, $\angle S \cong$ ____ because all right angles are congruent. Also, by the Lines Perpendicular to a Transversal Theorem, $\overline{PQ} \parallel$ ____. Then $\angle 1 \cong$ ____ and $\angle 2 \cong$ ____ by the ______________________ ________. So, all pairs of corresponding angles are __________.

The diagram shows $\overline{PQ} \cong$ ____ and $\overline{QR} \cong$ ____. By the ________________, $\overline{PR} \cong \overline{RP}$. All corresponding parts are __________, so $\triangle PQR \cong$ ______.

____, the two sections will be the same ____ and ______.

Your Notes

THEOREM 4.3: THIRD ANGLES THEOREM

If two angles of one triangle are congruent to two angles of another triangle, then the third angles are also ___________.

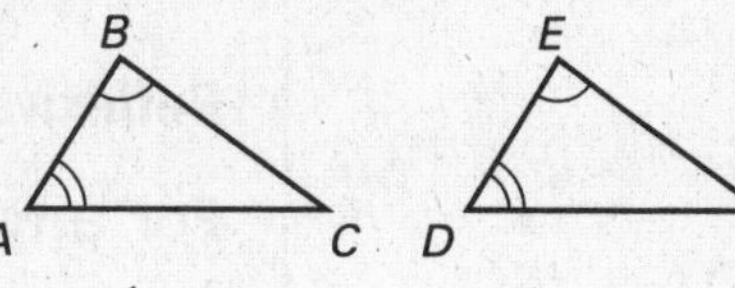

Example 4 ***Use the Third Angles Theorem***

Find $m\angle V$.

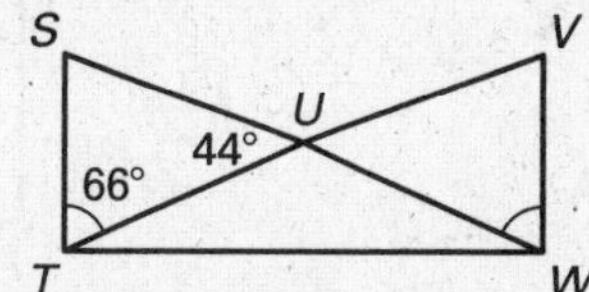

Solution

$\angle SUT \cong \angle VUW$ by the _______________.
The diagram shows that $\angle STU \cong$ _________, so by the Third Angles Theorem, $\angle S \cong$ _____. By the Triangle Sum Theorem, $m\angle S =$ _______________ $=$ _____. So, $m\angle S = m\angle V =$ _____ by the definition of congruent angles.

Example 5 ***Prove that triangles are congruent***

Write a proof.

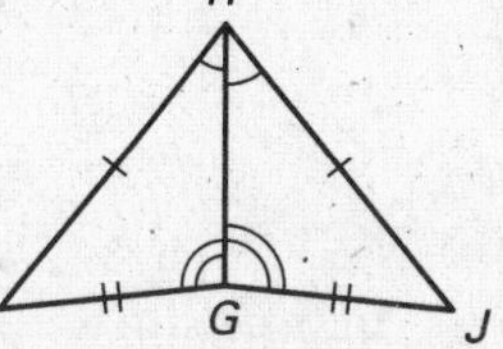

Given $\overline{FH} \cong \overline{JH}$, $\overline{FG} \cong \overline{JG}$,
$\angle FHG \cong \angle JHG$, $\angle FGH \cong \angle JGH$

Prove $\triangle FGH \cong \triangle JGH$

Plan for Proof

a. Use the Reflexive Property to show ___________.

b. Use the Third Angles Theorem to show ___________.

Plan in Action

	Statements	Reasons
	1. $\overline{FH} \cong \overline{JH}$, $\overline{FG} \cong \overline{JG}$	1. _______
a.	2. ___________	2. Reflexive Property of Congruence
	3. $\angle FHG \cong \angle JHG$, $\angle FGH \cong \angle JGH$	3. _______
b.	4. ___________	4. Third Angles Theorem
	5. $\triangle FGH \cong \triangle JGH$	5. _______________

Your Notes

THEOREM 4.4: PROPERTIES OF CONGRUENT TRIANGLES

Reflexive Property of Congruent Triangles

For any triangle ABC, $\triangle ABC \cong$ ________.

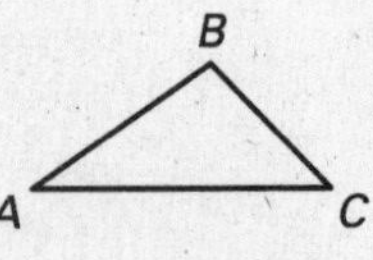

Symmetric Property of Congruent Triangles

If $\triangle ABC \cong \triangle DEF$, then ________________.

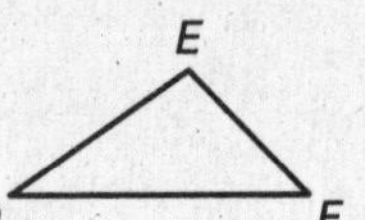

Transitive Property of Congruent Triangles

If $\triangle ABC \cong \triangle DEF$ and $\triangle DEF \cong \triangle JKL$, then ________________.

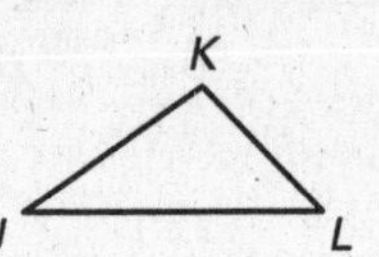

✔ ***Checkpoint*** **Complete the following exercises.**

3. In the diagram at the right, E is the midpoint of $\overline{AC}$ and $\overline{BD}$. Show that $\triangle ABE \cong \triangle CDE$.

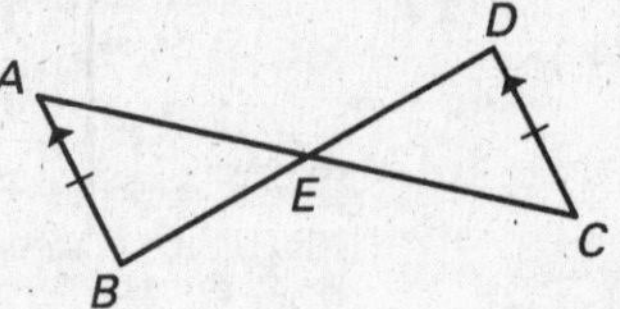

4. In the diagram, what is the measure of $\angle D$?

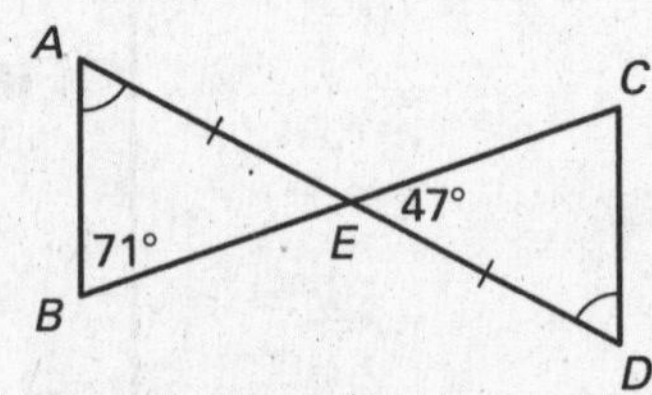

5. By the definition of congruence, what additional information is needed to know that $\triangle ABE \cong \triangle DCE$ in Exercise 4?

Homework

4.3 Prove Triangles Congruent by SSS

Goal • Use side lengths to prove triangles are congruent.

Your Notes

POSTULATE 19: SIDE-SIDE-SIDE (SSS) CONGRUENCE POSTULATE

If three sides of one triangle are congruent to three sides of a second triangle, then the two triangles are congruent.

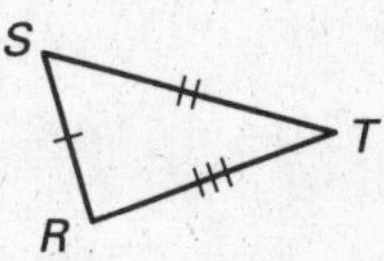

If Side $\overline{AB} \cong$ ______,

Side $\overline{BC} \cong$ ______, and

Side $\overline{CA} \cong$ ______,

then $\triangle ABC \cong$ ______.

Example 1 ***Use the SSS Congruence Postulate***

Write a proof.

Given $\overline{FJ} \cong \overline{HJ}$,
G is the midpoint of $\overline{FH}$.

Prove $\triangle FGJ \cong \triangle HGJ$

Proof It is given that $\overline{FJ} \cong$ ______. Point G is the midpoint of $\overline{FH}$, so ______. By the Reflexive Property, ______. So, by the ______, $\triangle FGJ \cong \triangle HGJ$.

Checkpoint Decide whether the congruence statement is true. *Explain* your reasoning.

1. $\triangle JKL \cong \triangle MKL$	2. $\triangle RST \cong \triangle TVW$
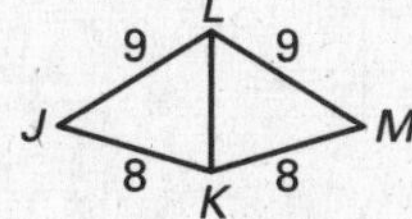	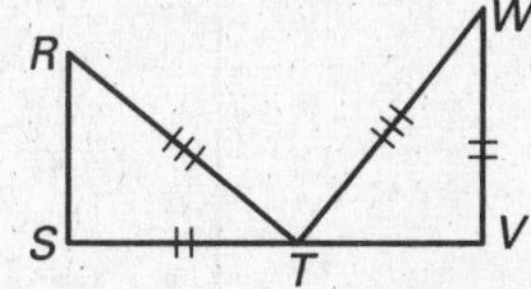

Your Notes

Example 2 Congruence in the coordinate plane

Determine whether $\triangle PQR$ is congruent to the other triangles shown at the right.

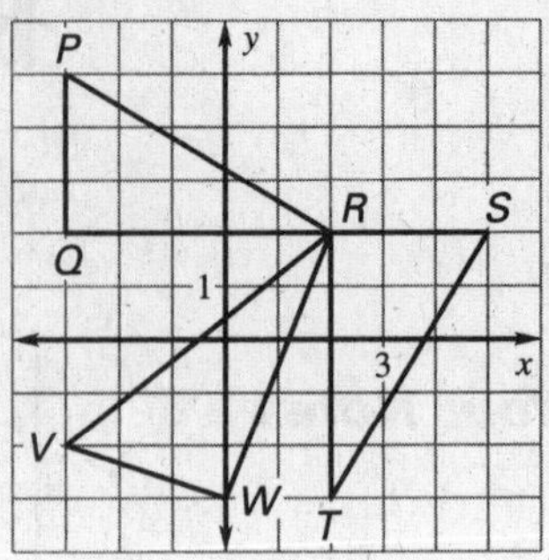

Solution

By counting, $PQ = 3$ and $QR = 5$.
Use the distance formula to find PR.

$d = \sqrt{(x_2 - x_1)^2 + (y_2 - y_1)^2}$

$PR = \sqrt{\_\_\_\_\_\_\_\_\_\_\_\_\_\_\_\_} = \sqrt{\_\_\_\_}$

By the SSS Congruence Postulate, any triangle with side lengths ____, ____, and ______ will be congruent to $\triangle PQR$. The distance from R to S is ___. The distance from R to T is ___. The distance from S to T is $\sqrt{\_\_\_\_\_\_\_\_\_\_\_\_\_\_\_\_} = \sqrt{\_\_\_\_}$. So, $\triangle PQR \cong$ ________.

The distance from W to V is $\sqrt{\_\_\_\_\_\_\_\_\_\_\_\_\_\_\_\_} = \sqrt{\_\_\_\_}$. No side of $\triangle PQR$ has a length of $\sqrt{\_\_\_\_}$, so $\triangle PQR$ ____ $\triangle VWR$.

Checkpoint **Complete the following exercise.**

3. $\triangle DFG$ has vertices $D(-2, 4)$, $F(4, 4)$, and $G(-2, 2)$. $\triangle LMN$ has vertices $L(-3, -3)$, $M(-3, 3)$, and $N(-1, -3)$. Graph the triangles in the same coordinate plane and show that they are congruent.

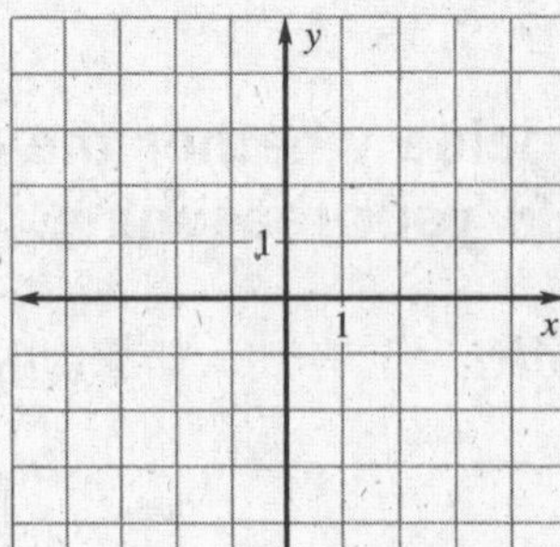

Your Notes

Example 3 ***Solve a real-world problem***

Stability *Explain* why the table with the diagonal legs is stable, while the one without the diagonal legs can collapse.

Solution

The table with the diagonal legs forms triangles with ______ side lengths. By the SSS Congruence Postulate, these triangles ______________________, so the table is ________. The table without the diagonal legs is ___________ because there are many possible quadrilaterals with the given side lengths.

✔ ***Checkpoint*** **Determine whether the figure is stable.** ***Explain*** **your reasoning.**

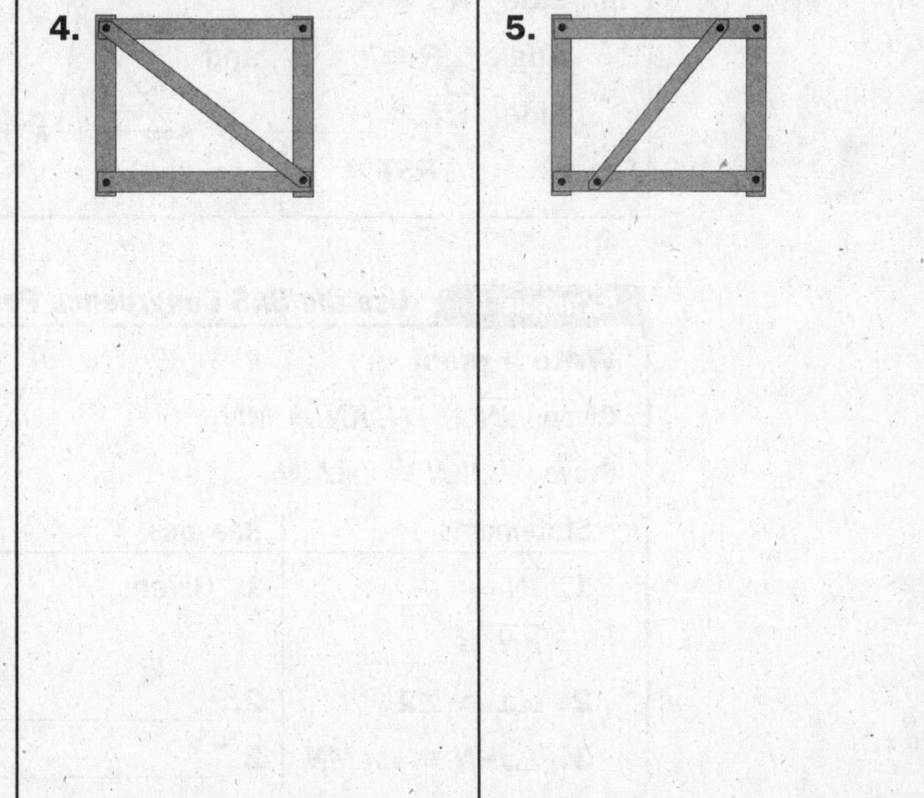

4.	5.

Homework

4.4 Prove Triangles Congruent by SAS and HL

Goal • Use sides and angles to prove congruence.

Your Notes

VOCABULARY

Leg of a right triangle

Hypotenuse

POSTULATE 20: SIDE-ANGLE-SIDE (SAS) CONGRUENCE POSTULATE

If two sides and the included angle of one triangle are congruent to two sides and the included angle of a second triangle, then the two triangles are congruent.

If **Side** $\overline{RS} \cong$ _____,

Angle $\angle R \cong$ _____, and

Side $\overline{RT} \cong$ _____,

then $\triangle RST \cong$ _____.

Example 1 ***Use the SAS Congruence Postulate***

Write a proof.

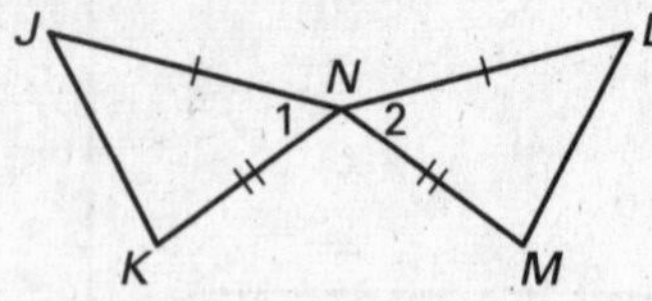

Given $\overline{JN} \cong \overline{LN}$, $\overline{KN} \cong \overline{MN}$

Prove $\triangle JKN \cong \triangle LMN$

Statements	Reasons
1. $\overline{JN} \cong$ _____, $\overline{KN} \cong$ _____	1. Given
2. $\angle 1 \cong \angle 2$	2. _____
3. $\triangle JKN \cong \triangle LMN$	3. _____

Your Notes

Example 2 ***Use SAS and properties of shapes***

In the diagram, *ABCD* is a rectangle. What can you conclude about $\triangle ABC$ and $\triangle CDA$?

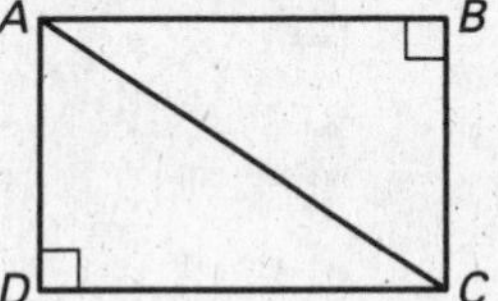

Solution

By the ______________________________,

$\angle B \cong \angle D$. Opposite sides of a rectangle are congruent, so __________ and __________.

$\triangle ABC$ and $\triangle CDA$ are congruent by the ____________________ __________.

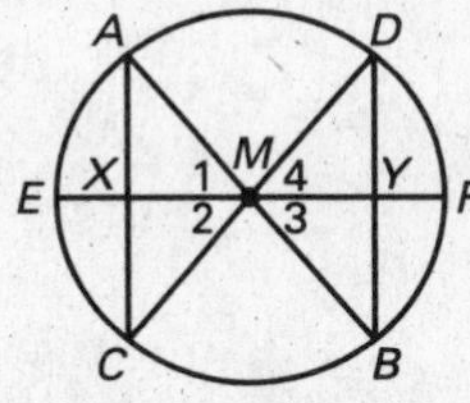

Checkpoint In the diagram, $\overline{AB}$, $\overline{CD}$, and $\overline{EF}$ pass through the center *M* of the circle. Also, $\angle 1 \cong \angle 2 \cong \angle 3 \cong \angle 4$.

1. Prove that $\triangle DMY \cong \triangle BMY$.

2. What can you conclude about $\overline{AC}$ and $\overline{BD}$?

Your Notes

THEOREM 4.5: HYPOTENUSE-LEG CONGRUENCE THEOREM

If the hypotenuse and a leg of a right triangle are congruent to the hypotenuse and a leg of a second triangle, then the two triangles are __________.

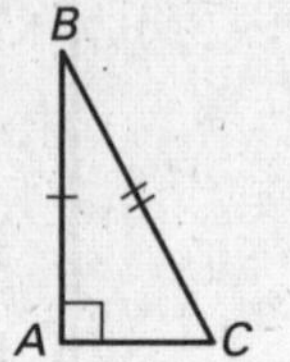

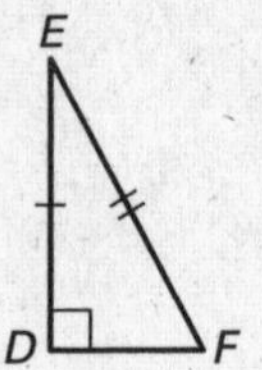

Example 3 *Use the Hypotenuse-Leg Theorem*

Write a proof.

Given $\overline{AC} \cong \overline{EC}$, $\overline{AB} \perp \overline{BD}$, $\overline{ED} \perp \overline{BD}$, $\overline{AC}$ is a bisector of $\overline{BD}$.

Prove $\triangle ABC \cong \triangle EDC$

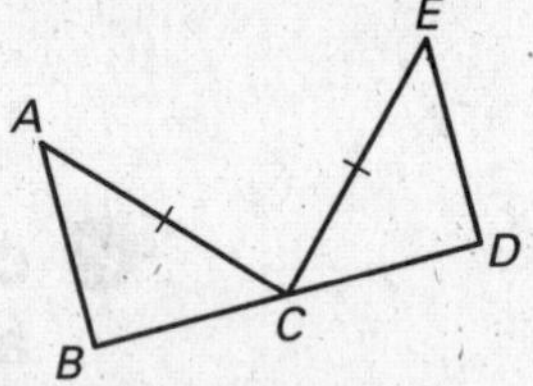

	Statements	Reasons
H	1. $\overline{AC} \cong \overline{EC}$	1. ________
	2. $\overline{AB} \perp \overline{BD}$, $\overline{ED} \perp \overline{BD}$	2. ________
	3. $\angle B$ and $\angle D$ are __________.	3. Definition of $\perp$ lines
	4. $\triangle ABC$ and $\triangle EDC$ are __________.	4. Definition of a ________ ________
	5. $\overline{AC}$ is a bisector of $\overline{BD}$.	5. ________
L	6. $\overline{BC} \cong \overline{DC}$	6. Definition of segment bisector
	7. $\triangle ABC \cong \triangle EDC$	7. ________________

Your Notes

Example 4 ***Choose a postulate or theorem***

Gate The entrance to a ranch has a rectangular gate as shown in the diagram. You know that $\triangle AFC \cong \triangle EFC$. What postulate or theorem can you use to conclude that $\triangle ABC \cong \triangle EDC$?

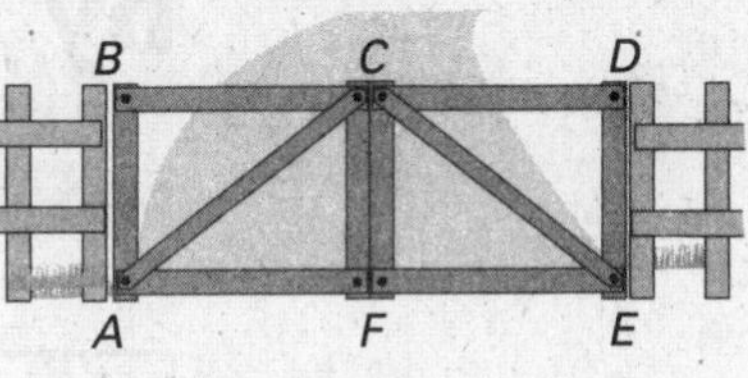

Solution

You are given that *ABDE* is a rectangle, so $\angle B$ and $\angle D$ are ______________. Because opposite sides of a rectangle are ____________, $\overline{AB} \cong$ _____. You are also given that $\triangle AFC \cong \triangle EFC$, so $\overline{AC} \cong$ _____. The hypotenuse and a leg of each triangle is congruent.

You can use the ____________________________ to conclude that $\triangle ABC \cong \triangle EDC$.

Checkpoint Complete the following exercises.

3. *Explain* why a diagonal of a rectangle forms a pair of congruent triangles.

4. In Example 4, suppose it is given that *ABCF* and *EDCF* are squares. What postulate or theorem can you use to conclude that $\triangle ABC \cong \triangle EDC$? *Explain.*

Homework

4.5 Prove Triangles Congruent by ASA and AAS

Goal • Use two more methods to prove congruences.

Your Notes

VOCABULARY

Flow proof

POSTULATE 21: ANGLE-SIDE-ANGLE (ASA) CONGRUENCE POSTULATE

If two angles and the included side of one triangle are congruent to two angles and the included side of a second triangle, then the two triangles are congruent.

If **Angle** $\angle A \cong$ _____,

Side $\overline{AC} \cong$ _____, **and**

Angle $\angle C \cong$ _____,

then $\triangle ABC \cong$ _______.

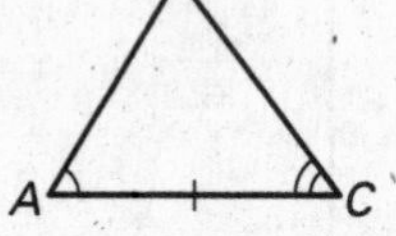

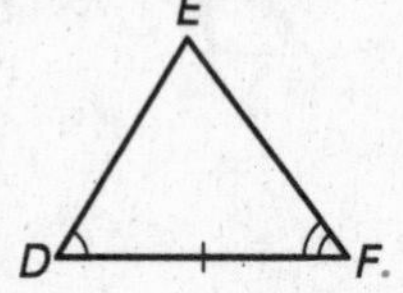

THEOREM 4.6: ANGLE-ANGLE-SIDE (AAS) CONGRUENCE THEOREM

If two angles and a non-included side of one triangle are congruent to two angles and the corresponding non-included side of a second triangle, then the two triangles are congruent.

If **Angle** $\angle A \cong$ _____,

Angle $\angle C \cong$ _____, **and**

Side $\overline{BC} \cong$ _____,

then $\triangle ABC \cong$ _______.

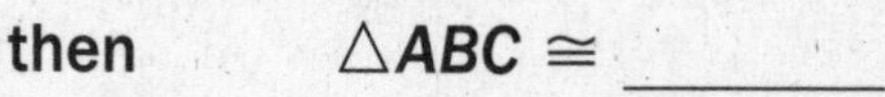

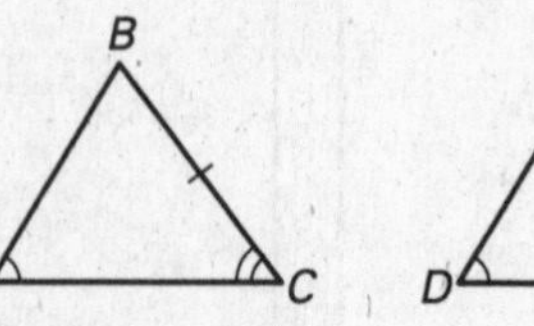

Your Notes

Example 1 *Identify congruent triangles*

Can the triangles be proven congruent with the information given in the diagram? If so, state the postulate or theorem you would use.

a. 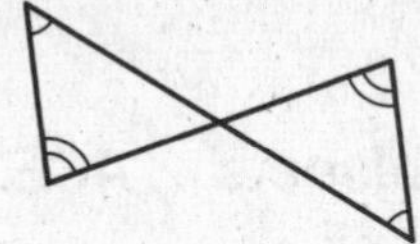

b. 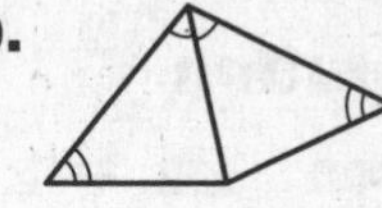

c. 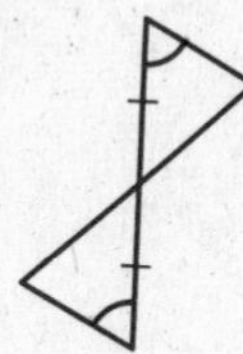

Solution

a. There is not enough information to prove the triangles are congruent, because no _______ are known to be congruent.

b. Two pairs of angles and a ____________ pair of sides are congruent. The triangles are congruent by the ____________________.

c. The vertical angles are congruent, so two pairs of angles and their ____________ are congruent. The triangles are congruent by the ____________ ____________.

Checkpoint Can $\triangle STW$ and $\triangle VWT$ be proven congruent with the information given in the diagram? If so, state the postulate or theorem you would use.

1. 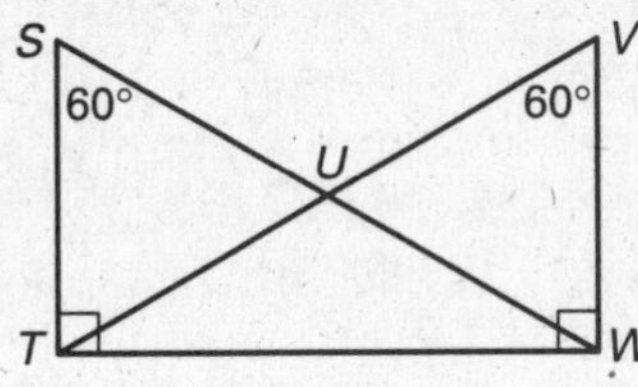

2. 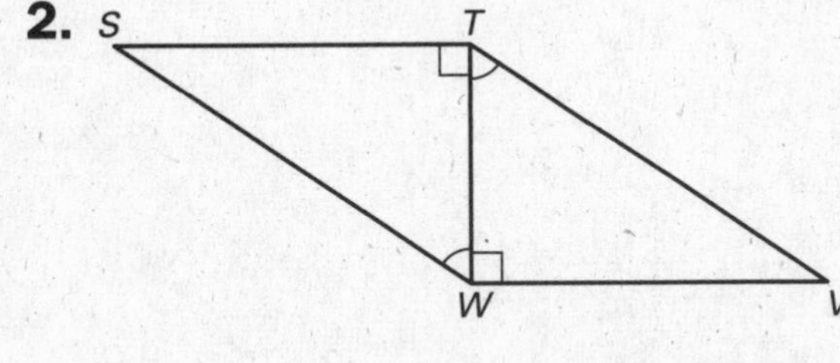

Your Notes

Example 2 *Write a flow proof*

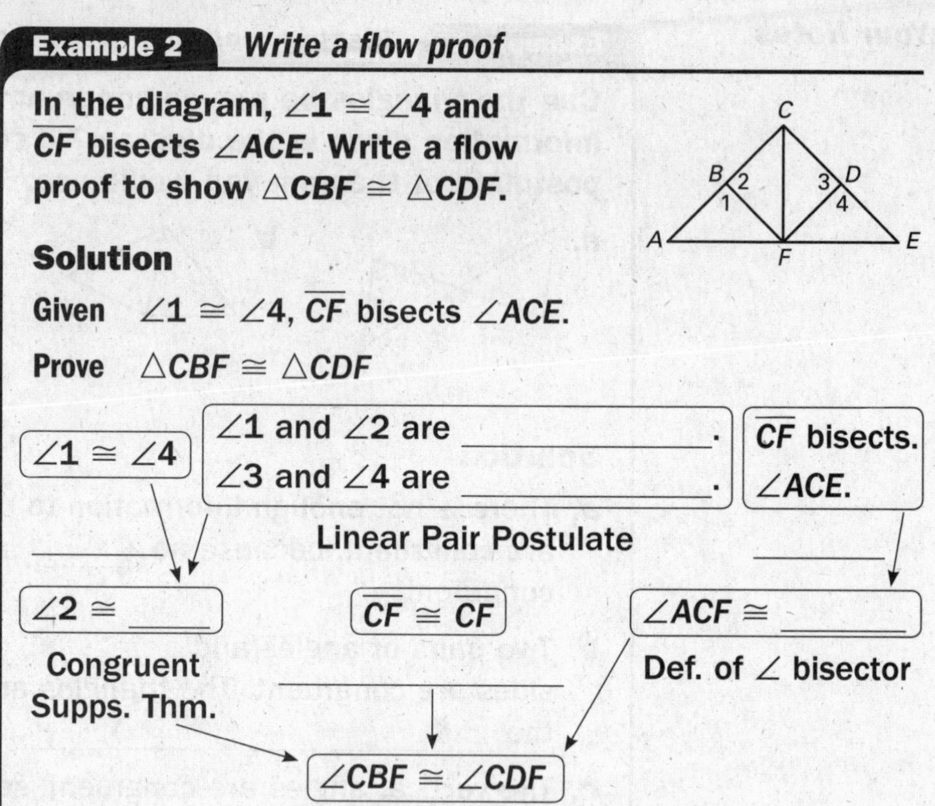

In the diagram, $\angle 1 \cong \angle 4$ and $\overline{CF}$ bisects $\angle ACE$. Write a flow proof to show $\triangle CBF \cong \triangle CDF$.

Solution

Given $\angle 1 \cong \angle 4$, $\overline{CF}$ bisects $\angle ACE$.

Prove $\triangle CBF \cong \triangle CDF$

$\angle 1 \cong \angle 4$

$\angle 1$ and $\angle 2$ are ________.
$\angle 3$ and $\angle 4$ are ________.

Linear Pair Postulate

$\overline{CF}$ bisects. $\angle ACE$.

____

$\angle 2 \cong$ ____

Congruent Supps. Thm.

$\overline{CF} \cong \overline{CF}$

____

$\angle ACF \cong$ ________

Def. of $\angle$ bisector

$\angle CBF \cong \angle CDF$

____

Checkpoint Complete the following exercise.

3. In Example 2, suppose it is given that $\overline{CF}$ bisects $\angle ACE$ and $\angle BFD$. Write a flow proof to show $\triangle CBF \cong \triangle CDF$.

Your Notes

Example 3 ***Choose a postulate or theorem***

Games You and a friend are trying to find a flag hidden in the woods. Your friend is standing 75 feet away from you. When facing each other, the angle from you to the flag is 72° and the angle from your friend to the flag is 53°. Is there enough information to locate the flag?

Solution

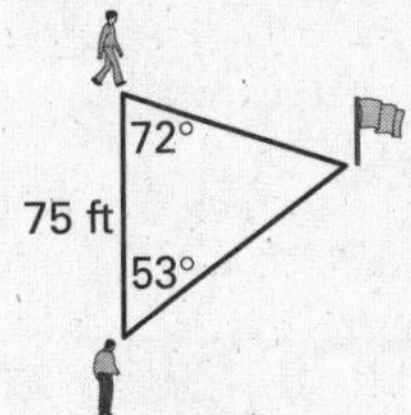

The locations of you, your friend, and the flag form a triangle. The measures of ____________ and an ______________ of the triangle are known.

By the ___________________________, all triangles with these measures are congruent. So, the triangle formed is unique and the flag location is given by the ____ ____.

Checkpoint Complete the following exercise.

4. **Theater** Two actors are standing apart from each other on the edge of a stage. Spotlights are located and pointed as shown in the diagram. Can one of the actors move to another location on the stage without changing any of the angles of the triangle, without changing the distance to the other actor, and without requiring a spotlight to move?

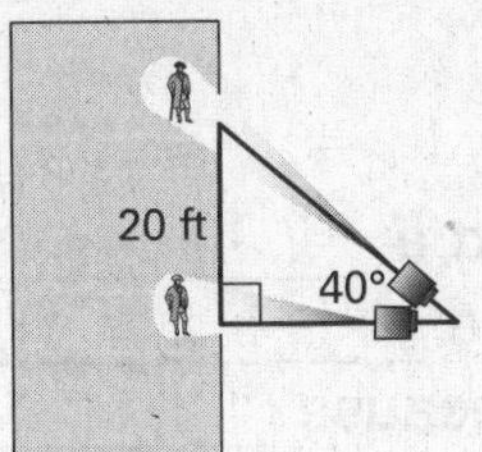

Homework

 Use Congruent Triangles

Goal • Use congruent triangles to prove corresponding parts congruent.

Your Notes

Example 1 ***Use congruent triangles***

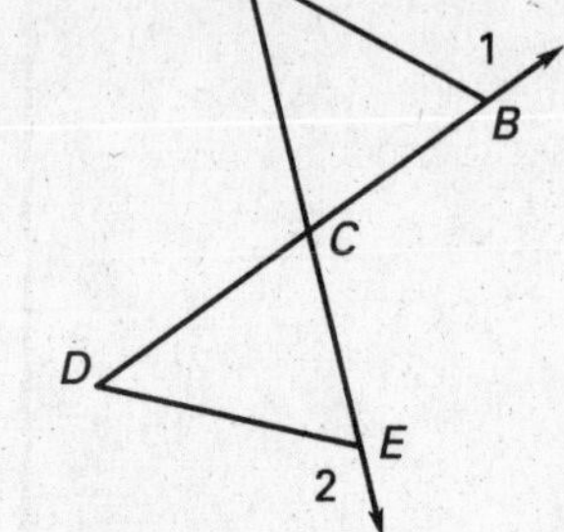

Explain **how you can use the given information to prove that the triangles are congruent.**

Given $\angle 1 \cong \angle 2$, $\overline{AB} \cong \overline{DE}$

Prove $\overline{DC} \cong \overline{AC}$

Solution

If you can show that ______________, you will know that $DC \cong AC$. First, copy the diagram and mark the given information. Then add the information that you can deduce. In this case, $\angle ABC$ and $\angle DEC$ are ______________ to congruent angles, so $\angle$______ $\cong \angle$______. Also, $\angle ACB \cong$ ______.

Mark given information.

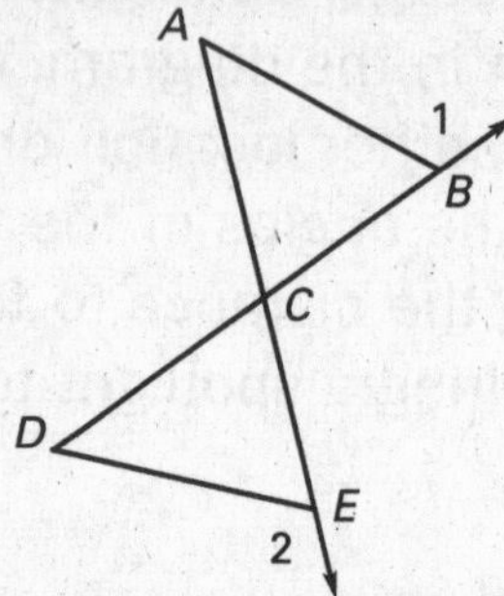

Add deduced information.

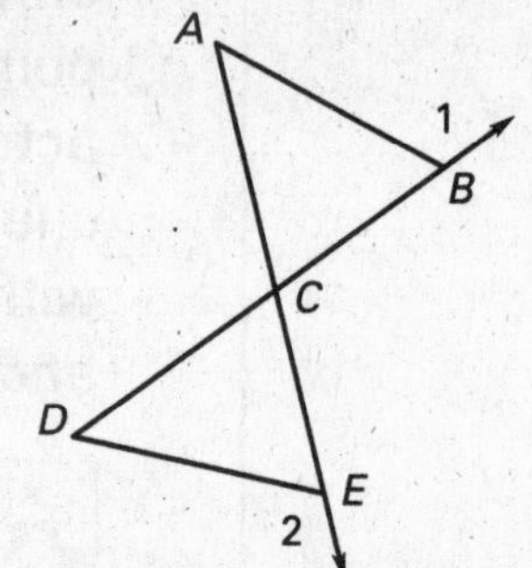

Two angle pairs and a ______________ side are congruent, so by the ______________________________, $\triangle ABC \cong \triangle DEC$. Because ____________________ of congruent triangles are congruent, $\overline{DC} \cong \overline{AC}$.

Your Notes

When you cannot easily measure a length directly, you can make conclusions about the length *indirectly*, usually by calculations based on known lengths.

Example 2 *Use congruent triangles for measurement*

Boats Use the following method to find the distance between two docked boats, from point *A* to point *B*.

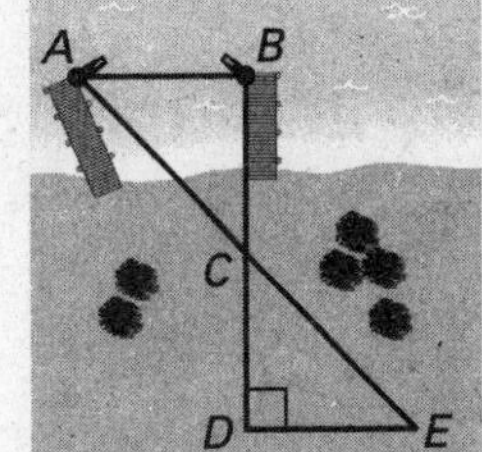

- Place a marker at *D* so that $\overline{AB} \perp \overline{BD}$.
- Find *C*, the midpoint of $\overline{BD}$.
- Locate the point *E* so that $\overline{BD} \perp \overline{DE}$ and *A*, *C*, and *E* are collinear.
- *Explain* how this plan allows you to find the distance.

Solution

Because $\overline{AB} \perp \overline{BD}$ and $\overline{BD} \perp \overline{DE}$, ____ and ____ are congruent right angles. Because *C* is the midpoint of $\overline{BD}$, ____ $\cong$ ____. The vertical angles ________ and ________ are congruent. So, $\triangle CBA \cong$ ________ by the ________________.

Then, because corresponding parts of congruent triangles are congruent, $\overline{BA} =$ ____. So, you can find the distance *AB* between the boats by measuring ____.

Checkpoint Complete the following exercises.

1. *Explain* how you can prove that $\overline{PR} \cong \overline{QS}$.

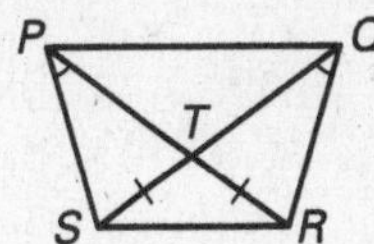

2. In Example 2, does it matter how far away from point *B* you place a marker at point *D*? *Explain*.

Your Notes

Example 3 *Plan a proof involving pairs of triangles*

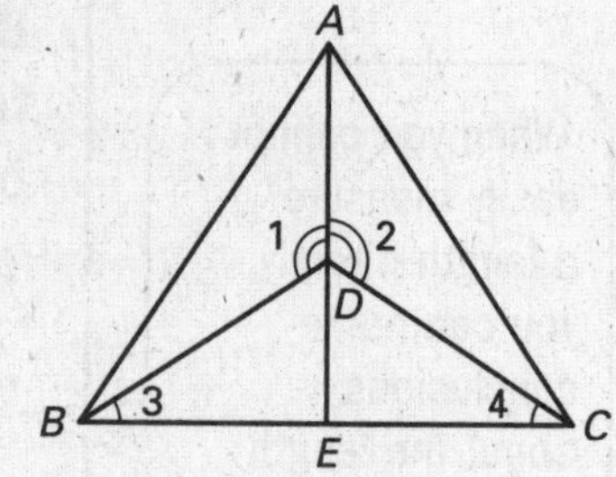

Use the given information to write a plan for proof.

Given $\angle 1 \cong \angle 2$, $\angle 3 \cong \angle 4$

Prove $\triangle ABD \cong \triangle ACD$

Solution

In $\triangle ABD$ and $\triangle ACD$, you know that $\angle 1 \cong$ ______ and $\overline{AD} \cong \overline{AD}$. If you can show that $\overline{BD} \cong \overline{CD}$, you can use the ____________________.

To prove that $\overline{BD} \cong \overline{CD}$, you can first prove that $\triangle BED \cong$ ________. You are given $\angle 1 \cong \angle 2$ and $\angle 3 \cong \angle 4$. $\overline{ED} \cong \overline{ED}$ by the Reflexive Property and $\angle BDE \cong$ ________ by the Congruent Supplements Theorem. You can use the ____________________ to prove that $\triangle BED \cong$ ________.

Plan for Proof Use the ____________________ to prove that $\triangle BED \cong$ ________. Then state that $\overline{BD} \cong \overline{CD}$. Use the ____________________ to prove that $\triangle ABD \cong \triangle ACD$.

✔ ***Checkpoint*** **Use the given information to write a plan for proof.**

3. Given $\overline{GH} \cong \overline{KJ}$, $\overline{FG} \cong \overline{LK}$, $\angle FJG$ and $\angle LHK$ are rt. $\angle$s.

Prove $\triangle FJK \cong \triangle LHG$

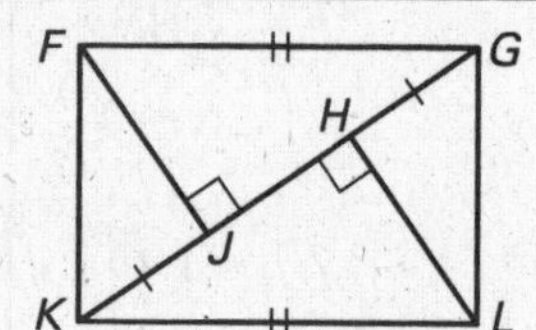

Your Notes

Example 4 *Prove a construction*

Write a proof to verify that the construction for copying an obtuse angle is valid.

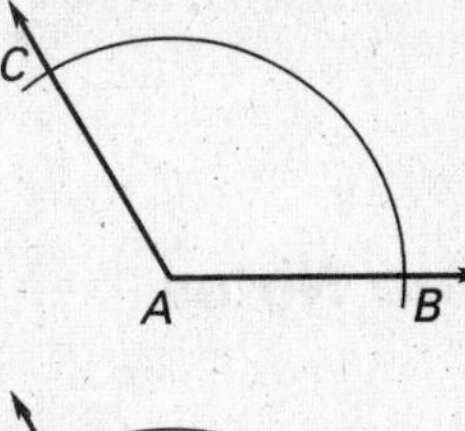

Solution

Add $\overline{BC}$ and $\overline{EF}$ to the diagram. In the construction, $\overline{AB}$, _____, _____, and _____ are determined by the same compass setting, as are $\overline{BC}$ and _____. So, you can assume the following as given statements.

Given $\overline{AB} \cong$ _____, $\overline{AC} \cong$ _____, $\overline{BC} \cong$ _____

Prove $\angle D \cong$ _____

Plan for Proof Show that $\triangle CAB \cong$ _____, so you can conclude that the corresponding parts $\angle D$ and _____ are congruent.

Plan for Action

Statements	Reasons
1. $\overline{AB} \cong$ _____, $\overline{AC} \cong$ _____, $\overline{BC} \cong$ _____	1. _____
2. $\triangle CAB \cong$ _____	2. SSS Congruence Postulate
3. $\angle D \cong$ _____	3. Corresp. parts of $\cong$ triangles are $\cong$.

✔ ***Checkpoint*** **Complete the following exercise.**

4. Write a paragraph proof to verify that the construction for bisecting a right angle is valid.

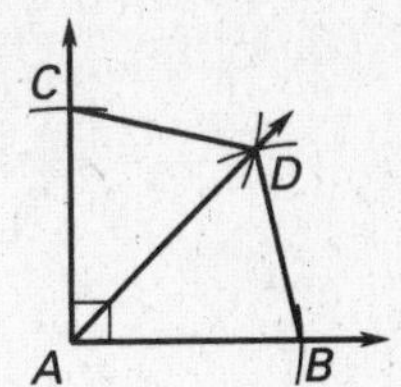

Homework

4.7 Use Isosceles and Equilateral Triangles

Goal • Use theorems about isosceles and equilateral triangles.

Your Notes

VOCABULARY

Legs

Vertex angle

Base

Base angles

THEOREM 4.7: BASE ANGLES THEOREM

If two sides of a triangle are congruent, then the angles opposite them are congruent.

If $\overline{AB} \cong \overline{AC}$, then $\angle B \cong$ ____.

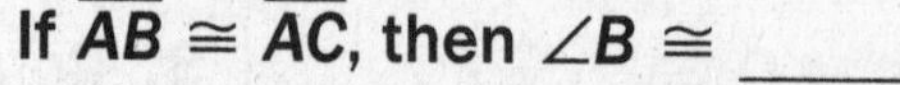

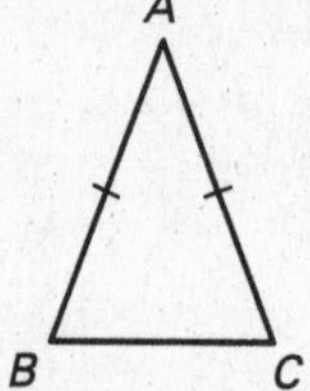

THEOREM 4.8: CONVERSE OF BASE ANGLES THEOREM

If two angles of a triangle are congruent, then the sides opposite them are congruent.

If $\angle B \cong \angle C$, then $\overline{AB} \cong$ ____.

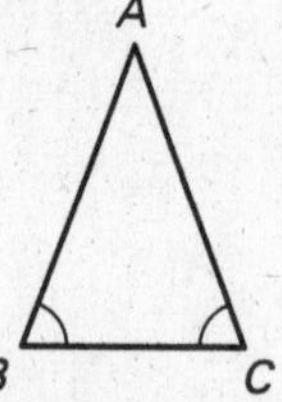

Example 1 ***Apply the Base Angles Theorem***

In $\triangle FGH$, $\overline{FH} \cong \overline{GH}$. Name two congruent angles.

Solution

$\overline{FH} \cong \overline{GH}$, so by the Base Angles Theorem, $\angle$___ $\cong \angle$___.

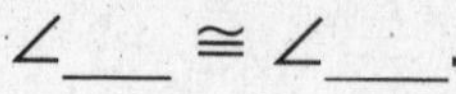

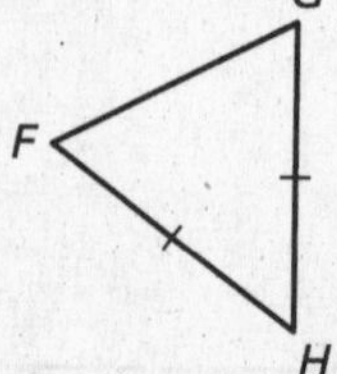

Your Notes

> The corollaries state that a triangle is *equilateral* if and only if it is *equiangular*.

COROLLARY TO THE BASE ANGLES THEOREM

If a triangle is equilateral, then it is ____________.

COROLLARY TO THE CONVERSE OF BASE ANGLES THEOREM

If a triangle is equiangular, then it is ____________.

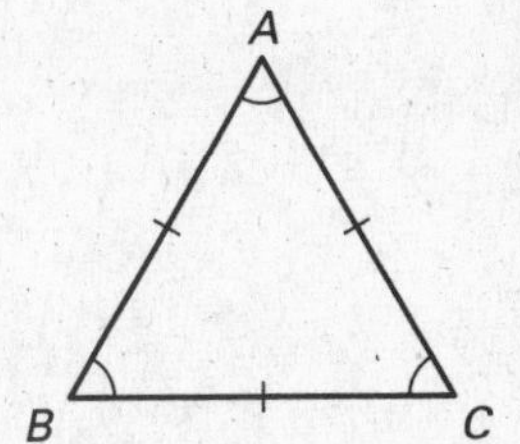

Example 2 *Find measures in a triangle*

Find the measures of $\angle R$, $\angle S$, and $\angle T$.

Solution

The diagram shows that $\triangle RST$ is ____________. Therefore, by the Corollary to the Base Angles Theorem, $\triangle RST$ is ____________. So, $m\angle R = m\angle S = m\angle T$.

$3(m\angle R) =$ ______ **Triangle Sum Theorem**

$m\angle R =$ ______ **Divide each side by 3.**

The measures of $\angle R$, $\angle S$, and $\angle T$ are all _____.

Example 3 *Use isosceles and equilateral triangles*

Find the values of x and y in the diagram.

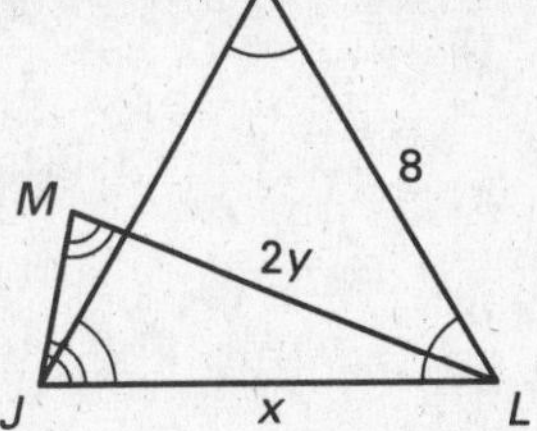

Solution

> You cannot use $\angle J$ to refer to $\angle LJM$ because three angles have J as their vertex.

Step 1 Find the value of x. Because $\triangle JKL$ is ____________, it is also ____________ and $\overline{KL} \cong$ ____. Therefore, $x =$ ___.

Step 2 Find the value of y. Because $\angle JML \cong$ ________, $\overline{LM} \cong$ ____, and $\triangle LMJ$ is isosceles. You know that $LJ =$ ___.

$LM =$ ____ **Definition of congruent segments**

$2y =$ ___ **Substitute 2y for LM and ___ for LJ.**

$y =$ ___ **Divide each side by 2.**

Your Notes

Example 4 ***Solve a multi-step problem***

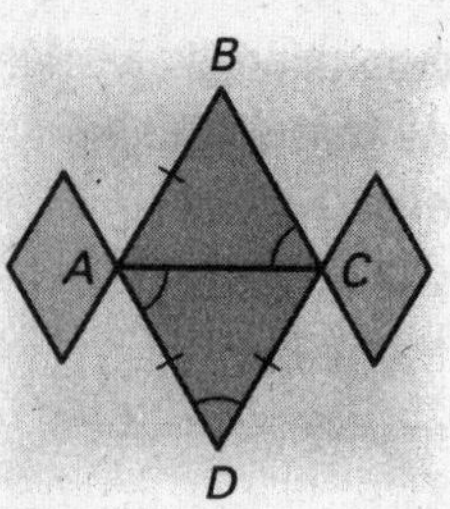

Quilting The pattern at the right is present in a quilt.

a. *Explain* why $\triangle ADC$ is equilateral.

b. Show that $\triangle CBA \cong \triangle ADC$.

Solution

a. By the Base Angles Theorem, $\angle DAC \cong$ ________. So, $\triangle ADC$ is ________. By the ________________________________, $\triangle ADC$ is equilateral.

b. By the Base Angles Theorem, $\angle ABC \cong$ ________. So, $\triangle CBA \cong \triangle ADC$ by the ________________.

Checkpoint **Complete the following exercises.**

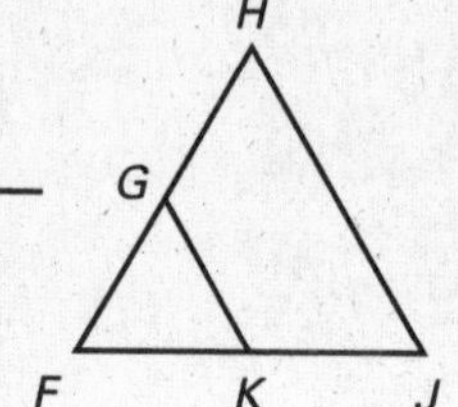

1. Copy and complete the statement: If $\overline{FH} \cong \overline{FJ}$, then $\angle \underline{?} \cong \angle \underline{?}$.

2. Copy and complete the statement: If $\triangle FGK$ is equiangular and $FG = 15$, then $GK = \underline{?}$.

3. Use parts (a) and (b) in Example 4 to show that $m\angle BAD = 120°$.

Homework

4.8 Perform Congruence Transformations

• Create an image congruent to a given triangle.

Your Notes

VOCABULARY

Transformation

Image

Translation

Reflection

Rotation

Congruence Transformation

Example 1 ***Identify transformations***

Name the type of transformation demonstrated in each picture.

a.

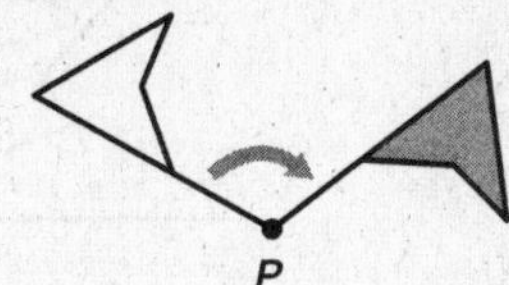

b.

c.

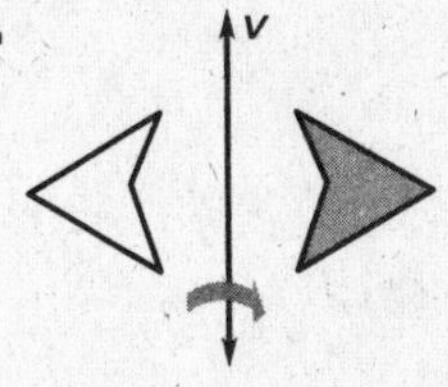

__________ about a point

__________ in a straight path

__________ in a vertical line

Your Notes

COORDINATE NOTATION FOR A TRANSLATION

You can describe a translation by the notation

$(x, y) \rightarrow (x + a, y + b)$

which shows that each point (x, y) of the unshaded figure is translated horizontally a units and vertically b units.

Example 2 ***Translate a figure in the coordinate plane***

Figure *ABCD* has the vertices $A(1, 2)$, $B(3, 3)$, $C(4, -1)$, and $D(1, -2)$. Sketch *ABCD* and its image after the translation $(x, y) \rightarrow (x - 4, y + 2)$.

Solution

First draw *ABCD*. Find the translation of each vertex by ______________ from its *x*-coordinate and ______________ to its *y*-coordinate. Then draw *ABCD* and its image.

$(x, y) \rightarrow (x - 4, y + 2)$

$A(1, 2) \rightarrow$ __________

$B(3, 3) \rightarrow$ __________

$C(4, -1) \rightarrow$ __________

$D(1, -2) \rightarrow$ __________

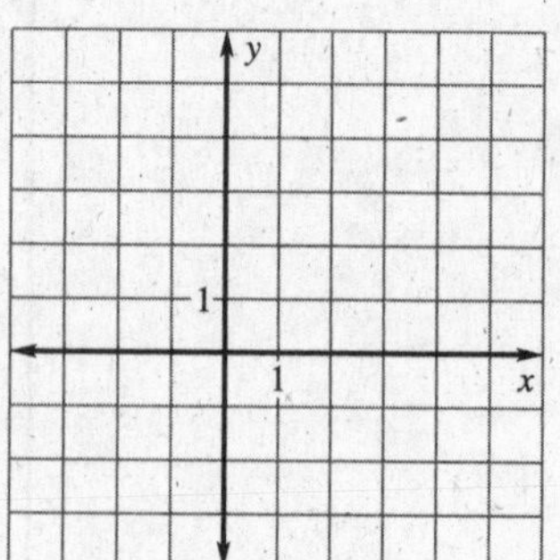

COORDINATE NOTATION FOR A REFLECTION

Reflection in the *x*-axis

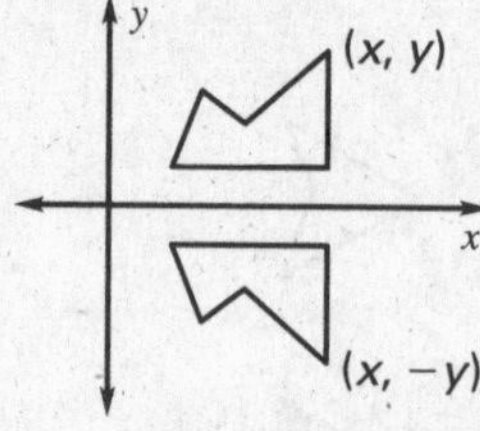

Multiply *y*-coordinate by −1.

$(x, y) \rightarrow (x, -y)$

Reflection in the *y*-axis

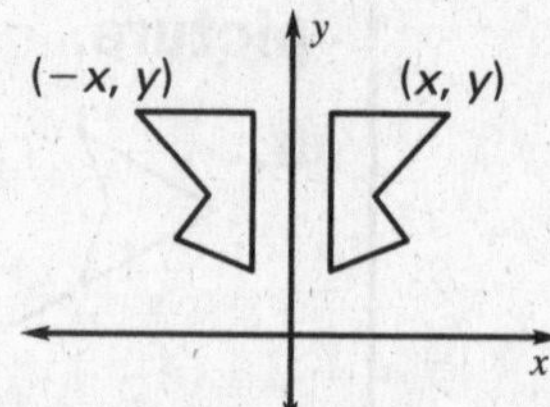

Multiply *x*-coordinate by −1.

$(x, y) \rightarrow (-x, y)$

Your Notes

Example 3 *Reflect a figure in the x-axis*

Shapes You are cutting figures out of paper. Use a reflection in the *x*-axis to draw the other half of the figure.

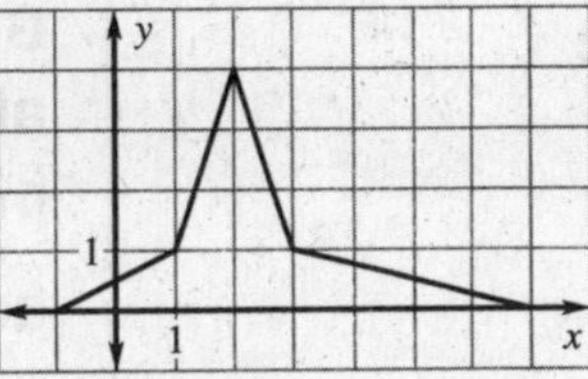

Solution

Multiply the ________________ of each vertex by −1 to find the corresponding vertex in the image. Then draw the image.

$(x, y) \rightarrow$ ________

$(-1, 0) \rightarrow$ ________

$(1, 1) \rightarrow$ ________

$(2, 4) \rightarrow$ ________

$(3, 1) \rightarrow$ ________

$(7, 0) \rightarrow$ ________

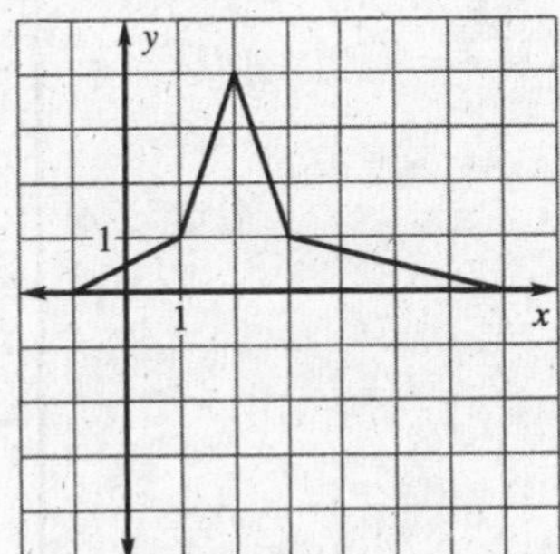

You can check your results by looking to see if each original point and its image are the same distance from the ________.

Checkpoint Complete the following exercises.

1. Name the type of transformation shown.

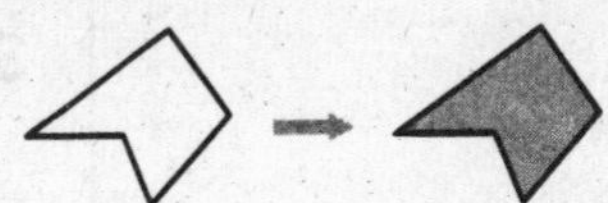

2. Figure *FGHJ* has the vertices *F*(0, 2), *G*(2, 3), *H*(3, 3), and *J*(0, −2). Sketch *FGHJ* and its image after (a) the translation $(x, y) \rightarrow (x - 3, y + 1)$ and (b) a reflection in the *y*-axis.

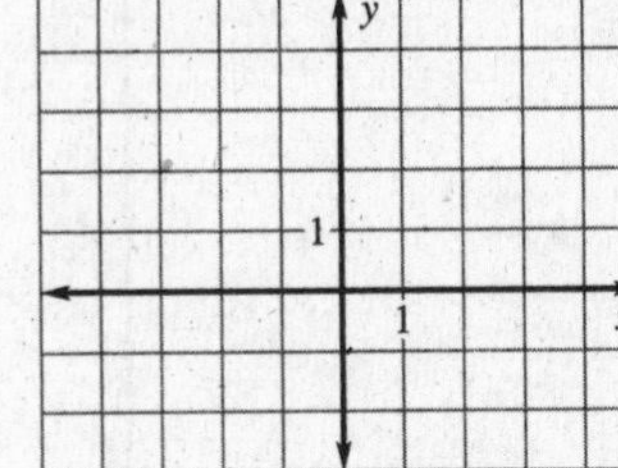

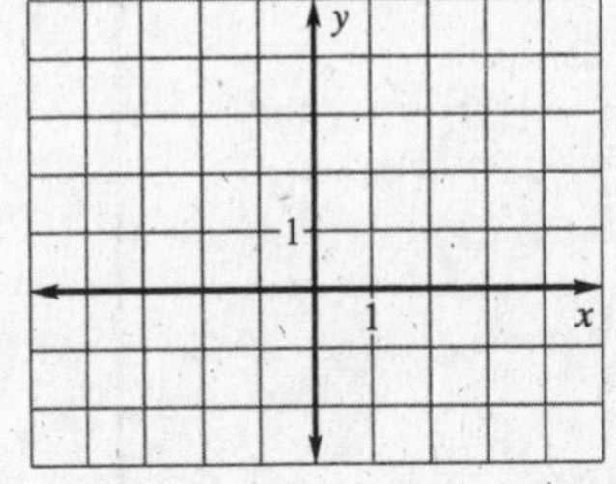

Your Notes

Example 4 *Identify a rotation*

Graph $\overline{JK}$ and $\overline{LM}$. Tell whether $\overline{LM}$ is a rotation of $\overline{JK}$ about the origin. If so, give the angle and direction of rotation.

a. $J(3, 1)$, $K(1, 4)$, $L(-1, 3)$, $M(-4, 1)$

b. $J(-2, 1)$, $K(-1, 5)$, $L(1, 1)$, $M(2, 5)$

Solution

a.

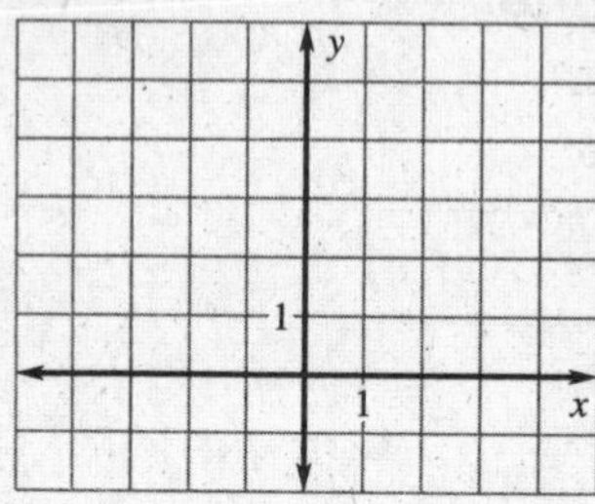

m∠JOL ____ m∠KOM

____ ______

____

____

b.

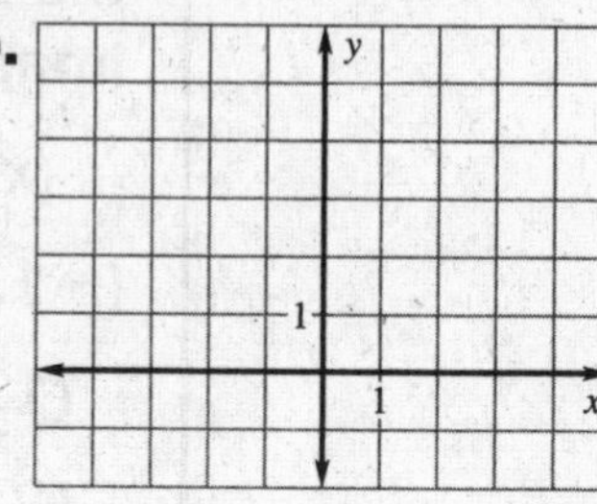

m∠JOL ___ m∠KOM

____

Checkpoint Graph $\overline{RS}$ and $\overline{TV}$. Tell whether $\overline{TV}$ is a rotation of $\overline{RS}$ about the origin. If so, give the angle of rotation.

3. $R(-3, -2)$, $S(-3, 2)$, $T(-1, 2)$, $V(3, 2)$ 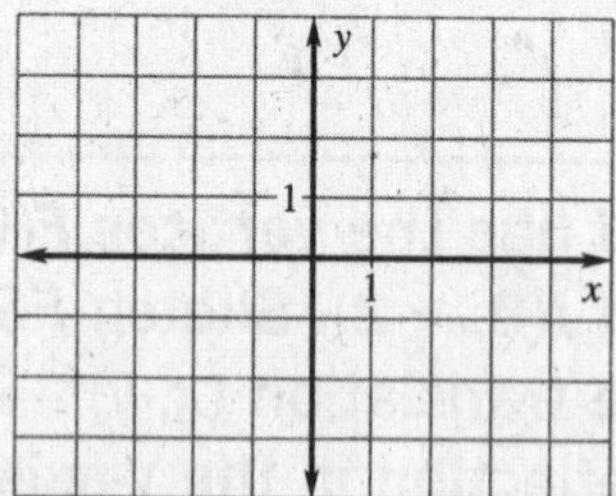	**4.** $R(-1, 1)$, $S(-4, 2)$, $T(1, -1)$, $V(4, -2)$ 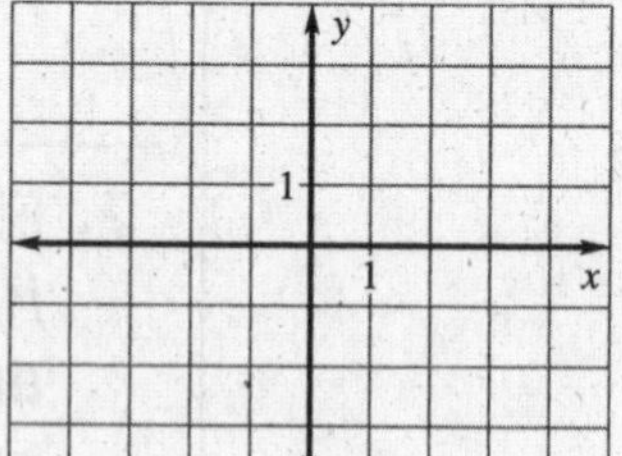

Your Notes

Example 5 ***Verify congruence***

The vertices of $\triangle PQR$ are $P(2, 2)$, $Q(3, 4)$, and $R(5, 2)$. The notation $(x, y) \rightarrow (x + 1, y - 6)$ describes the translation of $\triangle PQR$ to $\triangle XYZ$. Show that $\triangle PQR \cong \triangle XYZ$ to verify that the translation is a congruence transformation.

Solution

S You can see that PR = _____ = ___, so $\overline{PR} \cong$ _____.

A Using the slopes, $\overline{PQ} \parallel$ _____ and $\overline{QR} \parallel$ _____. If you extend $\overline{PQ}$ and $\overline{XZ}$ to form $\angle V$, the Corresponding Angles Postulate gives you _______ $\cong \angle V$ and $\angle V \cong$ _______. Then, _______ $\cong$ _______ by the Transitive Property of Congruence.

S Using the distance formula, PQ = _____ = _____ so $\overline{PQ} \cong$ _____. So, $\triangle PQR \cong \triangle XYZ$ by the _____ ____________________.

Because $\triangle PQR \cong \triangle XYZ$, the translation is a congruence transformation.

Checkpoint **Complete the following exercise.**

5. Show that $\triangle ABC \cong \triangle EDC$ to verify that the transformation is a congruence transformation.

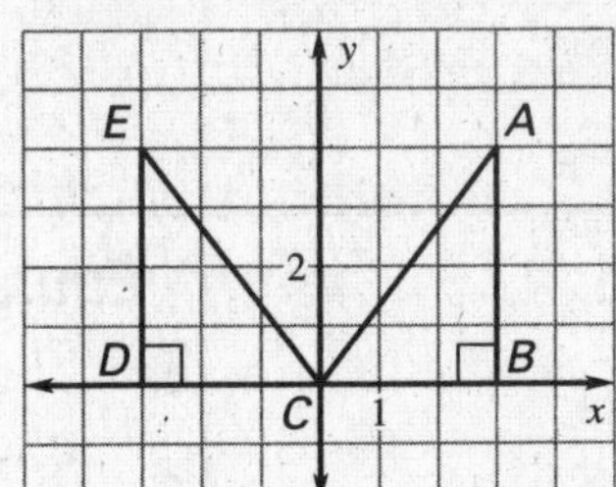

Homework

Words to Review

Give an example of the vocabulary word.

Triangle	**Scalene triangle**
Isosceles triangle	**Equilateral triangle**
Acute triangle	**Right triangle**
Obtuse triangle	**Equiangular triangle**

Interior angles	Exterior angles
Corollary to a theorem	Congruent figures
Corresponding parts	Leg of a right triangle, hypotenuse
Flow proof	Legs, base of an isosceles triangle

Vertex angle, base angles of an isosceles triangle	Transformation
Image	Translation
Reflection	Rotation
Congruence transformation	

Review your notes and Chapter 4 by using the Chapter Review on pages 282–285 of your textbook.

5.1 Midsegment Theorem and Coordinate Proof

- Use properties of midsegments and write coordinate proofs.

Your Notes

VOCABULARY

Midsegment of a triangle

Coordinate proof

THEOREM 5.1: MIDSEGMENT THEOREM

The segment connecting the midpoints of two sides of a triangle is __________ to the third side and is ______ as long as that side.

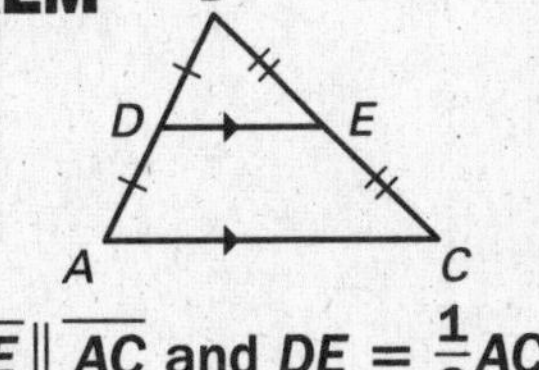

$\overline{DE} \parallel \overline{AC}$ and $DE = \frac{1}{2}AC$

Example 1 ***Use the Midsegment Theorem to find lengths***

Windows A large triangular window is segmented as shown. In the diagram, $\overline{DF}$ and $\overline{EF}$ are midsegments of $\triangle ABC$. Find DF and AB.

A
D F
45 in.
B E C
90 in.

In the diagram for Example 1, midsegment $\overline{DF}$ can be called "the midsegment opposite $\overline{BC}$."

Solution

DF = ___ • BC = ___ (______) = ______

AB = ___ • FE = ___ (______) = ______

Checkpoint Complete the following exercise.

1. In Example 1, consider $\triangle ADF$. What is the length of the midsegment opposite $\overline{DF}$?

Your Notes

Example 2 ***Use the Midsegment Theorem***

In the diagram at the right, $QS = SP$ and $PT = TR$. Show that $\overline{QR} \parallel \overline{ST}$.

Solution

Because $QS = SP$ and $PT = TR$, S is the ________ of $\overline{QP}$ and T is the ________ of $\overline{PR}$ by definition. Then $\overline{ST}$ is a ________ of $\triangle PQR$ by definition and $\overline{QR} \parallel \overline{ST}$ by the ________.

Checkpoint Complete the following exercise.

2. In Example 2, if V is the midpoint of $\overline{QR}$, what do you know about $\overline{SV}$?

Example 3 ***Place a figure in a coordinate plane***

Place each figure in a coordinate plane in a way that is convenient for finding side lengths. Assign coordinates to each vertex.

a. a square

b. an acute triangle

Solution

It is easy to find lengths of horizontal and vertical segments and distances from ______, so place one vertex at the ______ and one or more sides on an ______.

a. Let s represent the ______ ______.

b. You need to use ______ different variables.

The square represents a general square because the coordinates are based only on the definition of a square. If you use this square to prove a result, the result will be true for all squares.

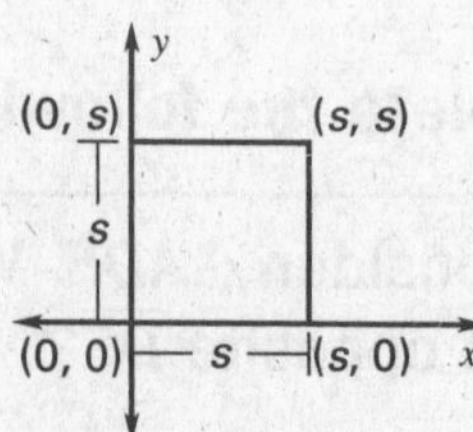

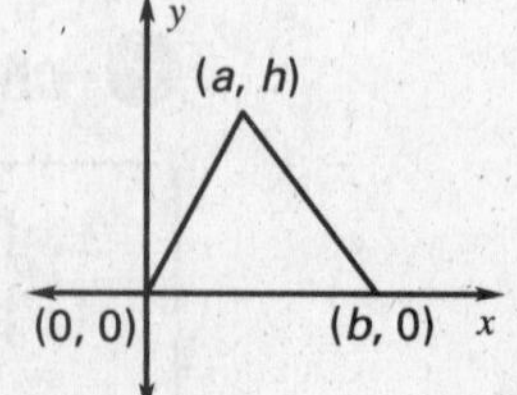

Your Notes

Example 4 ***Apply variable coordinates***

In Example 3 part (a), find the length and midpoint of a diagonal of the square.

Solution

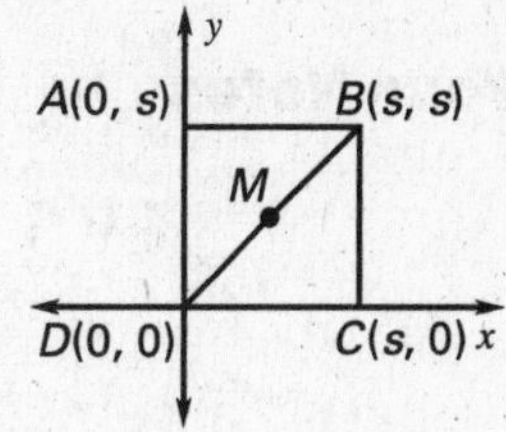

Draw a diagonal and its midpoint. Assign letters to the points.

Use the distance formula to find *BD*.

$BD =$ ____________________

$=$ __________ $=$ ______ $=$ ______

Use the midpoint formula to find the midpoint *M*.

$M\left(\_\_\_\_\_\_\_\_\_\_\right) = M\left(\_\_\_\_\right)$

Checkpoint **Complete the following exercises.**

3. Place an obtuse scalene triangle in a coordinate plane that is convenient for finding side lengths. Assign coordinates to each vertex.

4. In Example 4, find the length and midpoint of diagonal $\overline{AC}$. What do you notice? *Explain* why this is true for all squares.

Homework

5.2 Use Perpendicular Bisectors

Goal • Use perpendicular bisectors to solve problems.

Your Notes

VOCABULARY

Perpendicular bisector

Equidistant

Concurrent

Point of concurrency

Circumcenter

THEOREM 5.2: PERPENDICULAR BISECTOR THEOREM

In a plane, if a point is on the perpendicular bisector of a segment, then it is __________ from the endpoints of the segment.

If $\overleftrightarrow{CP}$ is the $\perp$ bisector of $\overline{AB}$, then $CA =$ _____.

THEOREM 5.3: CONVERSE OF THE PERPENDICULAR BISECTOR THEOREM

In a plane, if a point is equidistant from the endpoints of a segment, then it is on the ____________ ________ of the segment.

If $DA = DB$, then D lies on the __________ of $\overline{AB}$.

Your Notes

Example 1 ***Use the Perpendicular Bisector Theorem***

$\overleftrightarrow{AC}$ is the perpendicular bisector of $\overline{BD}$. Find AD.

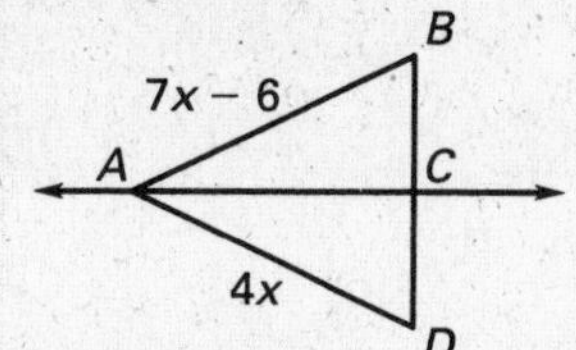

Solution

$AD =$ ____ **Perpendicular Bisector Theorem**

____ $=$ ______ **Substitute.**

$x =$ ___ **Solve for x.**

$AD =$ ____ $=$ _____ $=$ ___.

Example 2 ***Use perpendicular bisectors***

In the diagram, $\overleftrightarrow{KN}$ is the perpendicular bisector of $\overline{JL}$.

a. What segment lengths in the diagram are equal?

b. Is M on $\overleftrightarrow{KN}$?

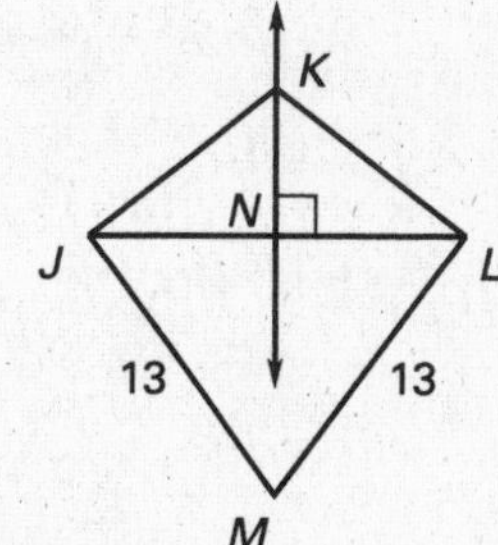

Solution

a. $\overleftrightarrow{KN}$ bisects $\overline{JL}$, so ____ $=$ ____. Because K is on the perpendicular bisector of $\overline{JL}$, ____ $=$ ____ by Theorem 5.2. The diagram shows that ____ $=$ ____ $= 13$.

b. Because $MJ = ML$, M is __________ from J and L. So, by the ______________________________ ________, M is on the perpendicular bisector of $\overline{JL}$, which is $\overleftrightarrow{KN}$.

✔ ***Checkpoint*** **In the diagram, $\overleftrightarrow{JK}$ is the perpendicular bisector of $\overline{GH}$.**

1. What segment lengths are equal?

____

2. Find GH.

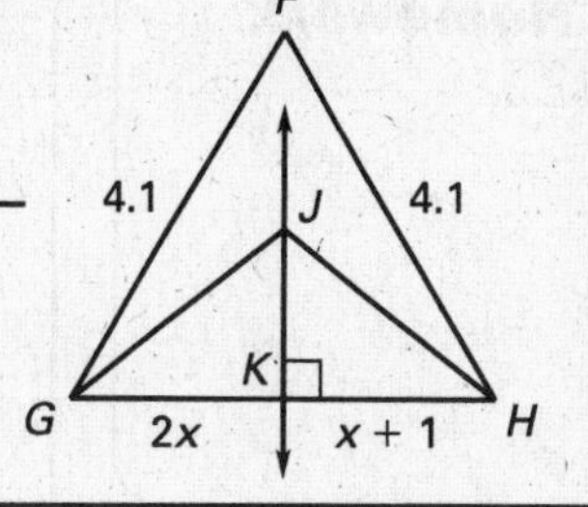

Your Notes

THEOREM 5.4: CONCURRENCY OF PERPENDICULAR BISECTORS OF A TRIANGLE

The perpendicular bisectors of a triangle intersect at a point that is equidistant from the vertices of the triangle.

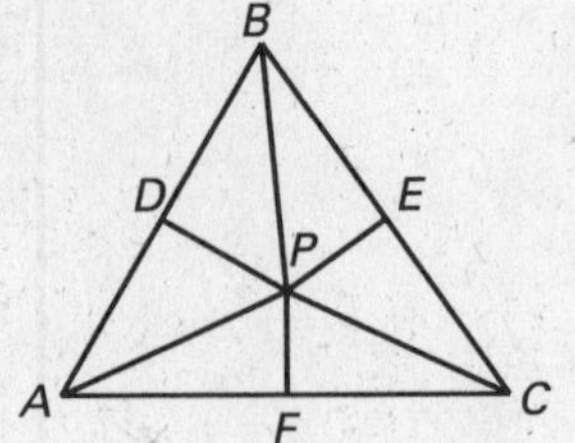

If $\overline{PD}$, $\overline{PE}$, and $\overline{PF}$ are perpendicular bisectors, then $PA =$ _____ $=$ _____.

Example 3 ***Use the concurrency of perpendicular bisectors***

Football Three friends are playing catch. You want to join and position yourself so that you are the same distance from your friends. Find a location for you to stand.

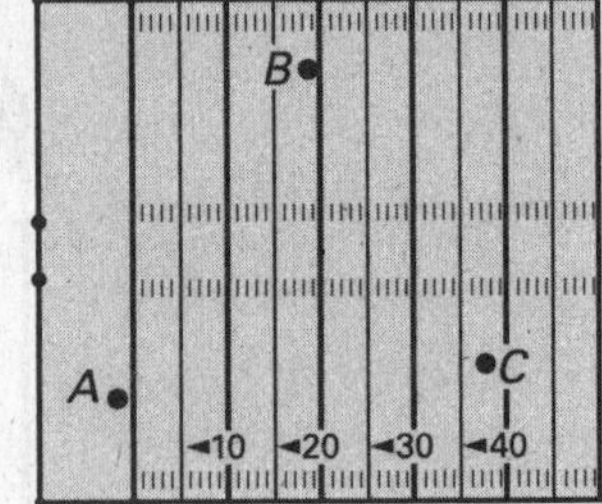

Solution

Theorem 5.4 shows you that you can find a point equidistant from three points by using the _______________ of the triangle formed by those points.

Copy the positions of points *A*, *B*, and *C* and connect those points to draw $\triangle ABC$. Then use a ruler and a protractor to draw the three _______________ of $\triangle ABC$. The point of concurrency *D* is a location for you to stand.

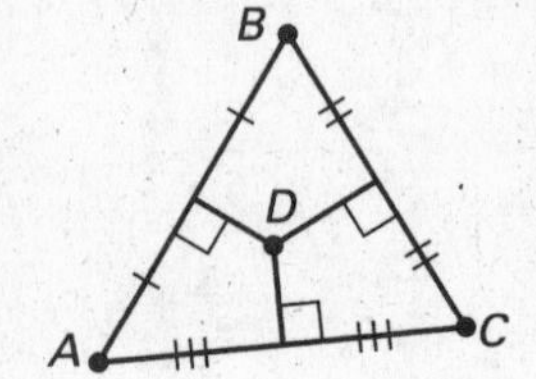

Checkpoint **Complete the following exercise.**

3. In Example 3, your friend at location *A* wants to move to a location that is the same distance from everyone else. Find a new location for *A*.

Homework

5.3 Use Angle Bisectors of Triangles

Goal • Use angle bisectors to find distance relationships.

Your Notes

VOCABULARY

Incenter

THEOREM 5.5: ANGLE BISECTOR THEOREM

If a point is on the bisector of an angle, then it is equidistant from the two ______ of the angle.

If $\overrightarrow{AD}$ bisects $\angle BAC$ and $\overline{DB} \perp \overrightarrow{AB}$ and $\overline{DC} \perp \overrightarrow{AC}$, then $DB =$ ____.

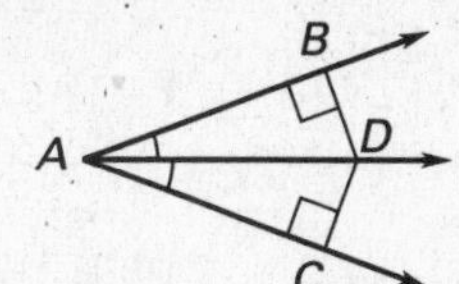

In Geometry, *distance* means the *shortest* length between two objects.

THEOREM 5.6: CONVERSE OF THE ANGLE BISECTOR THEOREM

If a point is in the interior of an angle and is equidistant from the sides of the angle, then it lies on the ________ of the angle.

If $\overline{DB} \perp \overrightarrow{AB}$ and $\overline{DC} \perp \overrightarrow{AC}$ and $DB = DC$, then $\overrightarrow{AD}$ ________ $\angle BAC$.

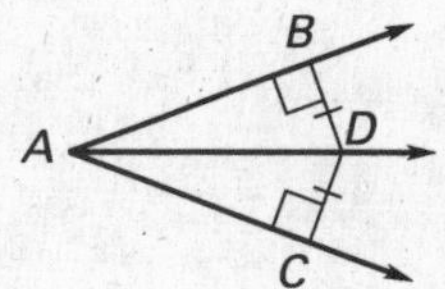

Example 1 ***Use the Angle Bisector Theorems***

Find the measure of $\angle CBE$.

Solution

Because $\overline{EC} \perp$ ____ and $\overline{ED} \perp$ ____ and $EC = ED = 21$, $\overrightarrow{BE}$ bisects $\angle CBD$ by the ________________ ________________. So, $m\angle CBE = m\angle$ ____ $=$ ____.

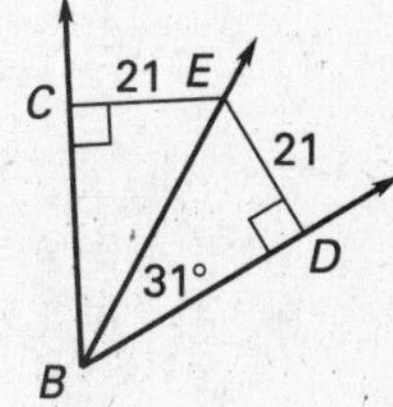

Your Notes

Example 2 ***Solve a real-world problem***

Web A spider's position on its web relative to an approaching fly and the opposite sides of the web forms congruent angles, as shown. Will the spider have to move farther to reach a fly toward the right edge or the left edge?

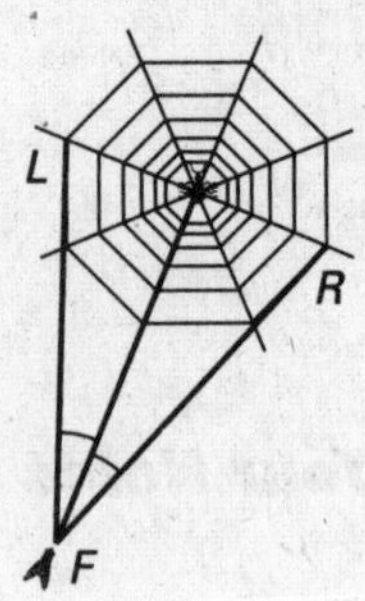

Solution

The congruent angles tell you that the spider is on the ________ of $\angle LFR$. By the ____________ ________, the spider is equidistant from $\overrightarrow{FL}$ and $\overrightarrow{FR}$.

So, the spider must move the ______________ to reach each edge.

Example 3 ***Use algebra to solve a problem***

For what value of *x* does *P* lie on the bisector of $\angle J$?

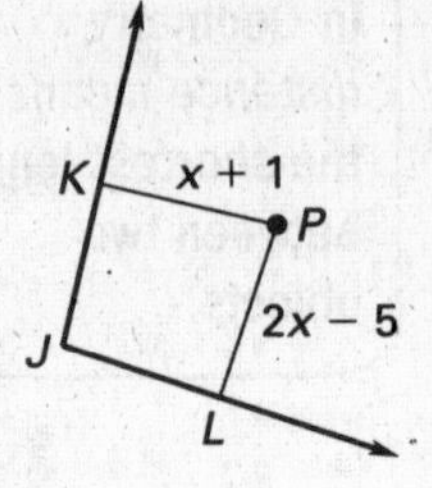

Solution

From the Converse of the Angle Bisector Theorem, you know that *P* lies on the bisector of $\angle J$ if *P* is equidistant from the sides of $\angle J$, so when ____ = ____.

____ = ____	**Set segment lengths equal.**
______ = ______	**Substitute expressions for segment lengths.**
___ = x	**Solve for *x*.**

Point *P* lies on the bisector of $\angle J$ when x = ___.

THEOREM 5.7: CONCURRENCY OF ANGLE BISECTORS OF A TRIANGLE

The angle bisectors of a triangle intersect at a point that is equidistant from the sides of the triangle.

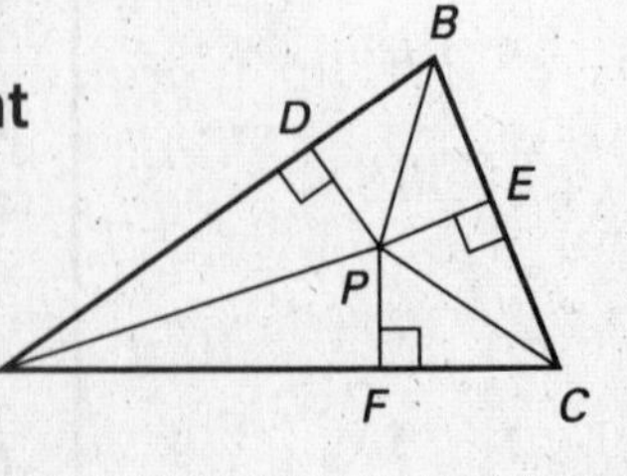

If $\overline{AP}$, $\overline{BP}$, and $\overline{CP}$ are angle bisectors of $\triangle ABC$, then PD = ____ = ____.

Your Notes

Example 4 ***Use the concurrency of angle bisectors***

In the diagram, L is the incenter of $\triangle FHJ$. Find LK.

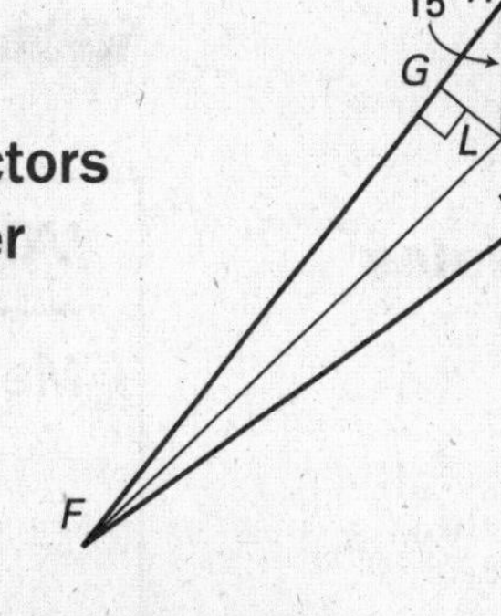

By the Concurrency of Angle Bisectors of a Triangle Theorem, the incenter L is ______________ from the sides of $\triangle FHJ$. So, to find LK, you can find ____ in $\triangle LHI$. Use the Pythagorean Theorem.

____ = __________ **Pythagorean Theorem**

____ = ____________ **Substitute known values.**

____ = _____ **Simplify.**

__ = ____ **Take the positive square root of each side.**

Because ____ = LK, LK = ___.

Checkpoint In Exercises 1 and 2, find the value of x.

1.

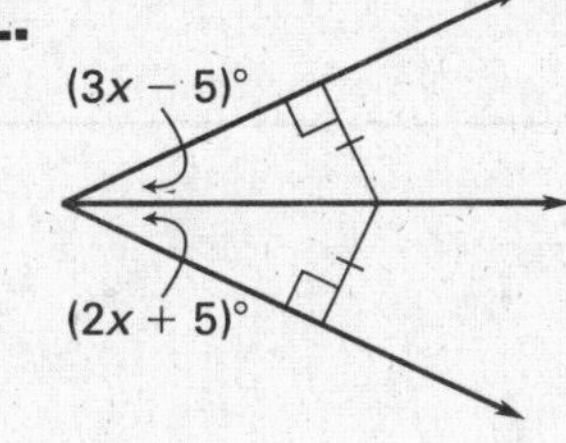

2.

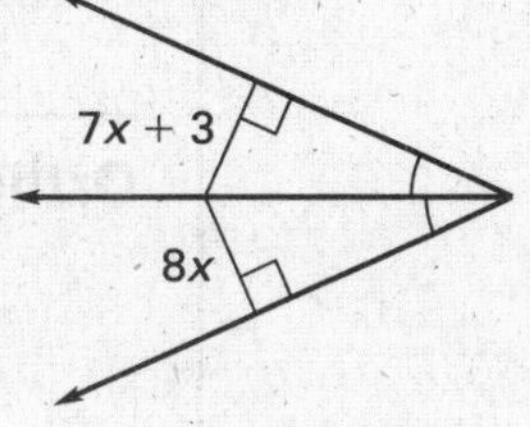

3. Do you have enough information to conclude that $\overrightarrow{AC}$ bisects $\angle DAB$? *Explain.*

B
A
C
D

4. In Example 4, suppose you are not given HL or HI, but you are given that $JL = 25$ and $JI = 20$. Find LK.

Homework

5.4 Use Medians and Altitudes

Goal • Use medians and altitudes of triangles.

Your Notes

VOCABULARY

Median of a triangle

Centroid

Altitude of a triangle

Orthocenter

THEOREM 5.8: CONCURRENCY OF MEDIANS OF A TRIANGLE

The medians of a triangle intersect at a point that is two thirds of the distance from each vertex to the midpoint of the opposite side.

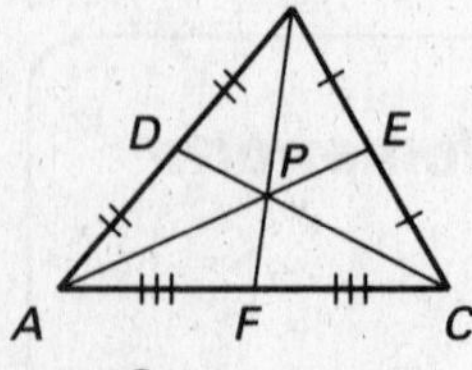

The medians of $\triangle ABC$ meet at P and $AP = \frac{2}{3}$_____, $BP = \frac{2}{3}$_____, and $CP = \frac{2}{3}$_____.

Your Notes

Example 1 ***Use the centroid of a triangle***

In $\triangle FGH$, M is the centroid and $GM = 6$. Find ML and GL.

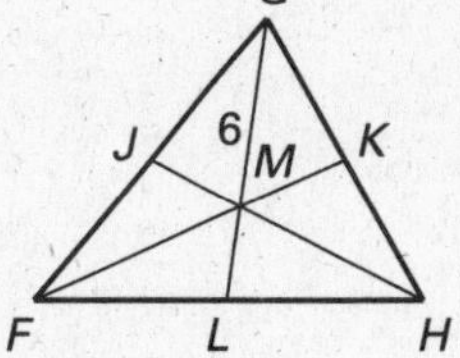

$\_\_\_\_ = \frac{\_\_\_}{\_\_\_} GL$ **Concurrency of Medians of a Triangle Theorem**

$\_\_\_ = \frac{\_\_\_}{\_\_\_} GL$ **Substitute ___ for GM.**

$\_\_\_\_ = GL$ **Multiply each side by the reciprocal, $\frac{\_\_\_}{\_\_\_}$.**

Then $ML = GL - \_\_\_\_ = \_\_\_ - \_\_\_ = \_\_\_$.

So, $ML = \_\_\_$ and $GL = \_\_\_$.

Checkpoint **Complete the following exercise.**

1. In Example 1, suppose $FM = 10$. Find MK and FK.

Example 2 ***Find the centroid of a triangle***

The vertices of $\triangle JKL$ are $J(1, 2)$, $K(4, 6)$, and $L(7, 4)$. Find the coordinates of the centroid P of $\triangle JKL$.

Sketch $\triangle JKL$. Then use the Midpoint Formula to find the midpoint M of $\overline{JL}$ and sketch median $\overline{KM}$.

Median $\overline{KM}$ was used in Example 2 because it is easy to find distances on a vertical segment. You can check by finding the centroid using a different median.

$M\left(\frac{\square}{2}, \frac{\square}{2}\right) = \_\_\_\_\_\_$

The centroid is ________ of the distance from each vertex to the midpoint of the opposite side.

The distance from vertex K to point M is $6 - \_\_\_ = \_\_\_$ units. So, the centroid is $\frac{\_\_\_}{\_\_\_}(\_\_\_) = \_\_\_$ units down from K on $\overline{KM}$.

The coordinates of the centroid P are $(4, 6 - \_\_\_)$, or $(\_\_\_\_\_)$.

Your Notes

THEOREM 5.9: CONCURRENCY OF ALTITUDES OF A TRIANGLE

The lines containing the altitudes of a triangle are __________.

The lines containing $\overline{AF}$, $\overline{BE}$, and $\overline{CD}$ meet at G.

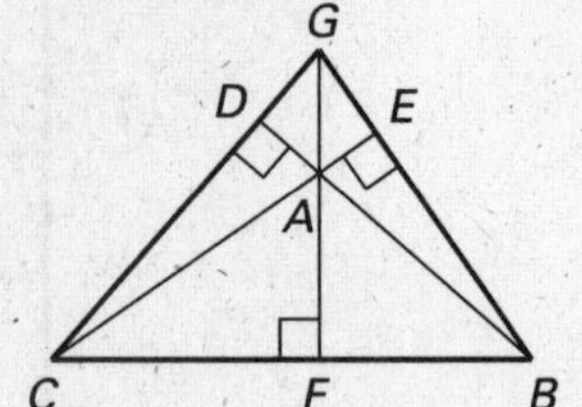

Example 3 ***Find the orthocenter***

Find the orthocenter *P* in the triangle.

Notice that in a right triangle the legs are also altitudes. The altitudes of the obtuse triangle are extended to find the orthocenter.

a.

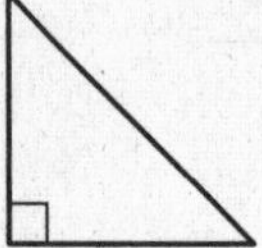

b.

Solution

a.

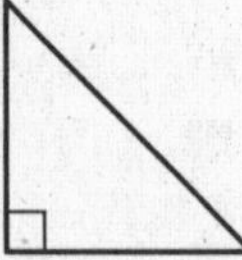

b.

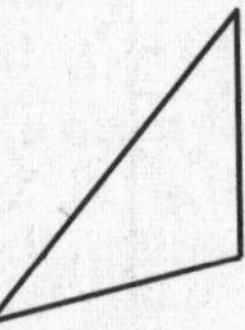

Checkpoint **Complete the following exercises.**

2. In Example 2, where do you need to move point K so that the centroid is $P(4, 5)$?

3. Find the orthocenter P in the triangle.

Your Notes

Example 4 ***Prove a property of isosceles triangles***

Prove that the altitude to the base of an isosceles triangle is a median.

Solution

Given $\triangle ABC$ is isosceles, with base $\overline{AC}$. $\overline{BD}$ is the altitude to base $\overline{AC}$.

Prove $\overline{BD}$ is a median of $\triangle ABC$.

Proof Legs $\overline{AB}$ and $\overline{CD}$ of $\triangle ABC$ are congruent. ________ and ________ are congruent right angles because $\overline{BD}$ is the ________ to $\overline{AC}$. Also, $\overline{BD} \cong \overline{BD}$. Therefore, $\triangle ADB \cong \triangle CDB$ by the ____________________.

$\overline{AD} \cong$ _____ because corresponding parts of congruent triangles are congruent. So, D is the ________ of $\overline{AC}$ by definition. Therefore, $\overline{BD}$ intersects $\overline{AC}$ at its ________, and $\overline{BD}$ is a median of $\triangle ABC$.

Checkpoint **Complete the following exercise.**

4. Prove that the altitude $\overline{BD}$ in Example 4 is also an angle bisector.

Homework

5.5 Use Inequalities in a Triangle

Goal • Find possible side lengths of a triangle.

Your Notes

Example 1 ***Relate side length and angle measure***

Mark the largest angle, longest side, smallest angle, and shortest side of the triangle shown at the right. What do you notice?

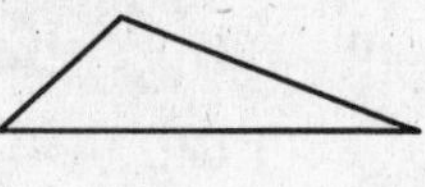

Solution

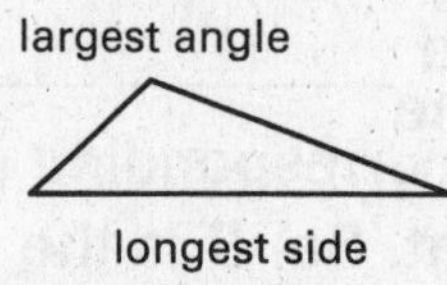

The longest side and largest angle are _______ each other.

The shortest side and smallest angle are _______ each other.

THEOREM 5.10

If one side of a triangle is longer than another side, then the angle opposite the longer side is _______ than the angle opposite the shorter side.

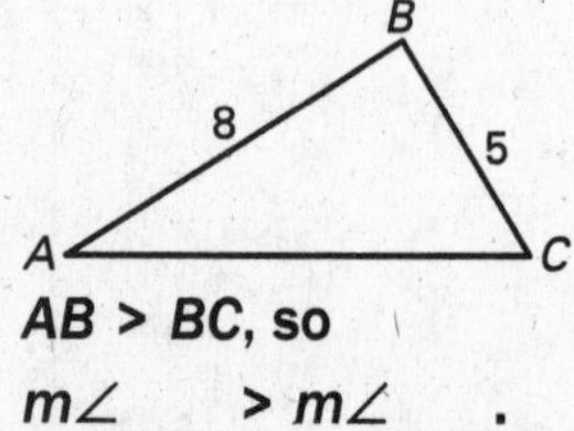

AB > *BC*, so
$m\angle$___ > $m\angle$___.

Be careful not to confuse the symbol ∠ meaning *angle* with the symbol < meaning *is less than*. Notice that the bottom edge of the angle symbol is horizontal.

THEOREM 5.11

If one angle of a triangle is larger than another angle, then the side opposite the larger angle is _______ than the side opposite the smaller angle.

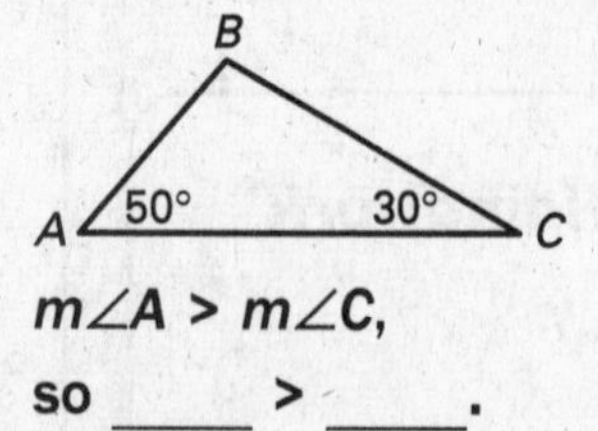

$m\angle A > m\angle C$,
so _____ > _____.

Your Notes

Example 2 ***Find angle measures***

Boating A long-tailed boat leaves a dock and travels 2500 feet to a cave, 5000 feet to a beach, then 6000 feet back to the dock as shown below. One of the angles in the path is about 55° and one is about 24°. What is the angle measure of the path made at the cave?

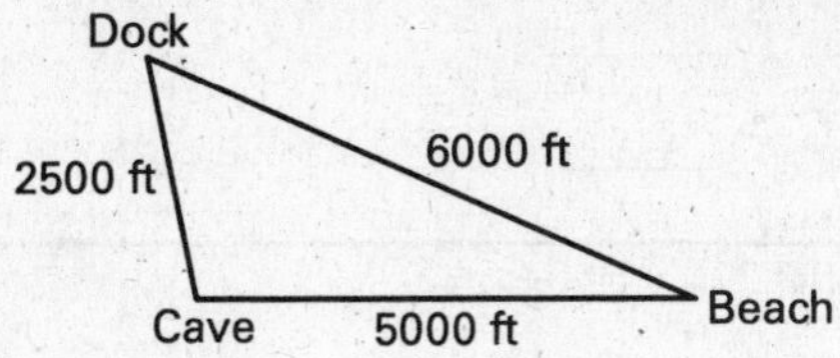

Solution

The cave is opposite the ________ side so, by Theorem 5.10, the cave angle is the ________ angle.

The angle measures sum to 180°, so the third angle measure is ________________ = ________.

The angle measure made at the cave is ______.

Checkpoint **Complete the following exercises.**

1. List the sides of $\triangle PQR$ in order from shortest to longest.

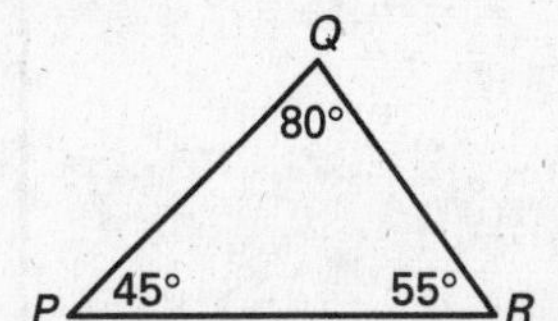

2. Another boat makes a trip whose path has sides of 1.5 miles, 2 miles, and 2.5 miles long and angles of 90°, about 53°, and about 37°. Sketch and label a diagram with the shortest side on the bottom and the right angle at the right.

Your Notes

THEOREM 5.12: TRIANGLE INEQUALITY THEOREM

The sum of the lengths of any two sides of a triangle is greater than the length of the third side.

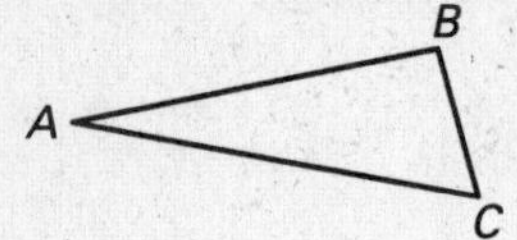

_____ + _____ > AC

AC + _____ > _____

_____ + AC > _____

Example 3 *Find possible side lengths*

A triangle has one side of length 14 and another of length 10. Describe the possible lengths of the third side.

Solution

Let x represent the length of the third side. Draw diagrams to help visualize the small and large values of x. Then use the Triangle Inequality Theorem to write and solve inequalities.

Small values of x

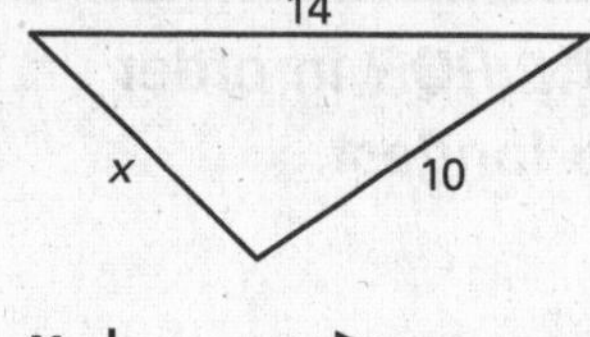

x + _____ > _____

x > _____

Large values of x

_____ + _____ > x

_____ > x, or x < _____

The length of the third side must be ______________________________.

Checkpoint Complete the following exercise.

Homework

3. A triangle has one side of 23 meters and another of 17 meters. *Describe* the possible lengths of the third side.

5.6 Inequalities in Two Triangles and Indirect Proof

• Use inequalities to make comparisons in two triangles.

Your Notes

VOCABULARY

Indirect Proof

THEOREM 5.13: HINGE THEOREM

If two sides of one triangle are congruent to two sides of another triangle, and the included angle of the first is larger than the included angle of the second, then the third side of the first is ________ than the third side of the second.

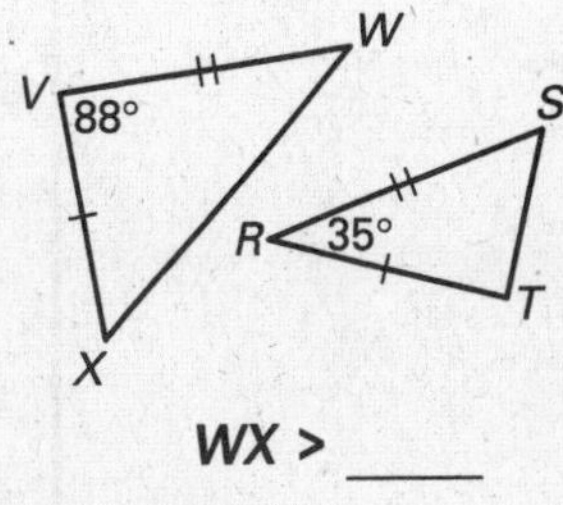

$WX >$ ____

THEOREM 5.14: CONVERSE OF THE HINGE THEOREM

If two sides of one triangle are congruent to two sides of another triangle, and the third side of the first is longer than the third side of the second, then the included angle of the first is ________ than the included angle of the second.

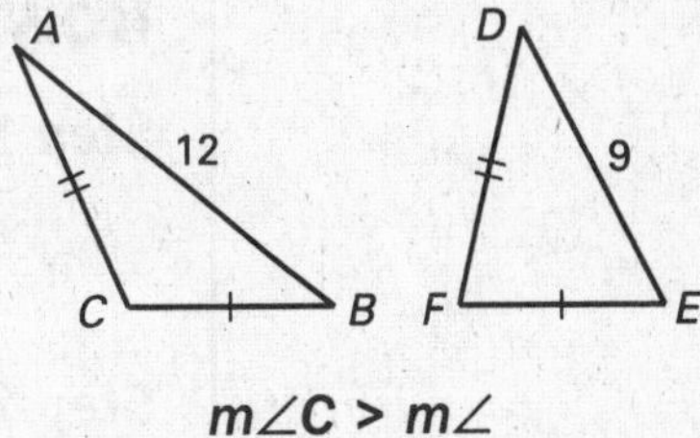

$m\angle C > m\angle$ ____

Your Notes

Example 1 *Use the Converse of the Hinge Theorem*

Given that $\overline{AD} \cong \overline{BC}$, how does $\angle 1$ compare to $\angle 2$?

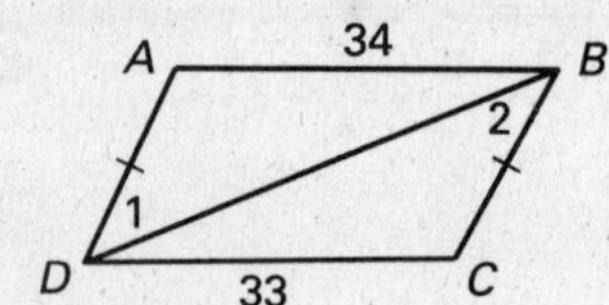

Solution

You are given that $\overline{AD} \cong \overline{BC}$ and you know that $\overline{BD} \cong \overline{BD}$ by the Reflexive Property. Because 34 > 33, _____ > _____. So, two sides of $\triangle ADB$ are congruent to two sides of $\triangle CBD$ and the third side in $\triangle ADB$ is ________.

By the Converse of the Hinge Theorem, $m\angle$___ > $m\angle$___.

Example 2 *Solve a multi-step problem*

Travel Car A leaves a mall, heads due north for 5 mi and then turns due west for 3 mi. Car B leaves the same mall, heads due south for 5 mi and then turns 80° toward east for 3 mi. Which car is farther from the mall?

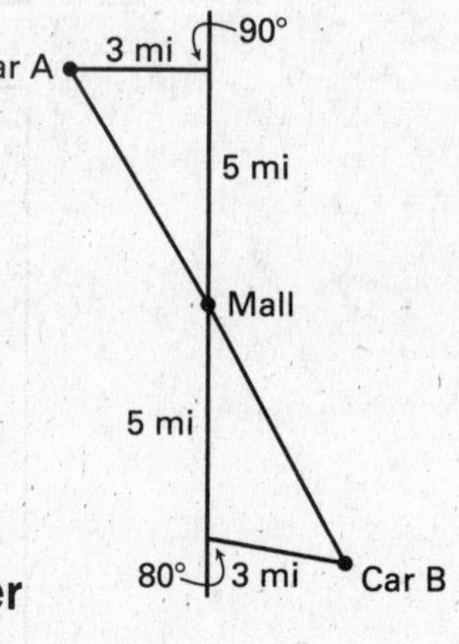

Draw a diagram. The distance driven and the distance back to the mall form two triangles, with __________ 5 mile sides and __________ 3 mile sides. Add the third side to the diagram.

Use linear pairs to find the included angles of _____ and _____.

Because 100° > 90°, Car ___ is farther from the mall than Car A by the _____________.

HOW TO WRITE AN INDIRECT PROOF

Step 1 **Identify** the statement you want to prove. **Assume** temporarily that this statement is _______ by assuming that the opposite is _____.

Step 2 **Reason** logically until you reach a contradiction.

Step 3 **Point out** that the desired conclusion must be _____ because the contradiction proves the temporary assumption _____.

Your Notes

Example 3 *Write an indirect proof*

Write an indirect proof to show that an odd number is not divisible by 6.

Given x is an odd number.

Prove x is not divisible by 6.

Solution

Step 1 Assume temporarily that ________________.
This means that $\frac{}{}$ = n for some whole number n.
So, multiplying both sides by 6 gives ___ = ____.

You have reached a contradiction when you have two statements that cannot both be true at the same time.

Step 2 If x is odd, then, by definition, x cannot be divided evenly by ____. However, ____ = ____ so $\frac{}{}$ = $\frac{}{}$ = ____. We know that ____ is a whole number because n is a whole number, so x can be divided evenly by ___. This contradicts the given statement that ________.

Step 3 Therefore, the assumption that x is divisible by 6 is ______, which proves that ________________ _____.

✔ ***Checkpoint*** **Complete the following exercises.**

1. If $m\angle ADB > m\angle CDB$ which is longer, $\overline{AB}$ or $\overline{CB}$?

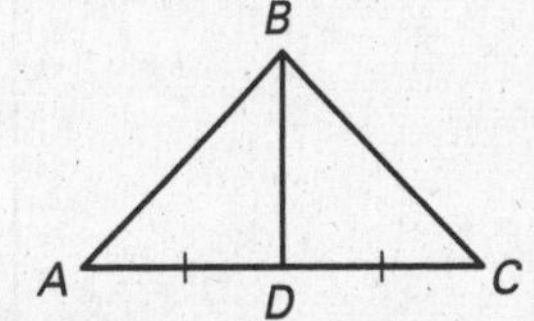

2. In Example 2, car C leaves the mall and goes 5 miles due west, then turns 85° toward south for 3 miles. Write the cars in order from the car closest to the mall to the car farthest from the mall.

3. Suppose you wanted to prove the statement "If $x + y \neq 5$ and $y = 2$, then $x \neq 3$." What temporary assumption could you make to prove the conclusion indirectly?

Homework

Words to Review

Give an example of the vocabulary word.

Midsegment of a triangle	Coordinate proof
Perpendicular bisector	**Equidistant**
Concurrent	**Point of concurrency**
Circumcenter	**Incenter**

Median of a triangle	Centroid
Altitude of a triangle	**Orthocenter**
Indirect proof	

Review your notes and Chapter 5 by using the Chapter Review on pages 344–347 of your textbook.

6.1 Ratios, Proportions, and the Geometric Mean

Goal • Solve problems by writing and solving proportions.

Your Notes

VOCABULARY

Ratio of *a* to *b*

Proportion

Means, extremes

Geometric mean

Example 1 ***Simplify ratios***

Simplify the ratio. *(See Table of Measures, p. 921)*

a. 76 cm : 8 cm **b.** $\frac{4\text{ ft}}{24\text{ in.}}$

Solution

a. Write 76 cm : 8 cm as $\frac{\square}{\square}$. Then divide out the units and simplify.

For help with conversion factors, see p. 886.

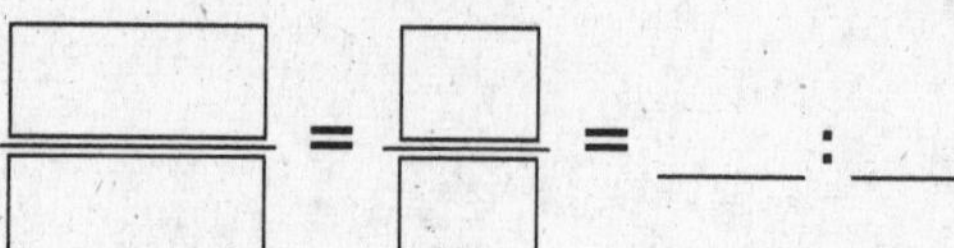

$\frac{\square}{\square} = \frac{\square}{\square} = $ ____ : ____

b. To simplify a ratio with unlike units, multiply by a conversion factor.

$$\frac{4\text{ ft}}{24\text{ in.}} = \frac{4\text{ ft}}{24\text{ in.}} \cdot \frac{\square}{\square} = \frac{\square}{\square} = \frac{\square}{\square}$$

Your Notes

Example 2 *Use a ratio to find a dimension*

Painting You are painting barn doors. You know that the perimeter of the doors is 64 feet and that the ratio of the length to the height is 3 : 5. Find the area of the doors.

Solution

Step 1 **Write** expressions for the length and height. Because the ratio of the length to height is 3 : 5, you can represent the length by ___x and the height by ___x.

Step 2 **Solve** an equation to find x.

$2\ell + 2w = P$	**Formula for perimeter**
$2(\_\_\_x) + 2(\_\_\_x) = \_\_\_\_$	**Substitute.**
$\_\_\_\_x = \_\_\_\_$	**Multiply and combine like terms.**
$x = \_\_\_$	**Divide each side by ____.**

Step 3 **Evaluate** the expressions for the length and height. Substitute the value of x into each expression.

Length: ___x = ___(___) = ____

Height: ___x = ___(___) = ____

The doors are ____ feet long and ____ feet high, so the area is ____ • ____ = _______.

✔ ***Checkpoint*** **In Exercises 1 and 2, simplify the ratio.**

1. 4 meters to 18 meters	**2.** 33 yd : 9 ft

3. The perimeter of a rectangular table is 21 feet and the ratio of its length to its width is 5 : 2. Find the length and width of the table.

Your Notes

Example 3 ***Use extended ratios***

The measures of the angles in $\triangle BCD$ are in the *extended ratio* of 2:3:4. Find the measures of the angles.

Solution

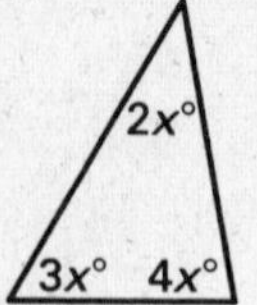

Begin by sketching the triangle. Then use the extended ratio of 2:3:4 to label the measures as ___x°, ___x°, and ___x°.

___x° + ___x° + ___x° = 180° **Triangle Sum Theorem**

___x = 180 **Combine like terms.**

x = ____ **Divide each side by ___.**

The angle measures are 2(____) = ____, 3(____) = ____, and 4(____) = ____.

✔ ***Checkpoint*** **Complete the following exercise.**

4. A triangle's angle measures are in the extended ratio of 1:4:5. Find the measures of the angles.

A PROPERTY OF PROPORTIONS

1. **Cross Products Property** In a proportion, the product of the extremes equals the product of the means.

If $\frac{a}{b} = \frac{c}{d}$ where $b \neq 0$ and $d \neq 0$, then ____ = ____.

$\frac{2}{3} = \frac{4}{6}$

3 • ___ = ___

2 • ___ = ___

Your Notes

> In part (a), you could multiply each side by the denominator, 16. Then $16 \cdot \frac{3}{4} = 16 \cdot \frac{x}{16}$ so _____ $= x$.

Example 4 ***Solve proportions***

Solve the proportion.

a. $\frac{3}{4} = \frac{x}{16}$ **Original proportion**

$3 \cdot$ _____ $=$ _____ $\cdot\, x$ **Cross Products Property**

_____ $=$ _____x **Multiply.**

_____ $= x$ **Divide each side by ___.**

b. $\frac{3}{x+1} = \frac{2}{x}$ **Original proportion**

___ $\cdot\, x =$ ___$(x + 1)$ **Cross Products Property**

___$x =$ ___$x +$ ___ **Distributive Property**

$x =$ ___ **Subtract ____ from each side.**

Example 5 ***Solve a real-world problem***

Bowling You want to find the total number of rows of boards that make up 24 lanes at a bowling alley. You know that there are 117 rows in 3 lanes. Find the total number of rows of boards that make up the 24 lanes.

Solution

Write and solve a proportion involving two ratios that compare the number of rows with the number of lanes.

$\frac{\_\_\_\_}{\_\_\_\_} = \frac{\_\_\_\_}{\_\_\_\_}$ ← number of rows / ← number of lanes **Write proportion.**

_____ $\cdot$ _____ $=$ ____ $\cdot$ ____ **Cross Products Property**

_____ $= n$ **Simplify.**

There are _____ rows of boards that make up the 24 lanes.

GEOMETRIC MEAN

The geometric mean of two positive numbers a and b is the positive number x that satisfies $\frac{a}{x} = \frac{x}{b}$.

So, $x^2 =$ ____ and $x = \sqrt{\_\_\_\_}$.

Your Notes

Example 6 *Find a geometric mean*

Find the geometric mean of 16 and 48.

Solution

$x =$ ______ **Definition of geometric mean**

$=$ ______ **Substitute ____ for *a* and ____ for *b*.**

$=$ ______ **Factor.**

$=$ ______ **Simplify.**

The geometric mean of 16 and 48 is ______ ≈ ______.

Checkpoint Complete the following exercises.

5. Solve $\frac{8}{y} = \frac{2}{5}$.

6. Solve $\frac{x - 3}{3} = \frac{2x}{9}$.

7. A small gymnasium contains 10 sets of bleachers. You count 192 spectators in 3 sets of bleachers and the spectators seem to be evenly distributed. Estimate the total number of spectators.

8. Find the geometric mean of 14 and 16.

Homework

6.2 Use Proportions to Solve Geometry Problems

Goal • Use proportions to solve geometry problems.

Your Notes

VOCABULARY

Scale drawing

Scale

ADDITIONAL PROPERTIES OF PROPORTIONS

2. **Reciprocal Property** If two ratios are equal, then their reciprocals are also equal.

   If $\frac{a}{b} = \frac{c}{d}$, then $\frac{b}{a} =$ ____.

3. If you interchange the means of a proportion, then you form another true proportion.

   If $\frac{a}{b} = \frac{c}{d}$, then $\frac{a}{c} =$ ____.

4. In a proportion, if you add the value of each ratio's denominator to its numerator, then you form another true proportion.

   If $\frac{a}{b} = \frac{c}{d}$, then $\frac{a+b}{b} =$ ______.

Your Notes

Example 1 *Use properties of proportions*

In the diagram, $\frac{AC}{DF} = \frac{BC}{EF}$. Write four true proportions.

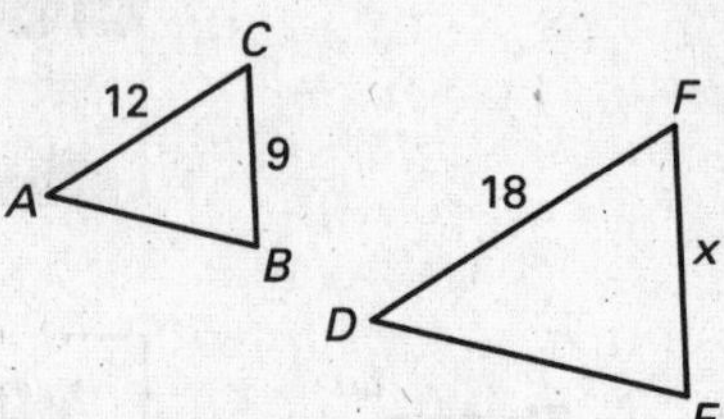

Because $\frac{AC}{DF} = \frac{BC}{EF}$, then $\frac{12}{18} =$ ____.

Reciprocal Property: The reciprocals are equal, so $\frac{18}{12} =$ ____.

Property 3: You can interchange the means, so $\frac{12}{9} =$ ____.

Property 4: You can add the denominators to the numerators, so ____ = ____.

Example 2 *Use proportions with geometric figures*

In the diagram, $\frac{JL}{LH} = \frac{JK}{KG}$.

Find *JH* and *JL*.

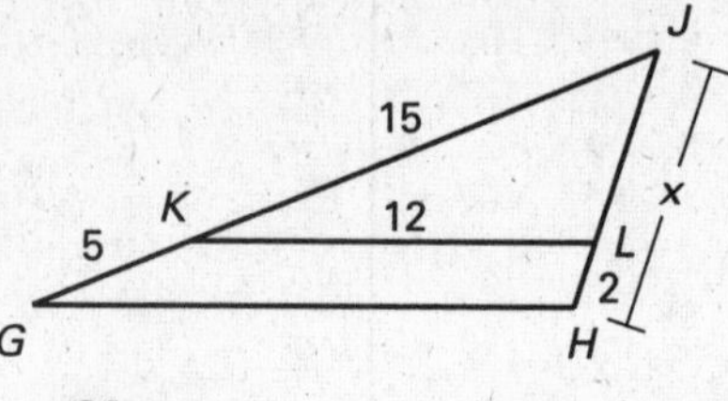

$\frac{JL}{LH} = \frac{JK}{KG}$	Given
____ = ____	Property of Proportions (Property 4)
____ = ____	Substitution Property of Equality
____ = ____	Cross Products Property
$x =$ ____	Solve for *x*.

So *JH* = ____ and *JL* = ____ = ____.

✔ ***Checkpoint*** **Complete the following exercises.**

1. In Example 1, find the value of *x*.	**2.** In Example 2, $\frac{KL}{GH} = \frac{JK}{JG}$. Find *GH*.

Your Notes

Example 3 ***Find the scale of a drawing***

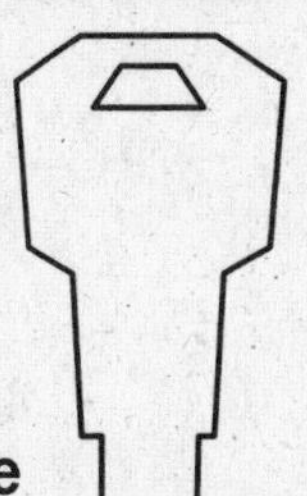

Keys The length of the key in the scale drawing is 7 centimeters. The length of the actual key is 4 centimeters. What is the scale of the drawing?

Solution

To find the scale, write the ratio of a length in the drawing to ________________, then rewrite the ratio so that the ____________ is 1.

$\frac{\text{length in drawing}}{\boxed{}} = \frac{}{} = \frac{}{} = \frac{}{}$

The scale of the drawing is ____________.

Checkpoint Complete the following exercise.

3. In Example 3, suppose the length of the key in the scale drawing is 6 centimeters. Find the new scale of the drawing.

Example 4 ***Use a scale drawing***

Maps The scale of the map at the right is 1 inch : 8 miles. Find the actual distance from Westbrook to Cooley.

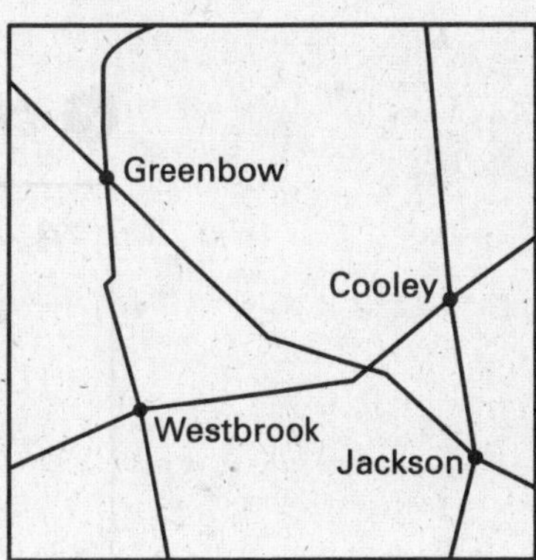

Solution

Use a ruler. The distance from Westbrook to Cooley on the map is about __________. Let x be the actual distance in miles.

$\frac{}{} = \frac{1\text{ in.}}{8\text{ mi}}$ ← distance on map / ← actual distance

$x =$ ________ **Cross Products Property**

$x =$ ____ **Simplify.**

The actual distance from Westbrook to Cooley is about __________.

Your Notes

Example 5 ***Solve a multi-step problem***

Scale Model You buy a 3-D scale model of the Sunsphere in Knoxville, TN. The actual building is 266 feet tall. Your model is 20 inches tall, and the diameter of the dome on your scale model is about 5.6 inches.

a. What is the diameter of the actual dome?

b. How many times as tall as your model is the actual building?

Solution

a. $\frac{20 \text{ in.}}{266 \text{ ft}} = \frac{5.6 \text{ in.}}{x \text{ ft}}$ ← measurement on model / ← measurement on actual building

$\_\_\_\_ x = \_\_\_\_\_\_$ **Cross Products Property**

$x \approx \_\_\_\_$ **Divide each side by ____.**

The diameter of the actual dome is about ______ feet.

b. To simplify a ratio with unlike units, multiply by a conversion factor.

$\frac{266 \text{ ft}}{20 \text{ in.}} = \_\_\_\_\_\_\_\_ = \_\_\_\_\_\_$

The actual building is _____ times as tall as the model.

Checkpoint **Complete the following exercises.**

4. Two landmarks are 130 miles from each other. The landmarks are 6.5 inches apart on a map. Find the scale of the map.

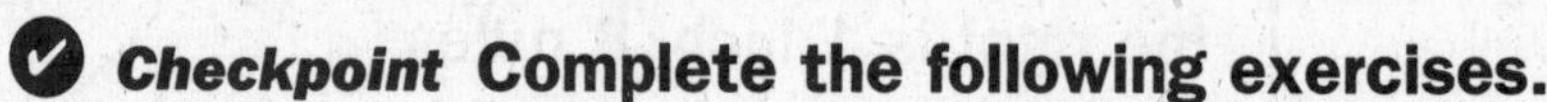

Homework

5. Your friend has a model of the Sunsphere that is 5 inches tall. What is the approximate diameter of the dome on your friend's model?

6.3 Use Similar Polygons

Goal • Use proportions to identify similar polygons.

Your Notes

VOCABULARY

Similar polygons

Scale factor of two similar polygons

Example 1 ***Use similarity statements***

In the diagram, $\triangle ABC \sim \triangle DEF$.

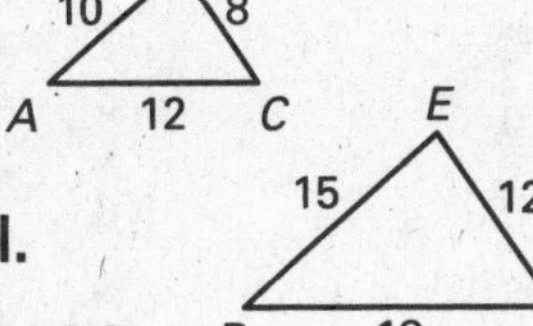

a. List all pairs of congruent angles.

b. Check that the ratios of corresponding side lengths are equal.

c. Write the ratios of the corresponding side lengths in a *statement of proportionality*.

In a *statement of proportionality*, any pair of ratios forms a true proportion.

Solution

a. $\angle A \cong \angle$ ____, $\angle B \cong \angle$ ____, $\angle C \cong \angle$ ____

b. $\frac{AB}{DE} = \frac{\_\_\_}{\_\_\_} = \_\_\_$ $\frac{BC}{EF} = \frac{\_\_\_}{\_\_\_} = \_\_\_$

$\frac{CA}{FD} = \frac{\_\_\_}{\_\_\_} = \_\_\_$

c. The ratios in part (b) are equal, so

____ = ____ = ____.

✔ ***Checkpoint*** **Complete the following exercise.**

1. Given $\triangle PQR \sim \triangle XYZ$, list all pairs of congruent angles. Write the ratios of the corresponding side lengths in a statement of proportionality.

Your Notes

Example 2 *Find the scale factor*

Determine whether the polygons are similar. If they are, write a similarity statement and find the scale factor of *ABCD* to *JKLM*.

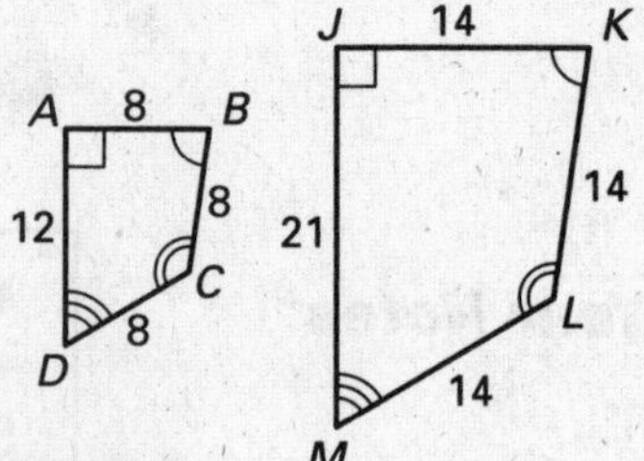

Solution

Step 1 Identify pairs of congruent angles.
From the diagram, you can see that $\angle B \cong \angle$___, $\angle C \cong \angle$___, and $\angle D \cong \angle$___. Angles ___ and ___ are right angles, so $\angle$___ $\cong \angle$___. So, the corresponding angles are ________.

Step 2 Show that corresponding side lengths are proportional.

$\frac{AB}{JK} = \frac{\quad}{\quad} = \frac{\quad}{\quad}$ $\qquad$ $\frac{BC}{KL} = \frac{\quad}{\quad} = \frac{\quad}{\quad}$

$\frac{CD}{LM} = \frac{\quad}{\quad} = \frac{\quad}{\quad}$ $\qquad$ $\frac{AD}{JM} = \frac{\quad}{\quad} = \frac{\quad}{\quad}$

The ratios are equal, so the corresponding side lengths are ________.

So $ABCD \sim$ ______. The scale factor of *ABCD* to *JKLM* is ___.

Example 3 *Use similar polygons*

In the diagram, $\triangle BCD \sim \triangle RST$. Find the value of x.

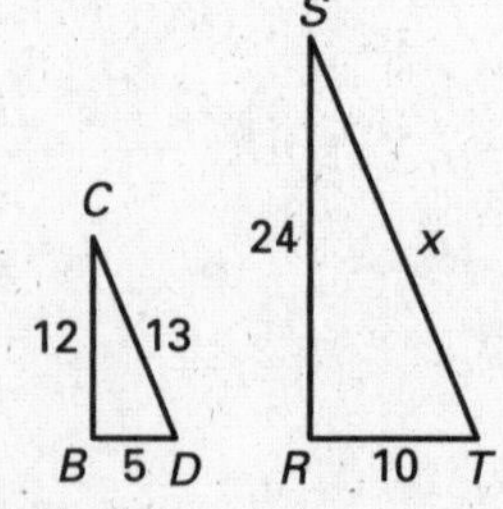

Solution

The triangles are similar, so the corresponding side lengths are ________.

$\frac{BC}{\square} = \frac{\square}{ST}$ **Write proportion.**

$\frac{12}{\square} = \frac{\square}{x}$ **Substitute.**

$12x =$ _____ **Cross Products Property**

$x =$ _____ **Solve for x.**

There are several ways to write the proportion. For example, you could write $\frac{BD}{RT} = \frac{CD}{ST}$.

Your Notes

Checkpoint In the diagram, $FGHJ \sim LMNP$.

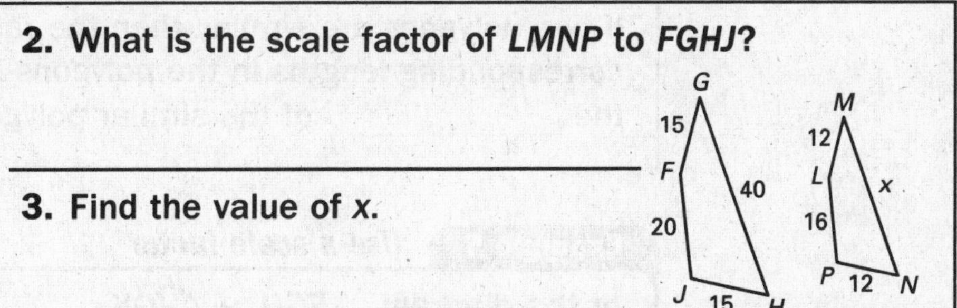

2. What is the scale factor of *LMNP* to *FGHJ*?

3. Find the value of *x*.

THEOREM 6.1: PERIMETERS OF SIMILAR POLYGONS

If two polygons are similar, then the ratio of their perimeters is equal to the ratios of their corresponding side lengths.

If $KLMN \sim PQRS$, then

$$\frac{KL + LM + MN + NK}{PQ + QR + RS + SP} = \frac{\_\_}{\_\_} = \frac{\_\_}{\_\_} = \frac{\_\_}{\_\_} = \frac{\_\_}{\_\_}.$$

Example 4 ***Find perimeters of similar figures***

Basketball A larger cement court is being poured for a basketball hoop in place of a smaller one. The court will be 20 feet wide and 25 feet long. The old court was similar in shape, but only 16 feet wide.

a. Find the scale factor of the new court to the old court.

b. Find the perimeters of the new court and the old court.

Solution

a. Because the new court will be similar to the old court, the scale factor is the ratio of the widths, $\frac{\_\_}{\_\_} = \frac{\_\_}{\_\_}$.

b. The new court's perimeter is ________ = ____ feet. Use Theorem 6.1 to find the perimeter *x* of the old court.

$\frac{90}{x} = \frac{\_\_}{\_\_}$ **Use Theorem 6.1 to write a proportion.**

$x =$ ____ **Simplify.**

The perimeter of the old court was ____ feet.

Your Notes

CORRESPONDING LENGTHS IN SIMILAR POLYGONS

If two polygons are similar, then the ratio of any two corresponding lengths in the polygons is equal to the ____________ of the similar polygons.

Example 5 ***Use a scale factor***

In the diagram, $\triangle FGH \sim \triangle JGK$. Find the length of the altitude $\overline{GL}$.

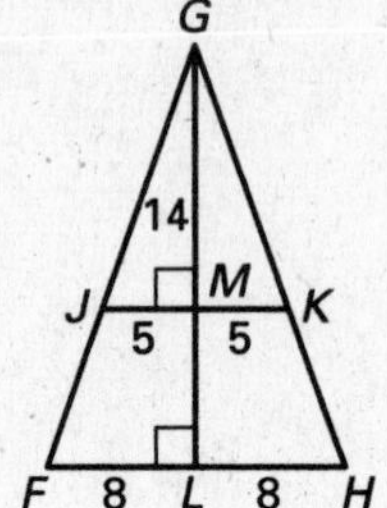

Solution

First, find the scale factor of $\triangle FGH$ to $\triangle JGK$.

$$\frac{FH}{\square} = \frac{\_\_\_}{\_\_\_} = \frac{\_\_}{\_\_} = \_\_$$

Because the ratio of the lengths of the altitudes in similar triangles is equal to the scale factor, you can write the following proportion.

$\frac{GL}{GM} = \_\_\_$ **Write proportion.**

$\frac{GL}{\square} = \_\_\_$ **Substitute ____ for GM.**

$GL = \_\_\_$ **Multiply each side by ____ and simplify.**

The length of altitude $\overline{GL}$ is ______.

Checkpoint **In the diagrams, $\triangle PQR \sim \triangle WXY$.**

4. Find the perimeter of $\triangle WXY$.

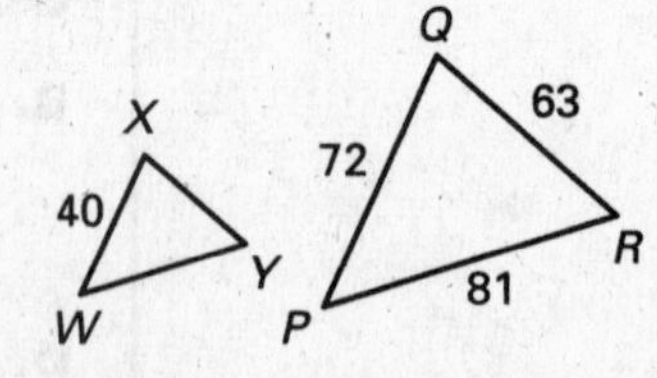

5. Find the length of median $\overline{QS}$.

Homework

6.4 Prove Triangles Similar by AA

Goal • Use the AA Similarity Postulate.

Your Notes

POSTULATE 22: ANGLE-ANGLE (AA) SIMILARITY POSTULATE

If two angles of one triangle are congruent to two angles of another triangle, then the two triangles are similar.

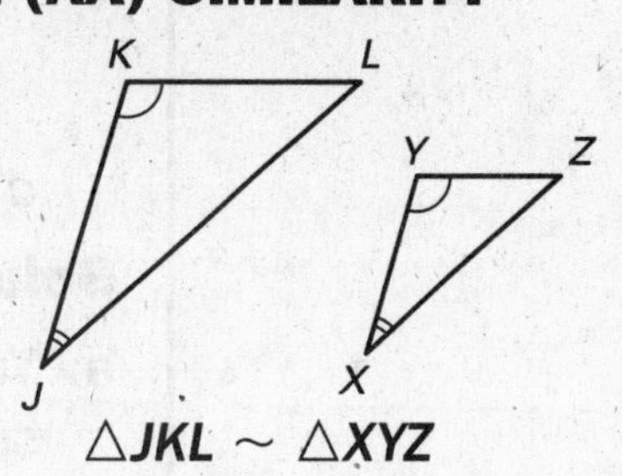

Example 1 ***Use the AA Similarity Postulate***

Determine whether the triangles are similar. If they are, write a similarity statement. *Explain* your reasoning.

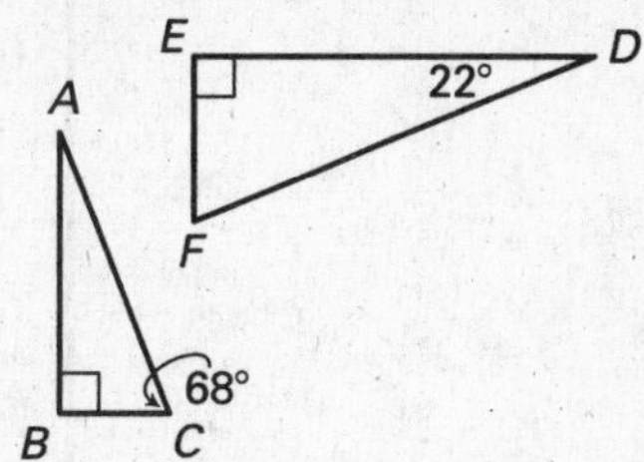

Solution

Because they are both right angles, $\angle$___ and $\angle$___ are congruent.

By the Triangle Sum Theorem,
_____ + _____ + $m\angle A = 180°$, so $m\angle A =$ _____.
Therefore, $\angle A$ and $\angle$___ are congruent.

So, $\triangle ABC \sim \triangle DEF$ by the ______________________.

Checkpoint **Determine whether the triangles are similar. If they are, write a similarity statement.**

1. **2.**

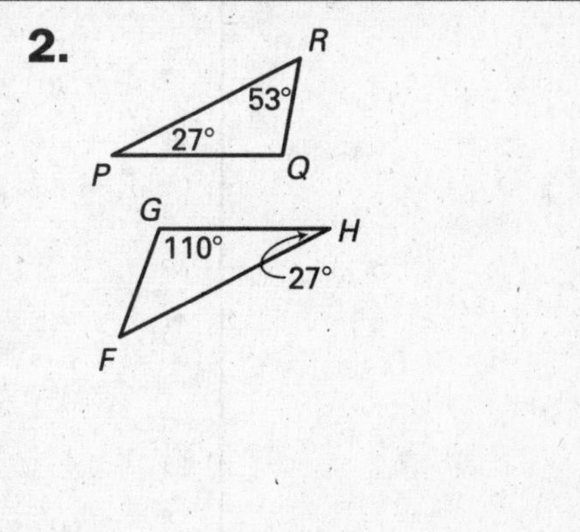

Your Notes

Example 2 *Show that triangles are similar*

Show that the two triangles are similar.

a. $\triangle RTV$ and $\triangle RQS$

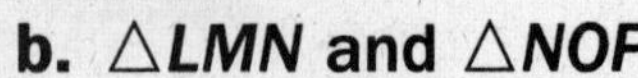

b. $\triangle LMN$ and $\triangle NOP$

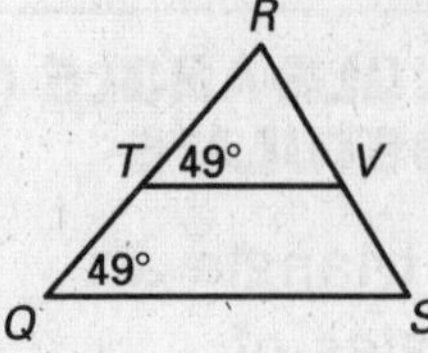

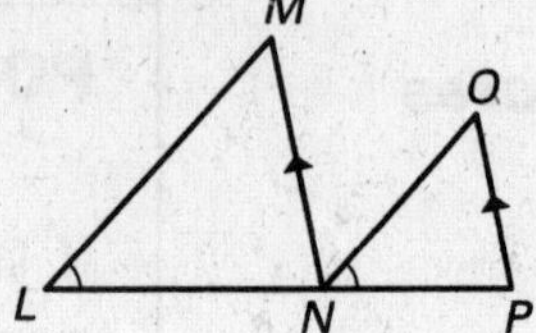

Solution

a. You may find it helpful to redraw the triangles separately.

Because $m\angle$______ and $m\angle$____ both equal 49°, $\angle$______ $\cong \angle$____. By the Reflexive Property, $\angle R \cong \angle$____.

So, $\triangle RTV \sim \triangle RQS$ by the ____________________.

b. The diagram shows $\angle L \cong \angle$______. It also shows that $\overline{MN} \parallel$ _____ so $\angle$______ $\cong \angle$____ by the Corresponding Angles Postulate.

So, $\triangle LMN \sim \triangle NOP$ by the ____________________.

✔ ***Checkpoint*** **Complete the following exercise.**

3. Show that $\triangle BCD \sim \triangle EFD$.

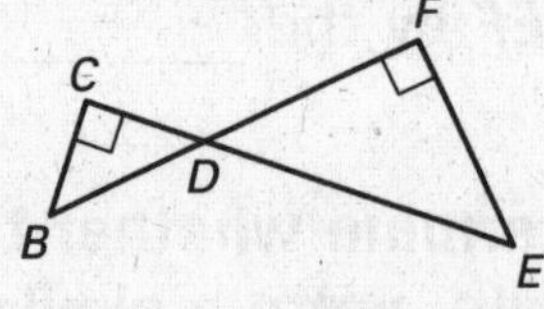

Your Notes

Example 3 — *Using similar triangles*

Height A lifeguard is standing beside the lifeguard chair on a beach. The lifeguard is 6 feet 4 inches tall and casts a shadow that is 48 inches long. The chair casts a shadow that is 6 feet long. How tall is the chair?

Solution

The lifeguard and the chair form sides of two right triangles with the ground, as shown below. The sun's rays hit the lifeguard and the chair at the same angle. You have two pairs of congruent ________, so the triangles are similar by the ______________________.

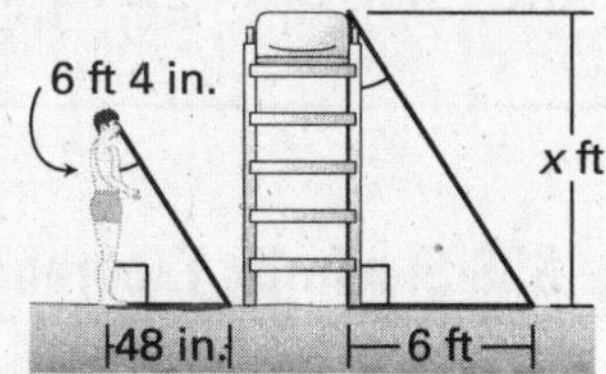

You can use a proportion to find the height x. Write 6 feet 4 inches as ____ inches so you can form two ratios of feet to inches.

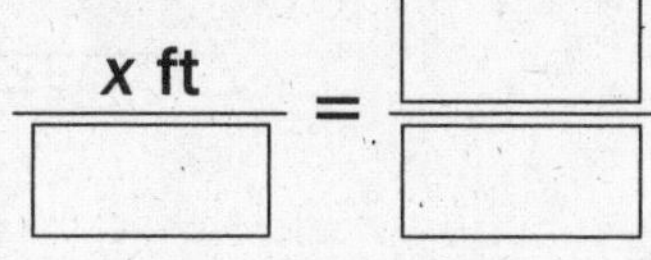

Write proportion of side lengths.

$\_\_\_\_ x = \_\_\_\_$ **Cross Products Property**

$x = \_\_\_\_$ **Solve for x.**

The chair is ____ feet tall.

✔ *Checkpoint* Complete the following exercise.

4. In Example 3, how long is the shadow of a person that is 4 feet 9 inches tall?

Homework

6.5 Prove Triangles Similar by SSS and SAS

Goal • Use the SSS and SAS Similarity Theorems.

Your Notes

THEOREM 6.2: SIDE-SIDE-SIDE (SSS) SIMILARITY THEOREM

If the corresponding side lengths of two triangles are ______________, then the triangles are similar.

If $\frac{AB}{RS} = \frac{BC}{ST} = \frac{CA}{TR}$, then $\triangle ABC \sim \triangle RST$.

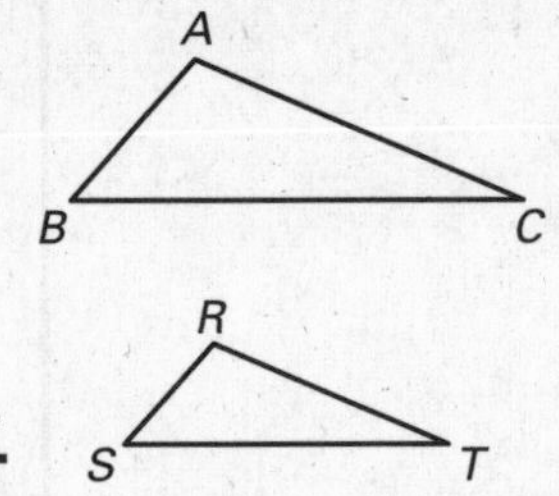

Example 1 **Use the SSS Similarity Theorem**

Is either $\triangle DEF$ or $\triangle GHJ$ similar to $\triangle ABC$?

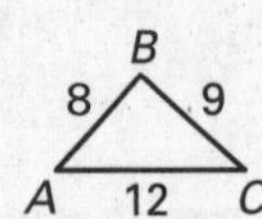

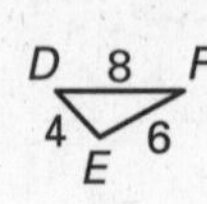

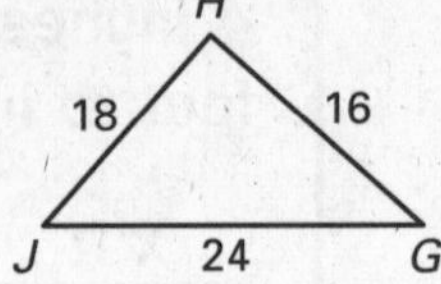

Solution

Compare $\triangle ABC$ and $\triangle DEF$ by finding ratios of corresponding side lengths.

When using the SSS Similarity Theorem, compare the shortest sides, the longest sides, and then the remaining sides.

Shortest sides	Longest sides	Remaining sides
$\frac{AB}{DE} = \frac{\_\_}{\_\_} = \_\_$	$\frac{CA}{FD} = \frac{\_\_}{\_\_} = \_\_$	$\frac{BC}{EF} = \frac{\_\_}{\_\_} = \_\_$

The ratios are ______________, so $\triangle ABC$ and $\triangle DEF$ are ______________.

Compare $\triangle ABC$ and $\triangle GHJ$ by finding ratios of corresponding side lengths.

Shortest sides	Longest sides	Remaining sides
$\frac{AB}{GH} = \frac{\_\_}{\_\_} = \_\_$	$\frac{CA}{JG} = \frac{\_\_}{\_\_} = \_\_$	$\frac{BC}{HJ} = \frac{\_\_}{\_\_} = \_\_$

All the ratios are ________, so $\triangle$______ $\sim \triangle$______.

Your Notes

Example 2 *Use the SSS Similarity Theorem*

Find the value of x that makes $\triangle ABC \sim \triangle DEF$.

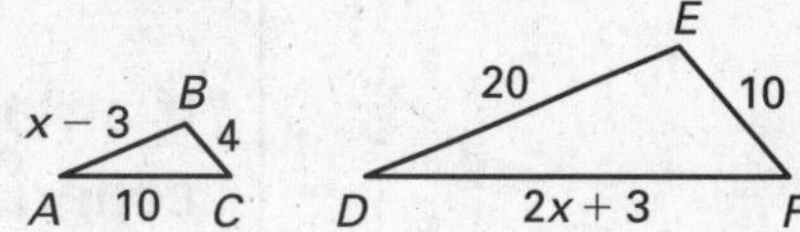

Solution

Step 1 **Find** the value of x that makes corresponding side lengths proportional.

$\frac{4}{\square} = \frac{x-3}{\square}$ **Write proportion.**

$4 \cdot \_\_\_\_ = \_\_\_\_(x - 3)$ **Cross Products Property**

$\_\_\_\_ = \_\_\_\_x - \_\_\_\_$ **Simplify.**

$\_\_\_\_ = x$ **Solve for x.**

Step 2 **Check** that the side lengths are proportional when $x = \_\_\_\_$.

$AB = x - 3 = \_\_\_\_$ $DF = 2x + 3 = \_\_\_\_$

$\frac{BC}{EF} \stackrel{?}{=} \frac{AB}{DE}$ $\_\_\_\_ = \_\_\_\_$ ✓ $\frac{BC}{EF} \stackrel{?}{=} \frac{AC}{DF}$ $\_\_\_\_ = \_\_\_\_$ ✓

When $x = \_\_\_\_$, the triangles are similar by the ________________.

✔ ***Checkpoint*** **Complete the following exercises.**

1. Which of the three triangles are similar?

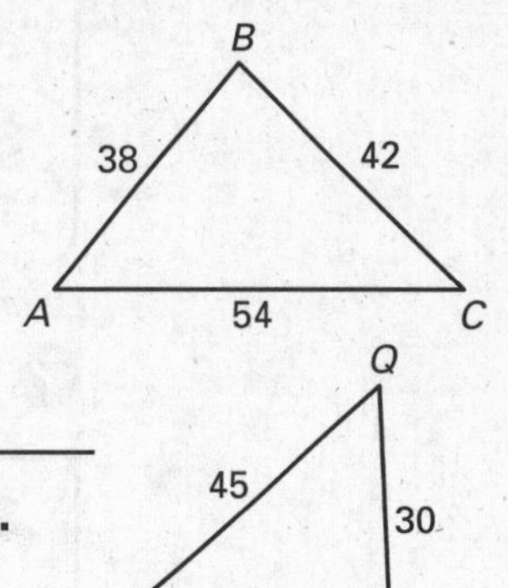

2. Suppose AB is not given in $\triangle ABC$. What value of AB would make $\triangle ABC$ similar to $\triangle QRP$?

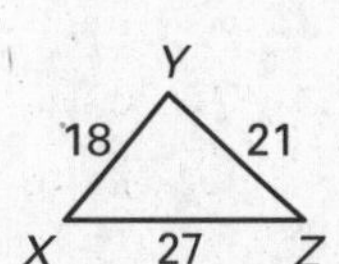

Your Notes

THEOREM 6.3: SIDE-ANGLE-SIDE (SAS) SIMILARITY THEOREM

If an angle of one triangle is congruent to an angle of a second triangle and the lengths of the sides including these angles are ______________, then the triangles are similar.

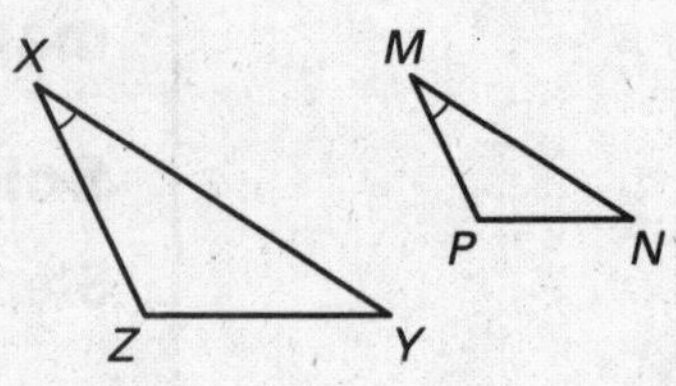

If $\angle X \cong \angle M$, and $\frac{ZX}{PM} = \frac{XY}{MN}$, then $\triangle XYZ \sim \triangle MNP$.

Example 3 ***Use the SAS Similarity Theorem***

Birdfeeder You are drawing a design for a birdfeeder. Can you construct the top so it is similar to the bottom using the angle measure and lengths shown?

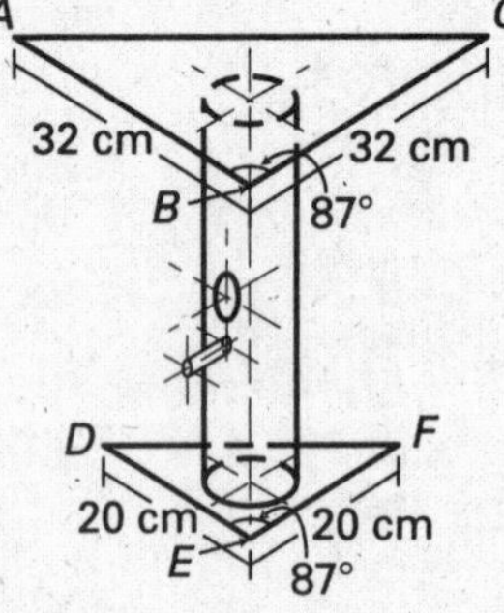

Solution

Both $m\angle$___ and $m\angle$___ equal 87°, so $\angle$___ $\cong$ $\angle$___. Next, compare the ratios of the lengths of the sides that include $\angle B$ and $\angle E$.

$$\frac{AB}{\square} = \frac{\square}{EF} = \frac{\quad}{\_\_\_} = \frac{\quad}{\_\_\_}$$

The lengths of the sides that include $\angle B$ and $\angle E$ are ______________.

So, by the ________________________, $\triangle ABC \sim \triangle DEF$. Yes, you can make the top similar to the bottom.

Checkpoint **Complete the following exercise.**

3. In Example 3, suppose you use equilateral triangles on the top and bottom. Are the top and bottom similar? *Explain.*

Your Notes

TRIANGLE SIMILARITY POSTULATE AND THEOREMS

AA Similarity Postulate If $\angle A \cong \angle D$ and $\angle B \cong \angle E$, then $\triangle ABC \sim \triangle DEF$.

SSS Similarity Theorem If $\frac{AB}{DE} = \frac{BC}{EF} = \frac{AC}{DF}$, then $\triangle ABC \sim \triangle DEF$.

SAS Similarity Theorem If $\angle A \cong \angle D$ and $\frac{AB}{DE} = \frac{AC}{DF}$, then $\triangle ABC \sim \triangle DEF$.

To identify corresponding parts, redraw the triangles so that the corresponding parts have the same orientation.

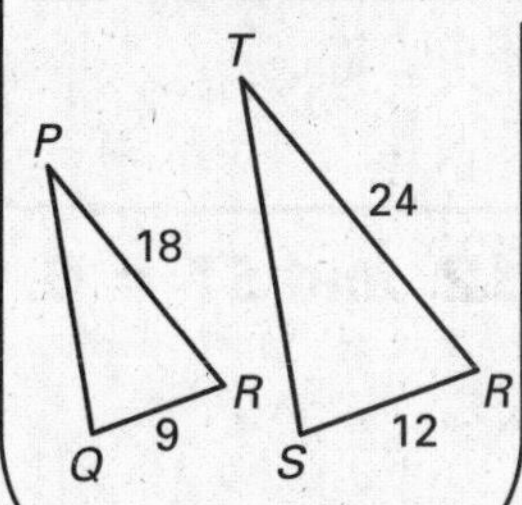

Example 4 **Choose a method**

Tell what method you would use to show that the triangles are similar.

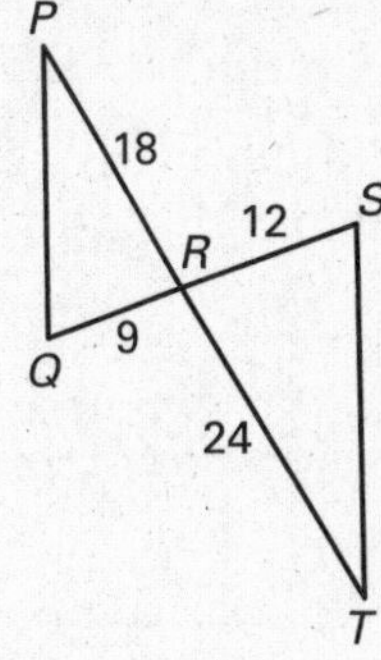

Solution

Find the ratios of the lengths of the corresponding sides.

Shorter sides __________

Longer sides __________

The corresponding side lengths are __________. The included angles $\angle PRQ$ and $\angle TRS$ are __________ because they are __________ angles. So, $\triangle PQR \sim \triangle TSR$ by the ____________________.

✔ ***Checkpoint*** **Complete the following exercise.**

4. *Explain* how to show $\triangle JKL \sim \triangle LKM$.

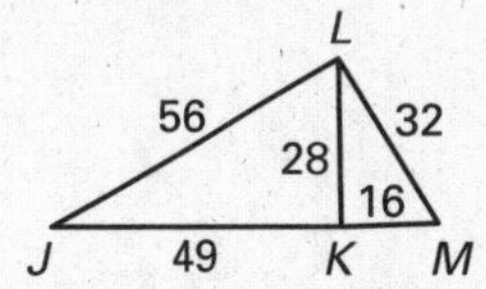

Homework

6.6 Use Proportionality Theorems

Goal • Use proportions with a triangle or parallel lines.

Your Notes

THEOREM 6.4: TRIANGLE PROPORTIONALITY THEOREM

If a line parallel to one side of a triangle intersects the other two sides, then it divides the two sides ________.

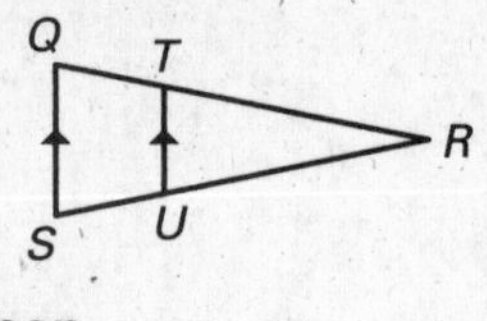

If $\overline{TU} \parallel \overline{QS}$, then $\frac{\_\_\_}{\_\_\_} = \frac{\_\_\_}{\_\_\_}$.

THEOREM 6.5: CONVERSE OF THE TRIANGLE PROPORTIONALITY THEOREM

If a line divides two sides of a triangle proportionally, then it is parallel to the ________.

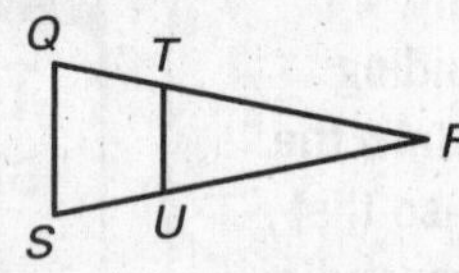

If $\frac{RT}{TQ} = \frac{RU}{US}$, then ____ ∥ ____.

Example 1 ***Find the length of a segment***

In the diagram, $\overline{QS} \parallel \overline{UT}$, $RQ = 10$, $RS = 12$, and $ST = 6$. What is the length of $\overline{QU}$?

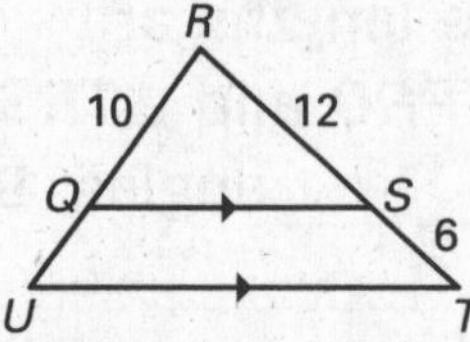

Solution

$\frac{RQ}{QU} = \frac{RS}{ST}$ ________________

$\frac{\square}{QU} = \frac{\square}{\square}$ **Substitute.**

____ = ____ • QU **Cross Products Property**

____ = QU **Divide each side by ____.**

Your Notes

Example 2 *Solve a real-world problem*

Aerodynamics A spoiler for a remote controlled car is shown where $AB = 31$ mm, $BC = 19$ mm, $CD = 27$ mm, and $DE = 23$ mm. *Explain* why $\overline{BD}$ is not parallel to $\overline{AE}$.

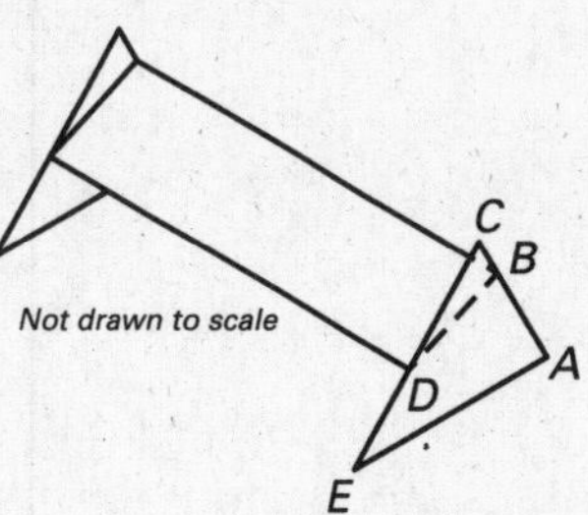

Solution

Find and simplify the ratios of lengths determined by $\overline{BD}$.

$\frac{CD}{DE} =$ ______ $\frac{CB}{BA} =$ ______

Because ______ $\neq$ ______, $\overline{BD}$ is not parallel to $\overline{AE}$.

Checkpoint Complete the following exercises.

1. Find the length of $\overline{KL}$.

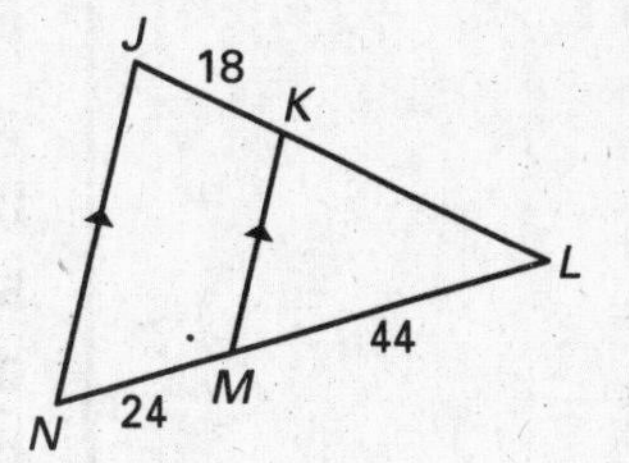

2. Determine whether $\overline{QT} \parallel \overline{RS}$.

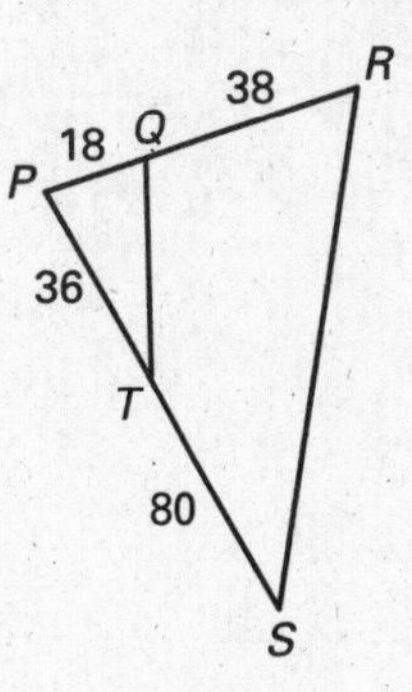

Your Notes

THEOREM 6.6

If three parallel lines intersect two transversals, then they divide the transversals ________.

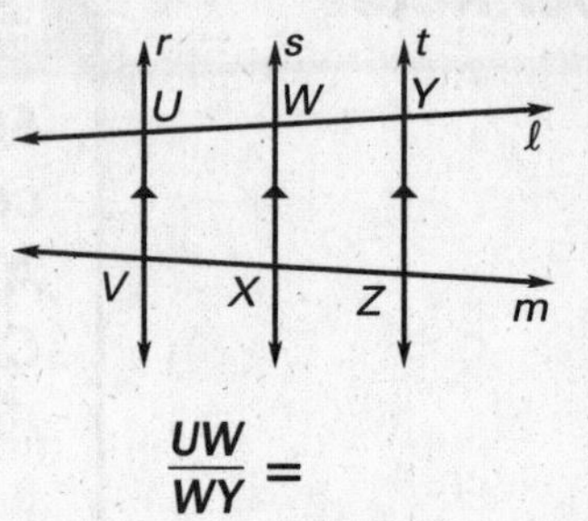

$\frac{UW}{WY} =$ ____

THEOREM 6.7

If a ray bisects an angle of a triangle, then it divides the opposite side into segments whose lengths are ________ to the lengths of the other two sides.

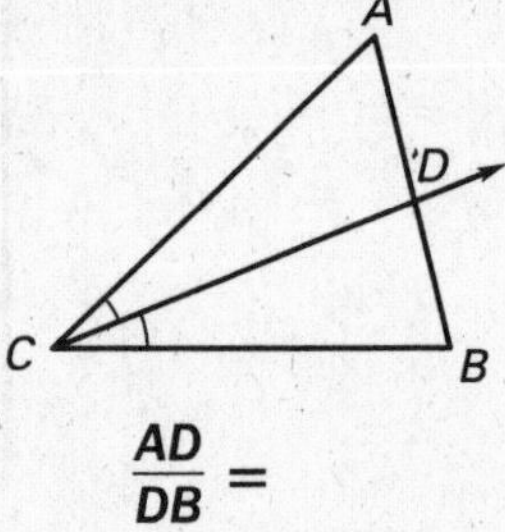

$\frac{AD}{DB} =$ ____

Example 3 *Use Theorem 6.6*

Farming A farmer's land is divided by a newly constructed interstate. The distances shown are in meters. Find the distance *CA* between the north border and the south border of the farmer's land.

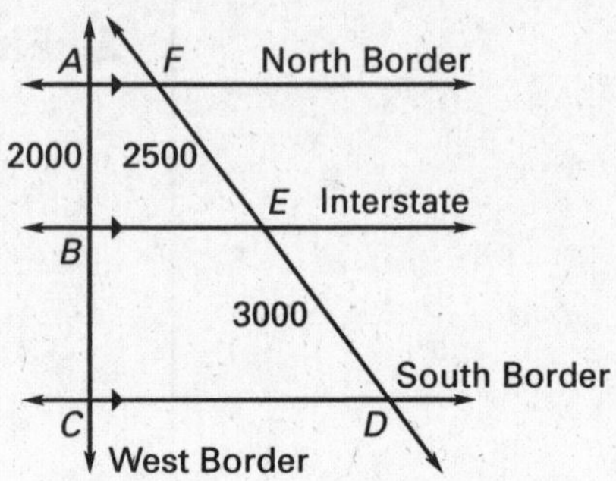

Use Theorem 6.6.

$\frac{CB}{BA} = \frac{DE}{EF}$ **Parallel lines divide transversals proportionally.**

$\frac{\boxed{}}{BA} = \frac{\boxed{}}{EF}$ **Property of proportions (Property 4)**

$\frac{CA}{\boxed{}} =$ ________ **Substitute.**

$\frac{CA}{\boxed{}} =$ ____ **Simplify.**

$CA =$ ____ **Multiply each side by ____ and simplify.**

The distance between the north border and the south border is ____ meters.

Your Notes

Example 4 *Use Theorem 6.7*

In the diagram, $\angle DEG \cong \angle GEF$. Use the given side lengths to find the length of $\overline{DG}$.

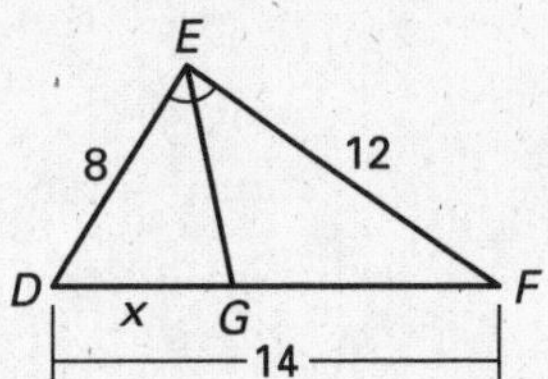

Solution

Because $\overrightarrow{EG}$ is an angle bisector of $\angle DEF$, you can apply Theorem 6.7. Let $GD = x$. Then $GF =$ _______.

$\frac{GF}{GD} = \frac{EF}{ED}$ **Angle bisector divides opposite side proportionally.**

$\frac{\boxed{}}{x} = \frac{}{\_\_\_\_}$ **Substitute.**

_____x = _____ − ____x **Cross Products Property**

x = _____ **Solve for *x*.**

✔ ***Checkpoint*** **Find the length of $\overline{AB}$.**

3.

4.

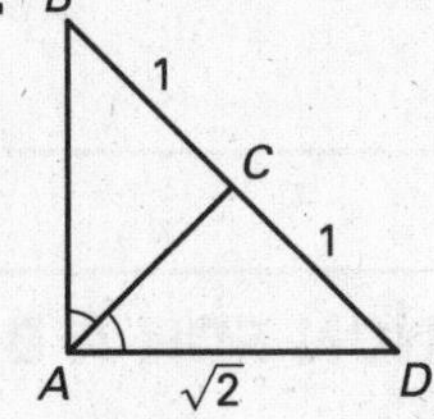

Homework

6.7 Perform Similarity Transformations

 • Perform dilations.

Your Notes

VOCABULARY

Dilation

Center of dilation

Scale factor of a dilation

Reduction

Enlargement

COORDINATE NOTATION FOR A DILATION

You can describe a dilation with respect to the origin with the notation $(x, y) \rightarrow (kx, ky)$, where k is the scale factor.

If $0 < k < 1$, the dilation is a __________. If $k > 1$, the dilation is an ____________.

Your Notes

All of the dilations in this lesson are in the coordinate plane and each center of dilation is the origin.

Example 1 ***Draw a dilation with a scale factor greater than 1***

Draw a dilation of quadrilateral *ABCD* with vertices *A*(2, 0), *B*(6, −4), *C*(8, 2), and *D*(6, 4). Use a scale factor of $\frac{1}{2}$.

First draw *ABCD*. Find the dilation of each vertex by multiplying its coordinates by ____. Then draw the dilation.

$(x, y) \rightarrow (\_\_\_x, \_\_\_y)$

A(2, 0) → *L*________

B(6, −4) → *M*________

C(8, 2) → *N*________

D(6, 4) → *P*________

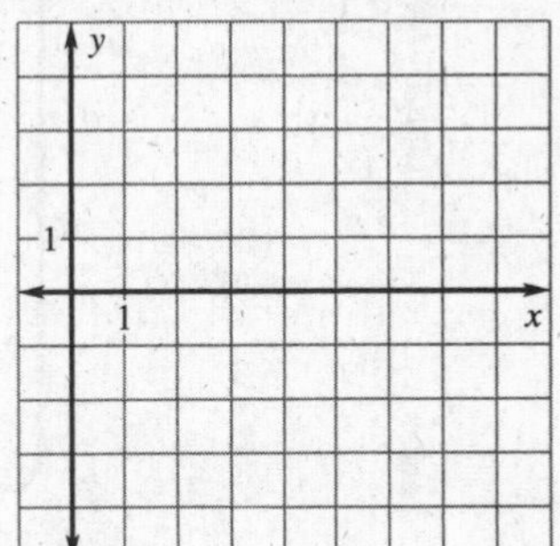

Example 2 ***Verify that a figure is similar to its dilation***

A triangle has the vertices *A*(2, −1), *B*(4, −1), and *C*(4, 2). The image of △*ABC* after a dilation with a scale factor of 2 is △*DEF*.

a. Sketch △*ABC* and △*DEF*.

b. Verify that △*ABC* and △*DEF* are similar.

Solution

a. The scale factor is greater than 1, so the dilation is an ____________.

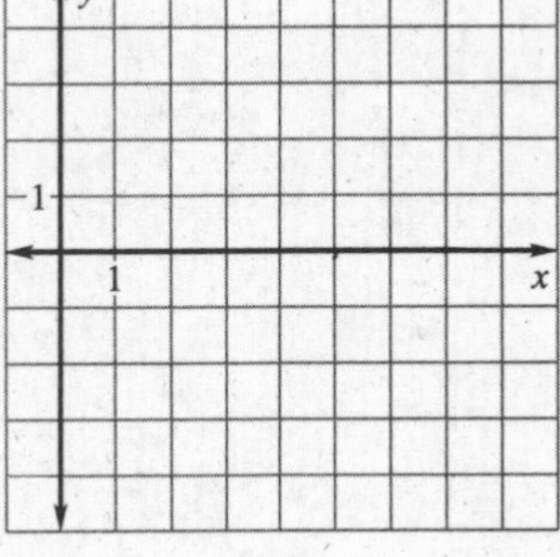

$(x, y) \rightarrow (\_\_\_x, \_\_\_y)$

A(2, −1) → ________

B(4, −1) → ________

C(4, 2) → ________

b. Because ∠___ and ∠___ are both right angles, ∠___ ≅ ∠___. Show that the lengths of the sides that include ∠___ and ∠___ are proportional.

$\frac{AB}{\square} \stackrel{?}{=} \frac{BC}{\square}$ $\qquad \frac{2}{\square} = \frac{3}{\square}$ ✓

The lengths are proportional. So, △*ABC* ~ △*DEF* by the ________________.

Your Notes

Example 3 *Find a scale factor*

Magnets You are making your own photo magnets. Your photo is 8 inches by 10 inches. The image on the magnet is 2.8 inches by 3.5 inches. What is the scale factor of the reduction?

Solution

The scale factor is the ratio of a side length of the ______________ to a side length of the ______________, or $\frac{\boxed{}}{8 \text{ in.}}$. In simplest form, the scale factor is $\frac{}{}$.

Checkpoint Complete the following exercises.

1. A triangle has the vertices $B(-1, -1)$, $C(0, 1)$, and $D(1, 0)$. Find the coordinates of L, M, and N so that $\triangle LMN$ is a dilation of $\triangle BCD$ with a scale factor of 4. Sketch $\triangle BCD$ and $\triangle LMN$.

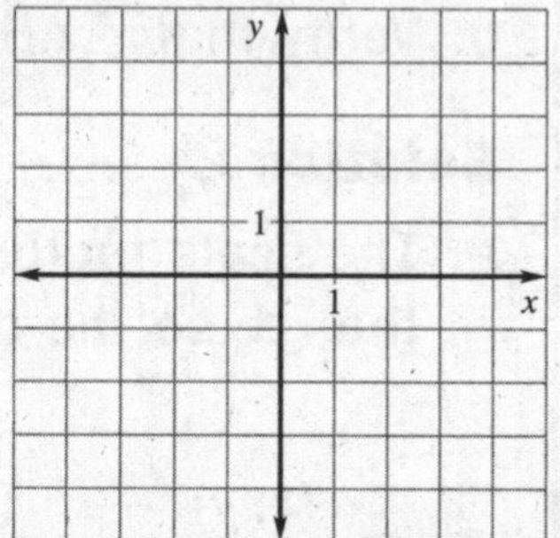

2. In Example 3, what is the scale factor of the reduction if your photo is 4 inches by 5 inches?

Your Notes

Example 4 *Find missing coordinates*

You want to create a quadrilateral *JKLM* that is similar to quadrilateral *PQRS*. What are the coordinates of *M*?

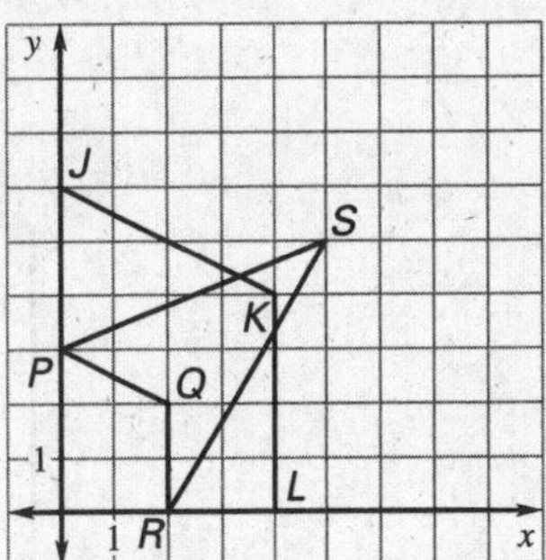

Solution

Determine if *JKLM* is a dilation of *PQRS* by checking whether the same scale factor can be used to obtain *J*, *K*, and *L* from *P*, *Q*, and *R*.

$(x, y) \rightarrow (kx, ky)$

P(______) → *J*(______) **k** = ___

Q(______) → *K*(______) **k** = ___

R(______) → *L*(______) **k** = ___

Because *k* is the same in each case, the image is a ________ with a scale factor of ___. So, you can use the scale factor to find the image *M* of point *S*.

S(______) → *M*(___ • ___, ___ • ___) = *M*(_______)

✔ *Checkpoint* Complete the following exercise.

3. You want to create a quadrilateral *QRST* that is similar to quadrilateral *WXYZ*. What are the coordinates of *T*?

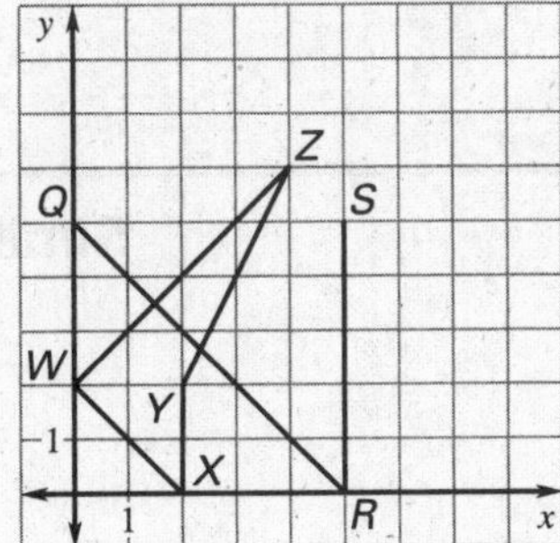

Homework

Words to Review

Give an example of the vocabulary word.

Ratio	Proportion
Means	Extremes
Geometric mean	Scale drawings
Scale	Similar polygons

Scale factor of two similar polygons	Dilation
Center of dilation	Scale factor of a dilation
Reduction	Enlargement

Review your notes and Chapter 6 by using the Chapter Review on pages 418–421 of your textbook.

7.1 Apply the Pythagorean Theorem

Goal • Find side lengths in right triangles.

Your Notes

VOCABULARY

Pythagorean triple

THEOREM 7.1: PYTHAGOREAN THEOREM

In a right triangle, the square of the length of the hypotenuse is equal to the sum of the squares of the lengths of the legs.

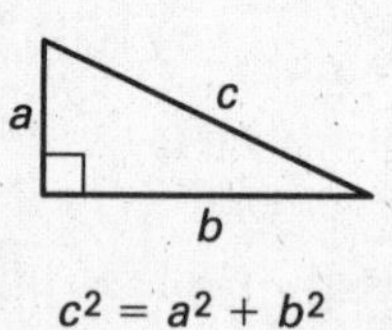

$c^2 = a^2 + b^2$

Example 1 *Find the length of a hypotenuse*

Find the length of the hypotenuse of the right triangle.

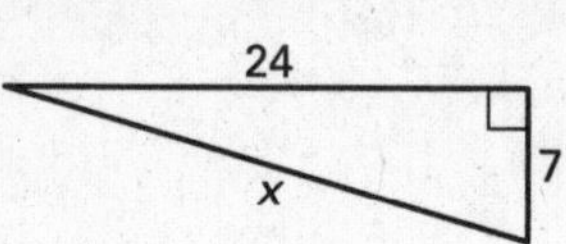

In the equation for the Pythagorean Theorem, "length of hypotenuse" and "length of leg" was shortened to "hypotenuse" and "leg".

Solution

$(\text{hypotenuse})^2 = (\text{leg})^2 + (\text{leg})^2$ **Pythagorean Theorem**

$x^2 = \_\_\_^2 + \_\_\_^2$ **Substitute.**

$x^2 = \_\_\_ + \_\_\_$ **Multiply.**

$x^2 = \_\_\_$ **Add.**

$x = \_\_\_$ **Find the positive square root.**

Checkpoint **Complete the following exercise.**

1. Find the length of the hypotenuse of the right triangle.

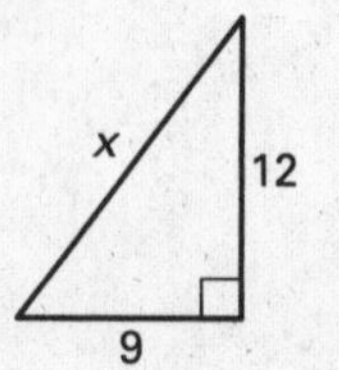

Your Notes

Example 2 *Find the length of a leg*

Door A 6 foot board rests under a doorknob and the base of the board is 5 feet away from the bottom of the door. Approximately how high above the ground is the doorknob?

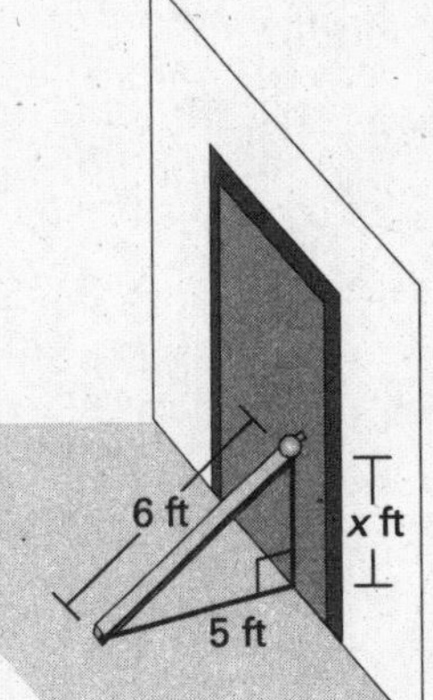

Solution

$$\left(\begin{array}{c}\text{Length}\\\text{of board}\end{array}\right)^2 = \left(\begin{array}{c}\text{Distance}\\\text{from door}\end{array}\right)^2 + \left(\begin{array}{c}\text{Height of}\\\text{doorknob}\end{array}\right)^2$$

$\_\_\_^2 = \_\_\_^2 + x^2$ **Substitute.**

$\_\_\_ = \_\_\_ + x^2$ **Multiply.**

$\_\_\_ = x^2$ **Subtract ___ from each side.**

$\_\_\_ = x$ **Find positive square root.**

$\_\_\_ \approx x$ **Approximate with a calculator.**

The board is resting against the doorknob at about ___ feet above the ground.

In real-world applications, it is usually appropriate to use a calculator to approximate the square root of a number. Round your answer to the nearest tenth.

✔ ***Checkpoint*** **Complete the following exercise.**

2. A 5 foot board rests under a doorknob and the base of the board is 3.5 feet away from the bottom of the door. Approximately how high above the ground is the doorknob?

Your Notes

Example 3 *Find the area of an isosceles triangle*

Find the area of the isosceles triangle with side lengths 16 meters, 17 meters, and 17 meters.

Solution

Step 1 Draw a sketch. By definition, the length of an altitude is the ______ of the triangle. In an isosceles triangle, the altitude to the base is also a perpendicular bisector. So, the altitude divides the triangle into two ______ triangles with the dimensions shown.

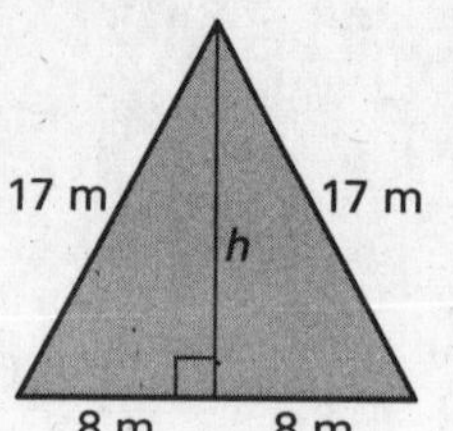

Step 2 Use the Pythagorean Theorem to find the height of the triangle.

$c^2 = a^2 + b^2$	**Pythagorean Theorem**
$\_\_\_^2 = \_\_\_^2 + h^2$	**Substitute.**
$\_\_\_ = \_\_\_ + h^2$	**Multiply.**
$\_\_\_ = h^2$	**Subtract ______ from each side.**
$\_\_\_ = h$	**Find the positive square root.**

Step 3 Find the area.

$$\text{Area} = \frac{1}{2}(\text{base})(\text{height}) = \frac{1}{2}(\_\_\_)(\_\_\_) = \_\_\_$$

The area of the triangle is ______ square meters.

COMMON PYTHAGOREAN TRIPLES AND SOME OF THEIR MULTIPLES

3, 4, 5	**5, 12, 13**	**8, 15, 17**	**7, 24, 25**
6, 8, 10	10, 24, 26	16, 30, 34	14, 48, 50
9, 12, 15	15, 36, 39	24, 45, 51	21, 72, 75
30, 40, 50	50, 120, 130	80, 150, 170	70, 240, 250
$3x, 4x, 5x$	$5x, 12x, 13x$	$8x, 15x, 17x$	$7x, 24x, 25x$

The most common Pythagorean triples are in bold. The other triples are the result of multiplying each integer in a bold face triple by the same factor.

You may find it helpful to memorize the basic Pythagorean triples, shown in **bold**, for standardized tests.

Your Notes

Example 4 ***Find length of a hypotenuse using two methods***

Find the length of the hypotenuse of the right triangle.

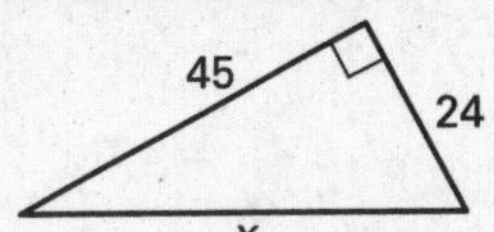

Solution

Method 1: Use a Pythagorean triple.

A common Pythagorean triple is 8, 15, ____. Notice that if you multiply the lengths of the legs of the Pythagorean triple by ___, you get the lengths of the legs of this triangle: 8 • ___ = 24 and 15 • ___ = 45. So, the length of the hypotenuse is ____ • ___ = ____.

Method 2: Use the Pythagorean Theorem.

$x^2 = 24^2 + 45^2$	**Pythagorean Theorem**
$x^2 =$ ______ + ______	**Multiply.**
$x^2 =$ ______	**Add.**
$x =$ ______	**Find the positive square root.**

Checkpoint **Complete the following exercises.**

3. Find the area of the triangle.

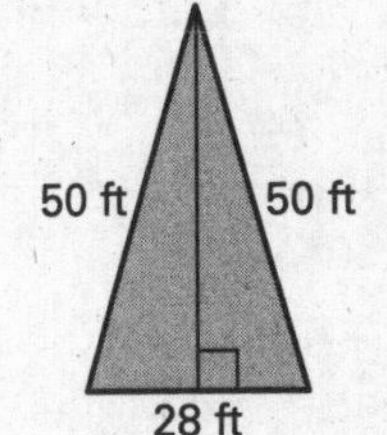

4. Use a Pythagorean triple to find the unknown side length of the right triangle.

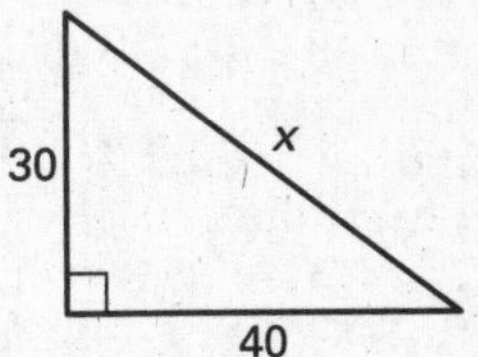

Homework

7.2 Use the Converse of the Pythagorean Theorem

Goal • Use the Converse of the Pythagorean Theorem to determine if a triangle is a right triangle.

Your Notes

THEOREM 7.2: CONVERSE OF THE PYTHAGOREAN THEOREM

If the square of the length of the longest side of a triangle is equal to the sum of the squares of the lengths of the other two sides, then the triangle is a ______ triangle.

If $c^2 = a^2 + b^2$, then $\triangle ABC$ is a ______ triangle.

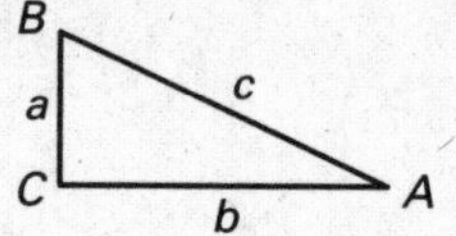

Example 1 *Verify right triangles*

Tell whether the given triangle is a right triangle.

a.

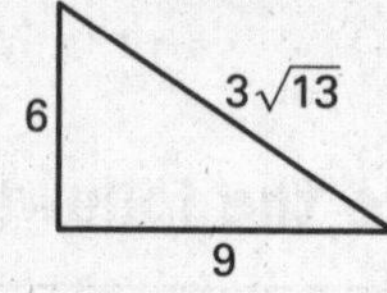

b.

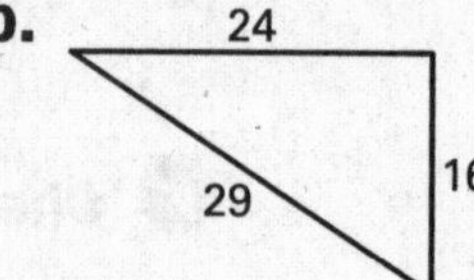

Solution

Let c represent the length of the longest side of the triangle. Check to see whether the side lengths satisfy the equation $c^2 = a^2 + b^2$.

a. $(\_\_\_\_)^2 \stackrel{?}{=} \_\_\_^2 + \_\_\_^2$

$\_\_\_ \cdot \_\_\_ \stackrel{?}{=} \_\_\_ + \_\_\_$

$\_\_\_ = \_\_\_$ ✓

The triangle ______ a right triangle.

b. $\_\_\_^2 \stackrel{?}{=} \_\_\_^2 + \_\_\_^2$

$\_\_\_ \stackrel{?}{=} \_\_\_ + \_\_\_$

$\_\_\_ \neq \_\_\_$

The triangle ______ a right triangle.

Your Notes

THEOREM 7.3

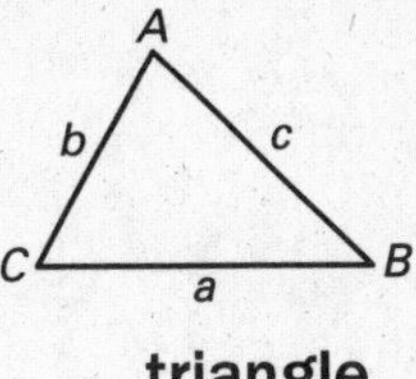

If the square of the length of the longest side of a triangle is less than the sum of the squares of the lengths of the other two sides, then the triangle ABC is an ________ triangle.

If $c^2 < a^2 + b^2$, then the triangle ABC is ______.

THEOREM 7.4

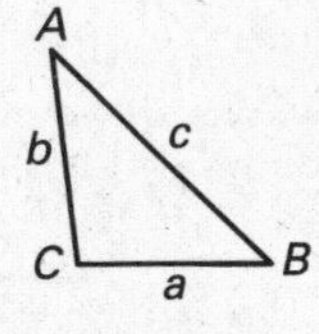

If the square of the length of the longest side of a triangle is greater than the sum of the squares of the lengths of the other two sides, then the triangle ABC is an ________ triangle.

If $c^2 > a^2 + b^2$, then the triangle ABC is ________.

Example 2 ***Classify triangles***

Can segments with lengths of 2.8 feet, 3.2 feet, and 4.2 feet form a triangle? If so, would the triangle be *acute*, *right*, or *obtuse*?

The Triangle Inequality Theorem states that the sum of the lengths of any two sides of a triangle is greater than the length of the third side.

Solution

Step 1 Use the Triangle Inequality Theorem to check that the segments can make a triangle.

$2.8 + 3.2 =$ ___	$2.8 + 4.2 =$ ___	$3.2 + 4.2 =$ ____
___ > 4.2	___ > 3.2	_____ > 2.8

Step 2 **Classify** the triangle by comparing the square of the length of the longest side with the sum of squares of the lengths of the shorter sides.

c^2 _?_ $a^2 + b^2$	**Compare c^2 with $a^2 + b^2$.**
____^{2} _?_ ____^{2} + ____^{2}	**Substitute.**
______ _?_ ____ + ______	**Simplify.**
________ ____ ________	**c^2 is ______ than $a^2 + b^2$.**

The side lengths 2.8 feet, 3.2 feet, and 4.2 feet form an ______ triangle.

Your Notes

Example 3 Use the Converse of the Pythagorean Theorem

Lights You are helping install a light pole in a parking lot. When the pole is positioned properly, it is perpendicular to the pavement. How can you check that the pole is perpendicular using a tape measure?

Solution

To show a line is perpendicular to a plane you must show that the line is perpendicular to ________ in the plane.

Think of the pole as a line and the pavement as a plane. Use a 3-4-5 right triangle and the Converse of the Pythagorean Theorem to show that the pole is perpendicular to different lines on the pavement.

First mark 3 feet up the pole and mark on the pavement 4 feet from the pole.

Use the tape measure to check that the distance between the two marks is ____ feet. The pole makes ________ angle with the line on the pavement.

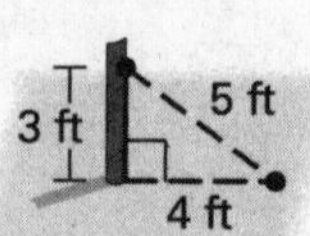

Finally, repeat the procedure to show that the pole is ____________ to another line on the pavement.

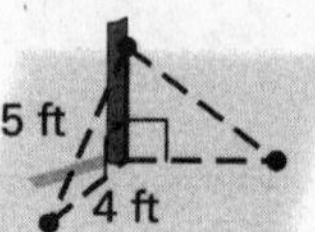

METHODS FOR CLASSIFYING A TRIANGLE BY ANGLES USING ITS SIDE LENGTHS

Theorem 7.2

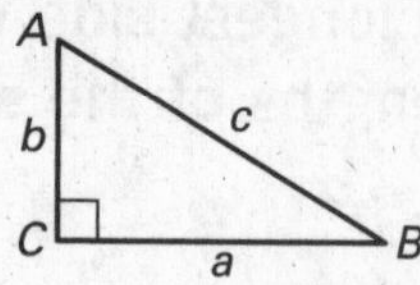

If $c^2 = a^2 + b^2$, then $m\angle C = 90°$ and $\triangle ABC$ is a ________ triangle.

Theorem 7.3

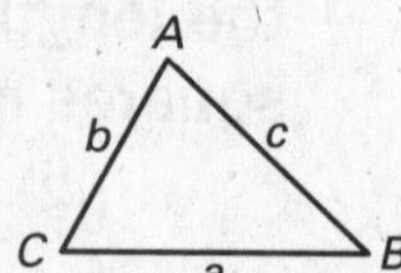

If $c^2 < a^2 + b^2$, then $m\angle C < 90°$ and $\triangle ABC$ is an ________ triangle.

Theorem 7.4

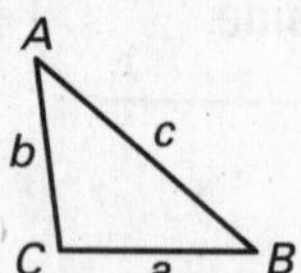

If $c^2 > a^2 + b^2$, then $m\angle C > 90°$ and $\triangle ABC$ is an ________ triangle.

Your Notes

Checkpoint In Exercises 1 and 2, tell whether the triangle is a right triangle.

1.

5 4

$2\sqrt{10}$

2.

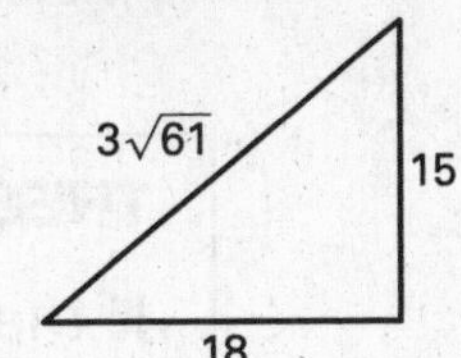

3. Can segments with lengths of 6.1 inches, 9.4 inches, and 11.3 inches form a triangle? If so, would the triangle be *acute*, *right*, or *obtuse*?

4. In Example 3, could you use triangles with side lengths 50 inches, 120 inches, and 130 inches to verify that you have perpendicular lines? *Explain*.

Homework

7.3 Use Similar Right Triangles

Goal • Use properties of the altitude of a right triangle.

Your Notes

THEOREM 7.5

If the altitude is drawn to the hypotenuse of a right triangle, then the two triangles formed are ________ to the original triangle and to each other.

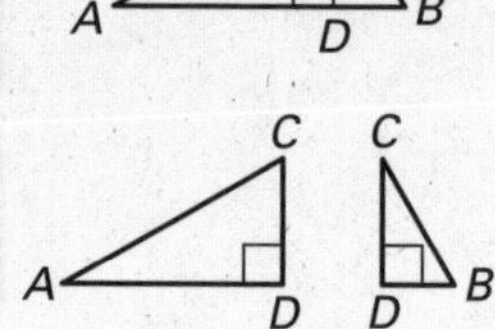

$\triangle CBD$ ___ $\triangle ABC$, $\triangle ACD$ ___ $\triangle ABC$, and $\triangle CBD$ ___ $\triangle ACD$.

Example 1 ***Identify similar triangles***

Identify the similar triangles in the diagram.

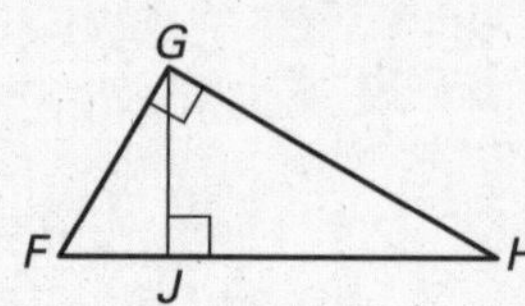

Solution

Sketch the three similar right triangles so that the corresponding angles and sides have the same orientation.

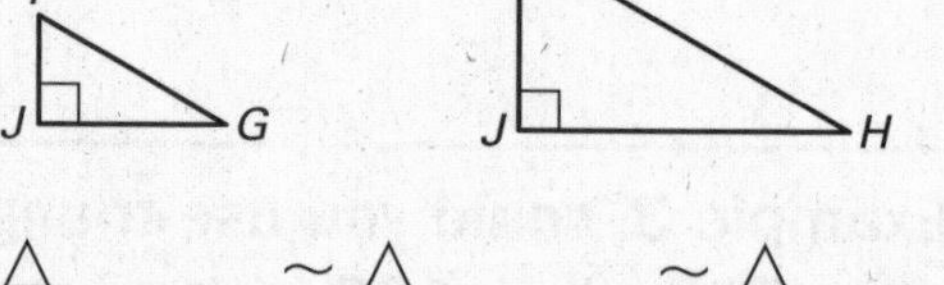

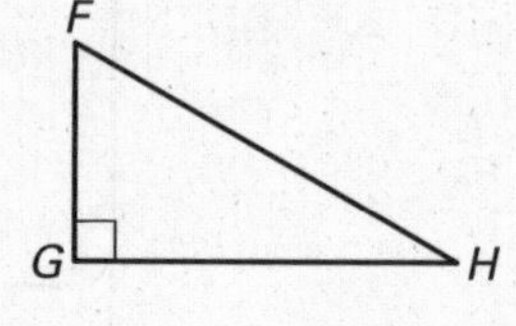

$\triangle$____ $\sim$ $\triangle$____ $\sim$ $\triangle$____

Checkpoint Complete the following exercise.

1. Identify the similar triangles in the diagram.

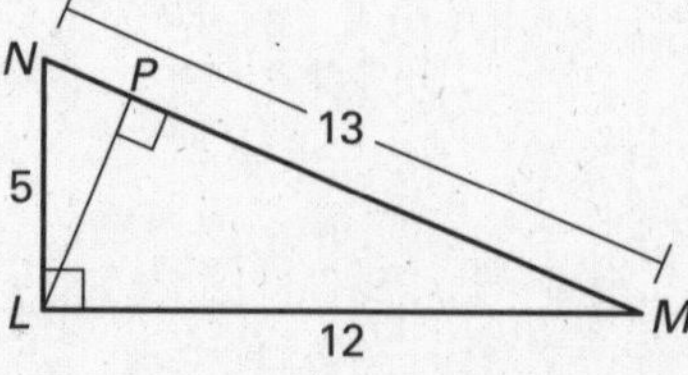

Your Notes

Example 2 ***Find the length of the altitude to the hypotenuse***

Stadium A cross section of a group of seats at a stadium shows a drainage pipe $\overline{BD}$ that leads from the seats to the inside of the stadium. What is the length of the pipe?

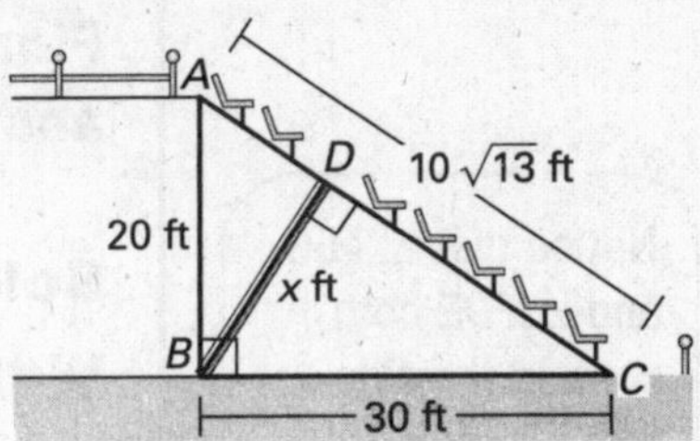

Solution

Step 1 Identify the similar triangles and sketch them.

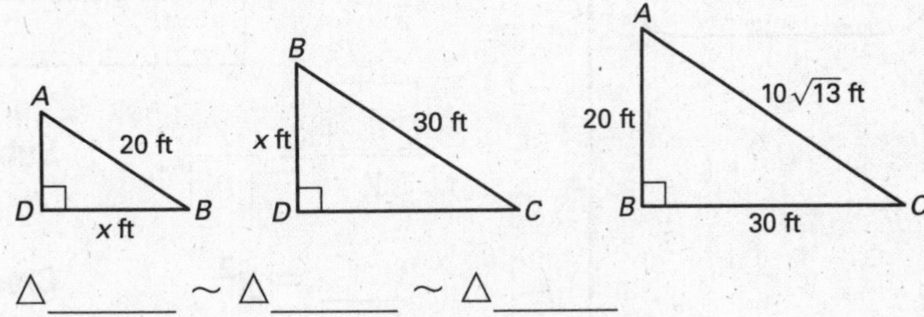

$\triangle$______ ~ $\triangle$______ ~ $\triangle$______

Notice that if you tried to write a proportion using $\triangle ADB$ and $\triangle BDC$, there would be two unknowns, so you would not be able to solve for x.

Step 2 Find the value of x. Use the fact that $\triangle BDC \sim \triangle ABC$ to write a proportion.

$\frac{BD}{\square} = \frac{\square}{AC}$ **Corresponding side lengths of similar triangles are in proportion.**

$\frac{x}{\square} = \frac{\quad}{\quad}$ **Substitute.**

______ x = ______ **Cross Products Property**

$x \approx$ ______ **Approximate.**

The length of the pipe is about ______ feet.

Checkpoint Complete the following exercise.

2. Identify the similar triangles. Then find the value of x.

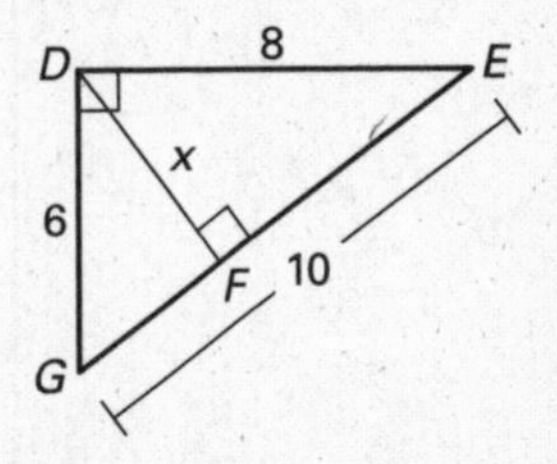

Your Notes

Example 3 ***Use a geometric mean***

Find the value of *y*. Write your answer in simplest radical form.

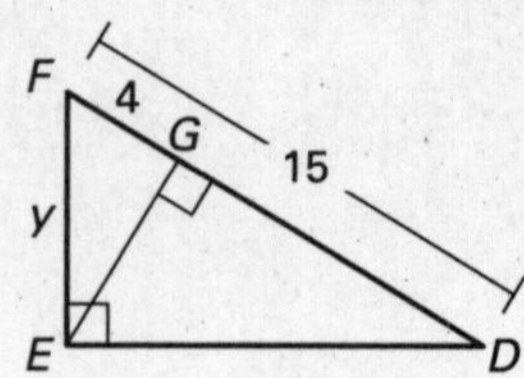

Notice that $\triangle FEG$ and $\triangle FDE$ both contain the side with length *y*, so these are the similar pair of triangles to use to solve for *y*.

Solution

Write a proportion.

$$\frac{\boxed{}}{\text{length of hyp. of } \triangle FEG} = \frac{\text{length of shorter leg of } \triangle FDE}{\boxed{}}$$

$\frac{\boxed{}}{y} = \frac{y}{\boxed{}}$ **Substitute.**

$\_\_\_ = y^2$ **Cross Products Property**

$\sqrt{\_\_\_} = y$ **Take positive square roots.**

$\_\_\sqrt{\_\_\_} = y$ **Simplify.**

THEOREM 7.6: GEOMETRIC MEAN (ALTITUDE) THEOREM

In a right triangle, the altitude from the right angle to the hypotenuse divides the hypotenuse into two segments.

The length of the altitude is the ________________ of the lengths of the two segments.

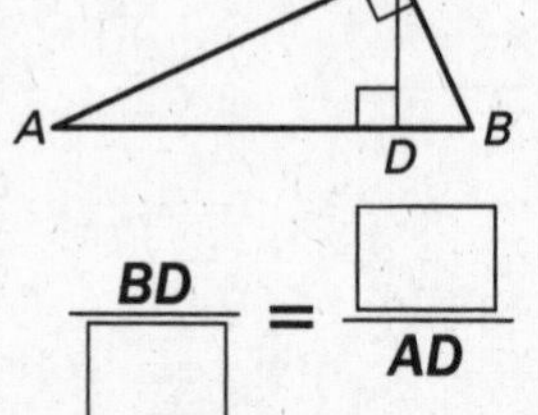

$$\frac{BD}{\boxed{}} = \frac{\boxed{}}{AD}$$

THEOREM 7.7: GEOMETRIC MEAN (LEG) THEOREM

In a right triangle, the altitude from the right angle to the hypotenuse divides the hypotenuse into two segments.

The length of each leg of the right triangle is the geometric mean of the lengths of the hypotenuse and the segment of the hypotenuse that is __________ to the leg.

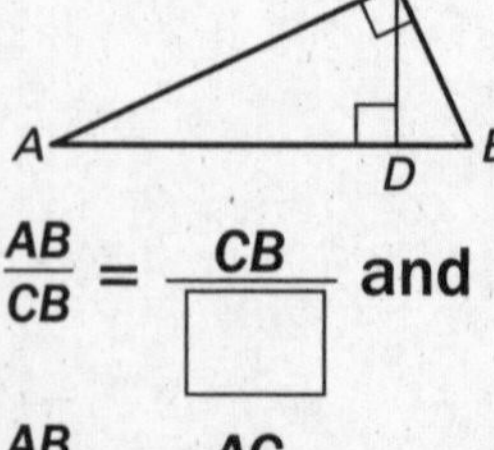

$\frac{AB}{CB} = \frac{CB}{\boxed{}}$ and

$\frac{AB}{AC} = \frac{AC}{\boxed{}}$

Your Notes

Example 4 ***Find a height using indirect measurement***

Overpass To find the clearance under an overpass, you need to find the height of a concrete support beam.

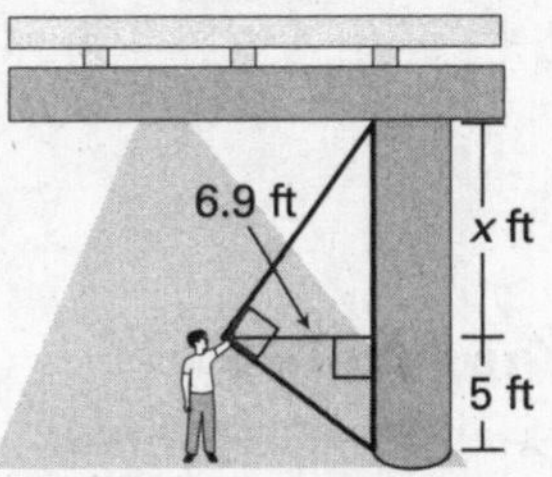

You use a cardboard square to line up the top and bottom of the beam. Your friend measures the vertical distance from the ground to your eye and the distance from you to the beam. Approximate the height of the beam.

Solution

By Theorem 7.6, you know that _____ is the geometric mean of ____ and ____.

$\frac{\_\_\_\_}{\_\_\_\_} = \frac{\_\_\_\_}{\_\_\_\_}$ **Write a proportion.**

$x \approx$ _____ **Solve for x.**

So, the clearance under the overpass is $5 + x \approx 5 +$ _____ $=$ _____ feet.

Checkpoint Complete the following exercises.

3. Find the value of y. Write your answer in simplest radical form.

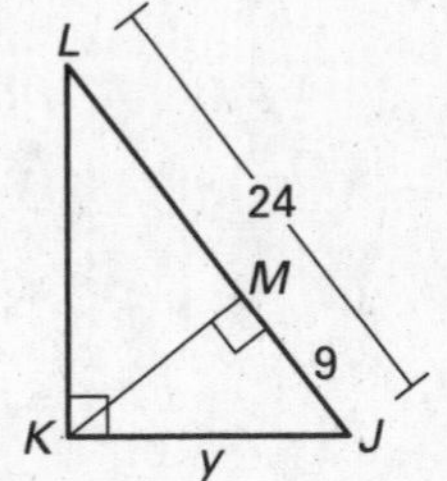

4. The distance from the ground to Larry's eyes is 4.5 feet. How far from the beam in Example 4 would he have to stand in order to measure its height?

Homework

7.4 Special Right Triangles

Goal • Use the relationships among the sides in special right triangles.

Your Notes

The extended ratio of the side lengths of a 45°-45°-90° triangle is $1:1:\sqrt{2}$.

THEOREM 7.8: 45°-45°-90° TRIANGLE THEOREM

In a 45°-45°-90° triangle, the hypotenuse is ____ times as long as each leg.

hypotenuse = leg • ____

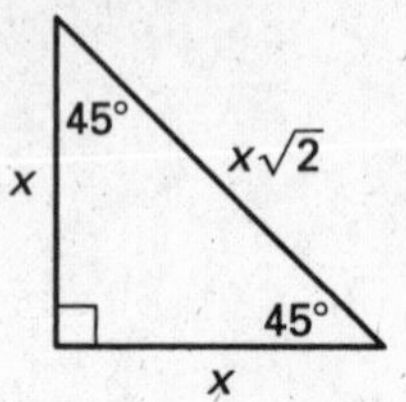

Example 1 ***Find hypotenuse length in a 45°-45°-90° triangle***

Find the length of the hypotenuse.

a.

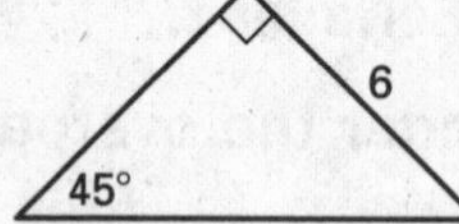

b.

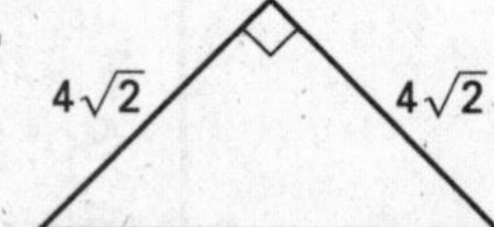

Solution

a. By the Triangle Sum Theorem, the measure of the third angle must be ____. Then the triangle is a ____-____-90° triangle, so by Theorem 7.8, the hypotenuse is ____ times as long as each leg.

hypotenuse = leg • ____   **____-____-90° Triangle Theorem**

= ____   **Substitute.**

b. By the Base Angles Theorem and the Corollary to the Triangle Sum Theorem, the triangle is a 45°-45°-90° triangle.

Remember the following properties of radicals: $\sqrt{a} \cdot \sqrt{b} = \sqrt{a \cdot b}$; $\sqrt{a \cdot a} = a$

hypotenuse = leg • ____   **45°-45°-90° Triangle Theorem**

= ____ • ____   **Substitute.**

= ____ • ____   **Product of square roots**

= ____   **Simplify.**

Your Notes

Example 2 *Find leg lengths in a 45°-45°-90° triangle*

Find the lengths of the legs in the triangle.

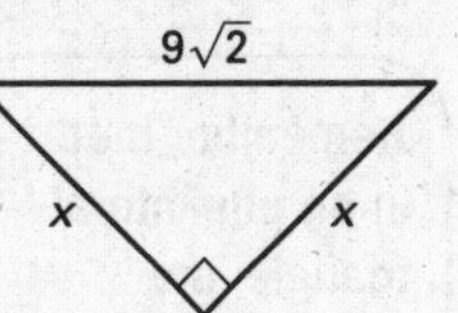

Solution

By the Base Angles Theorem and the Corollary to the Triangle Sum Theorem, the triangle is a 45°-45°-90° triangle.

hypotenuse = leg • ____ **45°-45°-90° Triangle Theorem**

____ = x • ____ **Substitute.**

$\frac{\_\_\_\_}{\square} = \frac{x\square}{\square}$ **Divide each side by ____.**

____ = x **Simplify.**

Checkpoint Find the value of the variable.

1.

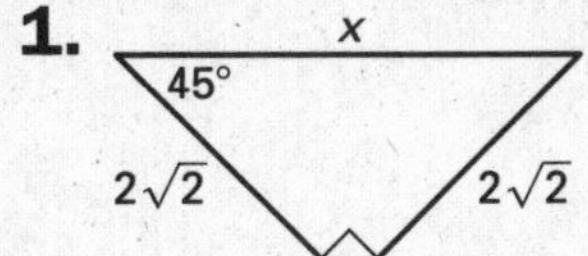

2.

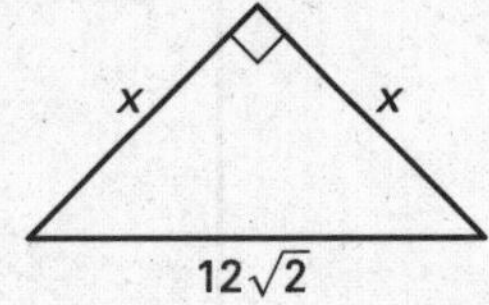

THEOREM 7.9: 30°-60°-90° TRIANGLE THEOREM

In a 30°-60°-90° triangle, the hypotenuse is ______ as long as the shorter leg, and the longer leg is ____ times as long as the shorter leg.

hypotenuse = ___ • shorter leg

longer leg = shorter leg • ____

60°
2x
x
30°
$x\sqrt{3}$

The extended ratio of the side lengths of a 30°-60°-90° triangle is $1:\sqrt{3}:2$.

Your Notes

Remember that in an equilateral triangle, the altitude to a side is also the median to that side. So, altitude $\overline{BD}$ ______ $\overline{AC}$.

Example 3 *Find the height of an equilateral triangle*

Music You make a guitar pick that resembles an equilateral triangle with side lengths of 32 millimeters. What is the approximate height of the pick?

Solution

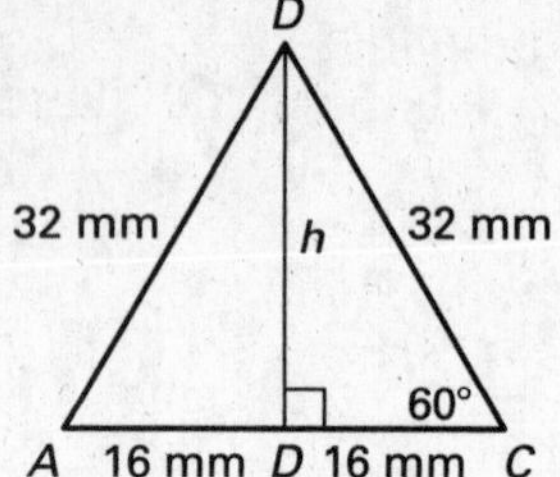

Draw the equilateral triangle described. Its altitude forms the longer leg of two ____-____-90° triangles. The length h of the altitude is approximately the height of the pick.

longer leg = shorter leg • ____

h = ____ • ____ ≈ ______ mm

Example 4 *Find lengths in a 30°-60°-90° triangle*

Find the values of x and y. Write your answer in simplest radical form.

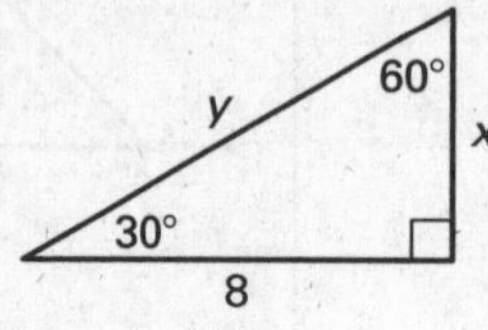

Solution

Step 1 Find the value of x.

longer leg = shorter leg • ____

____ = x____ **Substitute.**

____ = x **Divide each side by ____.**

____ • ____ = x **Multiply numerator and denominator by ____.**

____ = x **Multiply fractions.**

Step 2 Find the value of y.

hypotenuse = ____ • shorter leg

y = ____ • ____ = ______

Your Notes

Example 5 *Find a height*

Windshield wipers A car is turned off while the windshield wipers are moving. The 24 inch wipers stop, making a 60° angle with the bottom of the windshield. How far from the bottom of the windshield are the ends of the wipers?

Solution

The distance d is the length of the longer leg of a ____-____-90° triangle.

The length of the hypotenuse is ____ inches.

hypotenuse = ___ • shorter leg	____-____-90° Triangle Theorem
____ = ___ • s	Substitute.
____ = s	Divide each side by ___.
longer leg = shorter leg • ____	____-____-90° Triangle Theorem
d = ______	Substitute.
$d \approx$ _____	Approximate.

The ends of the wipers are about _____ inches from the bottom of the windshield.

Checkpoint In Exercises 3 and 4, find the value of the variable.

3.

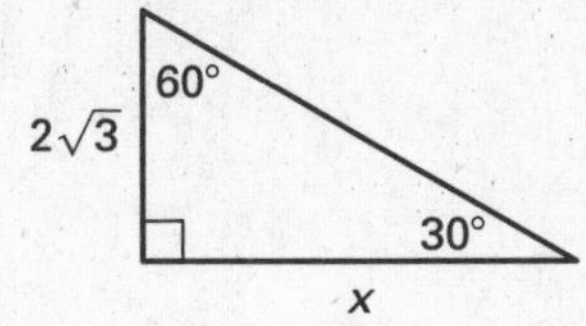

4.

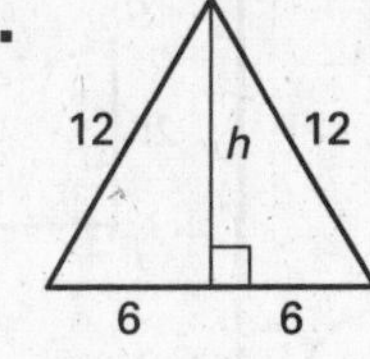

5. In Example 5, how far from the bottom of the windshield are the ends of the wipers if they make a 30° angle with the bottom of the windshield?

Homework

7.5 Apply the Tangent Ratio

Goal • Use the tangent ratio for indirect measurement.

Your Notes

VOCABULARY

Trigonometric ratio

Tangent

TANGENT RATIO

Remember these abbreviations:
tangent → tan
opposite → opp.
adjacent → adj.

Let $\triangle ABC$ be a right triangle with acute $\angle A$. The tangent of $\angle A$ (written as tan A) is defined as follows:

C, leg opposite ∠A, hypotenuse, B, leg adjacent to ∠A, A

$$\tan A = \frac{\text{length of leg opposite } \angle A}{\text{length of leg adjacent to } \angle A} = \frac{\square}{\square}$$

Example 1 ***Find tangent ratios***

Find tan *S* and tan *R*. Write each answer as a fraction and as a decimal rounded to four places, if necessary.

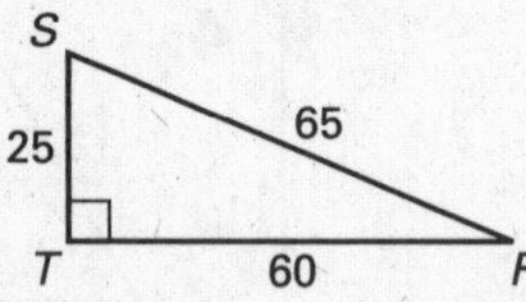

Unless told otherwise, round values of trigonometric ratios to the ten-thousandths' place and round lengths to the tenths' place.

Solution

$$\tan S = \frac{\text{opp. } \angle S}{\text{adj. to } \angle S} = \frac{\square}{\square} = \frac{\square}{\square} = \frac{\square}{\square} = \underline{\qquad}$$

$$\tan R = \frac{\text{opp. } \angle R}{\text{adj. to } \angle R} = \frac{\square}{\square} = \frac{\square}{\square} = \frac{\square}{\square} \approx \underline{\qquad}$$

Your Notes

Checkpoint **Find tan B and tan C. Write each answer as a fraction and as a decimal rounded to four places.**

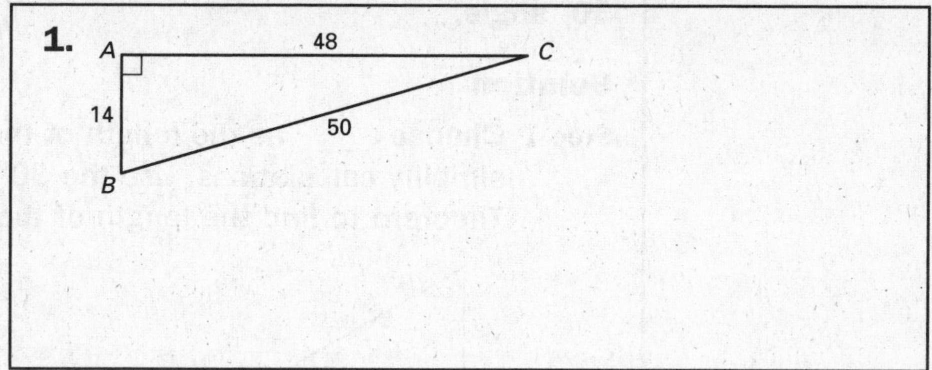

Example 2 *Find a leg length*

Find the value of x.

Use the tangent of an acute angle to find a leg length.

tan 31° = ______ **Write ratio for tangent of 31°.**

tan 31° = ______ **Substitute.**

___ • tan 31° = ____ **Multiply each side by ___.**

x = ______ **Divide each side by ______.**

x ≈ ______ **Use a calculator to find ______.**

x ≈ ______ **Simplify.**

Example 3 *Estimate height using tangent*

Lighthouse Find the height h of the lighthouse to the nearest foot.

______ = $\frac{\text{opp.}}{\text{adj.}}$ **Write ratio for ______.**

______ = ______ **Substitute.**

_____ • ______ = h **Multiply each side by _____.**

______ ≈ h **Use a calculator and simplify.**

Your Notes

Example 4 ***Use a special right triangle to find a tangent***

Use a special right triangle to find the tangent of a 30° angle.

Solution

Step 1 **Choose ____ as the length of the shorter leg to simplify calculations. Use the 30°-60°-90° Triangle Theorem to find the length of the longer leg.**

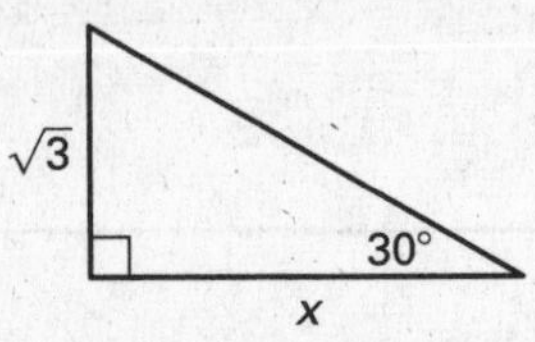

longer leg = ____________

x = __________ = ____

Step 2 **Find tan 30°.**

tan 30° = $\frac{\_\_\_\_}{\_\_\_\_}$ **Write ratio for tangent of 30°.**

tan 30° = $\frac{\_\_\_\_}{\_\_\_\_}$ **Substitute.**

The tangent of any 30° angle is $\frac{\_\_\_\_}{\_\_\_\_}$ ≈ ________.

The tangents of all 30° angles are the same constant ratio. Any right triangle with a 30° angle can be used to determine this value.

Checkpoint **In Exercises 2 and 3, find the value of x. Round to the nearest tenth.**

2.

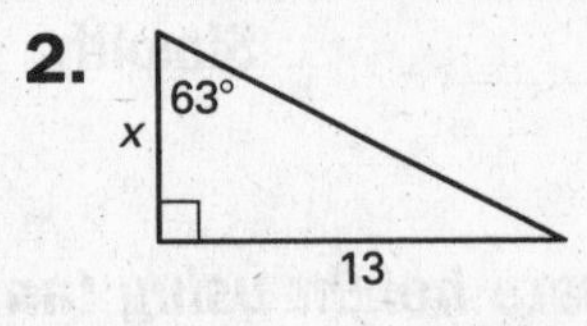

3.

x
21
59°

4. **In Example 4, suppose the length of the shorter leg is 1 instead of $\sqrt{3}$. Show that the tangent of 30° is still equal to $\frac{\sqrt{3}}{3}$.**

Homework

7.6 Apply the Sine and Cosine Ratios

Goal • Use the sine and cosine ratios.

Your Notes

VOCABULARY

Sine, cosine

Angle of elevation

Angle of depression

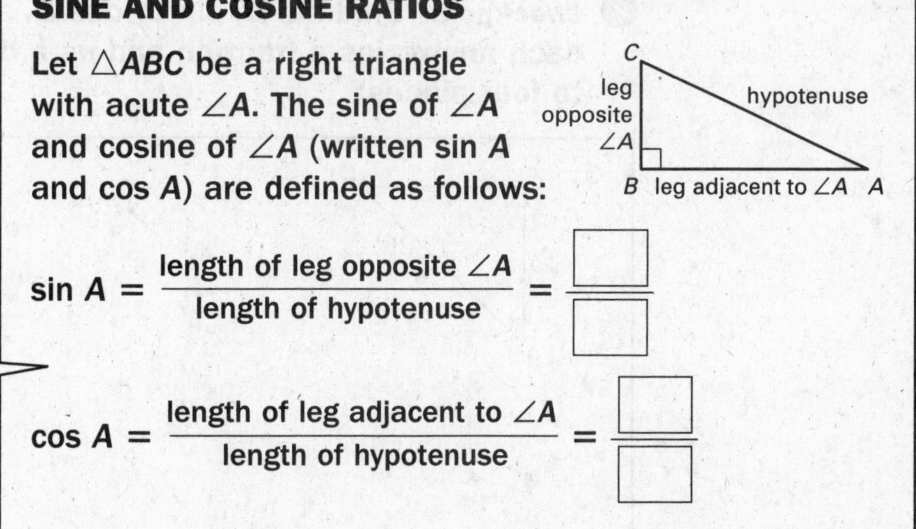

SINE AND COSINE RATIOS

Let $\triangle ABC$ be a right triangle with acute $\angle A$. The sine of $\angle A$ and cosine of $\angle A$ (written sin A and cos A) are defined as follows:

$$\sin A = \frac{\text{length of leg opposite } \angle A}{\text{length of hypotenuse}} = \frac{\square}{\square}$$

$$\cos A = \frac{\text{length of leg adjacent to } \angle A}{\text{length of hypotenuse}} = \frac{\square}{\square}$$

Remember these abbreviations:
sine → sin
cosine → cos
hypotenuse → hyp

Your Notes

Example 1 *Find sine ratios*

Find sin *U* and sin *W*. Write each answer as a fraction and as a decimal rounded to four places.

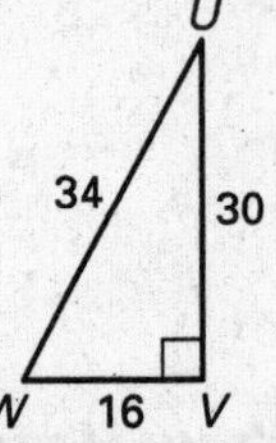

Solution

$\sin U = \dfrac{\text{opp. } \angle U}{\text{hyp.}} = \dfrac{\square}{\square} = \dfrac{\square}{\square} = \dfrac{\square}{\square} \approx$ ______

$\sin W = \dfrac{\text{opp. } \angle W}{\text{hyp.}} = \dfrac{\square}{\square} = \dfrac{\square}{\square} = \dfrac{\square}{\square} \approx$ ______

Example 2 *Find cosine ratios*

Find cos *S* and cos *R*. Write each answer as a fraction and as a decimal rounded to four places.

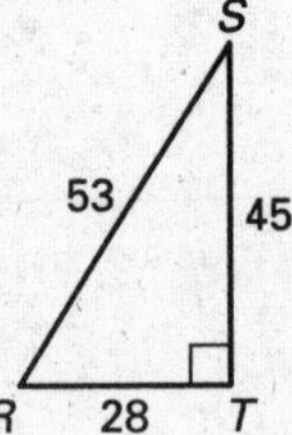

Solution

$\cos S = \dfrac{\text{adj. to } \angle S}{\text{hyp.}} \dfrac{\square}{\square} = \dfrac{\square}{\square} \approx$ ______

$\cos R = \dfrac{\text{adj. to } \angle R}{\text{hyp.}} \dfrac{\square}{\square} = \dfrac{\square}{\square} \approx$ ______

Checkpoint **Find sin *B*, sin *C*, cos *B*, and cos *C*. Write each answer as a fraction and as a decimal rounded to four places.**

1.

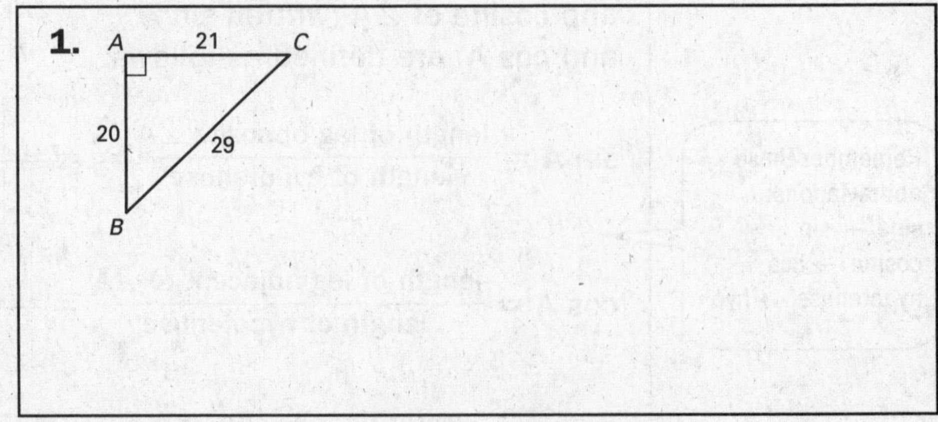

Your Notes

Example 3 *Use a trigonometric ratio to find a hypotenuse*

Basketball You walk from one corner of a basketball court to the opposite corner. Write and solve a proportion using a trigonometric ratio to approximate the distance of the walk.

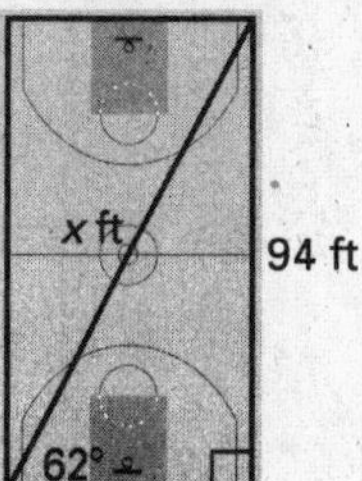

Solution

sin 62° = ______ **Write ratio for sine of 62°.**

sin 62° = ______ **Substitute.**

____ • ________ = ______ **Multiply each side by ____.**

x = ________ **Divide each side by ________.**

x ≈ ________ **Use a calculator to find ________.**

x ≈ ______ **Simplify.**

The distance of the walk is about ______ feet.

Example 4 *Find a hypotenuse using an angle of depression*

Roller Coaster You are at the top of a roller coaster 100 feet above the ground. The angle of depression is 44°. About how far do you ride down the hill?

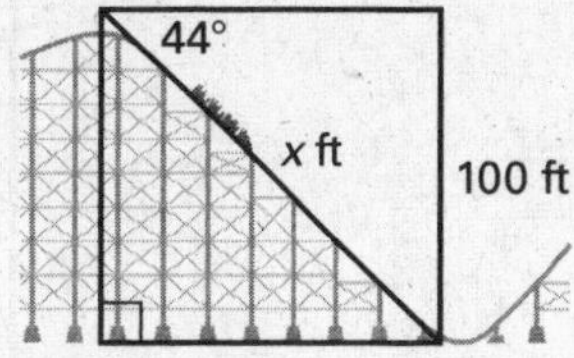

sin 44° = ______ **Write ratio for sine of 44°.**

sin 44° = ______ **Substitute.**

x • ________ = ______ **Multiply each side by ____.**

x = ________ **Divide each side by ________.**

x ≈ ________ **Use a calculator to find ________.**

x ≈ ______ **Simplify.**

You ride about ______ feet down the hill.

Your Notes

✔ ***Checkpoint*** **Complete the following exercises.**

2. In Example 3, use the cosine ratio to approximate the width of the basketball court.

3. Suppose the angle of depression in Example 4 is 72°. About how far would you ride down the hill?

Example 5 ***Find leg lengths using an angle of elevation***

Railroad A railroad crossing arm that is 20 feet long is stuck with an angle of elevation of 35°. Find the lengths x and y.

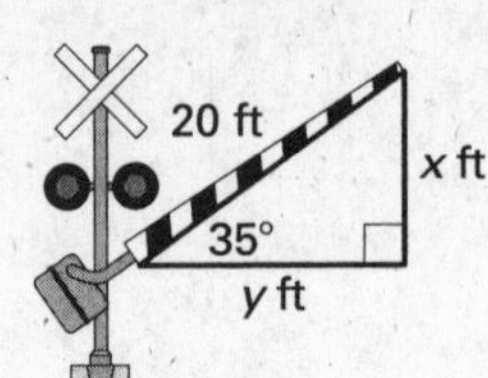

Solution

Step 1 Find x.

_______	$= \frac{\text{opp.}}{\text{hyp.}}$	**Write ratio for _______ of _____.**
_______	$=$ ____	**Substitute.**
_______	$= x$	**Multiply each side by ____.**
_______	$\approx x$	**Use a calculator to simplify.**

Step 2 Find y.

_______	$= \frac{\text{adj.}}{\text{hyp.}}$	**Write ratio for _______ of _____.**
_______	$=$ ____	**Substitute.**
_______	$= y$	**Multiply each side by ____.**
_______	$\approx y$	**Use a calculator to simplify.**

Your Notes

Example 6 ***Use a special right triangle to find a sin and cos***

Use a special right triangle to find the sine and cosine of a 30° angle.

Solution

Use the 30°-60°-90° Triangle Theorem to draw a right triangle with side lengths of 1, $\sqrt{3}$, and ___. Then set up sine and cosine ratios for the 30° angle.

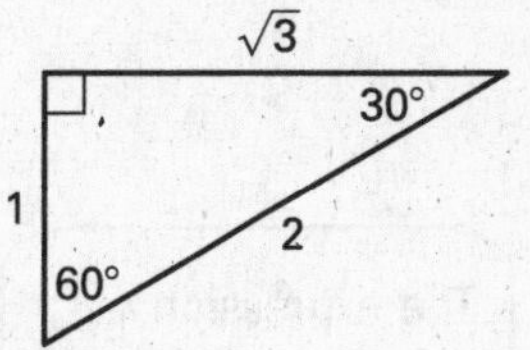

sin 30° = $\frac{\_\_\_}{\_\_\_}$ = $\frac{\_\_}{\_\_}$ = ______

cos 30° = $\frac{\_\_\_}{\_\_\_}$ = $\frac{\_\_}{\_\_}$ ≈ ______

✔ ***Checkpoint*** **Complete the following exercises.**

4. In Example 5, suppose the angle of elevation is 40°. What are the new lengths *x* and *y*?

5. Use a special right triangle to find the sine and cosine of a 60° angle.

Homework

7.7 Solve Right Triangles

Goal • Use inverse tangent, sine, and cosine ratios.

Your Notes

VOCABULARY

Solve a right triangle

INVERSE TRIGONOMETRIC RATIOS

The expression "$\tan^{-1} x$" is read as "the inverse tangent of x."

Let $\angle A$ be an acute angle.

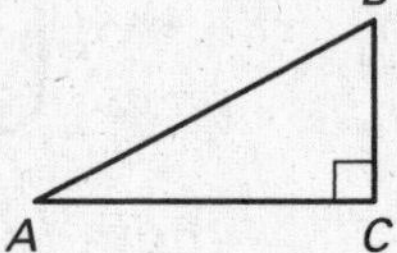

Inverse Tangent If $\tan A = x$, then $\tan^{-1} x = m\angle A$. $\quad \tan^{-1} \frac{BC}{AC} = m\angle A$

Inverse Sine If $\sin A = y$, then $\sin^{-1} y = m\angle A$. $\quad \sin^{-1} \frac{BC}{AB} = m\angle A$

Inverse Cosine If $\cos A = z$, then $\cos^{-1} z = m\angle A$. $\quad \cos^{-1} \frac{AC}{AB} = m\angle A$

Example 1 ***Use an inverse tangent to find an angle measure***

Use a calculator to approximate the measure of $\angle A$ to the nearest tenth of a degree.

C, 16, B, 20, A

Because $\tan A = \frac{\_\_\_}{\_\_\_} = \frac{\_\_\_}{\_\_\_} = \_\_\_\_\_$,

$\tan^{-1}$ _____ $= m\angle A$. Using a calculator,

$\tan^{-1}$ _____ $\approx$ ________________.

So, the measure of $\angle A$ is approximately ______.

✓ ***Checkpoint*** **Complete the following exercise.**

1. In Example 1, use a calculator and an inverse tangent to approximate $m\angle C$ to the nearest tenth of a degree.

Your Notes

Example 2 ***Use an inverse sine and an inverse cosine***

Let $\angle A$ and $\angle B$ be acute angles in two right triangles. Use a calculator to approximate the measures of $\angle A$ and $\angle B$ to the nearest tenth of a degree.

a. $\sin A = 0.76$ **b.** $\cos B = 0.17$

Solution

a. $m\angle A =$ ______ $\approx$ ______ **b.** $m\angle B =$ ______ $\approx$ ______

Example 3 ***Solve a right triangle***

Solve the right triangle. Round decimal answers to the nearest tenth.

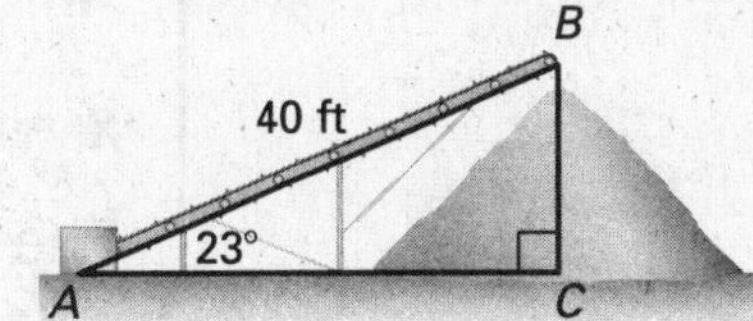

Solution

Step 1 Find $m\angle B$ by using the Triangle Sum Theorem.

______ $= 90° + 23° + m\angle B$

______ $= m\angle B$

Step 2 Approximate BC using a ______ ratio.

______ $= \frac{BC}{40}$ **Write ratio for ______.**

______ $= BC$ **Multiply each side by ______.**

______ $\approx BC$ **Approximate ______.**

______ $\approx BC$ **Simplify and round answer.**

Step 3 Approximate AC using a ______ ratio.

______ $= \frac{AC}{40}$ **Write ratio for ______.**

______ $= AC$ **Multiply each side by ______.**

______ $\approx AC$ **Approximate ______.**

______ $\approx AC$ **Simplify and round answer.**

The angle measures are ______, ______, and ______. The side lengths are ______ feet, about ______ feet, and about ______ feet.

Your Notes

Example 4 ***Solve a real-world problem***

Model Train You are building a track for a model train. You want the track to incline from the first level to the second level, 4 inches higher, in 96 inches. Is the angle of elevation less than 3°?

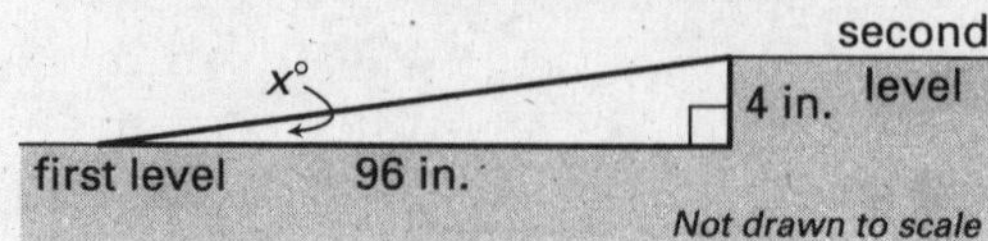

Solution

Use the tangent and inverse tangent ratios to find the degree measure x of the incline.

$\tan x° =$ ______ $=$ ______ $\approx$ ______

$x \approx$ ______________ $\approx$ ______

The incline is about ______, so it ______________ 3°.

Checkpoint Complete the following exercises.

2. Find $m\angle D$ to the nearest tenth of a degree if $\sin D = 0.48$.

3. Solve a right triangle that has a 50° angle and a 15 inch hypotenuse.

4. In Example 4, suppose another incline rises 8 inches in 120 inches. Is the incline less than 3°?

Homework

Words to Review

Give an example of the vocabulary word.

Pythagorean triple	Trigonometric ratio
Tangent	Sine
Cosine	Angle of elevation, Angle of depression
Solve a right triangle	Inverse tangent
Inverse sine	Inverse cosine

Review your notes and Chapter 7 by using the Chapter Review on pages 494–497 of your textbook.

8.1 Find Angle Measures in Polygons

Goal • Find angle measures in polygons.

Your Notes

VOCABULARY

Diagonal

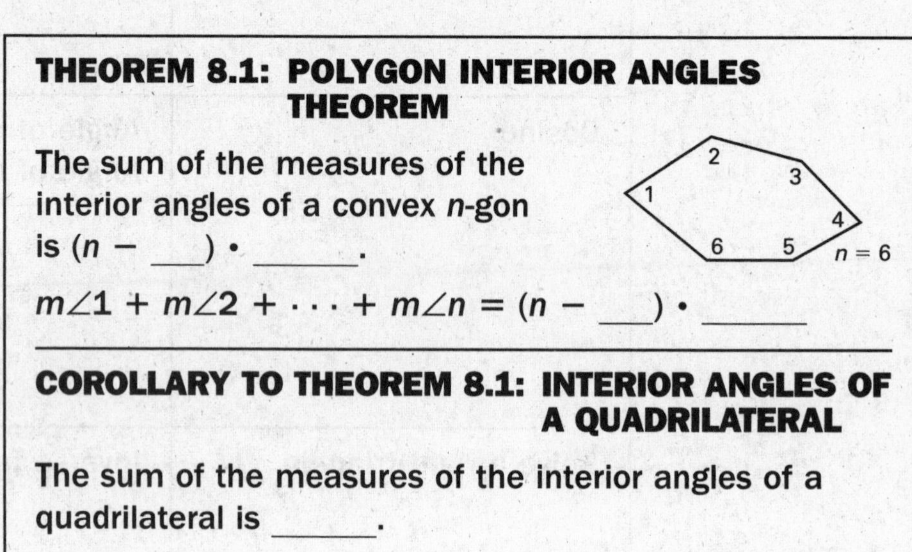

THEOREM 8.1: POLYGON INTERIOR ANGLES THEOREM

The sum of the measures of the interior angles of a convex n-gon is $(n - \_\_\_) \cdot \_\_\_\_\_$.

$m\angle 1 + m\angle 2 + \cdots + m\angle n = (n - \_\_\_) \cdot \_\_\_\_\_$

COROLLARY TO THEOREM 8.1: INTERIOR ANGLES OF A QUADRILATERAL

The sum of the measures of the interior angles of a quadrilateral is _____.

Example 1 ***Find the sum of angle measures in a polygon***

Find the sum of the measures of the interior angles of a convex hexagon.

Solution

A hexagon has ___ sides. Use the Polygon Interior Angles Theorem.

$(n - \_\_\_) \cdot \_\_\_\_\_$	$= (\_\_\_ - \_\_\_) \cdot \_\_\_\_\_$	**Substitute ___ for *n*.**
	$= \_\_\_ \cdot \_\_\_\_\_$	**Subtract.**
	$= \_\_\_\_\_$	**Multiply.**

The sum of the measures of the interior angles of a hexagon is _____.

Your Notes

Example 2 *Find the number of sides of a polygon*

The sum of the measures of the interior angles of a convex polygon is 1260°. Classify the polygon by the number of sides.

Solution

Use the Polygon Interior Angles Theorem to write an equation involving the number of sides *n*. Then solve the equation to find the number of sides.

$(n - \_\_\_) \cdot \_\_\_\_\_ = \_\_\_\_\_$ **Polygon Interior Angles Theorem**

$n - \_\_\_ = \_\_\_$ **Divide each side by _____.**

$n = \_\_\_$ **Add ___ to each side.**

The polygon has ___ sides. It is a _________.

Example 3 *Find an unknown interior angle measure*

Find the value of *x* in the diagram shown.

x° 71° 135° 112°

Solution

The polygon is a quadrilateral. Use the Corollary to the Polygon Interior Angles Theorem to write an equation involving *x*. Then solve the equation.

$x° + \_\_\_\_\_ + \_\_\_\_\_ + \_\_\_\_ = \_\_\_\_\_$ **Corollary to Theorem 8.1**

$x + \_\_\_\_ = \_\_\_\_$ **Combine like terms.**

$x = \_\_\_\_$ **Subtract _____ from each side.**

✔ ***Checkpoint*** **Complete the following exercise.**

1. Find the sum of the measures of the interior angles of the convex decagon.

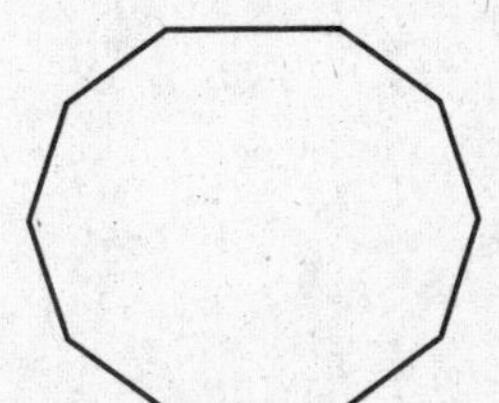

Your Notes

✔ *Checkpoint* Complete the following exercises.

2. The sum of the measures of the interior angles of a convex polygon is 1620°. Classify the polygon by the number of sides.

3. Use the diagram at the right. Find $m\angle K$ and $m\angle L$.

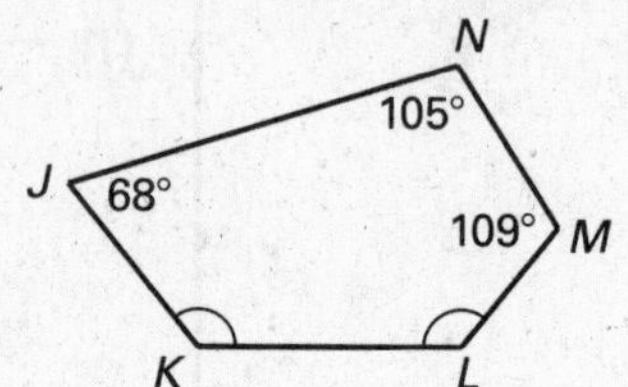

THEOREM 8.2: POLYGON EXTERIOR ANGLES THEOREM

The sum of the measures of the exterior angles of a convex polygon, one angle at each vertex, is ______.

$m\angle 1 + m\angle 2 + \cdots + m\angle n =$ ______

Example 4 ***Find unknown exterior angle measures***

Find the value of x in the diagram shown.

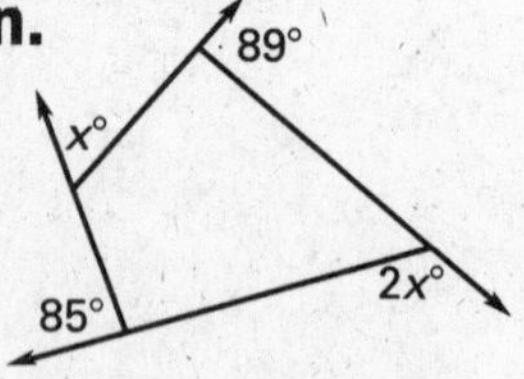

Solution

Use the Polygon Exterior Angles Theorem to write and solve an equation.

$x° +$ ______ $+$ ______ $+$ ______ $=$ ______	**Polygon Exterior Angles Theorem.**
______$x +$ ______ $=$ ______	**Combine like terms.**
$x =$ ______	**Solve for x.**

Your Notes

Example 5 ***Find angle measures in regular polygons***

Lamps The base of a lamp is in the shape of a regular 15-gon. Find (a) the measure of each interior angle and (b) the measure of each exterior angle.

Solution

a. Use the Polygon Interior Angles Theorem to find the sum of the measures of the interior angles.

$(n - \_\_\_) \cdot \_\_\_\_\_ = (\_\_\_\_ - \_\_\_) \cdot \_\_\_\_\_$

$= \_\_\_\_\_$

Then find the measure of one interior angle. A regular 15-gon has ____ congruent interior angles. Divide ______ by ____: ______ ÷ ____ = ______.

The measure of each interior angle in the 15-gon is _____.

b. By the Polygon Exterior Angles Theorem, the sum of the measures of the exterior angles, one angle at each vertex, is _____. Divide ______ by ____: ______ ÷ ____ = _____.

The measure of each exterior angle in the 15-gon is _____.

✓ ***Checkpoint*** Complete the following exercises.

4. A convex pentagon has exterior angles with measures 66°, 77°, 82°, and 62°. What is the measure of an exterior angle at the fifth vertex?

5. Find the measure of (a) each interior angle and (b) each exterior angle of a regular nonagon.

Homework

8.2 Use Properties of Parallelograms

Goal • Find angle and side measures in parallelograms.

Your Notes

VOCABULARY

Parallelogram

THEOREM 8.3

If a quadrilateral is a parallelogram, then its opposite sides are congruent.

If *PQRS* is a parallelogram, then 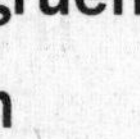
____ $\cong \overline{RS}$ and $\overline{QR} \cong$ ____.

THEOREM 8.4

If a quadrilateral is a parallelogram, then its opposite angles are congruent.

If *PQRS* is a parallelogram, then
$\angle P \cong$ ____ and ____ $\cong \angle S$.

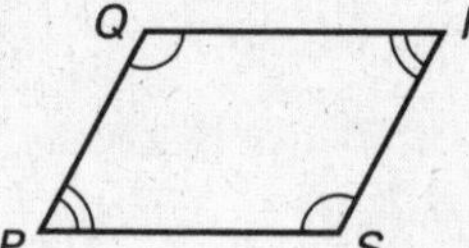

Example 1 ***Use properties of parallelograms***

Find the values of *x* and *y*.

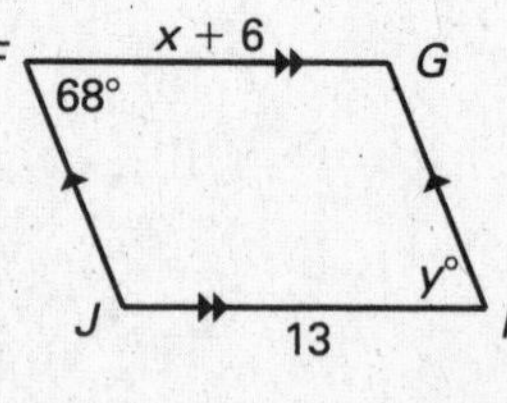

Solution

FGHJ is a parallelogram by the definition of a parallelogram. Use Theorem 8.3 to find the value of *x*.

$FG =$ ____	**Opposite sides of a ▱ are ≅.**
$x + 6 =$ ____	**Substitute $x + 6$ for *FG* and ____ for ____.**
$x =$ ____	**Subtract 6 from each side.**

By Theorem 8.4, $\angle F \cong$ ____, or $m\angle F =$ ____. So, $y° =$ ____.

In ▱*FGHJ*, $x =$ ____ and $y =$ ____.

Your Notes

THEOREM 8.5

If a quadrilateral is a parallelogram, then its consecutive angles are ______________.

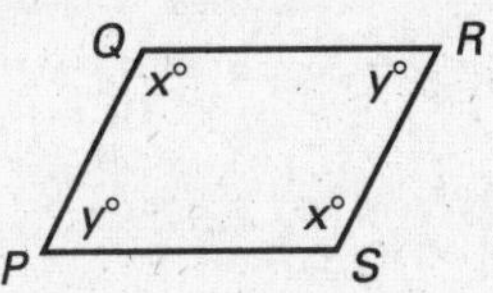

If *PQRS* is a parallelogram, then $x° + y° =$ ______.

Example 2 ***Use properties of a parallelogram***

Gates As shown, a gate contains several parallelograms. Find $m\angle ADC$ when $m\angle DAB = 65°$.

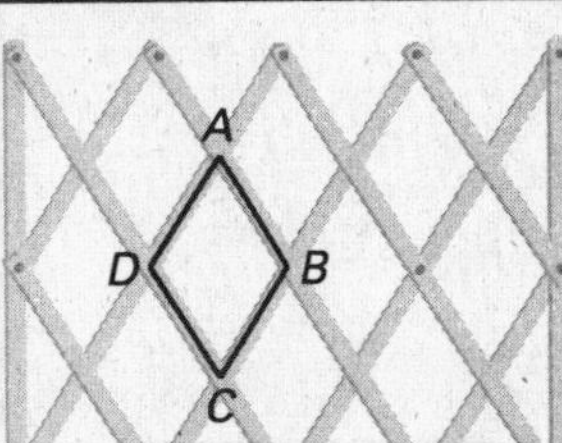

Solution

By Theorem 8.5, the consecutive angle pairs in $\square ABCD$ are ______________. So, $m\angle ADC + m\angle DAB =$ ______. Because $m\angle DAB = 65°$, $m\angle ADC =$ ______ $-$ ______ $=$ ______.

✔ ***Checkpoint*** **Find the indicated measure in $\square KLMN$ shown at the right.**

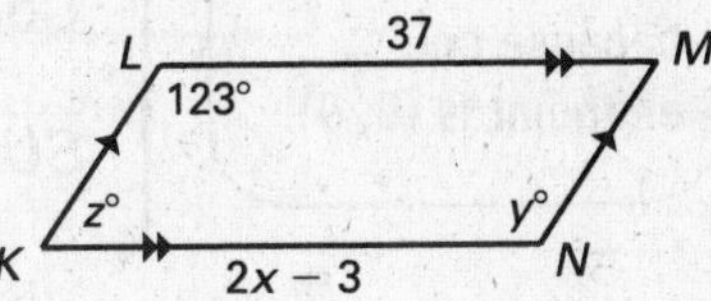

1. x	**2.** y
3. z	

Your Notes

THEOREM 8.6

If a quadrilateral is a parallelogram, then its diagonals ________ each other.

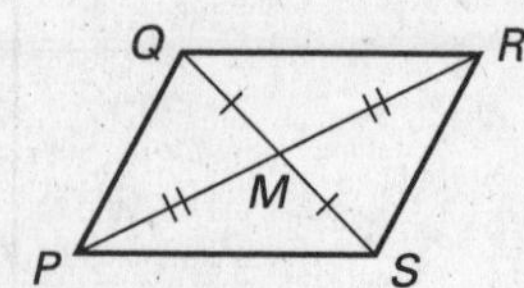

$\overline{QM} \cong$ ______ and $\overline{PM} \cong$ ______

Example 3 *Use properties of a parallelogram*

The diagonals of ▱STUV intersect at point W. Find the coordinates of W.

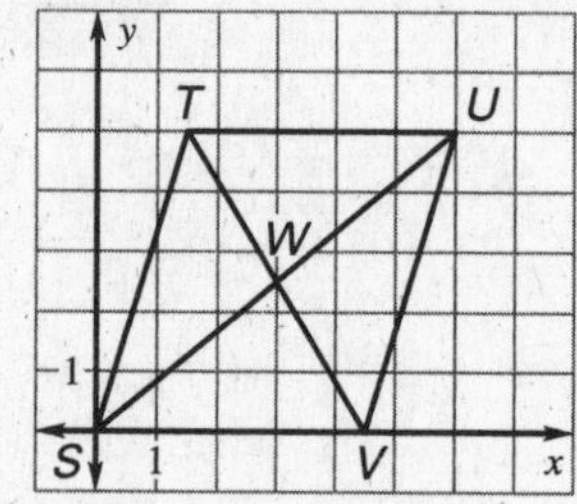

Solution

By Theorem 8.6, the diagonals of a parallelogram ______ each other. So, W is the __________ of the diagonals $\overline{TV}$ and $\overline{SU}$. Use the ______________.

Coordinates of midpoint W of $\overline{SU}$ = (____________) = (______)

> In Example 3, you can use either diagonal to find the coordinates of W. Using $\overline{SU}$ simplifies calculations because one endpoint is (0, 0).

✔ ***Checkpoint*** **Complete the following exercises.**

4. The diagonals of ▱VWXY intersect at point Z. Find the coordinates of Z.

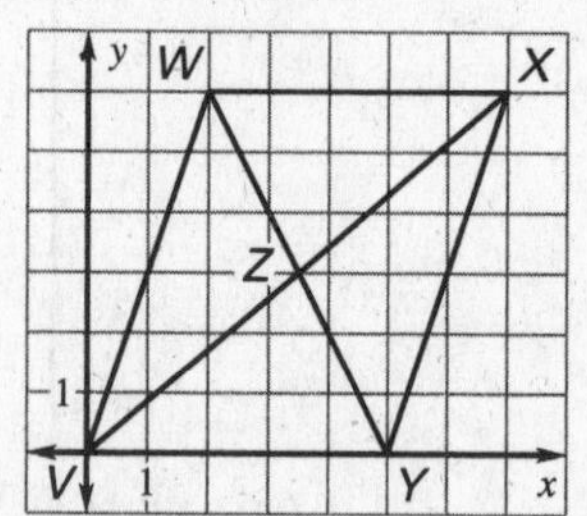

5. Given that ▱FGHJ is a parallelogram, find MH and FH.

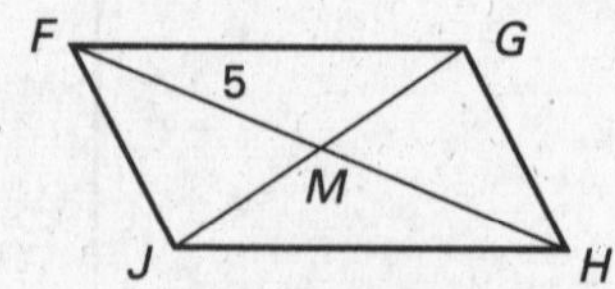

Homework

8.3 Show that a Quadrilateral is a Parallelogram

Goal • Use properties to identify parallelograms.

Your Notes

THEOREM 8.7

If both pairs of opposite ________ of a quadrilateral are congruent, then the quadrilateral is a parallelogram.

If $\overline{AB} \cong$ ______ and $\overline{BC} \cong$ ______, then *ABCD* is a parallelogram.

THEOREM 8.8

If both pairs of opposite ________ of a quadrilateral are congruent, then the quadrilateral is a parallelogram.

If $\angle A \cong$ ______ and $\angle B \cong$ ______, then *ABCD* is a parallelogram.

Example 1 ***Solve a real-world problem***

Basketball In the diagram at the right, $\overline{AB}$ and $\overline{DC}$ represent adjustable supports of a basketball hoop. *Explain* why $\overline{AD}$ is always parallel to $\overline{BC}$.

A 18 in.
36 in.
B
D
36 in.
18 in.
C

Solution

The shape of quadrilateral *ABCD* changes as the adjustable supports move, but its ____________ do not change. Both pairs of opposite ________ are congruent, so *ABCD* is a parallelogram by ______________.

By the definition of a parallelogram, $\overline{AD} \parallel$ ______.

Your Notes

THEOREM 8.9

If one pair of opposite sides of a quadrilateral are __________ and __________, then the quadrilateral is a parallelogram.

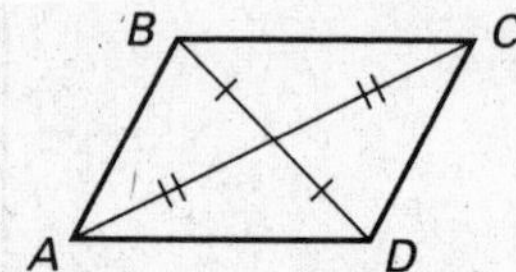

If $\overline{BC}$ ___ $\overline{AD}$ and $\overline{BC}$ ____ $\overline{AD}$, then *ABCD* is a parallelogram.

THEOREM 8.10

If the diagonals of a quadrilateral _______ each other, then the quadrilateral is a parallelogram.

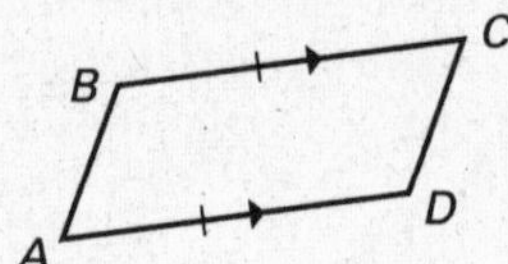

If $\overline{BD}$ and $\overline{AC}$ ________ each other, then *ABCD* is a parallelogram.

Example 2 ***Identify a parallelogram***

Lights The headlights of a car have the shape shown at the right. *Explain* how you know that $\angle B \cong \angle D$.

B C A D

Solution

In the diagram, $\overline{BC} \parallel$ _____ and $\overline{BC} \cong$ _____. By ______________, quadrilateral *ABCD* is a parallelogram. By ______________, you know that opposite angles of a parallelogram are congruent. So, $\angle B \cong$ _____.

Checkpoint **Complete the following exercises.**

1. In quadrilateral *GHJK*, $m\angle G = 55°$, $m\angle H = 125°$, and $m\angle J = 55°$. Find $m\angle K$. What theorem can you use to show that *GHJK* is a parallelogram?

2. What theorem can you use to show that the quadrilateral is a parallelogram?

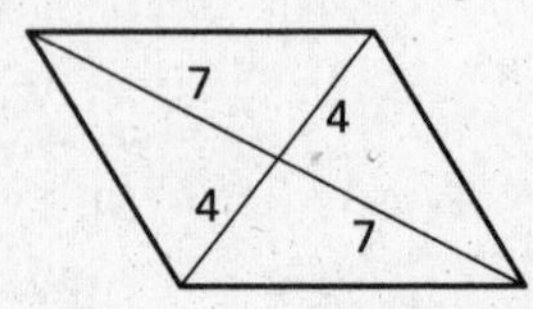

Your Notes

Example 3 *Use algebra with parallelograms*

For what value of x is quadrilateral $PQRS$ a parallelogram?

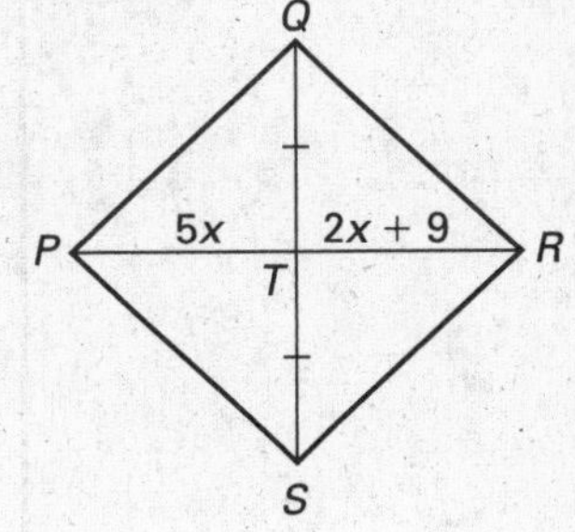

Solution

By Theorem 8.10, if the diagonals of $PQRS$ ______ each other, then it is a parallelogram. You are given that $\overline{QT} \cong$ ____. Find x so that $\overline{PT} \cong$ ____.

$PT =$ ____	**Set the segment lengths equal.**
$5x =$ ______	**Substitute $5x$ for PT and ______ for ____.**
___$x =$ ___	**Subtract ____ from each side.**
$x =$ ___	**Divide each side by ___.**

When $x =$ ___, $PT = 5($___$) =$ ____ and $RT = 2($___$) + 9 =$ ____.

Quadrilateral $PQRS$ is a parallelogram when $x =$ ___.

CONCEPT SUMMARY: WAYS TO PROVE A QUADRILATERAL IS A PARALLELOGRAM

1. Show both pairs of opposite sides are parallel. **(Definition)**

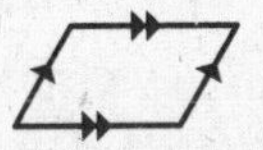

2. Show both pairs of opposite sides are congruent. **(Theorem 8.7)**

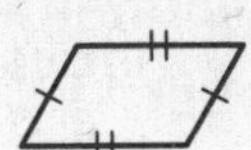

3. Show both pairs of opposite angles are congruent. **(Theorem 8.8)**

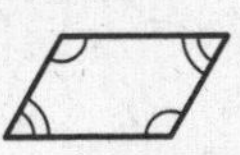

4. Show one pair of opposite sides are congruent and parallel. **(Theorem 8.9)**

5. Show the diagonals bisect each other. **(Theorem 8.10)**

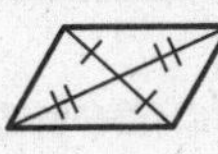

Your Notes

Example 4 ***Use coordinate geometry***

Show that quadrilateral *KLMN* is a parallelogram.

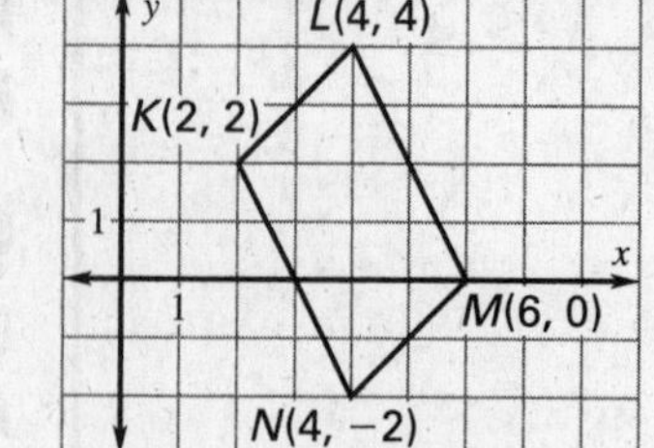

Solution

One way is to show that a pair of sides are congruent and parallel. Then apply ______.

First use the Distance Formula to show that $\overline{KL}$ and $\overline{MN}$ are ______.

$KL = \sqrt{\qquad\qquad} = \sqrt{\quad}$

$MN = \sqrt{\qquad\qquad} = \sqrt{\quad}$

Because $KL = MN = \sqrt{\quad}$, $\overline{KL}$ ___ $\overline{MN}$.

Then use the slope formula to show that $\overline{KL}$ ___ $\overline{MN}$.

Slope of $\overline{KL} = \frac{\square}{\square} =$ ___

Slope of $\overline{MN} = \frac{\square}{\square} =$ ___

$\overline{KL}$ and $\overline{MN}$ have the same slope, so they are ______.

$\overline{KL}$ and $\overline{MN}$ are congruent and parallel. So, *KLMN* is a parallelogram by ______.

Checkpoint **Complete the following exercises.**

3. For what value of *x* is quadrilateral *DFGH* a parallelogram?

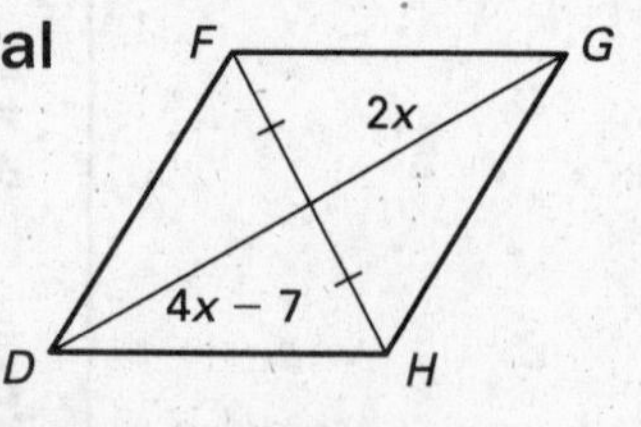

4. *Explain* another method that can be used to show that quadrilateral *KLMN* in Example 4 is a parallelogram.

Homework

8.4 Properties of Rhombuses, Rectangles, and Squares

Goal • Use properties of rhombuses, rectangles, and squares.

Your Notes

VOCABULARY

Rhombus

Rectangle

Square

RHOMBUS COROLLARY

A quadrilateral is a rhombus if and only if it has four congruent ______.

ABCD is a rhombus if and only if $\overline{AB} \cong \overline{BC} \cong \overline{CD} \cong \overline{AD}$.

RECTANGLE COROLLARY

A quadrilateral is a rectangle if and only if it has four ______.

ABCD is a rectangle if and only if $\angle A$, $\angle B$, $\angle C$, and $\angle D$ are right angles.

SQUARE COROLLARY

A quadrilateral is a square if and only if it is a ______ and a ______.

ABCD is a square if and only if $\overline{AB} \cong \overline{BC} \cong \overline{CD} \cong \overline{AD}$ and $\angle A$, $\angle B$, $\angle C$, and $\angle D$ are right angles.

Your Notes

Example 1 ***Use properties of special quadrilaterals***

For any rhombus *RSTV*, decide whether the statement is always or sometimes true. Draw a sketch and explain your reasoning.

a. $\angle S \cong \angle V$ **b.** $\angle T \cong \angle V$

Solution

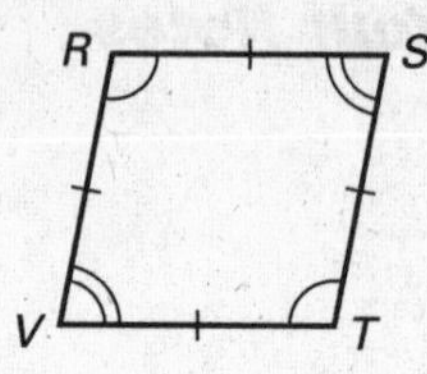

a. By definition, a rhombus is a parallelogram with four congruent ______. By Theorem 8.4, opposite angles of a parallelogram are __________. So, $\angle S \cong \angle V$. The statement is ________ true.

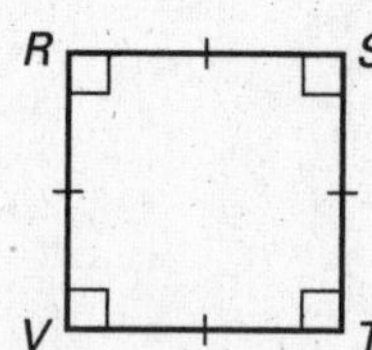

b. If rhombus *RSTV* is a ________, then all four angles are congruent right angles. So $\angle T \cong \angle V$ if *RSTV* is a ________. Because not all rhombuses are also _________, the statement is ___________ true.

Example 2 ***Classify special quadrilaterals***

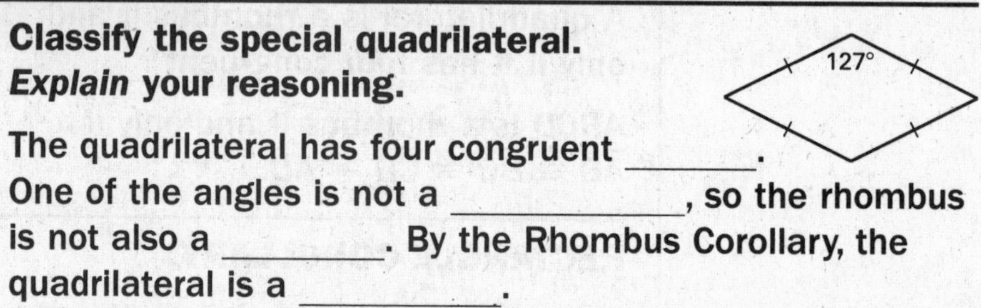

Classify the special quadrilateral.
Explain **your reasoning.**

The quadrilateral has four congruent ______. One of the angles is not a ____________, so the rhombus is not also a ______. By the Rhombus Corollary, the quadrilateral is a ________.

Checkpoint **Complete the following exercises.**

1. For any square *CDEF*, is it *always* or *sometimes* true that $\overline{CD} \cong \overline{DE}$? *Explain* your reasoning.

2. A quadrilateral has four congruent sides and four congruent angles. Classify the quadrilateral.

Your Notes

THEOREM 8.11

A parallelogram is a rhombus if and only if its diagonals are ______________.

▱*ABCD* is a rhombus if and only if ______ ⊥ ______.

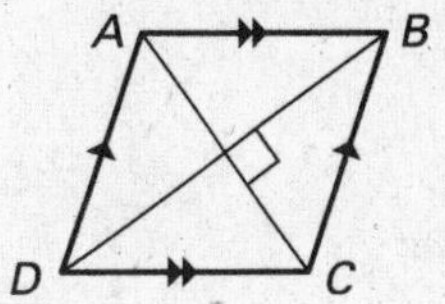

THEOREM 8.12

A parallelogram is a rhombus if and only if each diagonal bisects a pair of opposite angles.

▱*ABCD* is a rhombus if and only if $\overline{AC}$ bisects ∠______ and ∠______ and $\overline{BD}$ bisects ∠______ and ∠______.

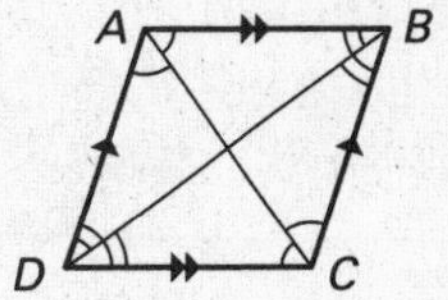

THEOREM 8.13

A parallelogram is a rectangle if and only if its diagonals are ______________.

▱*ABCD* is a rectangle if and only if ______ ≅ ______.

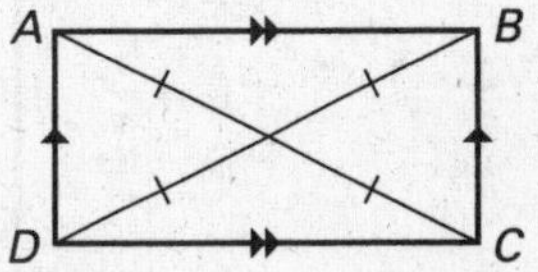

Example 3 ***List properties of special parallelograms***

Sketch rhombus *FGHJ*. List everything you know about it.

Solution

By definition, you need to draw a figure with the following properties:

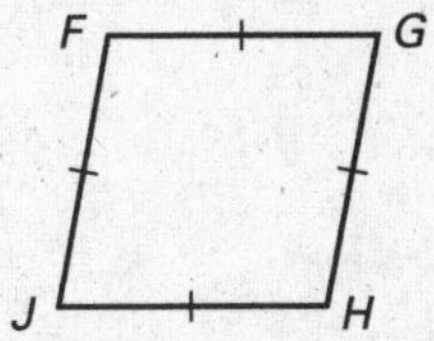

- The figure is a ______________.
- The figure has four congruent ________.

Because *FGHJ* is a parallelogram, it has these properties:

- Opposite sides are __________ and ______________.
- Opposite angles are ____________. Consecutive angles are ________________.
- Diagonals ________ each other.

By Theorem 8.11, the diagonals of *FGHJ* are ________________. By Theorem 8.12, each diagonal bisects a pair of ________________.

Your Notes

Example 4 ***Solve a real-world problem***

Framing You are building a frame for a painting. The measurements of the frame are shown at the right.

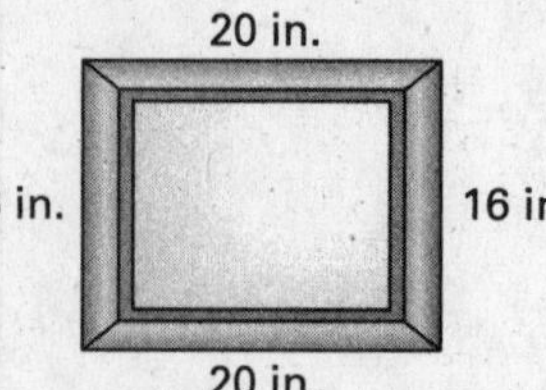

a. The frame must be a rectangle. Given the measurements in the diagram, can you assume that it is? *Explain.*

b. You measure the diagonals of the frame. The diagonals are about 25.6 inches. What can you conclude about the shape of the frame?

Solution

a. No, you cannot. The boards on opposite sides are the same length, so they form a ______________. But you do not know whether the angles are ______________.

b. By Theorem 8.13, the diagonals of a rectangle are ____________. The diagonals of the frame are ____________, so the frame forms a ____________.

Checkpoint Complete the following exercises.

3. Sketch rectangle *WXYZ*. List everything that you know about it.

4. Suppose the diagonals of the frame in Example 4 are not congruent.

Could the frame still be a rectangle? *Explain.*

Homework

8.5 Use Properties of Trapezoids and Kites

Goal • Use properties of trapezoids and kites.

Your Notes

VOCABULARY

Trapezoid

Bases of a trapezoid

Base angles of a trapezoid

Legs of a trapezoid

Isosceles trapezoid

Midsegment of a trapezoid

Kite

Your Notes

Example 1 ***Use a coordinate plane***

Show that *CDEF* is a trapezoid.

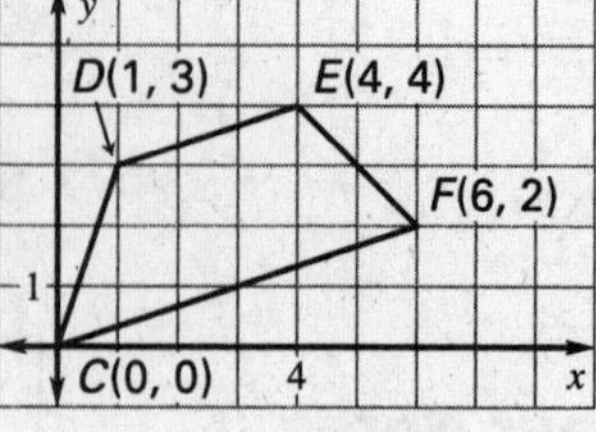

Solution

Compare the slopes of opposite sides.

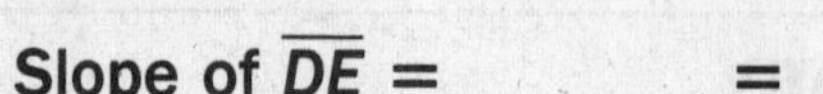

Slope of $\overline{DE}$ = ______ = ______

Slope of $\overline{CF}$ = ______ = ______ = ______

The slopes of $\overline{DE}$ and $\overline{CF}$ are the same, so $\overline{DE}$ ___ $\overline{CF}$.

Slope of $\overline{EF}$ = ______ = ______ = ______

Slope of $\overline{CD}$ = ______ = ______ = ______

The slopes of $\overline{EF}$ and $\overline{CD}$ are not the same, so $\overline{EF}$ is ______________ to $\overline{CD}$.

Because quadrilateral *CDEF* has exactly one pair of ______________, it is a trapezoid.

THEOREM 8.14

If a trapezoid is isosceles, then each pair of base angles is ______________.

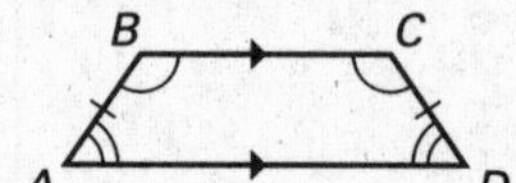

If trapezoid *ABCD* is isosceles, then $\angle A \cong \angle$___ and $\angle$___ $\cong \angle C$.

THEOREM 8.15

If a trapezoid has a pair of congruent ______________, then it is an isosceles trapezoid.

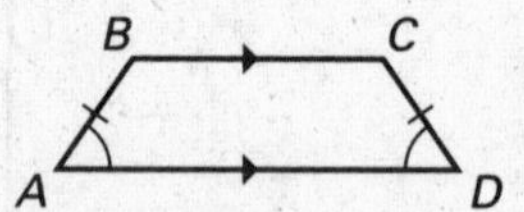

If $\angle A \cong \angle D$ (or if $\angle B \cong \angle C$), then trapezoid *ABCD* is isosceles.

THEOREM 8.16

A trapezoid is isosceles if and only if its diagonals are ______________.

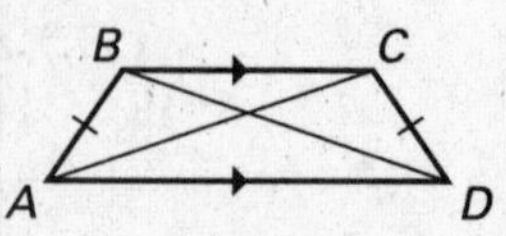

Trapezoid *ABCD* is isosceles if and only if ______ $\cong$ ______.

Your Notes

Example 2 ***Use properties of isosceles trapezoids***

Kitchen A shelf fitting into a cupboard in the corner of a kitchen is an isosceles trapezoid. Find $m\angle N$, $m\angle L$, and $m\angle M$.

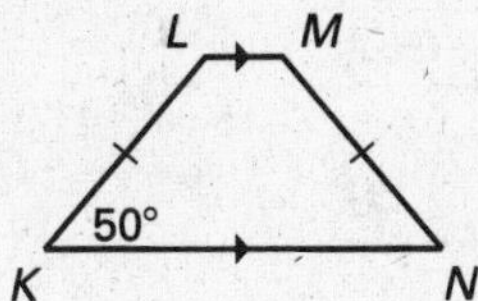

Solution

Step 1 Find $m\angle N$. *KLMN* is an ________________, so $\angle N$ and $\angle$___ are congruent base angles, and $m\angle N = m\angle$___ = _____.

Step 2 Find $m\angle L$. Because $\angle K$ and $\angle L$ are consecutive interior angles formed by $\overleftrightarrow{KL}$ intersecting two parallel lines, they are ______________. So, $m\angle L$ = _____ − _____ = _____.

Step 3 Find $m\angle M$. Because $\angle M$ and $\angle$___ are a pair of base angles, they are congruent, and $m\angle M = m\angle$___ = _____.

So, $m\angle N$ = _____, $m\angle L$ = _____, and $m\angle M$ = _____.

✔ ***Checkpoint*** **Complete the following exercises.**

1. In Example 1, suppose the coordinates of point *E* are (7, 5). What type of quadrilateral is *CDEF*? *Explain.*

2. Find $m\angle C$, $m\angle A$, and $m\angle D$ in the trapezoid shown.

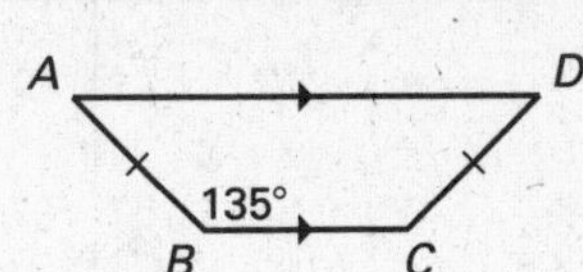

Your Notes

THEOREM 8.17: MIDSEGMENT THEOREM FOR TRAPEZOIDS

The midsegment of a trapezoid is parallel to each base and its length is one half the sum of the lengths of the bases.

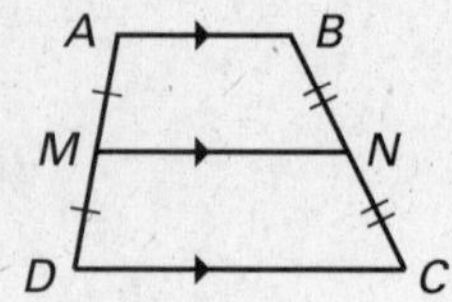

If $\overline{MN}$ is the midsegment of trapezoid $ABCD$, then $\overline{MN} \parallel$ ______, $\overline{MN} \parallel$ ______, and $MN = \frac{__}{__}($______ + ______$)$.

Example 3 ***Use the midsegment of a trapezoid***

In the diagram, $\overline{MN}$ is the midsegment of trapezoid $PQRS$. Find MN.

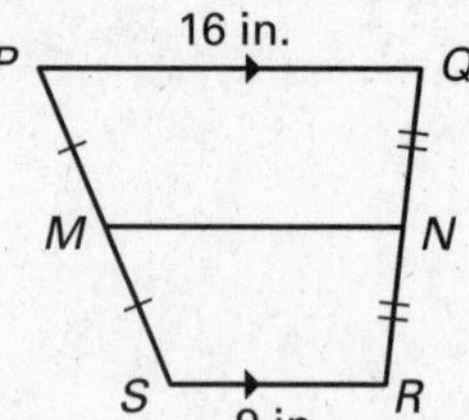

Solution

Use Theorem 8.17 to find MN.

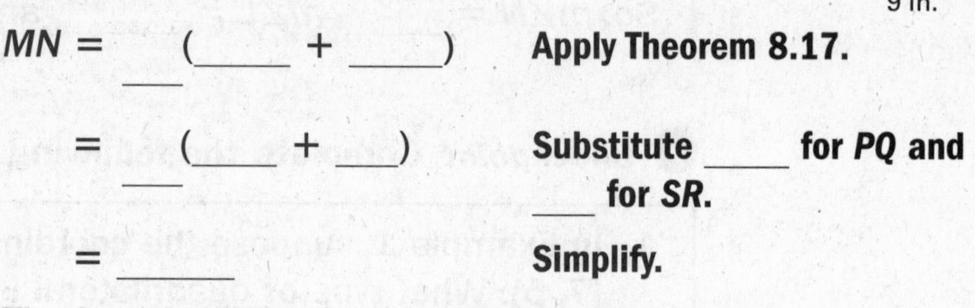

$MN = \frac{__}{__}($____ + ____$)$ **Apply Theorem 8.17.**

$= \frac{__}{__}($___ + ___$)$ **Substitute** ____ **for** ***PQ*** **and** ____ **for** ***SR*****.**

$=$ ______ **Simplify.**

The length MN is ______ inches.

Checkpoint Complete the following exercise.

3. Find MN in the trapezoid at the right.

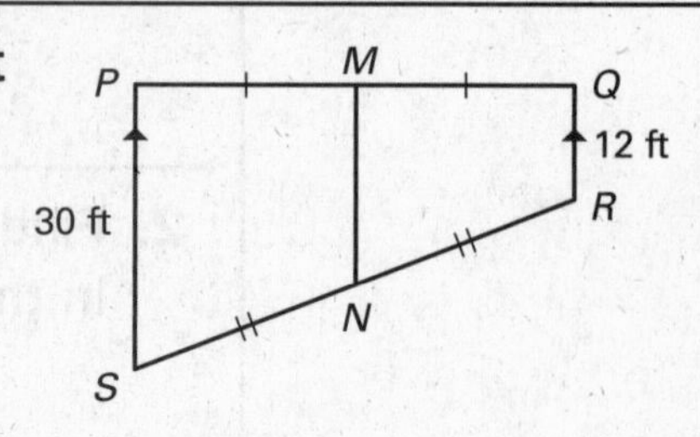

Your Notes

THEOREM 8.18

If a quadrilateral is a kite, then its diagonals are ______________.

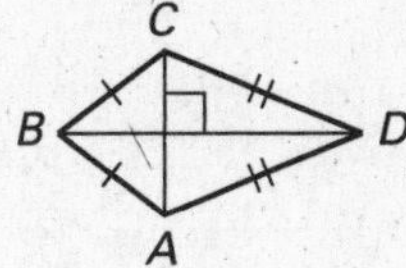

If quadrilateral $ABCD$ is a kite, then ____ $\perp$ ____.

THEOREM 8.19

If a quadrilateral is a kite, then exactly one pair of opposite angles are congruent.

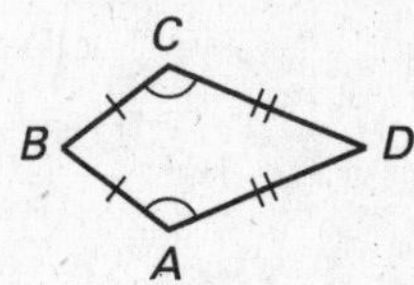

If quadrilateral $ABCD$ is a kite and $\overline{BC} \cong \overline{BA}$, then $\angle A$ ___ $\angle C$ and $\angle B$ ___ $\angle D$.

Example 4 ***Apply Theorem 8.19***

Find $m\angle T$ in the kite shown at the right.

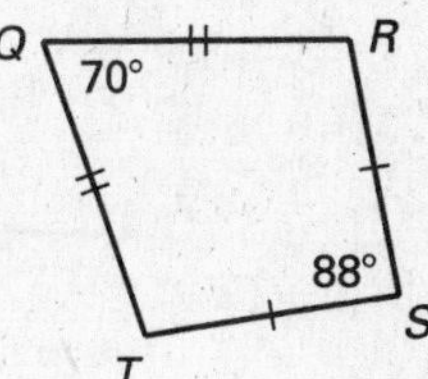

Solution

By Theorem 8.19, $QRST$ has exactly one pair of ____________ opposite angles. Because $\angle Q \not\cong \angle S$, $\angle$___ and $\angle T$ must be congruent. So, $m\angle$___ $= m\angle T$. Write and solve an equation to find $m\angle T$.

$m\angle T + m\angle R +$ ____ $+$ ____ $=$ ____ **Corollary to Theorem 8.1**

$m\angle T + m\angle T +$ ____ $+$ ____ $=$ ____ **Substitute $m\angle T$ for $m\angle R$.**

___$(m\angle T) +$ ____ $=$ ____ **Combine like terms.**

$m\angle T =$ ____ **Solve for $m\angle T$.**

Homework

✔ ***Checkpoint*** **Complete the following exercise.**

4. Find $m\angle G$ in the kite shown at the right.

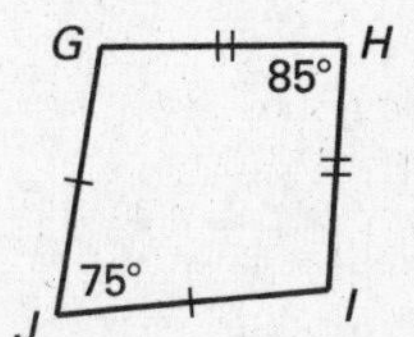

8.6 Identify Special Quadrilaterals

 • Identify special quadrilaterals.

Your Notes

Example 1 ***Identify quadrilaterals***

Quadrilateral *ABCD* has both pairs of opposite sides congruent. What types of quadrilaterals meet this condition?

Solution

There are many possibilities.

______ ______ ______ ______

Opposite sides are congruent. All sides are congruent.

Checkpoint **Complete the following exercise.**

1. Quadrilateral *JKLM* has both pairs of opposite angles congruent. What types of quadrilaterals meet this condition?

In Example 2, *ABCD* is shaped like a square. But you must rely only on marked information when you interpret a diagram.

Example 2 ***Identify a quadrilateral***

What is the most specific name for quadrilateral *ABCD*?

A B D C

Solution

The diagram shows that both pairs of opposite sides are congruent. By Theorem 8.7, *ABCD* is a ______________. All sides are congruent, so *ABCD* is a ___________ by definition.

__________ are also rhombuses. However, there is no information given about the angle measures of *ABCD*. So, you cannot determine whether it is a _________.

Your Notes

Example 3 ***Identify a quadrilateral***

Is enough information given in the diagram to show that quadrilateral *FGHJ* is an isosceles trapezoid? *Explain*.

Solution

Step 1 Show that *FGHJ* is a __________. ∠*G* and ∠*H* are ______________ but ∠*F* and ∠*G* are not. So, _____ ∥ _____, but $\overline{FJ}$ is not ________ to $\overline{GH}$. By definition, *FGHJ* is a __________.

Step 2 Show that trapezoid *FGHJ* is __________. ∠*F* and ∠*G* are a pair of congruent ____________. So, *FGHJ* is an _________________ by Theorem 8.15.

Yes, the diagram is sufficient to show that *FGHJ* is an isosceles trapezoid.

Checkpoint **Complete the following exercises.**

2. What is the most specific name for quadrilateral *QRST*? *Explain* your reasoning.

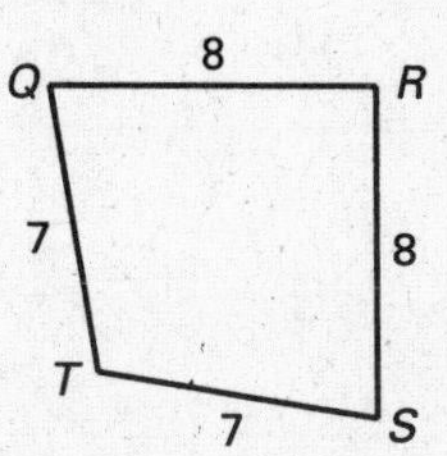

3. Is enough information given in the diagram to show that quadrilateral *BCDE* is a rectangle? *Explain*.

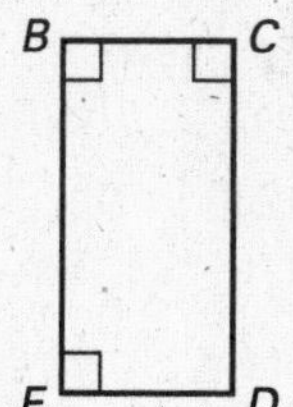

Homework

Words to Review

Give an example of the vocabulary word.

Diagonal	Parallelogram
Rhombus	Rectangle
Square	Trapezoid
Bases, Legs, and Base angles of a trapezoid	Isosceles trapezoid
Midsegment of a trapezoid	Kite

Review your notes and Chapter 8 by using the Chapter Review on pages 560–563 of your textbook.

9.1 Translate Figures and Use Vectors

Goal • Use a vector to translate a figure.

Your Notes

VOCABULARY

Image

Preimage

Isometry

Vector

Initial point

Terminal point

Horizontal component

Vertical component

Component form

Your Notes

You can use *prime notation* to name an image. For example, if the preimage is $\triangle ABC$, then its image is $\triangle A'B'C'$, read as "*triangle A prime, B prime, C prime.*"

Example 1 ***Translate a figure in the coordinate plane***

Graph quadrilateral *ABCD* with vertices *A*(−2, 6), *B*(2, 4), *C*(2, 1), and *D*(−2, 3). Find the image of each vertex after the translation $(x, y) \to (x + 3, y - 3)$. Then graph the image using prime notation.

Solution

First, draw *ABCD*. Find the translation of each vertex by ________ 3 to its *x*-coordinate and ____________ 3 from its *y*-coordinate. Then graph the image.

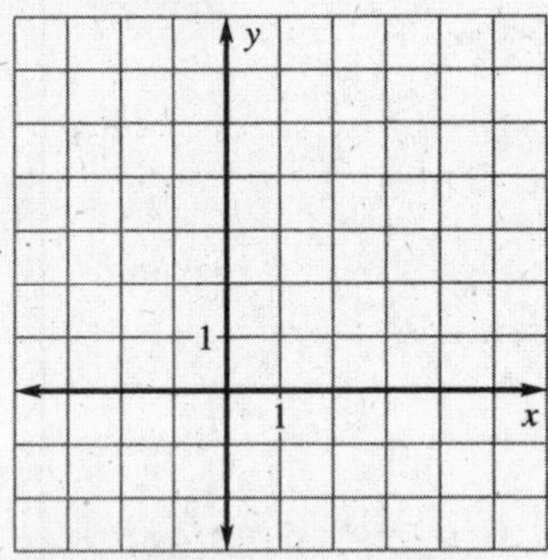

$(x, y) \to (x + 3, y - 3)$

$A(-2, 6) \to A'($______$)$

$B(2, 4) \to B'($______$)$

$C(2, 1) \to C'($______$)$

$D(-2, 3) \to D'($______$)$

Example 2 ***Write a translation rule and verify congruence***

Write a rule for the translation of $\triangle ABC$ to $\triangle A'B'C'$. Then verify that the transformation is an isometry.

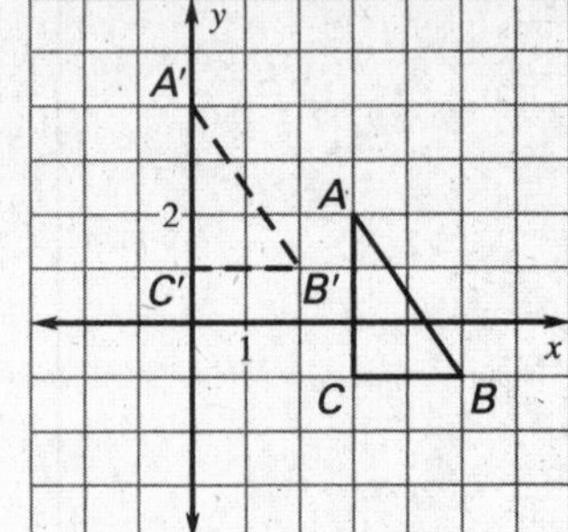

Solution

To go from *A* to *A'*, move 3 units _____ and 2 units _____. So, a rule for the translation is $(x, y) \to ($______________$)$.

Use the SAS Congruence Postulate. Notice that $CB = C'B' =$ ___, and $AC = A'C' =$ ___. The slopes of $\overline{CB}$ and $\overline{C'B'}$ are ___, and the slopes of $\overline{CA}$ and $\overline{C'A'}$ are ____________, so the sides are ______________. Therefore, $\angle C$ and $\angle C'$ are ________________. So, $\triangle ABC$ ___ $\triangle A'B'C'$. The translation is an isometry.

THEOREM 9.1: TRANSLATION THEOREM

A translation is an isometry.

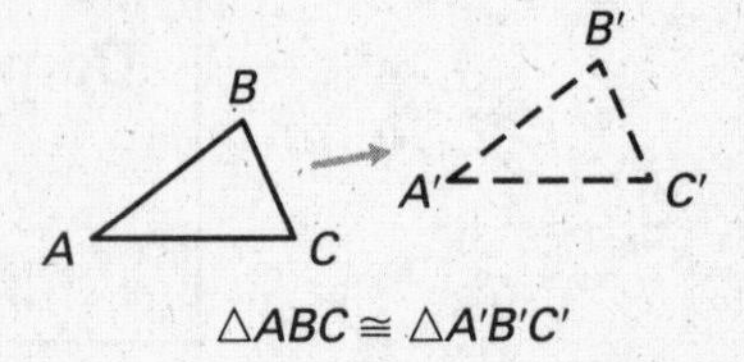

$\triangle ABC \cong \triangle A'B'C'$

Your Notes

✓ ***Checkpoint*** **Complete the following exercises.**

1. Draw $\triangle PQR$ with vertices $P(4, 2)$, $Q(6, 2)$, and $R(4, -2)$. Find the image of each vertex after the translation $(x, y) \rightarrow (x - 4, y + 1)$. Graph the image using prime notation.

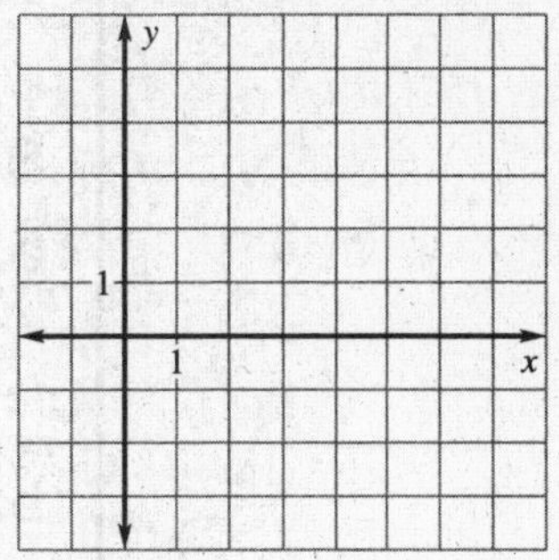

2. In Example 2, write a rule to translate $\triangle A'B'C'$ back to $\triangle ABC$.

VECTORS

The diagram shows a vector named $\overrightarrow{FG}$, read as "vector *FG*."

The initial point, or starting point, of the vector is ___.

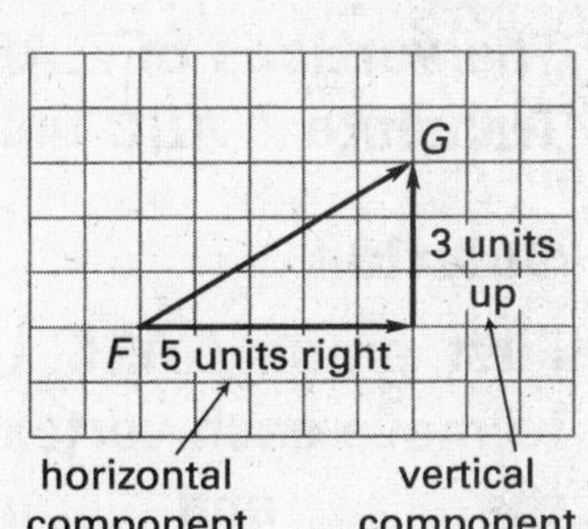

The terminal point, or ending point, of the vector is ___.

The component form of a vector combines the horizontal and vertical components. So, the component form of $\overrightarrow{FG}$ is ______.

Use brackets to write the component form of the vector $\langle r, s\rangle$. Use parentheses to write the coordinates of the point (p, q).

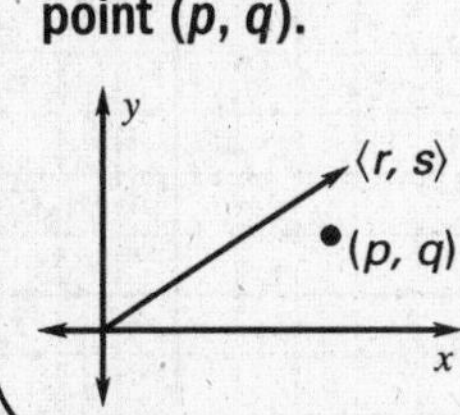

Your Notes

Example 3 ***Identify vector components***

Name the vector and write its component form.

a. 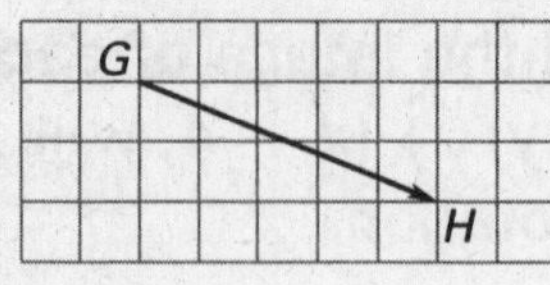

b. 

Solution

a. The vector is $\overrightarrow{GH}$. From initial point ___ to terminal point ___, you move ___ units ______ and ___ units ______. So, the component form is ________.

b. The vector is $\overrightarrow{RS}$. From initial point ___ to terminal point ___, you move ___ units _____ and ___ units __________. So, the component form is ________.

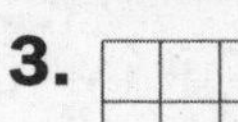

Checkpoint **Name the vector and write its component form.**

3. 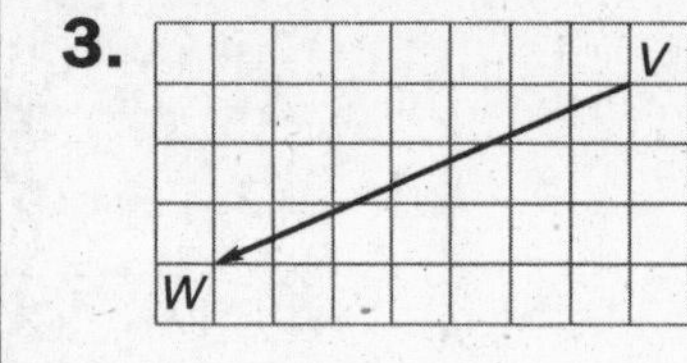

4. 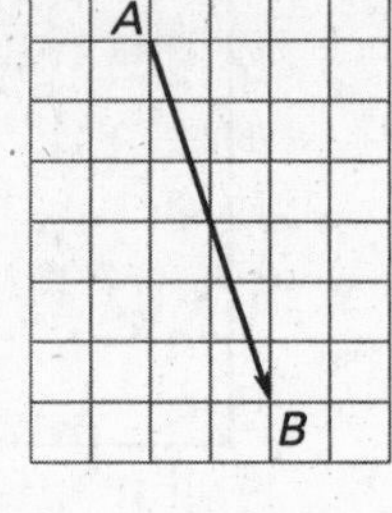

Example 4 ***Use a vector to translate a figure***

The vertices of $\triangle ABC$ are $A(0, 4)$, $B(2, 3)$, and $C(1, 0)$. Translate $\triangle ABC$ using the vector $\langle -4, 1 \rangle$.

Notice that the vector can have different initial points. The vector describes only the direction and magnitude of the translation.

Solution

First, graph $\triangle ABC$. Use $\langle -4, 1 \rangle$ to move each vertex ___ units to the _____ and ___ unit _____. Label the image vertices. Draw $\triangle A'B'C'$. Notice that the vectors drawn from preimage to image vertices are ________.

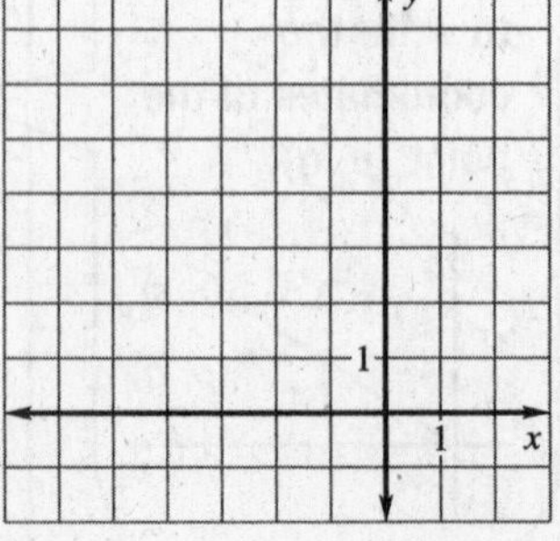

Your Notes

Example 5 *Solve a multi-step problem*

Construction A car heads out from point A toward point D. The car encounters construction at B, 8 miles east and 12 miles south of its starting point. The detour route leads the car to point C, as shown.

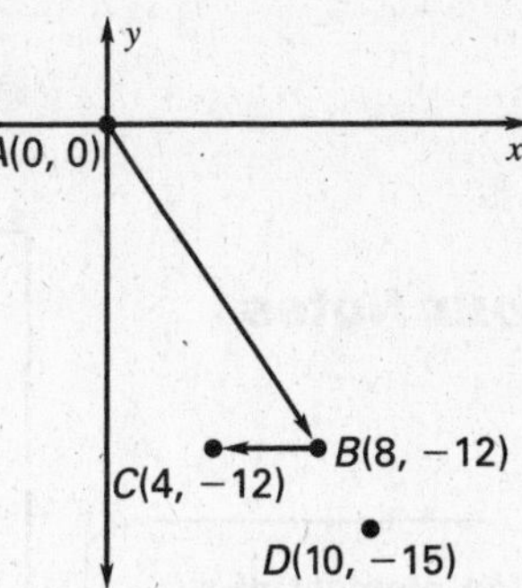

a. Write the component form of $\overrightarrow{AB}$.

b. Write the component form of $\overrightarrow{BC}$.

c. Write the component form of the vector that describes the straight line path from the car's current position C to its intended destination D.

a. The component form of the vector from $A(0, 0)$ to $B(8, -12)$ is

$\overrightarrow{AB}$ = ______________ = ______________.

b. The component form of the vector from $B(8, -12)$ to $C(4, -12)$ is

$\overrightarrow{BC}$ = ______________ = ______________.

c. The car is currently at point C and needs to travel to D. The component form of the vector from $C(4, -12)$ to $D(10, -15)$ is

$\overrightarrow{CD}$ = ______________ = ______________.

✔ ***Checkpoint*** **Complete the following exercises.**

5. The vertices of $\triangle ABC$ are $A(-1, -1)$, $B(0, 2)$, and $C(1, -1)$. Translate $\triangle ABC$ using the vector $\langle 5, 2 \rangle$.

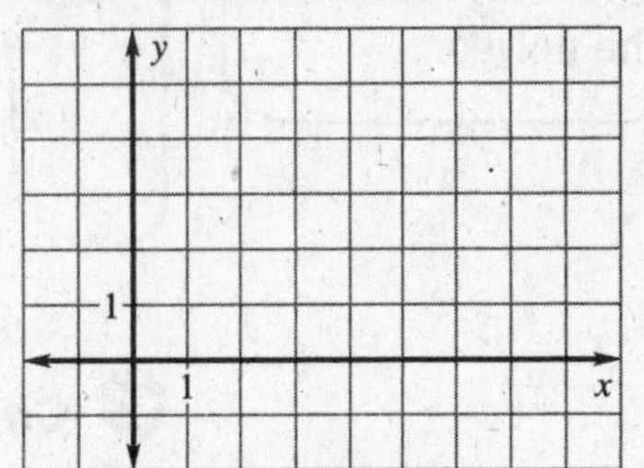

6. In Example 5, suppose there is no construction. Write the component form of the vector that describes the straight path from the car's starting point A to its final destination D.

Homework

9.2 Use Properties of Matrices

Goal • Perform translations using matrix operations.

Your Notes

VOCABULARY
Matrix
Element
Dimensions

An element of a matrix may also be called an *entry*.

Example 1 ***Represent figures using matrices***

Write a matrix to represent the point or polygon.

a. Point *A*

b. Quadrilateral *ABCD*

Solution

a. Point matrix for *A*

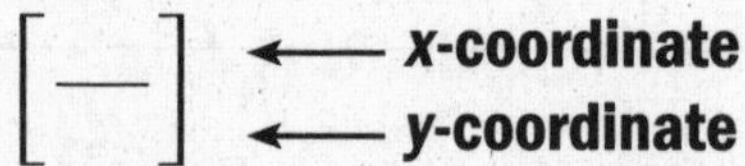

The columns in a polygon matrix follow the consecutive order of the vertices of the polygon.

b. Polygon matrix for *ABCD*

A B C D

[___ ___ ___ ___] ← ***x*-coordinates**
[___ ___ ___ ___] ← ***y*-coordinates**

Checkpoint **Complete the following exercise.**

1. Write a matrix to represent $\triangle RST$ with vertices $R(-5, -4)$, $S(-1, 2)$, and $T(3, 1)$.

Your Notes

Example 2 Add and subtract matrices

a. $\begin{bmatrix} 4 & -2 \\ 2 & -3 \end{bmatrix} + \begin{bmatrix} 1 & 2 \\ 5 & -6 \end{bmatrix} = \begin{bmatrix} \_\_\_\_ & \_\_\_\_ \\ \_\_\_\_ & \_\_\_\_ \end{bmatrix}$

$= \begin{bmatrix} \_\_ & \_\_ \\ \_\_ & \_\_ \end{bmatrix}$

b. $\begin{bmatrix} 7 & 4 & 5 \\ 1 & -2 & 8 \end{bmatrix} - \begin{bmatrix} 3 & -6 & 5 \\ 0 & 7 & 1 \end{bmatrix}$

$= \begin{bmatrix} \_\_\_\_ & \_\_\_\_ & \_\_\_\_ \\ \_\_\_\_ & \_\_\_\_ & \_\_\_\_ \end{bmatrix}$

$= \begin{bmatrix} \_\_ & \_\_ & \_\_ \\ \_\_ & \_\_ & \_\_ \end{bmatrix}$

Example 3 Represent a translation using matrices

The matrix $\begin{bmatrix} 2 & 3 & 4 \\ -3 & 2 & 0 \end{bmatrix}$ represents $\triangle ABC$. Find the image matrix that represents the translation of $\triangle ABC$ 4 units left and 1 unit down. Then graph $\triangle ABC$ and its image.

In order to add two matrices, they must have the same dimensions, so the translation matrix here must have three columns like the polygon matrix.

Solution

The translation matrix is $\begin{bmatrix} \_\_\_\_\_\_\_\_ \end{bmatrix}$.

Add this to the polygon matrix for the preimage to find the image matrix.

$\begin{bmatrix} \quad \\ \quad \end{bmatrix} + \overset{\quad A \quad B \quad C}{\begin{bmatrix} 2 & 3 & 4 \\ -3 & 2 & 0 \end{bmatrix}} = \overset{A' \quad B' \quad C'}{\begin{bmatrix} \quad \\ \quad \end{bmatrix}}$

Translation matrix **Polygon matrix** **Image matrix**

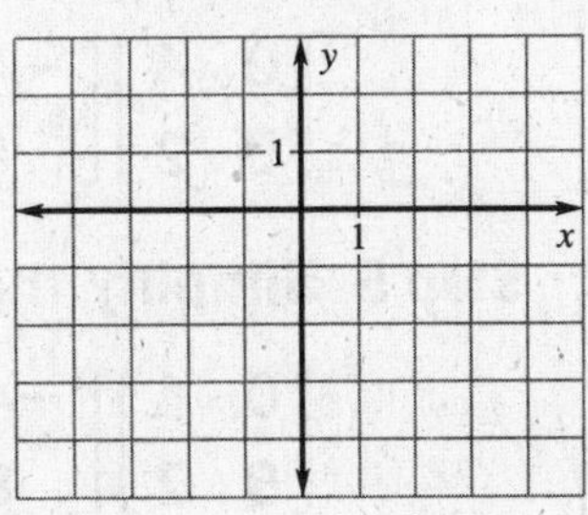

Your Notes

Example 4 ***Multiply matrices***

Multiply $\begin{bmatrix} 0 & 4 \\ 5 & 2 \end{bmatrix}\begin{bmatrix} -4 & 1 \\ 8 & -3 \end{bmatrix}$.

Solution

The matrices are both 2 × 2, so their product is defined. Use the following steps to find the elements of the product matrix.

Step 1 **Multiply** the numbers in the ________ of the first matrix by the numbers in the ________ of the second matrix. Put the result in the first row, first column of the product matrix.

$\begin{bmatrix} 0 & 4 \\ 5 & 2 \end{bmatrix}\begin{bmatrix} -4 & 1 \\ 8 & -3 \end{bmatrix} = \begin{bmatrix} \_\_\_\_\_\_ & ? \\ ? & ? \end{bmatrix}$

Step 2 **Multiply** the numbers in the ________ of the first matrix by the numbers in the ________ of the second matrix. Put the result in the first row, second column of the product matrix.

$\begin{bmatrix} 0 & 4 \\ 5 & 2 \end{bmatrix}\begin{bmatrix} -4 & 1 \\ 8 & -3 \end{bmatrix} = \begin{bmatrix} \_\_\_\_\_\_ & \_\_\_\_\_\_ \\ ? & ? \end{bmatrix}$

Step 3 **Multiply** the numbers in the ________ of the first matrix by the numbers in the ________ of the second matrix. Put the result in the second row, first column of the product matrix.

$\begin{bmatrix} 0 & 4 \\ 5 & 2 \end{bmatrix}\begin{bmatrix} -4 & 1 \\ 8 & -3 \end{bmatrix} = \begin{bmatrix} \_\_\_\_\_\_ & \_\_\_\_\_\_ \\ \_\_\_\_\_\_ & ? \end{bmatrix}$

Step 4 **Multiply** the numbers in the ________ of the first matrix by the numbers in the ________ of the second matrix. Put the result in the second row, second column of the product matrix.

$\begin{bmatrix} 0 & 4 \\ 5 & 2 \end{bmatrix}\begin{bmatrix} -4 & 1 \\ 8 & -3 \end{bmatrix} = \begin{bmatrix} \_\_\_\_\_\_ & \_\_\_\_\_\_ \\ \_\_\_\_\_\_ & \_\_\_\_\_\_ \end{bmatrix}$

Step 5 **Simplify** the product matrix.

$\begin{bmatrix} 0 & 4 \\ 5 & 2 \end{bmatrix}\begin{bmatrix} -4 & 1 \\ 8 & -3 \end{bmatrix} = \begin{bmatrix} \_\_\_ & \_\_\_ \\ \_\_\_ & \_\_\_ \end{bmatrix}$

Your Notes

✔ ***Checkpoint*** **Complete the following exercises.**

2. Subtract $\begin{bmatrix} 3 & -5 \\ 8 & -4 \end{bmatrix} - \begin{bmatrix} 9 & 7 \\ -3 & 1 \end{bmatrix}$.

3. The matrix $\begin{bmatrix} -3 & -1 & 0 \\ -1 & 3 & 0 \end{bmatrix}$ represents $\triangle ABC$. Find the image matrix that represents the translation of $\triangle ABC$ 3 units right and 2 units up. Then graph $\triangle ABC$ and its image.

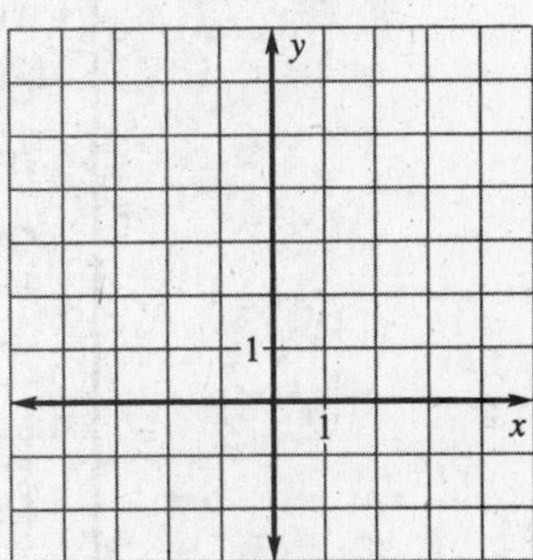

4. Multiply $\begin{bmatrix} 6 & 3 \\ 2 & -1 \end{bmatrix}\begin{bmatrix} 1 & 0 \\ 0 & -1 \end{bmatrix}$.

Your Notes

Example 5 *Solve a real-world problem*

Hockey A men's hockey team m needs 7 sticks, 30 pucks, and 4 helmets. A women's team w needs 5 sticks, 25 pucks, and 5 helmets. A hockey stick costs $30, a puck costs $4, and a helmet costs $50. Use matrix multiplication to find the total cost of equipment for each team.

Solution

Write equipment needs and costs per item in matrix form. You will use matrix multiplication, so form the matrices so that the number of columns of the ____________ matrix matches the number of rows of the ____________ matrix.

You could solve this problem arithmetically, multiplying the number of sticks by the price of sticks, and so on, then adding the costs for each team.

Equipment • **Cost** = **Total Cost**

	Sticks Pucks Helmets			Dollars			Dollars
m	[ ]	•	Stick	[ ]	=	m	?
w			Puck			w	?
			Helmet				

You can find the total cost of equipment for each team by multiplying the equipment matrix by the cost per item matrix. The equipment matrix is ___ × ___ and the cost per item matrix is ___ × ___, so their product is a ___ × ___ matrix.

[ ] [ ] = [ ] = [ ]

The total cost of equipment for the men's team is ______, and the total cost for the women's team is ______.

Checkpoint Complete the following exercise.

5. In Example 5, find the total costs if a stick costs $50, a puck costs $2, and a helmet costs $70.

Homework

9.3 Perform Reflections

Goal • Reflect a figure in any given line.

Your Notes

VOCABULARY

Line of reflection

Example 1 ***Graph reflections in horizontal and vertical lines***

The vertices of $\triangle ABC$ are $A(1, 2)$, $B(3, 0)$, and $C(5, 3)$. Graph the reflection of $\triangle ABC$ described.

a. In the line n: $x = 2$

b. In the line m: $y = 3$

Solution

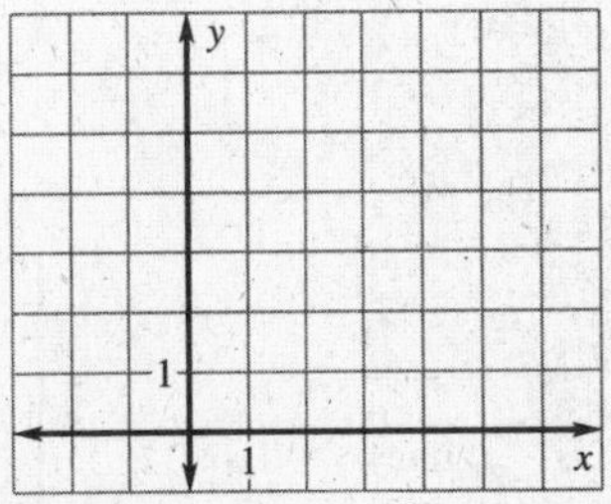

a. Point A is 1 unit _____ of n, so its reflection A' is 1 unit _____ of n at (___, ___). Also, B' is 1 unit _____ of n at (___, ___), and C' is 3 units _____ of n at (_____, ____).

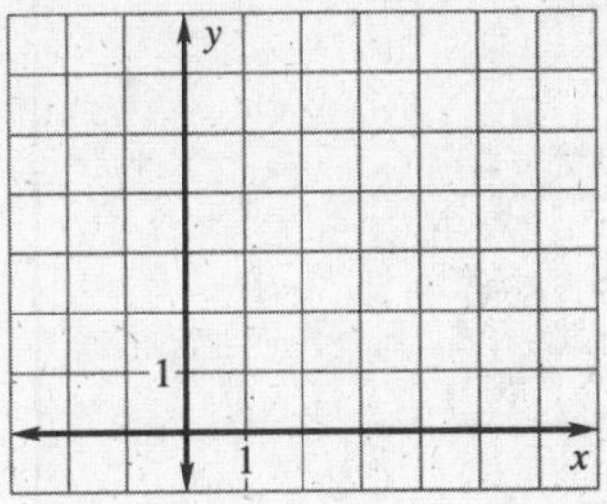

b. Point A is 1 unit _______ m, so A' is 1 unit _______ m at (___, ___). Also, B' is 3 units _______ m at (___, ___). Because point C is on line m, you know that C = ____.

✔ ***Checkpoint*** **Complete the following exercise.**

1. Graph the reflection of $\triangle ABC$ from Example 1 in the line $y = 2$.

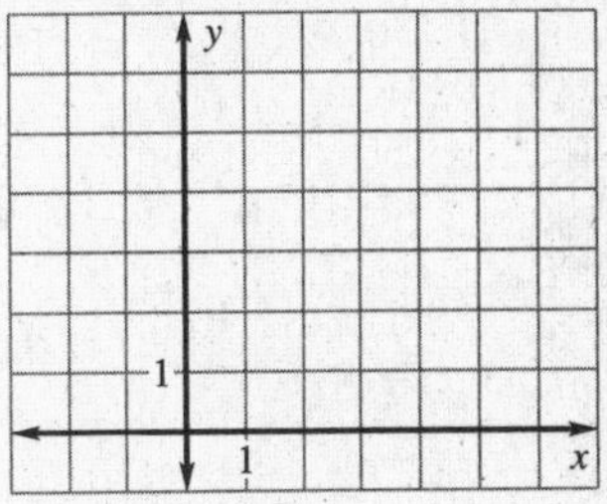

Your Notes

The product of the slopes of perpendicular lines is -1.

Example 2 *Graph a reflection in $y = x$*

The endpoints of $\overline{CD}$ are $C(-2, 2)$ and $D(1, 2)$. Reflect the segment in the line $y = x$. Graph the segment and its image.

Solution

The slope of $y = x$ is ___. The segment from C to its image, $\overline{CC'}$, is ______________ to the line of reflection $y = x$, so the slope of $\overline{CC'}$ will be _____ (because $1(-1) =$ _____). From C, move ___ units right and ___ units down to $y = x$. From that point, move ___ units right and ___ units down to locate C'(___, _____).

The slope of $\overline{DD'}$ will also be _____. From D, move _____ units right and _____ units down to $y = x$. Then move _____ units right and _____ units down to locate D'(___, ___).

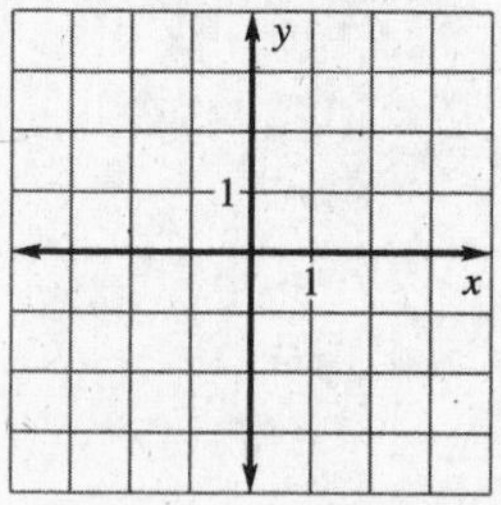

COORDINATE RULES FOR REFLECTIONS

- If (a, b) is reflected in the x-axis, its image is the point (___, _____).
- If (a, b) is reflected in the y-axis, its image is the point (_____, ___).
- If (a, b) is reflected in the line $y = x$, its image is the point (___, ___).
- If (a, b) is reflected in the line $y = -x$, its image is the point (_____, _____).

Your Notes

Example 3 ***Graph a reflection in y = −x***

Reflect $\overline{CD}$ from Example 2 in the line $y = -x$. Graph $\overline{CD}$ and its image.

Solution

Use the coordinate rule for reflecting in the line $y = -x$.

$(a, b) \rightarrow (-b, -a)$

$C(-2, 2) \rightarrow C'($_____, _____$)$

$D(1, 2) \rightarrow D'($_____, _____$)$

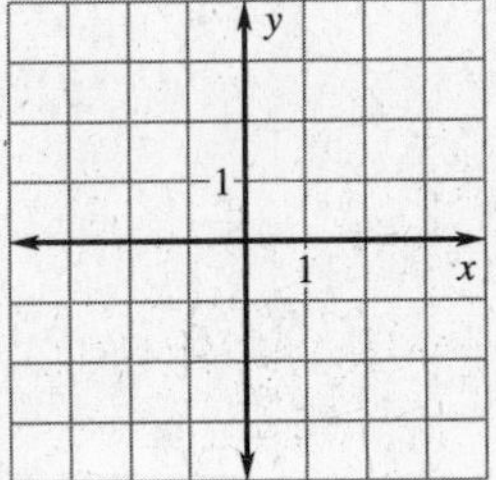

Checkpoint **The endpoints of $\overline{JK}$ are $J(-1, -2)$ and $K(1, -2)$. Reflect the segment in the given line. Graph the segment and its image.**

2. $y = x$

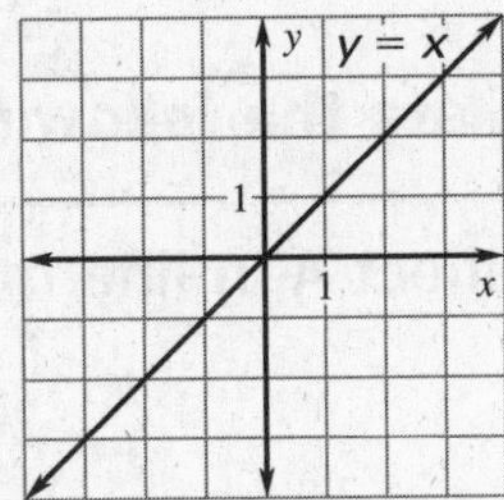

3. $y = -x$

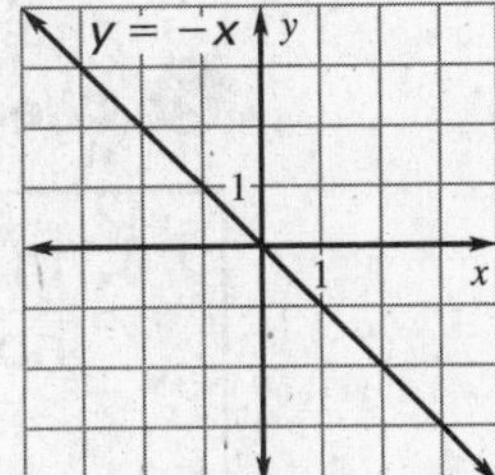

THEOREM 9.2: REFLECTION THEOREM

A reflection is an isometry.

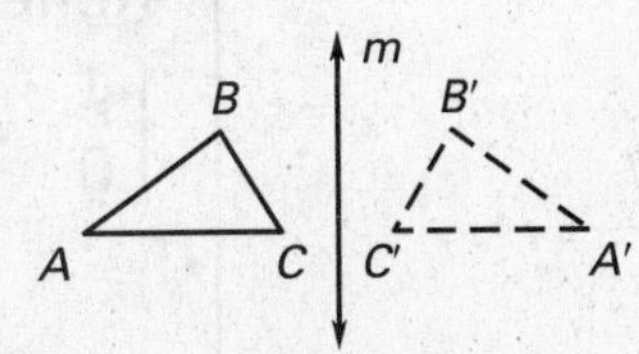

Your Notes

Example 4 *Find a minimum distance*

Tools Workers are retrieving tools that they need for a project. One will enter the building at point *A* and the other at point *B*. Where should they park on driveway *m* to minimize the distance they will walk?

m

Solution

Reflect *B* in line *m* to obtain *B′*. Then draw $\overline{AB'}$. Label the __________ of $\overline{AB'}$ and *m* as *C*. Because *AB′* is the ________ distance between *A* and *B′* and *BC* = _____, park at point ___ to minimize the combined distance, *AC* + *BC*, they have to walk.

A B

m

Checkpoint Complete the following exercise.

4. In Example 4, reflect *A* in line *m*. What do you notice?

A B

m

REFLECTION MATRICES

Reflection in the *x*-axis.

$$\begin{bmatrix} 1 & 0 \\ 0 & -1 \end{bmatrix}$$

Reflection in the *y*-axis.

$$\begin{bmatrix} -1 & 0 \\ 0 & 1 \end{bmatrix}$$

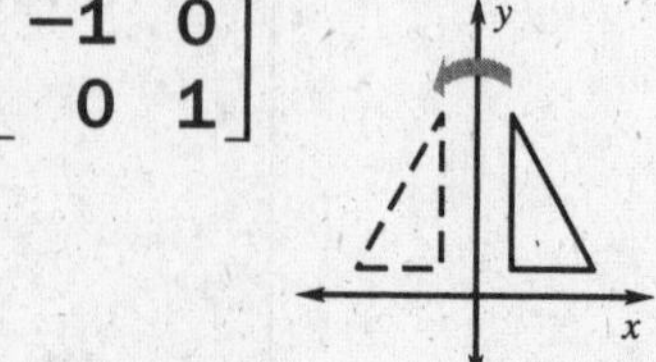

Your Notes

Example 5 ***Use matrix multiplication to reflect a polygon***

The vertices of △*DEF* are *D*(1, 2), *E*(2, 3), and *F*(4, 1). Find the reflection of △*DEF* in the *y*-axis using matrix multiplication. Graph △*DEF* and its image.

Solution

Step 1 **Multiply** the polygon matrix by the matrix for a reflection in the *y*-axis.

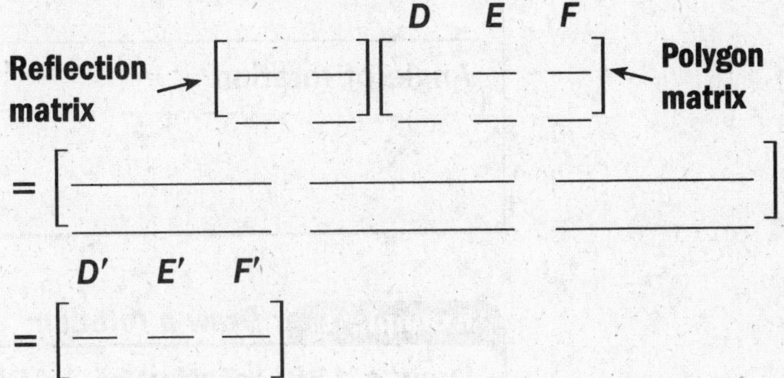

Step 2 **Graph** △*DEF* and △*D′E′F′*.

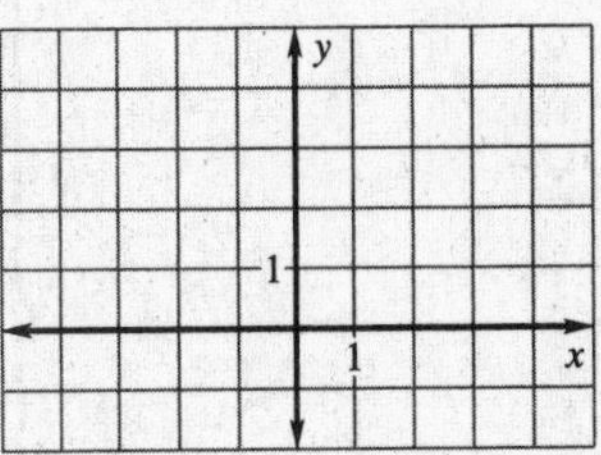

✓ ***Checkpoint*** **Complete the following exercise.**

5. The vertices of △*QRS* are *Q*(−1, 4), *R*(0, 1), and *S*(2, 3). Find the reflection of △*QRS* in the *x*-axis using matrix multiplication.

Homework

9.4 Perform Rotations

Goal • Rotate figures about a point.

Your Notes

VOCABULARY

Center of rotation

Angle of rotation

Example 1 ***Draw a rotation***

Draw a 150° rotation of △*ABC* about *P*.

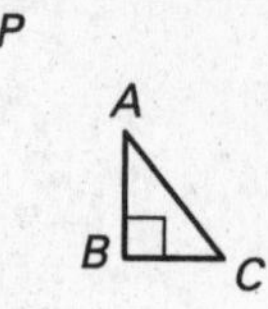

Solution

Step 1 **Draw** a segment from *A* to *P*.

Step 2 **Draw** a ray to form a 150° angle with $\overline{PA}$.

Step 3 **Draw** *A′* so that *PA′* = *PA*.

Step 4 **Repeat** Steps 1–3 for each vertex. Draw △*A′B′C′*.

Checkpoint **Complete the following exercise.**

1. Draw a 60° rotation of △*GHJ* about *P*.

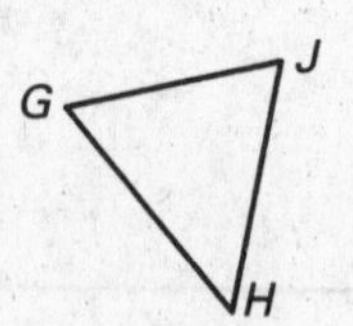

Your Notes

COORDINATE RULES FOR ROTATIONS ABOUT THE ORIGIN

When a point (a, b) is rotated counterclockwise about the origin, the following are true:

1. For a rotation of 90°,
$(a, b) \rightarrow$ (_____, ____).

2. For a rotation of 180°,
$(a, b) \rightarrow$ (_____, _____).

3. For a rotation of 270°,
$(a, b) \rightarrow$ (____, _____).

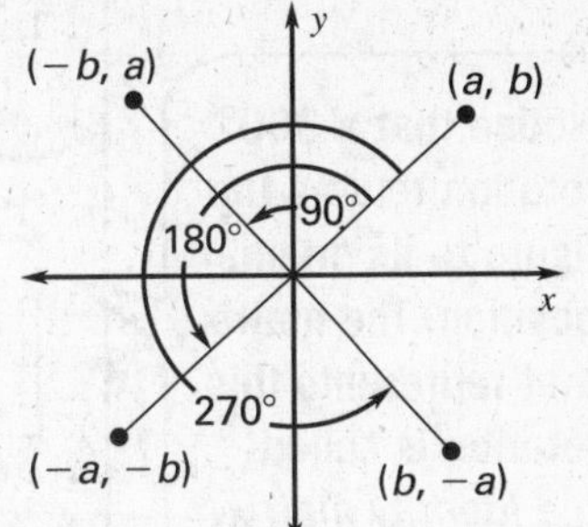

Example 2 *Rotate a figure using the coordinate rules*

Graph quadrilateral *KLMN* with vertices *K*(3, 2), *L*(4, 2), *M*(4, −3), and *N*(2, −1). Then rotate the quadrilateral 270° about the origin.

Solution

Graph *KLMN*. Use the coordinate rule for a 270° rotation to find the images of the vertices.

$(a, b) \rightarrow (b, -a)$

$K(3, 2) \rightarrow K'$(____, _____)

$L(4, 2) \rightarrow L'$(____, _____)

$M(4, -3) \rightarrow M'$(_____, _____)

$N(2, -1) \rightarrow N'$(_____, _____)

Graph the image $K'L'M'N'$.

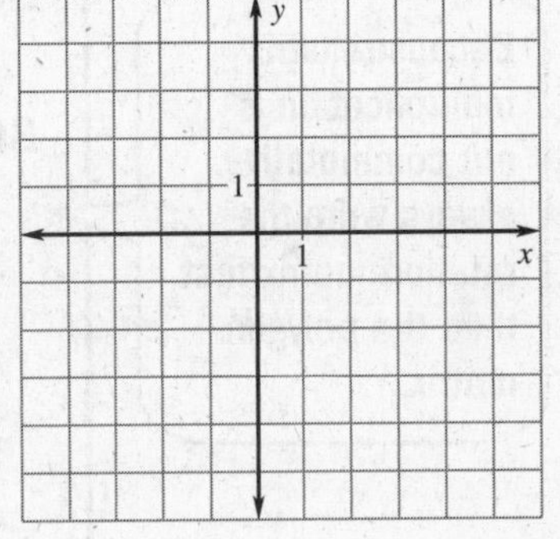

✔ ***Checkpoint*** **Complete the following exercise.**

2. Graph *KLMN* in Example 2. Then rotate the quadrilateral 90° about the origin.

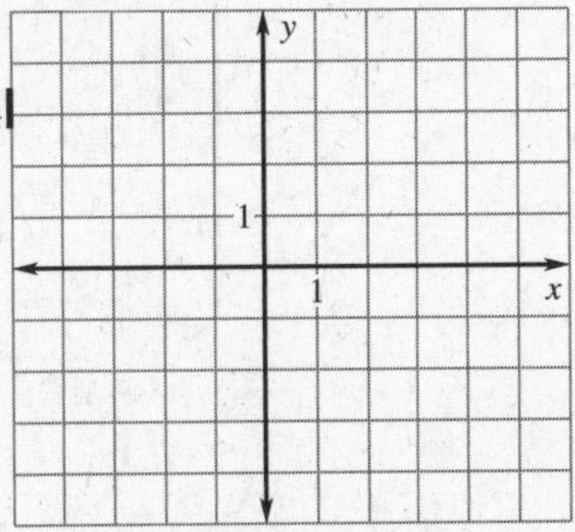

Your Notes

ROTATION MATRICES (COUNTERCLOCKWISE)

90° rotation

$$\begin{bmatrix} 0 & -1 \\ 1 & 0 \end{bmatrix}$$

180° rotation

$$\begin{bmatrix} -1 & 0 \\ 0 & -1 \end{bmatrix}$$

270° rotation

$$\begin{bmatrix} 0 & 1 \\ -1 & 0 \end{bmatrix}$$

360° rotation

$$\begin{bmatrix} 1 & 0 \\ 0 & 1 \end{bmatrix}$$

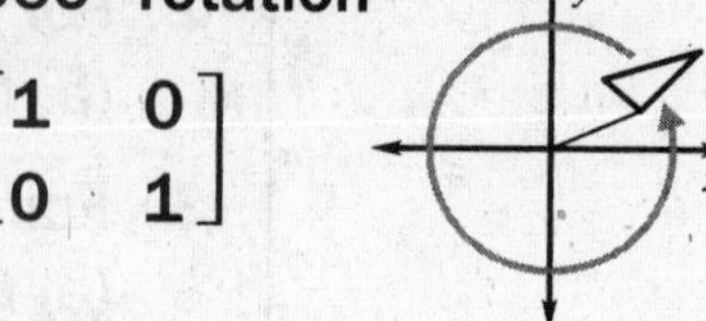

Notice that a 360° rotation returns the figure to its original position. The matrix that represents this rotation is called the *identity matrix*.

Example 3 ***Use matrices to rotate a figure***

Trapezoid *DEFG* has vertices *D*(−1, 3), *E*(1, 3), *F*(2, 1), and *G*(1, 0). Find the image matrix for a 180° rotation of *DEFG* about the origin. Graph *DEFG* and its image.

Solution

Step 1 Write the polygon matrix:

$$\begin{array}{cccc} D & E & F & G \end{array}$$
$$\begin{bmatrix} \_\_ & \_\_ & \_\_ & \_\_ \\ \_\_ & \_\_ & \_\_ & \_\_ \end{bmatrix}$$

Step 2 Multiply by the matrix for a 180° rotation.

Because matrix multiplication is not commutative, always write the rotation matrix first, then the polygon matrix.

$$\begin{bmatrix} \_\_ & \_\_ \\ \_\_ & \_\_ \end{bmatrix} \overset{\begin{array}{cccc} D & E & F & G \end{array}}{\begin{bmatrix} \_\_ & \_\_ & \_\_ & \_\_ \\ \_\_ & \_\_ & \_\_ & \_\_ \end{bmatrix}} = \overset{\begin{array}{cccc} D' & E' & F' & G' \end{array}}{\begin{bmatrix} \_\_ & \_\_ & \_\_ & \_\_ \\ \_\_ & \_\_ & \_\_ & \_\_ \end{bmatrix}}$$

Rotation matrix — **Polygon matrix** — **Image matrix**

Step 3 Graph the preimage *DEFG*.
Graph the image *D′E′F′G′*.

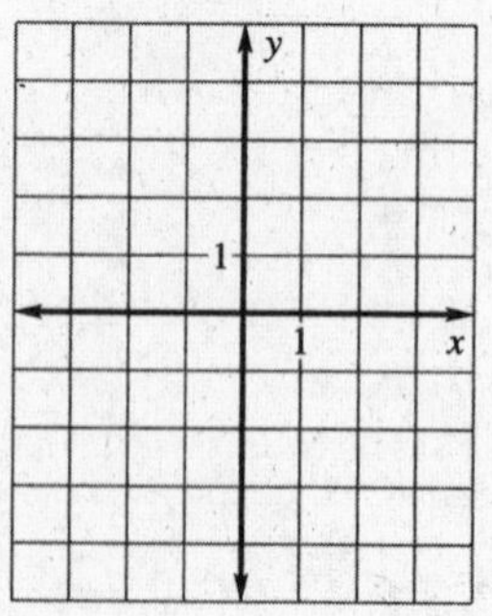

Your Notes

THEOREM 9.3: ROTATION THEOREM

A rotation is an isometry.

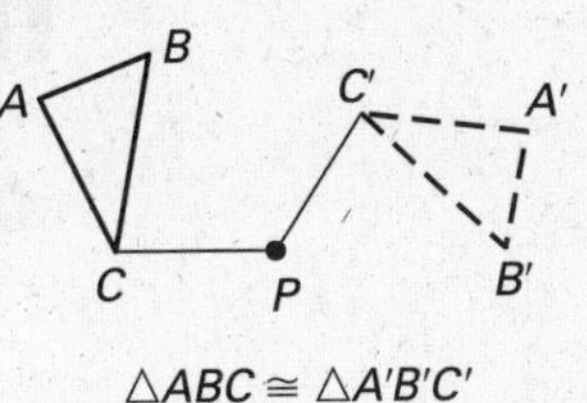

Example 4 ***Find side lengths in a rotation***

The quadrilateral is rotated about *P*. Find the value of *y*.

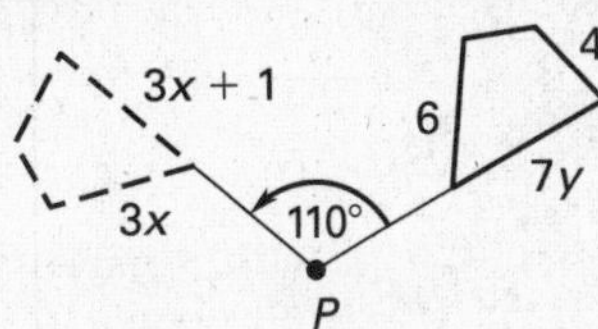

Solution

By Theorem 9.3, the rotation is an __________, so corresponding side lengths are _______. Then $3x =$ ___, so $x =$ ___. Now set up an equation to solve for y.

___$y =$ ________	**Corresponding lengths in an isometry are equal.**
___$y =$ __________	**Substitute ___ for *x*.**
$y =$ ___	**Solve for *y*.**

✓ ***Checkpoint*** **Complete the following exercises.**

3. Use the quadrilateral in Example 3. Find the image matrix after a 270° rotation about the origin.

4. The triangle is rotated about *P*. Find the value of *b*.

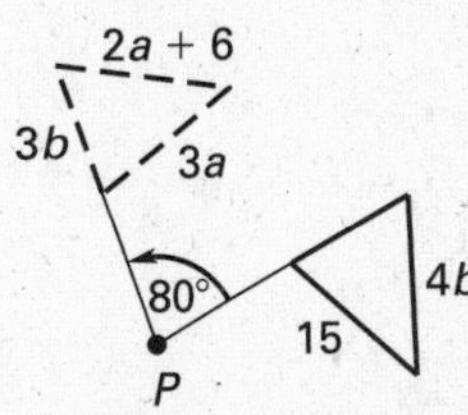

Homework

9.5 Apply Compositions of Transformations

Goal • Perform combinations of two or more transformations.

Your Notes

VOCABULARY

Glide reflection

Composition of transformations

Example 1 ***Find the image of a glide reflection***

The vertices of $\triangle ABC$ are $A(2, 1)$, $B(5, 3)$, and $C(6, 2)$. Find the image of $\triangle ABC$ after the glide reflection.

Translation: $(x, y) \rightarrow (x - 8, y)$

Reflection: in the x-axis

The line of reflection must be parallel to the direction of the translation to be a glide reflection.

Solution

Begin by graphing $\triangle ABC$. Then graph $\triangle A'B'C'$ after a translation 8 units _____. Finally, graph $\triangle A''B''C''$ after a reflection in the x-axis.

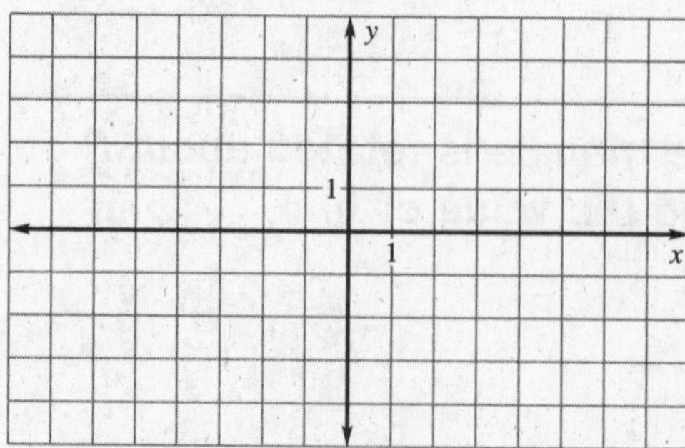

Your Notes

THEOREM 9.4: COMPOSITION THEOREM

The composition of two (or more) isometries is an isometry.

Example 2 ***Find the image of a composition***

> Unless you are told otherwise, do the transformations in the order given.

The endpoints of $\overline{CD}$ are $C(-2, 6)$ and $D(-1, 3)$. Graph the image of $\overline{CD}$ after the composition.

Reflection: in the *y*-axis
Rotation: 90° about the origin

Solution

Step 1 Graph $\overline{CD}$.

Step 2 Reflect $\overline{CD}$ in the *y*-axis. $\overline{C'D'}$ has endpoints $C'($___, ___$)$ and $D'($___, ___$)$.

Step 3 Rotate $\overline{C'D'}$ 90° about the origin. $\overline{C''D''}$ has endpoints $C''($_____, ___$)$ and $D''($_____, ___$)$.

✔ ***Checkpoint*** **Complete the following exercises.**

1. Suppose $\triangle ABC$ in Example 1 is translated 5 units down, then reflected in the *y*-axis. What are the coordinates of the vertices of the image?

2. Graph $\overline{CD}$ from Example 2. Do the rotation first, followed by the reflection.

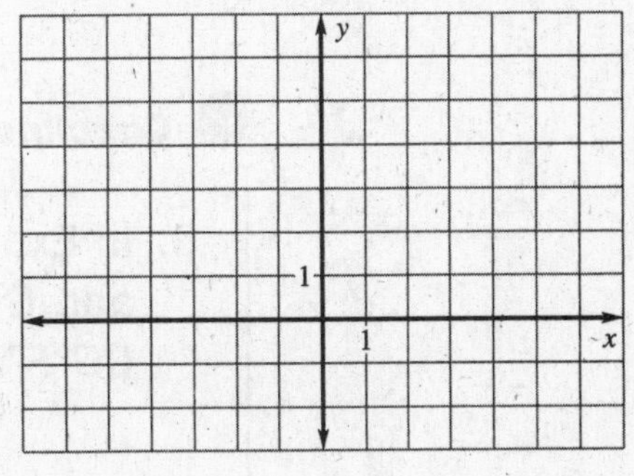

Your Notes

THEOREM 9.5: REFLECTIONS IN PARALLEL LINES THEOREM

If lines k and m are parallel, then a reflection in line k followed by a reflection in line m is the same as a ____________.

If P'' is the image of P, then:

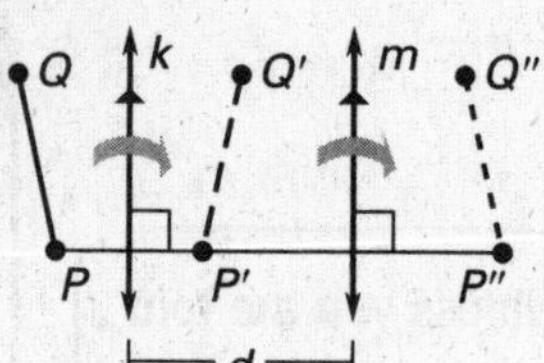

1. $\overline{PP''}$ is perpendicular to k and m, and
2. $PP'' = 2d$, where d is the distance between k and m.

Example 3 ***Use Theorem 9.5***

In the diagram, a reflection in line k maps $\overline{GF}$ to $\overline{G'F'}$. A reflection in line m maps $\overline{G'F'}$ to $\overline{G''F''}$. Also, $FA = 6$ and $DF'' = 3$.

a. Name any segments congruent to each segment: $\overline{GF}$, $\overline{FA}$, and $\overline{GB}$.

b. Does $AD = BC$? *Explain.*

c. What is the length of $\overline{GG''}$?

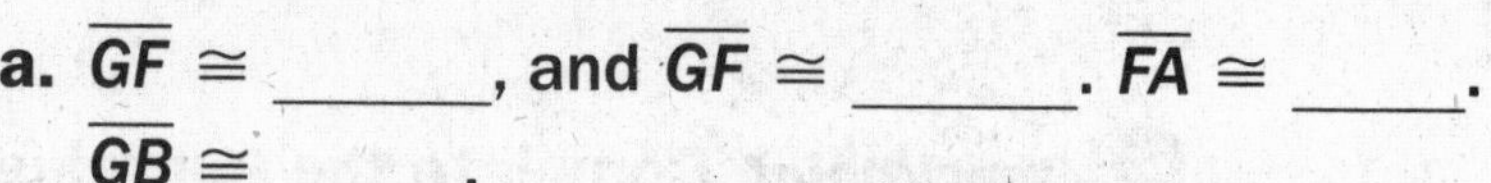

a. $\overline{GF} \cong$ ______, and $\overline{GF} \cong$ ______. $\overline{FA} \cong$ _____.
$\overline{GB} \cong$ _____.

b. _____, AD ____ BC because $\overline{GG''}$ and $\overline{FF''}$ are ____________ to both k and m, so $\overline{BC}$ and $\overline{AD}$ are opposite sides of a __________.

c. By the properties of reflections, $F'A =$ ___ and $F'D =$ ___. Theorem 9.5 implies that $GG'' = FF'' =$ ___ • _____, so the length of $\overline{GG''}$ is ___(___ + ___), or ____ units.

✔ *Checkpoint* Complete the following exercise.

3. In Example 3, suppose you are given that $BC = 10$ and $G'F' = 6$. What is the perimeter of quadrilateral $GG''F''F$?

Your Notes

THEOREM 9.6: REFLECTIONS IN INTERSECTING LINES THEOREM

If lines k and m intersect at point P, then a reflection in k followed by a reflection in m is the same as a __________ about ___.

The angle of rotation is $2x°$, where $x°$ is the measure of the acute or right angle formed by k and m.

Example 4 ***Use Theorem 9.6***

In the diagram, the figure is reflected in line k. The image is then reflected in line m. Describe a single transformation that maps F to F''.

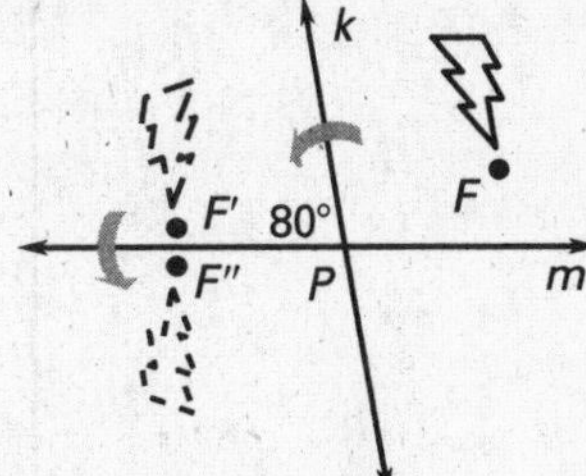

Solution

The measure of the acute angle formed between lines k and m is _____. So, by Theorem 9.6, a single transformation that maps F to F'' is a ______ rotation about _________.

You can check that this is correct by tracing lines k and m and point F, then rotating the point ______.

✔ ***Checkpoint*** **Complete the following exercise.**

4. In the diagram below, the preimage is reflected in line k, then in line m. Describe a single transformation that maps G to G''.

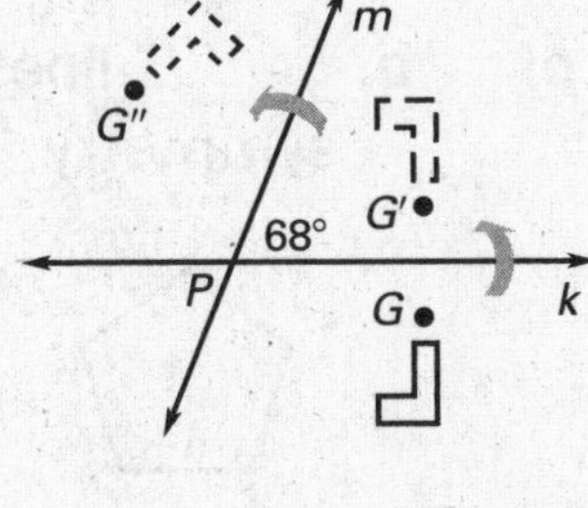

Homework

9.6 Identify Symmetry

Goal • Identify line and rotational symmetries of a figure.

Your Notes

VOCABULARY

Line symmetry

Line of symmetry

Rotational symmetry

Center of symmetry

Example 1 ***Identify lines of symmetry***

How many lines of symmetry does the figure have?

a. **b.** **c.**

Solution

a. ______ lines of symmetry **b.** ______ lines of symmetry **c.** ______ line of symmetry

Notice that the lines of symmetry are also lines of reflection.

Your Notes

Example 2 *Identify rotational symmetry*

Does the figure have rotational symmetry? If so, *describe* any rotations that map the figure onto itself.

a. Square

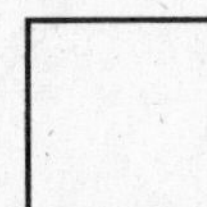

b. Regular hexagon

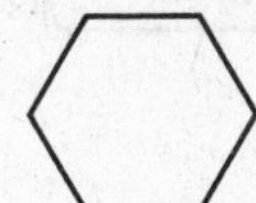

c. Kite

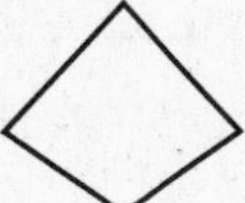

Solution

a. The square _____ rotational symmetry. The center is the intersection of the diagonals. Rotations of _____ or ______ about the center map the square onto itself.

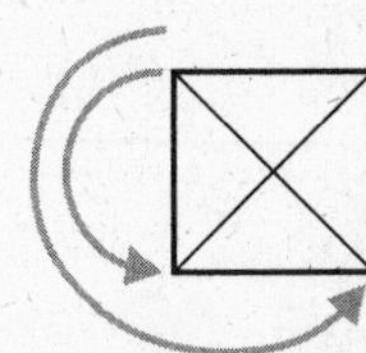

b. The regular hexagon _____ rotational symmetry. The center is the intersection of the diagonals. Rotations of _____, ______, or ______ about the center all map the hexagon onto itself.

c. The kite ______________ rotational symmetry because no rotation of ______ or less maps the kite onto itself.

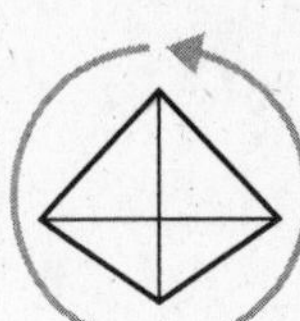

Example 3 *Identify symmetry*

Identify the line symmetry and rotational symmetry of the figure at the right.

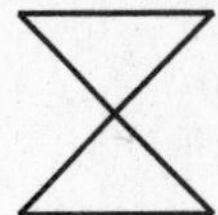

Solution

The figure _____ line symmetry. ______ lines of symmetry can be drawn for the figure.

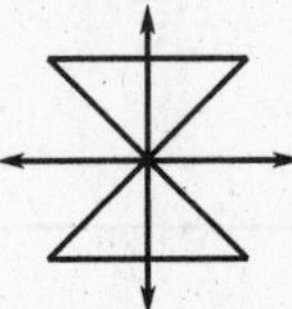

For a figure with *s* lines of symmetry, the smallest rotation that maps the figure onto itself has the measure ______. So, the figure has _____, or ______ rotational symmetry.

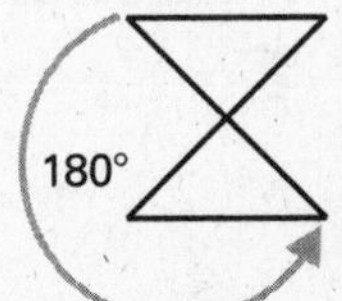

Your Notes

✔ ***Checkpoint*** **How many lines of symmetry does the figure have?**

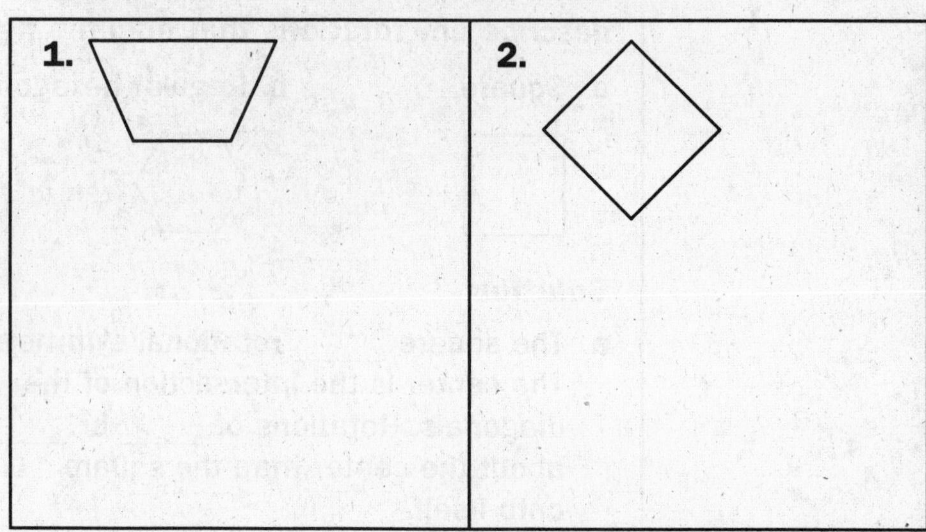

In Exercises 3 and 4, does the figure have rotational symmetry? If so, *describe* any rotations that map the figure onto itself.

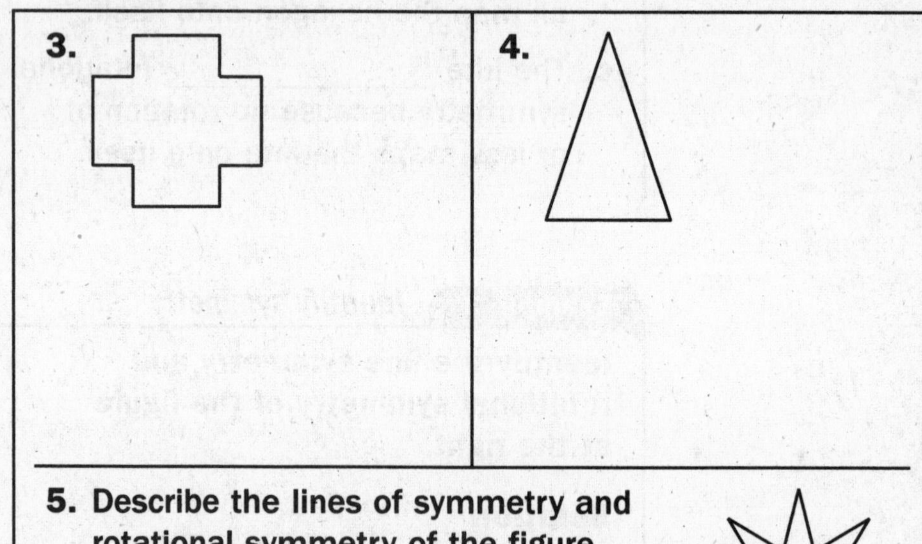

5. Describe the lines of symmetry and rotational symmetry of the figure at the right.

Homework

9.7 Identify and Perform Dilations

• Use drawing tools and matrices to draw dilations.

Your Notes

VOCABULARY

Scalar multiplication

Example 1 *Identify dilations*

Find the scale factor of the dilation. Then tell whether the dilation is a *reduction* or an *enlargement*.

a.

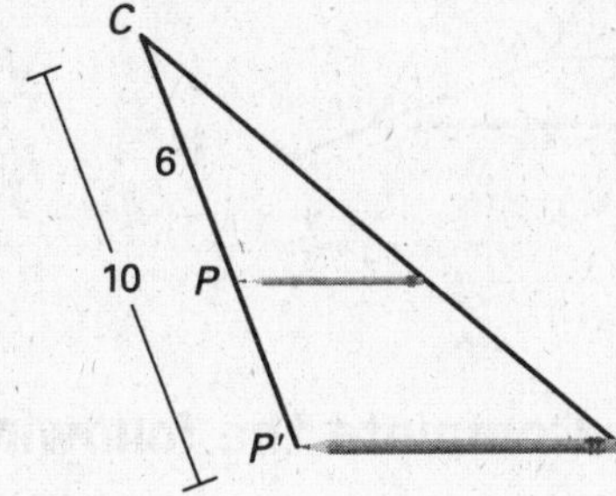

b.

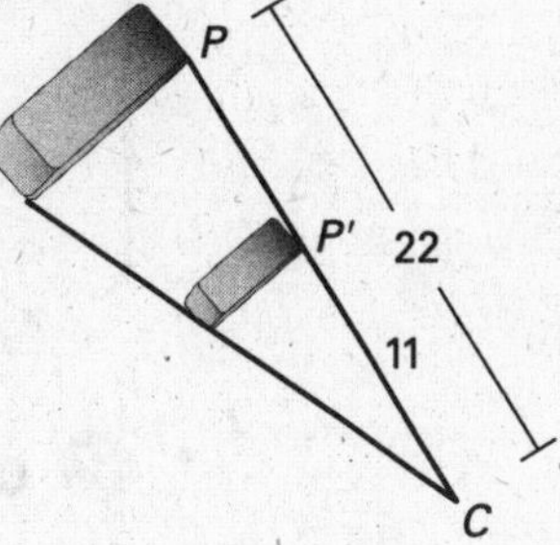

Solution

a. Because $\frac{CP'}{CP} =$ ____, the scale factor is $k =$ ____.
The image P' is an __________.

b. Because $\frac{CP'}{CP} =$ ____, the scale factor is $k =$ ____.
The image P' is a __________.

Checkpoint Complete the following exercise.

1. In a dilation, $CP' = 4$ and $CP = 20$. Tell whether the dilation is a *reduction* or an *enlargement* and find its scale factor.

Your Notes

Example 2 *Draw a dilation*

Draw and label $\square LMNP$. Then construct a dilation of $\square LMNP$ with point L as the center of dilation and a scale factor of $\frac{1}{2}$.

Solution

Step 1 Draw $LMNP$. Draw rays from L through vertices M, N, and P.

Step 2 Open the compass to the length of $\overline{LM}$. Locate M' on $\overrightarrow{LM}$ so $LM' =$ ____ (LM). Locate N' and P' the same way.

Step 3 Add a second label L' to point L. Draw the sides of $L'M'N'P'$.

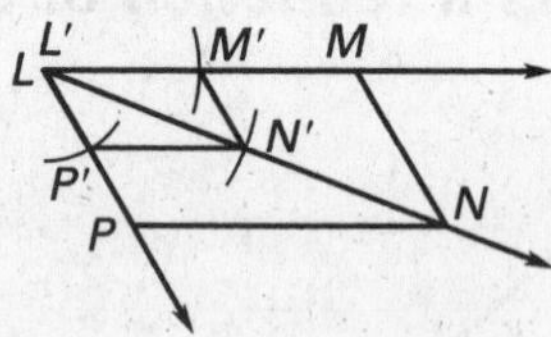

Checkpoint Complete the following exercise.

2. Draw and label $\triangle PQR$. Then construct a dilation of $\triangle PQR$ with P as the center of dilation and a scale factor of 2.

Your Notes

Example 3 *Scalar multiplication*

Simplify the product: $3\begin{bmatrix} 0 & 5 & 4 \\ 2 & -2 & -1 \end{bmatrix}$.

Solution

$3\begin{bmatrix} 0 & 5 & 4 \\ 2 & -2 & -1 \end{bmatrix} = \begin{bmatrix} \_\_\_ & \_\_\_ & \_\_\_ \\ \_\_\_ & \_\_\_ & \_\_\_ \end{bmatrix}$ **Multiply each element in the matrix by ___.**

$= \begin{bmatrix} \_\_ & \_\_ \\ \_\_ & \_\_ & \_\_ \end{bmatrix}$ **Simplify.**

Checkpoint **Simplify the product.**

3. $4\begin{bmatrix} -6 & 3 & 2 \\ 5 & -1 & 4 \end{bmatrix}$	**4.** $-3\begin{bmatrix} 5 & -1 & -2 \\ -2 & 0 & 4 \end{bmatrix}$

Example 4 *Use scalar multiplication in a dilation*

The vertices of quadrilateral *ABCD* are *A*(−3, 0), *B*(0, 6), *C*(3, 6), and *D*(3, 3). Use scalar multiplication to find the image of *ABCD* after a dilation with its center at the origin and a scale factor of $\frac{1}{3}$. Graph *ABCD* and its image.

Solution

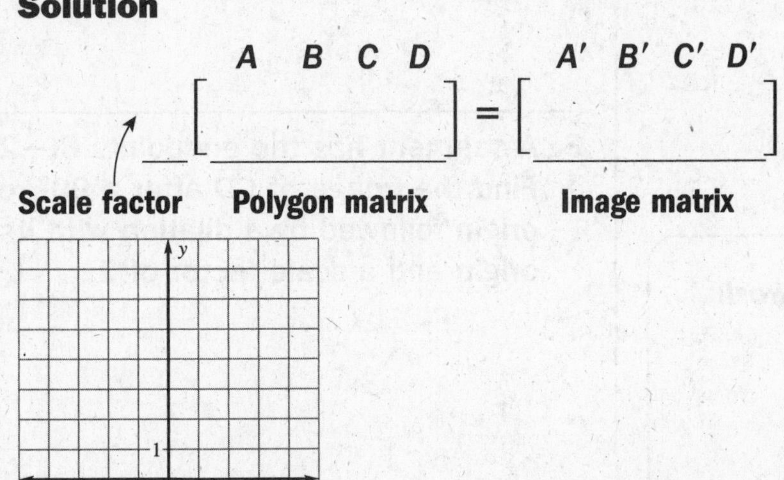

Your Notes

Example 5 ***Find the image of a composition***

The vertices of $\triangle KLM$ are $K(-3, 0)$, $L(-2, 1)$, and $M(-1, -1)$. Find the image of $\triangle KLM$ after the given composition.

Translation: $(x, y) \rightarrow (x + 4, y + 2)$
Dilation: centered at the origin with a scale factor of 2

Solution

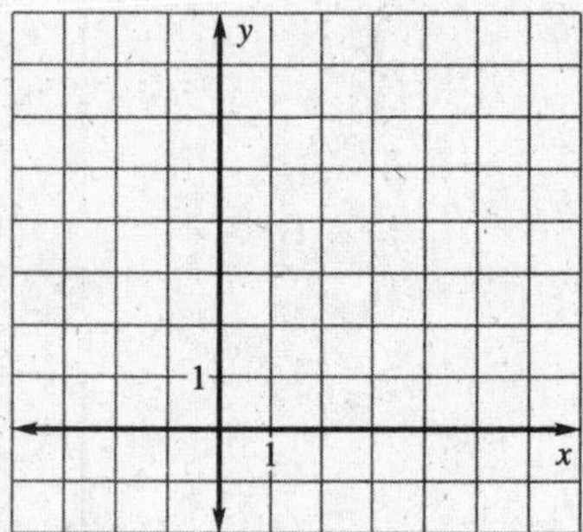

Step 1 Graph the preimage $\triangle KLM$ in the coordinate plane.

Step 2 Translate $\triangle KLM$ 4 units to the ________ and 2 units ______. Label it $\triangle K'L'M'$.

Step 3 Dilate $\triangle K'L'M'$ using the ________ as the center and a scale factor of 2 to find $\triangle K''L''M''$.

Checkpoint **Complete the following exercises.**

5. The vertices of $\triangle RST$ are $R(-4, 3)$, $S(-1, -2)$, and $T(2, 1)$. Use scalar multiplication to find the vertices of $\triangle R'S'T'$ after a dilation with its center at the origin and a scale factor of 2.

6. A segment has the endpoints $C(-2, 2)$ and $D(2, 2)$. Find the image of $\overline{CD}$ after a 90° rotation about the origin followed by a dilation with its center at the origin and a scale factor of 2.

Homework

Words to Review

Give an example of the vocabulary word.

Image	Preimage
Isometry	Vector
Initial point, Terminal point	Horizontal component, Vertical component
Component form	Matrix, Element
Dimensions	Line of reflection

Center of rotation	Angle of rotation
Glide reflection	Composition of transformations
Line symmetry, Line of symmetry	Rotational symmetry
Center of symmetry	Scalar multiplication

Review your notes and Chapter 9 by using the Chapter Review on pages 636–639 of your textbook.

10.1 Use Properties of Tangents

Goal • Use properties of a tangent to a circle.

Your Notes

VOCABULARY

Circle

Center

Radius

Chord

Diameter

Secant

Tangent

Example 1 ***Identify special segments and lines***

Tell whether the line, ray, or segment is best described as a *radius*, *chord*, *diameter*, *secant*, or *tangent* of $\odot C$.

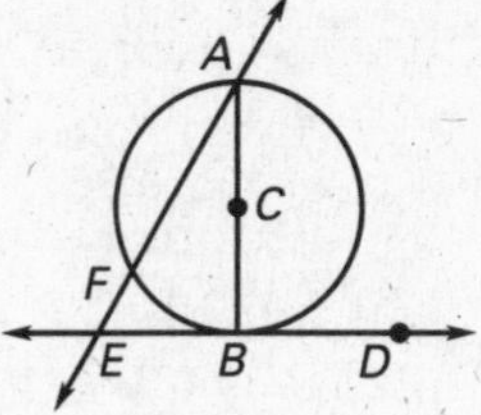

a. $\overline{BC}$ 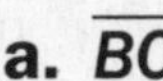 **b.** $\overleftrightarrow{EA}$ **c.** $\overrightarrow{DE}$

Solution

a. $\overline{BC}$ is a ________ because *C* is the center and *B* is a point on the circle.

b. $\overleftrightarrow{EA}$ is a ________ because it is a line that intersects the circle in two points.

c. $\overrightarrow{DE}$ is a ________ ray because it is contained in a line that intersects the circle at only one point.

Your Notes

Example 2 ***Find lengths in circles in a coordinate plane***

Use the diagram to find the given lengths.

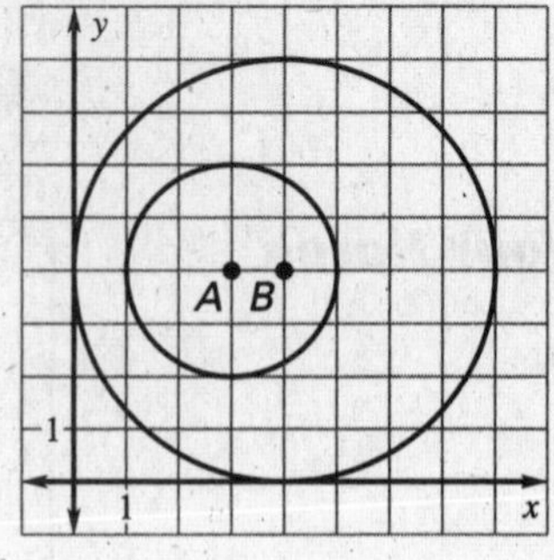

a. Radius of ⊙A

b. Diameter of ⊙A

c. Radius of ⊙B

d. Diameter of ⊙B

Solution

a. The radius of ⊙A is ___ units.

b. The diameter of ⊙A is ___ units.

c. The radius of ⊙B is ___ units.

d. The diameter of ⊙B is ___ units.

Checkpoint **Complete the following exercises.**

1. In Example 1, tell whether $\overline{AB}$ is best described as a *radius, chord, diameter, secant,* or *tangent. Explain.*

2. Use the diagram to find (a) the radius of ⊙C and (b) the diameter of ⊙D.

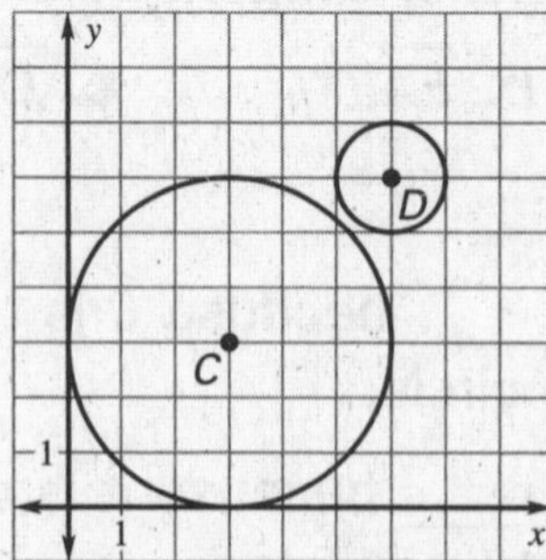

Your Notes

Example 3 *Draw common tangents*

Tell how many common tangents the circles have and draw them.

a. 

b. 

c. 

Solution

a. ___ common tangents

b. ___ common tangents

c. ___ common tangent

Checkpoint Tell how many common tangents the circles have and draw them.

3. 	4. 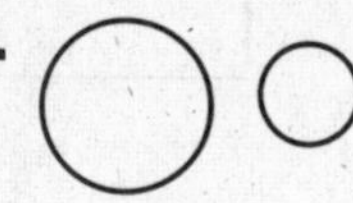

THEOREM 10.1

In a plane, a line is tangent to a circle if and only if the line is ________________ to a radius of the circle at its endpoint on the circle.

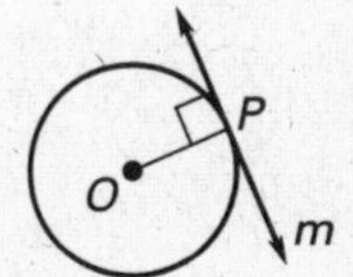

Your Notes

Example 4 ***Verify a tangent to a circle***

In the diagram, $\overline{RS}$ is a radius of $\odot R$. Is $\overline{ST}$ tangent to $\odot R$?

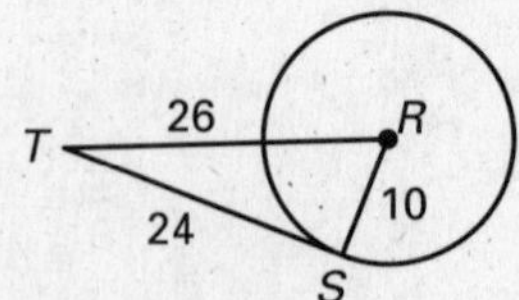

Solution

Use the Converse of the Pythagorean Theorem. Because $10^2 + 24^2 = 26^2$, $\triangle RST$ is a ______________ and $\overline{RS} \perp$ ____ . So, _____ is perpendicular to a radius of $\odot R$ at its endpoint on $\odot R$. By ________________, $\overline{ST}$ is tangent to $\odot R$.

✔ ***Checkpoint*** $\overline{RS}$ **is a radius of $\odot R$. Is $\overline{ST}$ tangent to $\odot R$?**

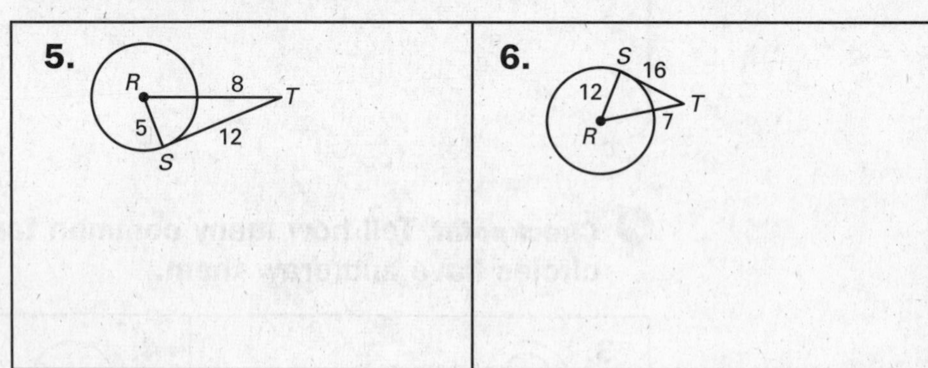

Example 5 ***Find the radius of a circle***

In the diagram, B is a point of tangency. Find the radius r of $\odot C$.

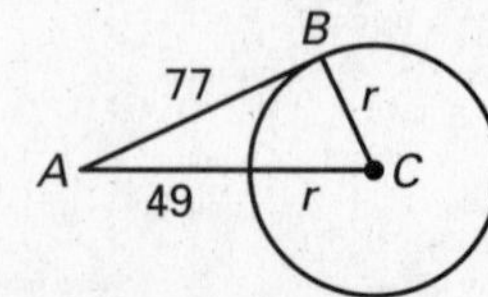

Solution

You know from Theorem 10.1 that $\overline{AB} \perp \overline{BC}$, so $\triangle ABC$ is a ________________. You can use the Pythagorean Theorem.

$AC^2 = BC^2 + AB^2$	**Pythagorean Theorem**
$(r + 49)^2 = r^2 + 77^2$	**Substitute.**
$r^2 +$ ____ $r +$ ______ $= r^2 +$ ______	**Multiply.**
____ $r =$ ______	**Subtract r^2 from each side.**
$r =$ ______	**Divide each side by ____.**

Your Notes

THEOREM 10.2

Tangent segments from a common external point are ________.

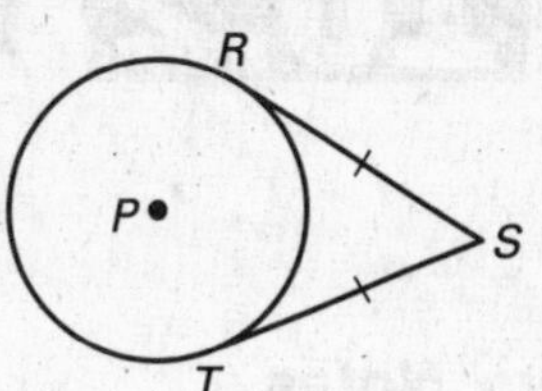

Example 6 *Use Theorem 10.2*

$\overline{QR}$ is tangent to ⊙C at R and $\overline{QS}$ is tangent to ⊙C at S. Find the value of x.

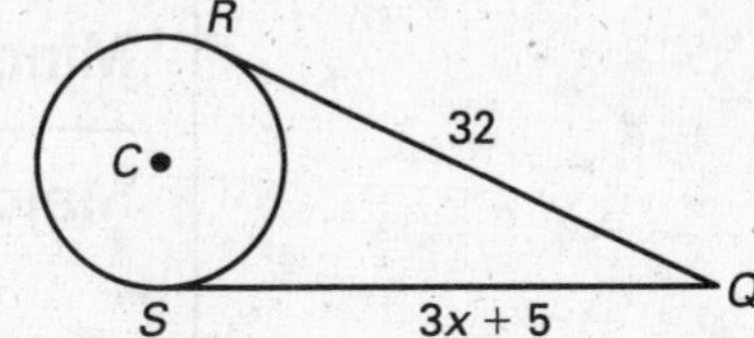

Solution

$QR = QS$	**Tangent segments from the same point are congruent.**
____ = ______	**Substitute.**
____ = x	**Solve for x.**

Checkpoint **Complete the following exercises.**

7. In the diagram, K is a point of tangency. Find the radius r of ⊙L.

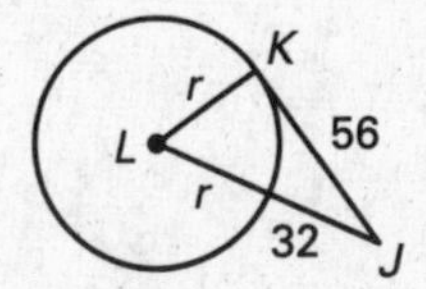

8. $\overline{RS}$ is tangent to ⊙C at S and $\overline{RT}$ is tangent to ⊙C at T. Find the value(s) of x.

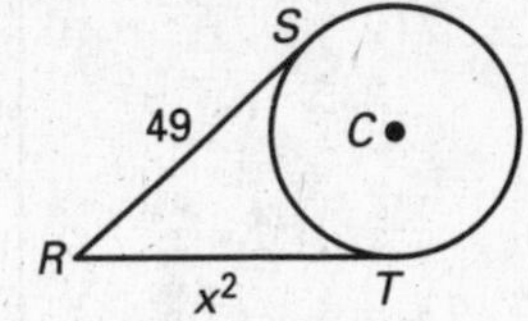

Homework

10.2 Find Arc Measures

Goal • Use angle measures to find arc measures.

Your Notes

VOCABULARY

Central angle

Minor arc

Major arc

Semicircle

Measure of a minor arc

Measure of a major arc

Congruent circles

Congruent arcs

MEASURING ARCS

The measure of a minor arc is the measure of its central angle. The expression $m\overset{\frown}{AB}$ is read as "the measure of arc AB."

The measure of the entire circle is _____. The measure of a major arc is the difference between _____ and the measure of the related minor arc. The measure of a semicircle is _____.

A, C, 50°, B, D

$m\overset{\frown}{AB} = 50°$

$m\overset{\frown}{ADB} = 310°$

Your Notes

Example 1 *Find measures of arcs*

Find the measure of each arc of $\odot C$, where $\overline{DF}$ is a diameter.

a. $\overset{\frown}{DE}$ **b.** $\overset{\frown}{DFE}$ **c.** $\overset{\frown}{DEF}$

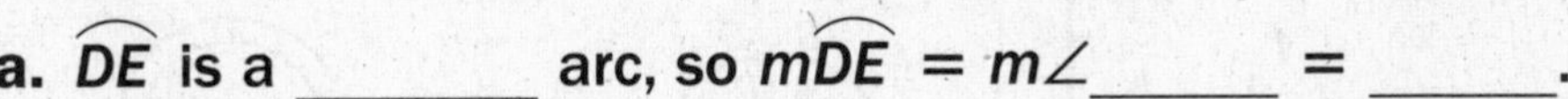

a. $\overset{\frown}{DE}$ is a ________ arc, so $m\overset{\frown}{DE} = m\angle$______ = ______.

b. $\overset{\frown}{DFE}$ is a ________ arc, so
$m\overset{\frown}{DFE}$ = ______ − ______ = ______.

c. $\overline{DF}$ is a diameter, so $\overset{\frown}{DEF}$ is a ___________, and
$m\overset{\frown}{DEF}$ = ______.

Checkpoint Complete the following exercise.

1. Find $m\overset{\frown}{RTS}$ in the diagram at the right.

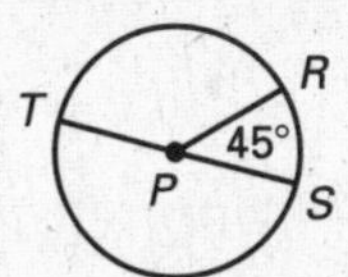

POSTULATE 23: ARC ADDITION POSTULATE

The measure of an arc formed by two adjacent arcs is the sum of the measures of the two arcs.

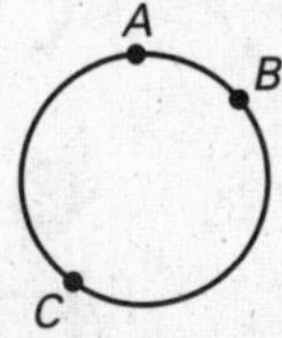

$m\overset{\frown}{ABC} = m$______ + m______

Example 2 *Find measures of arcs*

Money You join a new bank and divide your money several ways, as shown in the circle graph at the right. Find the indicated arc measures.

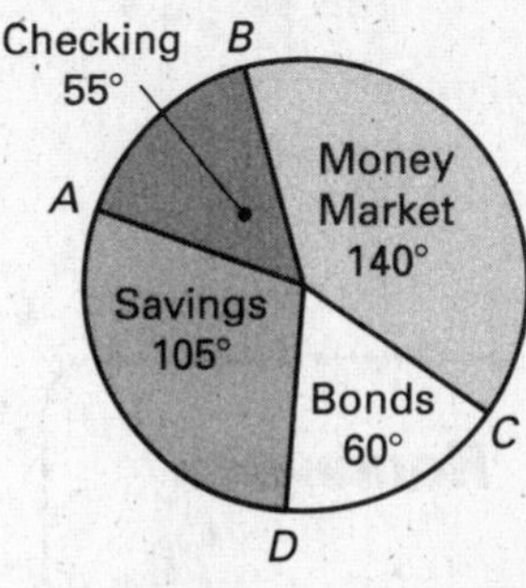

a. $m\overset{\frown}{BD}$ **b.** $m\overset{\frown}{BCD}$

The measure of a minor arc is less than 180°. The measure of a major arc is greater than 180°.

Solution

a. $m\overset{\frown}{BD} = m\overset{\frown}{BA} + m\overset{\frown}{AD}$
= ______ + ______
= ______

b. $m\overset{\frown}{BCD} = 360° - m\overset{\frown}{BD}$
= 360° − ______
= ______

Your Notes

Example 3 ***Identify congruent arcs***

Tell whether the given arcs are congruent. *Explain* why or why not.

a. $\overset{\frown}{BC}$ and $\overset{\frown}{DE}$ **b.** $\overset{\frown}{AB}$ and $\overset{\frown}{CD}$ **c.** $\overset{\frown}{FG}$ and $\overset{\frown}{HJ}$

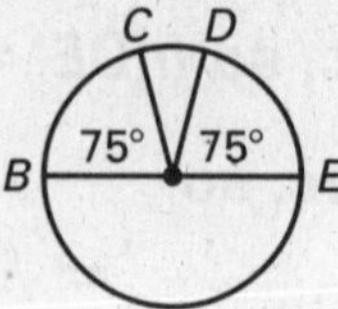

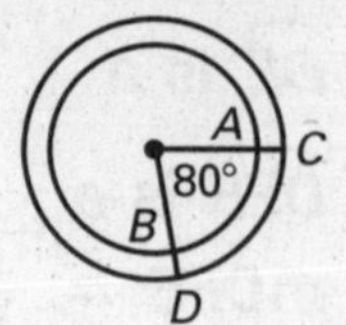

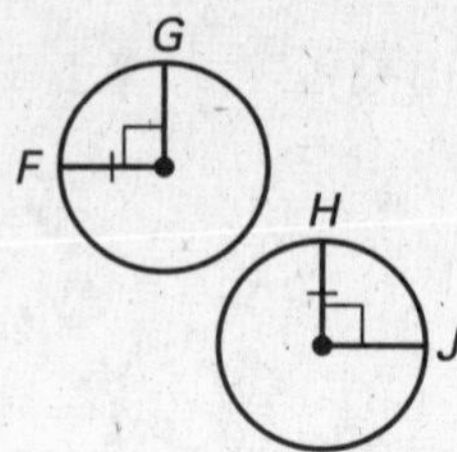

Solution

a. $\overset{\frown}{BC}$ ____ $\overset{\frown}{DE}$ because they are in ________________ and $m\overset{\frown}{BC}$ ____ $m\overset{\frown}{DE}$.

b. $\overset{\frown}{AB}$ and $\overset{\frown}{CD}$ have the same ____________, but they are ________________ because they are arcs of circles that are ______________.

c. $\overset{\frown}{FG}$ ____ $\overset{\frown}{HJ}$ because they are in ________________ and $m\overset{\frown}{FG}$ ____ $m\overset{\frown}{HJ}$.

✔ *Checkpoint* Complete the following exercises.

2. In Example 2, find (a) $m\overset{\frown}{BCA}$ and (b) $m\overset{\frown}{ABC}$.

3. In the diagram at the right, is $\overset{\frown}{PQ} \cong \overset{\frown}{SR}$? *Explain* why or why not.

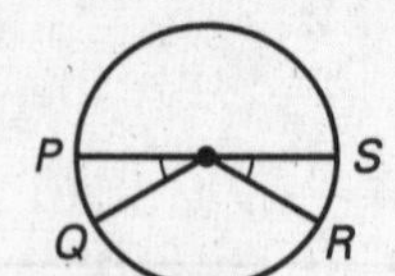

Homework

10.3 Apply Properties of Chords

Goal • Use relationships of arcs and chords in a circle.

Your Notes

THEOREM 10.3

In the same circle, or in congruent circles, two minor arcs are congruent if and only if their corresponding chords are congruent.

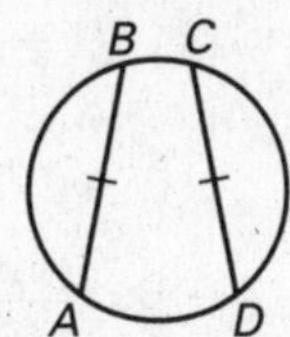

$\widehat{AB} \cong \widehat{CD}$ if and only if _____ $\cong$ _____.

Example 1 ***Use congruent chords to find an arc measure***

In the diagram, $\odot A \cong \odot D$, $\overline{BC} \cong \overline{EF}$, and $m\widehat{EF} = 125°$. Find $m\widehat{BC}$.

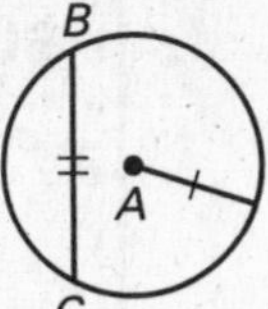

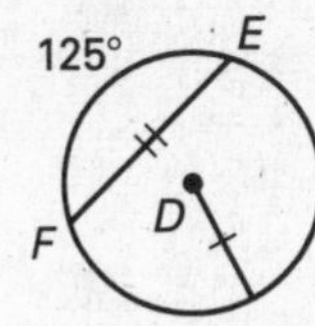

Solution

Because $\overline{BC}$ and $\overline{EF}$ are congruent __________ in congruent __________, the corresponding minor arcs $\widehat{BC}$ and $\widehat{EF}$ are ______________.

So, $m\widehat{BC} = m\widehat{EF} =$ _____.

THEOREM 10.4

If one chord is a perpendicular bisector of another chord, then the first chord is a diameter.

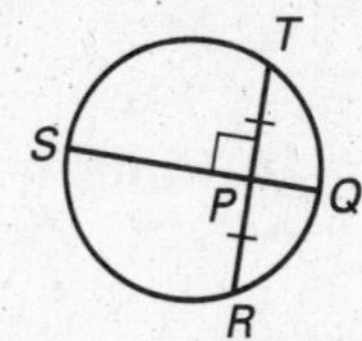

If $\overline{QS}$ is a perpendicular bisector of $\overline{TR}$, then _____ is a diameter of the circle.

THEOREM 10.5

If a diameter of a circle is perpendicular to a chord, then the diameter bisects the chord and its arc.

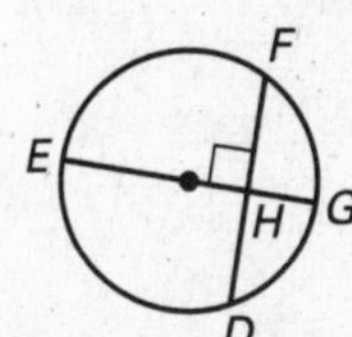

If $\overline{EG}$ is a diameter and $\overline{EG} \perp \overline{DF}$, then $\overline{HD} \cong \overline{HF}$ and _____ $\cong$ _____.

Your Notes

Example 2 *Use perpendicular bisectors*

Journalism A journalist is writing a a story about three sculptures, arranged as shown at the right. Where should the journalist place a camera so that it is the same distance from each sculpture?

Solution

Step 1 **Label** the sculptures *A*, *B*, and *C*. Draw segments $\overline{AB}$ and $\overline{BC}$.

Step 2 **Draw** the ______________________ of $\overline{AB}$ and $\overline{BC}$. By ______________, these are diameters of the circle containing *A*, *B*, and *C*.

Step 3 **Find** the point where these bisectors __________. This is the center of the circle through *A*, *B*, and *C*, and so it is ____________ from each point.

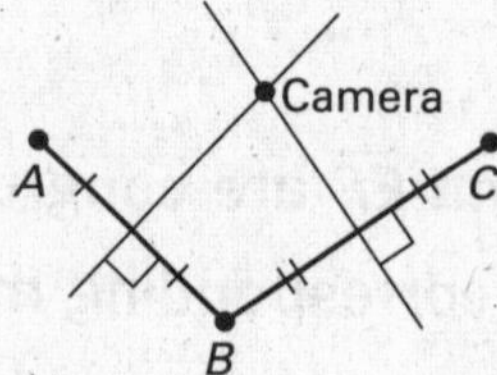

Example 3 *Use a diameter*

Use the diagram of ⊙*E* to find the length of $\overline{BD}$. Tell what theorem you use.

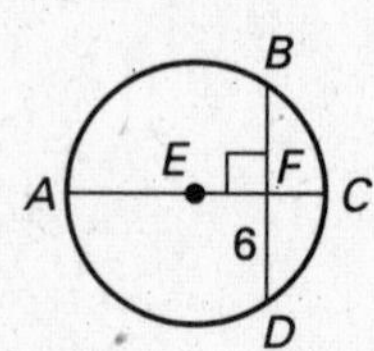

Solution

Diameter $\overline{AC}$ is ______________ to $\overline{BD}$. So, by Theorem 10.5, $\overline{AC}$ __________ $\overline{BD}$, and BF = ____.
Therefore, BD = 2(____) = 2(____) = ____.

THEOREM 10.6

In the same circle, or in congruent circles, two chords are congruent if and only if they are equidistant from the center.

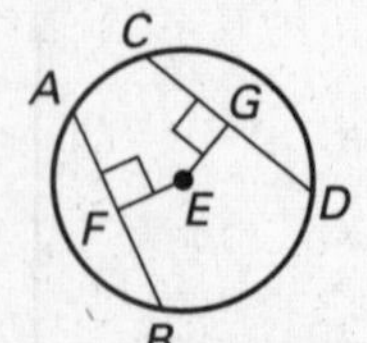

$\overline{AB} \cong \overline{CD}$ if and only if ____ = ____.

Your Notes

Example 4 *Use Theorem 10.6*

In the diagram of $\odot F$, $AB = CD = 12$. Find EF.

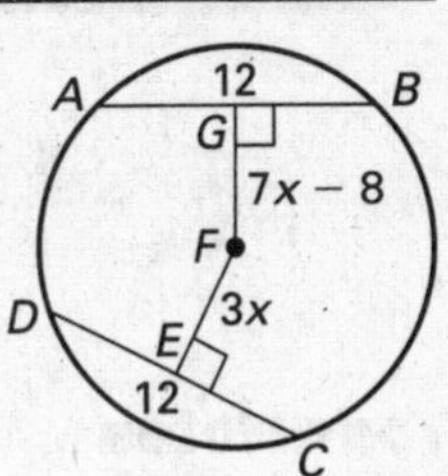

Solution

Chords $\overline{AB}$ and $\overline{CD}$ are congruent, so by Theorem 10.6 they are __________ from F. Therefore, $EF =$ _____.

$EF =$ _____	**Use Theorem 10.6.**
$3x =$ _______	**Substitute.**
$x =$ ___	**Solve for x.**

So, $EF = 3x = 3($___$) =$ ___.

Checkpoint **Complete the following exercises.**

1. If $m\overset{\frown}{TV} = 121°$, find $m\overset{\frown}{RS}$.

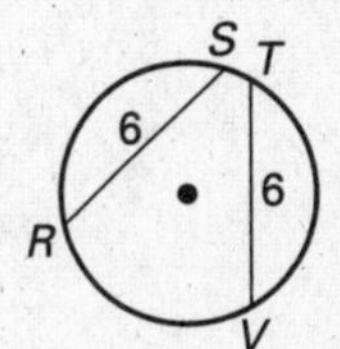

2. Find the measures of $\overset{\frown}{CB}$, $\overset{\frown}{BE}$, and $\overset{\frown}{CE}$.

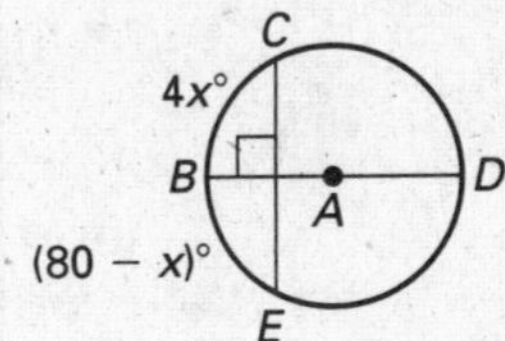

3. In the diagram in Example 4, suppose $AB = 27$ and $EF = GF = 7$. Find CD.

Homework

10.4 Use Inscribed Angles and Polygons

Goal • Use inscribed angles of circles.

Your Notes

VOCABULARY

Inscribed angle

Intercepted arc

Inscribed polygon

Circumscribed circle

THEOREM 10.7: MEASURE OF AN INSCRIBED ANGLE THEOREM

The measure of an inscribed angle is one half the measure of its intercepted arc.

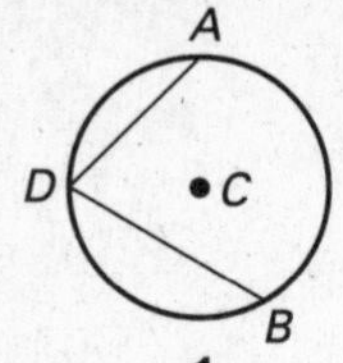

$m\angle ADB = \frac{1}{2}$ ________

Example 1 ***Use inscribed angles***

Find the indicated measure in $\odot P$.

a. $m\angle S$ **b.** $m\overset{\frown}{RQ}$

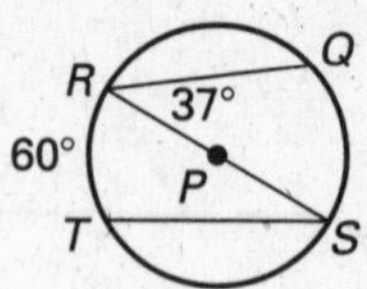

Solution

a. $m\angle S = \frac{1}{2}$ ________ $= \frac{1}{2}($______$) =$ ______

b. $m\overset{\frown}{QS} = 2m\angle$ ____ $= 2 \cdot$ ______ $=$ ______.

Because $\overset{\frown}{RQS}$ is a semicircle,

$m\overset{\frown}{RQ} = 180° -$ ________ $= 180° -$ ______ $=$ _______.

Your Notes

Example 2 *Find the measure of an intercepted arc*

Find $m\overparen{HJ}$ and $m\angle HGJ$. What do you notice about $\angle HGJ$ and $\angle HFJ$?

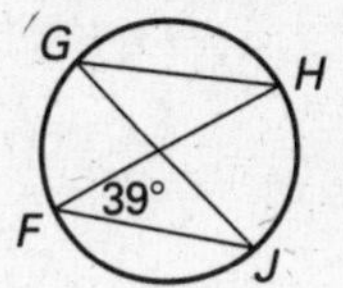

Solution

From Theorem 10.7, you know that

$m\overparen{HJ} = 2m\angle$ ______ $= 2($ ______ $) =$ ______.

Also, $m\angle HGJ = \frac{1}{2}$ ______ $= \frac{1}{2}($ ______ $) =$ ______.

So $\angle HGJ$ ______ $\angle HFJ$.

THEOREM 10.8

If two inscribed angles of a circle intercept the same arc, then the angles are congruent.

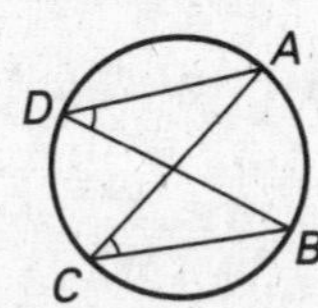

$\angle ADB \cong \angle$ ______

Example 3 *Use Theorem 10.8*

Name two pairs of congruent angles in the figure.

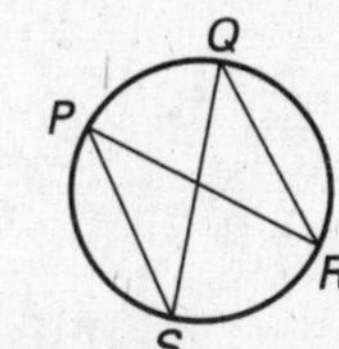

Solution

Notice that $\angle QRP$ and $\angle$ ______ intercept the same arc, and so $\angle QRP \cong \angle$ ______ by Theorem 10.8. Also, $\angle RQS$ and $\angle$ ______ intercept the same arc, so $\angle RQS \cong \angle$ ______.

✔ ***Checkpoint*** **Find the indicated measure.**

1. $m\angle GHJ$	2. $m\overparen{CD}$	3. $m\angle RTS$
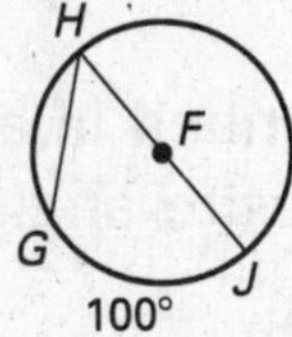	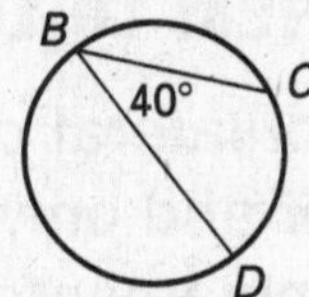	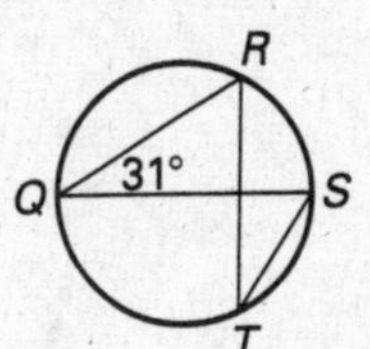

Your Notes

THEOREM 10.9

If a right triangle is inscribed in a circle, then the hypotenuse is a diameter of the circle. Conversely, if one side of an inscribed triangle is a diameter of the circle, then the triangle is a right triangle and the angle opposite the diameter is the right angle.

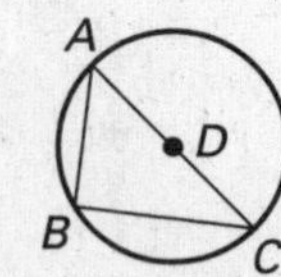

$m\angle ABC = 90°$ if and only if ______ is a diameter of the circle.

Example 4 ***Use a circumscribed circle***

Security A security camera rotates 90° and needs to be able to view the width of a wall. The camera is placed in a spot where the only thing viewed when rotating is the wall. You want to change the camera's position. Where else can it be placed so that the wall is viewed in the same way?

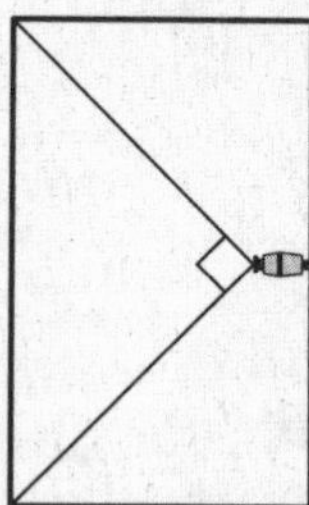

Solution

From Theorem 10.9, you know that if a right triangle is inscribed in a circle, then the hypotenuse of the triangle is a __________ of the circle. So, draw the circle that has the width of the wall as a __________. The wall fits perfectly with your camera's 90° rotation from any point on the __________ in front of the wall.

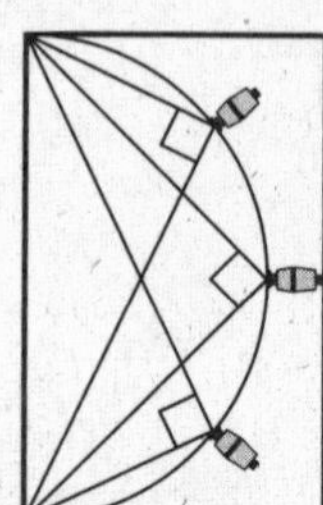

THEOREM 10.10

A quadrilateral can be inscribed in a circle if and only if its opposite angles are supplementary.

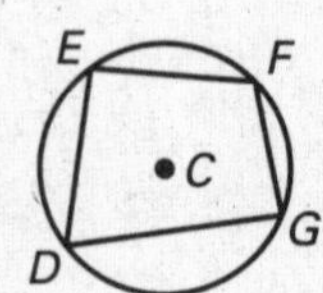

D, *E*, *F*, and *G* lie on $\odot C$ if and only if $m\angle D + m\angle F = m\angle E + m\angle G =$ ______.

Your Notes

Example 5 *Use Theorem 10.10*

Find the value of each variable.

a.

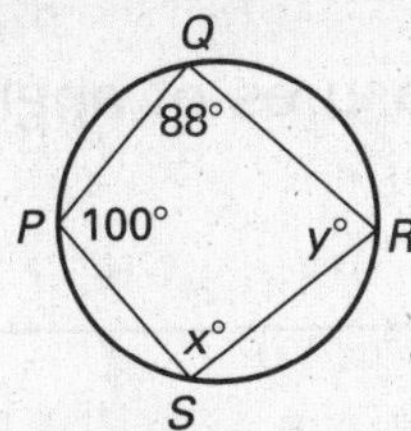

b.

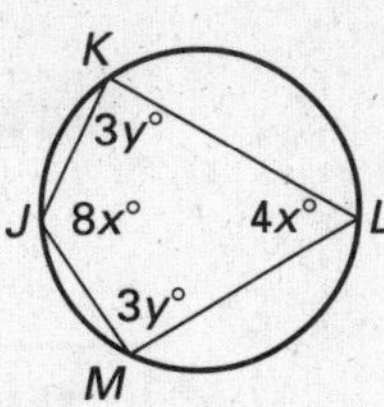

Solution

a. *PQRS* is inscribed in a circle, so opposite angles are ______.

$m\angle P + m\angle R =$ ______ $m\angle Q + m\angle S =$ ______

$100° + y° =$ ______ $88° + x° =$ ______

$y =$ ____ $x =$ ____

b. *JKLM* is inscribed in a circle, so opposite angles are ______.

$m\angle J + m\angle L =$ ______ $m\angle K + m\angle M =$ ______

$8x° + 4x° =$ ______ $3y° + 3y° =$ ______

$12x =$ ______ $6y =$ ______

$x =$ ____ $y =$ ____

✔ ***Checkpoint*** **Complete the following exercises.**

4. A right triangle is inscribed in a circle. The radius of the circle is 5.6 centimeters. What is the length of the hypotenuse of the right triangle?

5. Find the values of *a* and *b*.

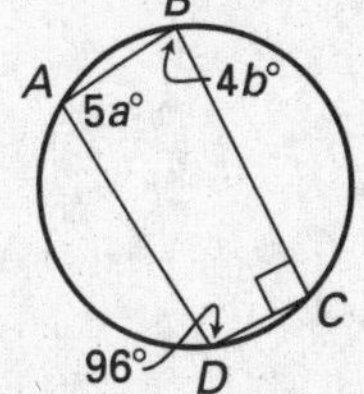

Homework

10.5 Apply Other Angle Relationships in Circles

 Goal • Find the measures of angles inside or outside a circle.

Your Notes

THEOREM 10.11

If a tangent and a chord intersect at a point on a circle, then the measure of each angle formed is one half the measure of its intercepted arc.

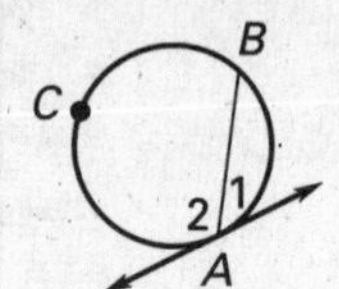

$m\angle 1 = \frac{1}{2}$________

$m\angle 2 = \frac{1}{2}$________

Example 1 ***Find angle and arc measures***

Line *m* is tangent to the circle. Find the indicated measure.

a. $m\angle 1$

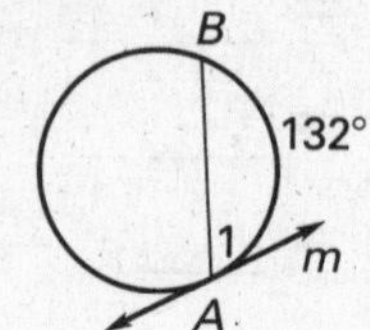

b. $m\widehat{EFD}$

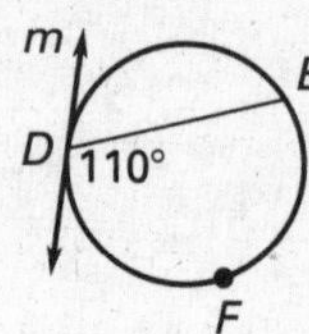

Solution

a. $m\angle 1 =$ ____ $(132°) =$ ______

b. $m\widehat{EFD} =$ ____ $(110°) =$ ______

THEOREM 10.12: ANGLES INSIDE THE CIRCLE THEOREM

If two chords intersect *inside* a circle, then the measure of each angle is one half the *sum* of the measures of the arcs intercepted by the angle and its vertical angle.

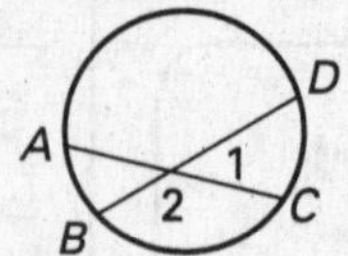

$m\angle 1 = \frac{1}{2}(m$_____ $+ m$_____$)$

$m\angle 2 = \frac{1}{2}(m$_____ $+ m$_____$)$

Your Notes

THEOREM 10.13: ANGLES OUTSIDE THE CIRCLE THEOREM

If a tangent and a secant, two tangents, or two secants intersect *outside* a circle, then the measure of the angle formed is one half the *difference* of the measures of the intercepted arcs.

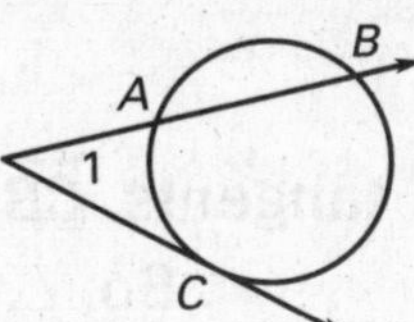

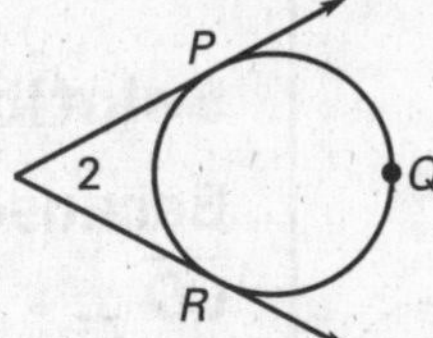

$m\angle 1 = \frac{1}{2}(m\overset{\frown}{BC} - m\overset{\frown}{AC})$ $\quad$ $m\angle 2 = \frac{1}{2}(m\overset{\frown}{PQR} - m\overset{\frown}{PR})$

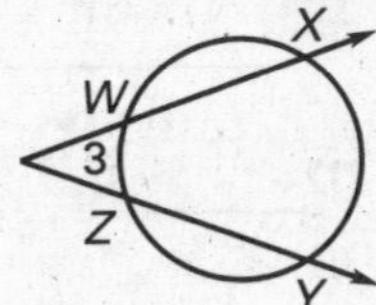

$m\angle 3 = \frac{1}{2}(m\overset{\frown}{XY} - m\overset{\frown}{WZ})$

Example 2 ***Find an angle measure inside a circle***

Find the value of *x*.

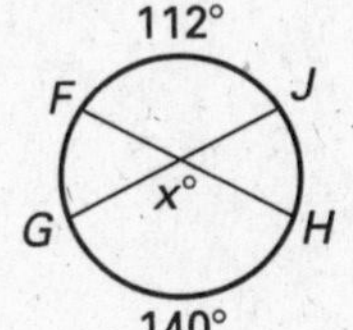

The chords $\overline{FH}$ and $\overline{GJ}$ intersect inside the circle.

$x° = \frac{1}{2}(m\_\_\_\_ + m\_\_\_\_)$ **Use Theorem 10.12.**

$x° = \frac{1}{2}(\_\_\_\_ + \_\_\_\_)$ **Substitute.**

$x = \_\_\_\_$ **Simplify.**

Example 3 ***Find an angle measure outside a circle***

Find the value of *x*.

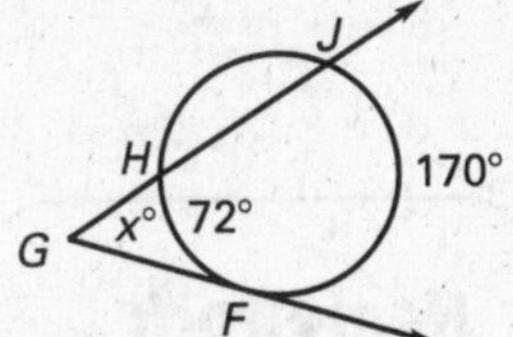

The tangent $\overrightarrow{GF}$ and the secant $\overrightarrow{GJ}$ intersect outside the circle.

$m\angle FGH = \frac{1}{2}(m\_\_\_\_ - m\_\_\_\_)$ **Use Theorem 10.13.**

$x° = \frac{1}{2}(\_\_\_\_ - \_\_\_\_)$ **Substitute.**

$x = \_\_\_\_$ **Simplify.**

Your Notes

Example 4 *Solve a real-world problem*

Airplane You are flying in an airplane about 5 miles above the ground. What is the measure of arc *BD*, the part of Earth that you can see? (Earth's radius is about 4000 miles.)

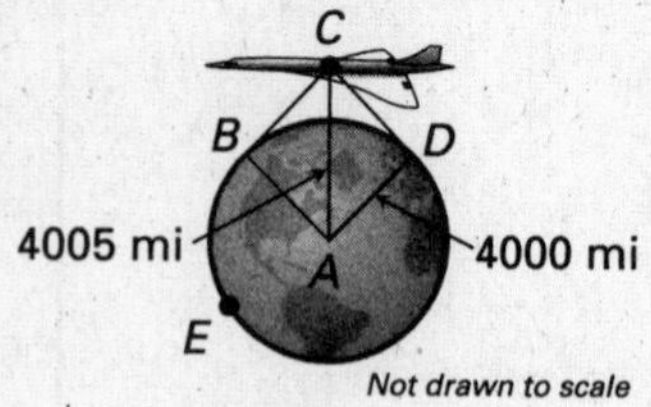

Solution

Because $\overline{CB}$ and $\overline{CD}$ are tangents, $\overline{CB} \perp$ ____ and $\overline{CD} \perp$ ____. Also, $\overline{BC} \cong$ ____. So, $\triangle ABC \cong$ ____ by the HL Congruence Theorem, and $\angle BCA \cong$ ____. Solve right triangle *CBA* to find that $m\angle BCA \approx$ ____. So, $m\angle BCD \approx 2($____$) =$ ____. Let $m\overparen{BD} = x°$.

Because the value for $m\angle BCD$ is an approximation, use the symbol $\approx$ instead of $=$.

$m\angle BCD = \frac{1}{2}(m$____ $- m$____$)$ **Use Theorem 10.13.**

____ $\approx \frac{1}{2}[($____$) -$ ____$]$ **Substitute.**

$x \approx$ ____ **Solve for x.**

From the airplane, you can see an arc of about ____.

Checkpoint Find the indicated measure or the value of the variable.

1. $m\overparen{ACB}$ (A, B, 120°, C)	2. (F, $x°$, J, 52°, G, H, 144°)
3. (26°, G, H, 30°, J, F, $y°$, K)	4. (D, 2, 4, C, E, $a°$, A)

Homework

10.6 Find Segment Lengths in Circles

Goal • Find segment lengths in circles.

Your Notes

VOCABULARY

Segments of a chord

Secant segment

External segment

THEOREM 10.14: SEGMENTS OF CHORDS THEOREM

If two chords intersect in the interior of a circle, then the product of the lengths of the segments of one chord is equal to the product of the lengths of the segments of the other chord.

$EA \cdot$ ____ $= EC \cdot$ ____

Example 1 ***Find lengths using Theorem 10.14***

Find *ML* and *JK*.

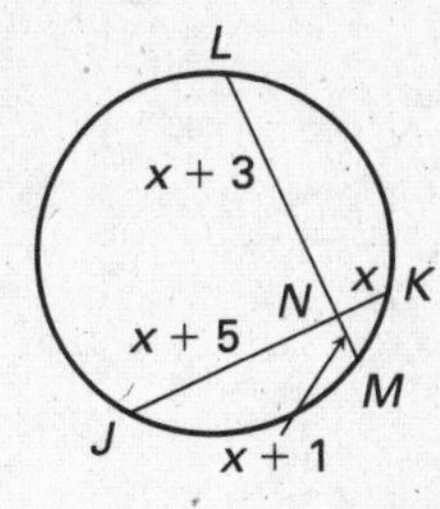

$NK \cdot NJ =$ ____ $\cdot$ ____

$x \cdot (x + 5) = ($____$) \cdot ($____$)$

$x^2 + 5x =$ ________

$x =$ ___

Find *ML* and *JK* by substitution.

$ML = ($____$) + ($____$)$
$=$ ___ $+$ ___ $+$ ___ $+$ ___
$=$ ____

$JK =$ ___ $+ ($____$)$
$=$ ___ $+$ ___ $+$ ___
$=$ ____

Your Notes

THEOREM 10.15: SEGMENTS OF SECANTS THEOREM

If two secant segments share the same endpoint outside a circle, then the product of the lengths of one secant segment and its external segment equals the product of the lengths of the other secant segment and its external segment.

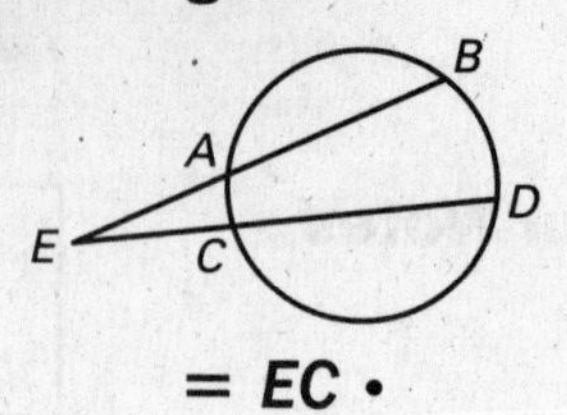

$EA \cdot$ ____ $= EC \cdot$ ____

Example 2 *Use Theorem 10.15*

Find the value of x.

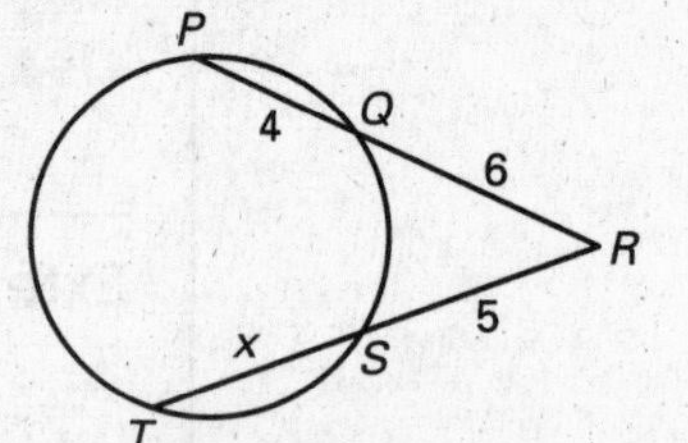

Solution

$RQ \cdot RP = RS \cdot RT$		**Use Theorem** ____.
___ $\cdot$ (___ + ___) = ___ $\cdot$ (x + ___)		**Substitute.**
___ = ___ x + ___		**Simplify.**
___ $= x$		**Solve for x.**

✔ ***Checkpoint*** **Find the value of x.**

1.

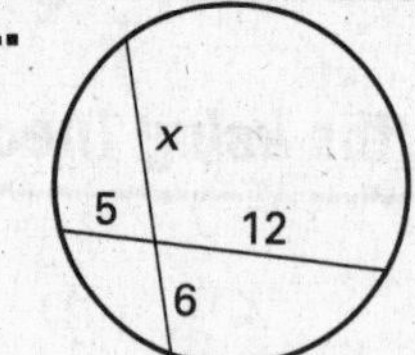

2.

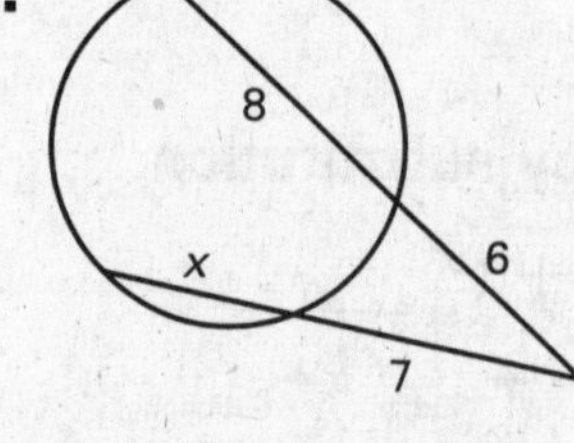

Your Notes

THEOREM 10.16: SEGMENTS OF SECANTS AND TANGENTS THEOREM

If a secant segment and a tangent segment share an endpoint outside a circle, then the product of the lengths of the secant segment and its external segment equals the square of the length of the tangent segment.

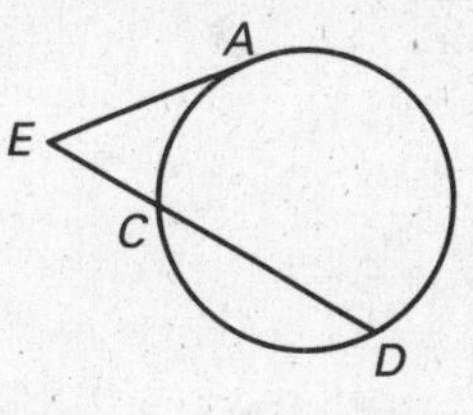

$EA^2 =$ ____ • ____

Example 3 ***Find lengths using Theorem 10.16***

Use the figure at the right to find *RS*.

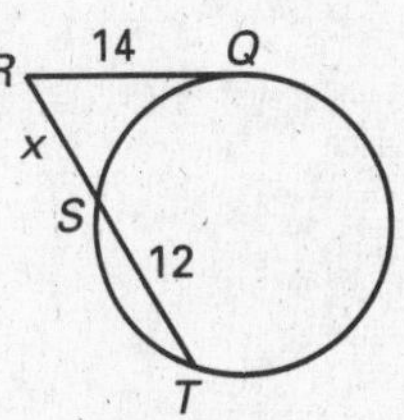

Solution

$RQ^2 = RS \cdot RT$ **Use Theorem ______.**

____$^2 = x \cdot (x +$ ____$)$ **Substitute.**

______ $= x^2 +$ ____x **Simplify.**

$0 = x^2 +$ ____$x -$ ______ **Write in standard form.**

$x = \dfrac{\_\_\_\_ \pm \sqrt{\_\_\_\_^2 - 4(\_\_\_)(\_\_\_\_\_\_)}}{2(\_\_\_)}$ **Use quadratic formula.**

$x =$ ____________ **Simplify.**

Lengths cannot be __________, so use the __________ solution.

So, $x =$ ____________ ≈ ______, and $RS \approx$ ______.

Checkpoint **Complete the following exercise.**

3. Use the figure at the right to find *JK*.

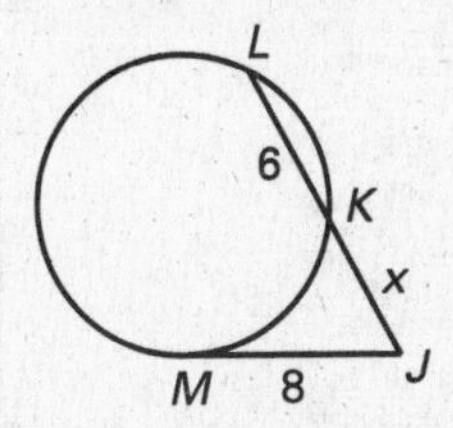

Your Notes

Example 4 ***Solve a real-world problem***

Fountain You are standing at point *C*, 45 feet from the Point State Park fountain in Pittsburgh, PA. The distance from you to a point of tangency on the fountain is 105 feet. Find the distance *CA* between you and your friend at point *A*.

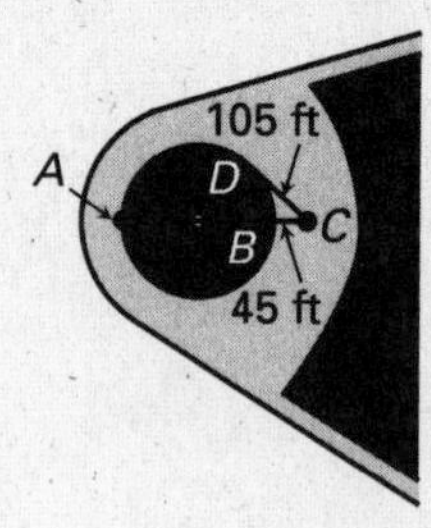

Solution

_____ • *CA* = _____ **Use Theorem 10.16.**

_____ • *CA* = _____ **Substitute.**

CA = _____ **Solve for *CA*.**

You are _____ feet from your friend.

Checkpoint **Complete the following exercise.**

4. In Example 4, suppose $\overline{AB}$ is a diameter of the fountain. Use the diagram below and Theorem 10.16 to find the radius of the fountain.

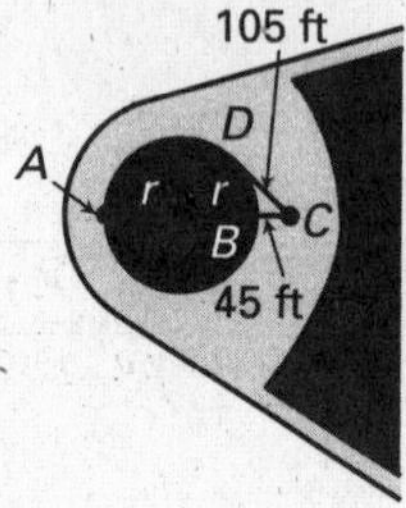

Homework

10.7 Write and Graph Equations of Circles

Goal • Write equations of circles in the coordinate plane.

Your Notes

VOCABULARY

Standard equation of a circle

Example 1 ***Write an equation of a circle***

Write the equation of the circle shown.

Solution

The radius is ___ and the center is at __________.

$x^2 + y^2 = \_\_^2$ **Equation of circle**

$x^2 + y^2 = \_\_^2$ **Substitute.**

$x^2 + y^2 = \_\_$ **Simplify.**

The equation of the circle is $x^2 + y^2 = \_\_$.

Checkpoint **Complete the following exercise.**

1. Write an equation of the circle shown.

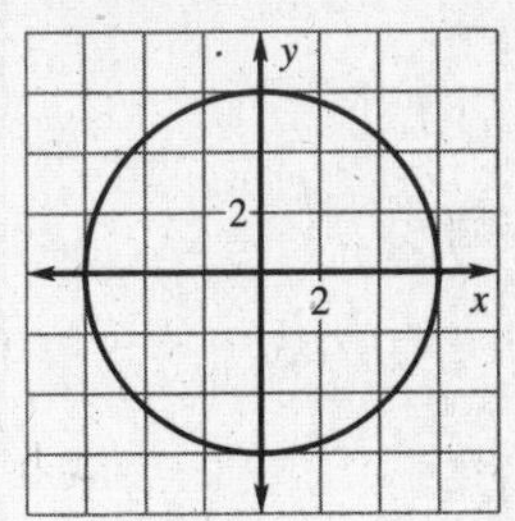

Your Notes

STANDARD EQUATION OF A CIRCLE

The standard equation of a circle with center (h, k) and radius r is:

$(x - h)^2 + (y - k)^2 = r^2$

Example 2 ***Write the standard equation of a circle***

Write the standard equation of a circle with center (0, −5) and radius 3.7.

$(x - h)^2 + (y - k)^2 = r^2$	**Standard equation of a circle**
$(x - \_\_\_)^2 + (y - (\_\_\_\_))^2 = \_\_\_\_^2$	**Substitute.**
$x^2 + (y + \_\_\_)^2 = \_\_\_\_\_$	**Simplify.**

Example 3 ***Write the standard equation of a circle***

The point (−3, 4) is on a circle with center (−1, 2). Write the standard equation of the circle.

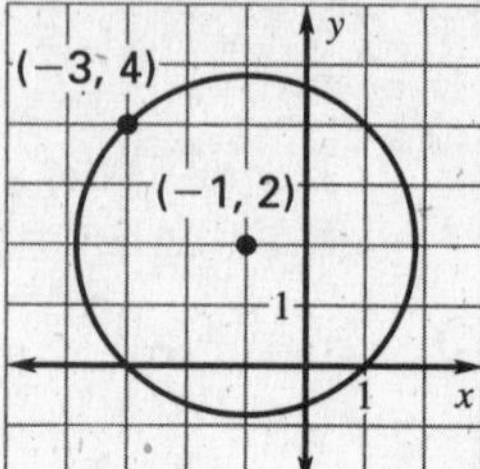

Solution

To write the standard equation, you need to know the values of h, k, and r. To find r, find the distance between the ________ and the point (−3, 4) on the circle.

$r = \sqrt{[-3 - (\_\_\_\_)]^2 + (\_\_\_ - 2)^2}$	**Distance formula**
$= \sqrt{(\_\_\_\_)^2 + \_\_\_\_^2}$	**Simplify.**
$= \_\_\_\_\_$	**Simplify.**

Substitute $(h, k) = (-1, 2)$ and $r =$ _____ into the standard equation of a circle.

$(x - h)^2 + (y - k)^2 = r^2$	**Standard equation of a circle**
$(x - (\_\_\_\_))^2 + (y - \_\_\_)^2 = (\_\_\_\_)^2$	**Substitute.**
$(x + \_\_\_)^2 + (y - \_\_\_)^2 = \_\_\_$	**Simplify.**

The standard equation of the circle is $(x + \_\_\_)^2 + (y - \_\_\_)^2 = \_\_\_$.

Your Notes

If you know the equation of a circle, you can graph the circle by identifying its center and radius.

Example 4 Graph a circle

The equation of a circle is $(x - 2)^2 + (y + 3)^2 = 16$. Graph the circle.

Solution

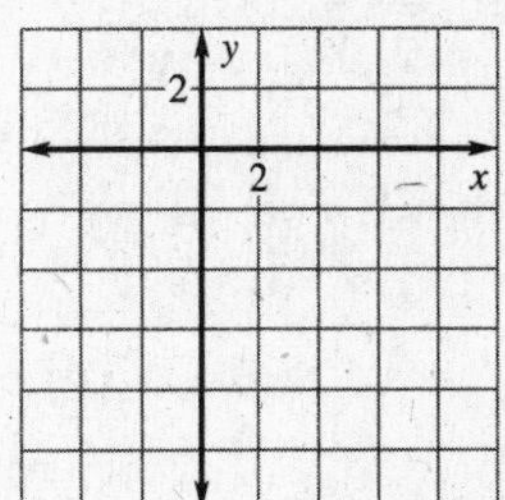

Rewrite the equation to find the center and radius.

$$(x - 2)^2 + (y + 3)^2 = 16$$

$$(x - 2)^2 + [y - (\quad)]^2 =$$

The center is (____, ____) and the radius is ___. Use a compass to graph the circle.

Checkpoint Complete the following exercises.

2. Write the standard equation of a circle with center $(-3, -5)$ and radius 6.1.

3. The point $(-1, 2)$ is on a circle with center $(3, -3)$. Write the standard equation of the circle.

4. The equation of a circle is $(x + 2)^2 + (y - 1)^2 = 9$. Graph the circle.

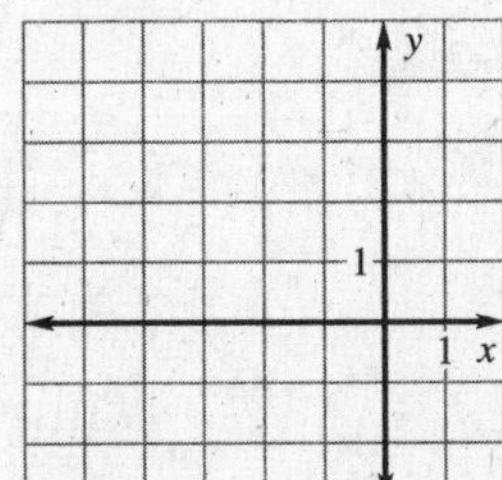

Your Notes

Example 5 ***Use graphs of circles***

Time Capsule You bury a time capsule and use a grid to write directions for finding it. Use the following measurements to find the burial location of the time capsule.

- The capsule is about 11 feet from the oak tree at $A(0, 0)$.
- The capsule is 8 feet from the flagpole at $B(0, 8)$.
- The capsule is 4 feet from the mailbox at $C(-12, 8)$.

Solution

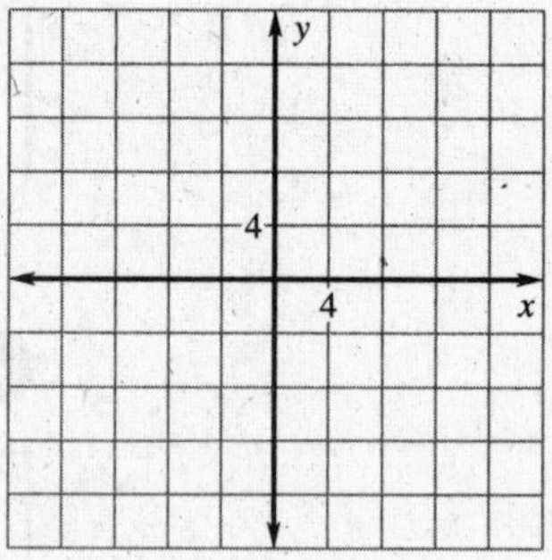

The set of all points equidistant from a given point is a circle, so the burial location is located on each of the following circles.

$\odot A$ with center (___, ___) and radius ____

$\odot B$ with center (___, ___) and radius ___

$\odot C$ with center (_____, ___) and radius ___

To find the burial location, graph the circles on a graph where units are measured in feet. Estimate the point of ____________ of all three circles.

The burial location is at about (_____, ___).

Checkpoint Complete the following exercise.

5. In Example 4, suppose the mailbox is at $C(12, 8)$ and the time capsule is 4 feet away. Find the burial location of the time capsule.

Homework

Words to Review

Give an example of the vocabulary word.

Circle	Center, radius, diameter of a circle
Chord	Secant
Tangent	Central angle
Minor arc, Major arc	Semicircle
Measure of a minor arc	Measure of a major arc

Congruent circles	Congruent arcs
Inscribed angle	Intercepted arc
Inscribed polygon	Circumscribed circle
Segments of a chord	Secant segment
External segment	Standard equation of a circle

Review your notes and Chapter 10 by using the Chapter Review on pages 708–711 of your textbook.

Areas of Triangles and Parallelograms

Goal • Find areas of triangles and parallelograms.

Your Notes

VOCABULARY

Bases of a parallelogram

Height of a parallelogram

POSTULATE 24: AREA OF A SQUARE POSTULATE

The area of a square is the ________ of the length of one of its sides.

POSTULATE 25: AREA CONGRUENCE POSTULATE

If two polygons are ___________, then they have the same area.

POSTULATE 26: AREA ADDITION POSTULATE

The area of a region is the _______ of the areas of its nonoverlapping parts.

THEOREM 11.1: AREA OF A RECTANGLE

The area of a rectangle is the product of its ______ and ________.

THEOREM 11.2: AREA OF A PARALLELOGRAM

The area of a parallelogram is the product of a ______ and its corresponding ________.

THEOREM 11.3: AREA OF A TRIANGLE

The area of a triangle is _________ the product of a ______ and its corresponding ________.

Your Notes

Example 1 *Use a formula to find area*

Find the area of ▱*ABCD*.

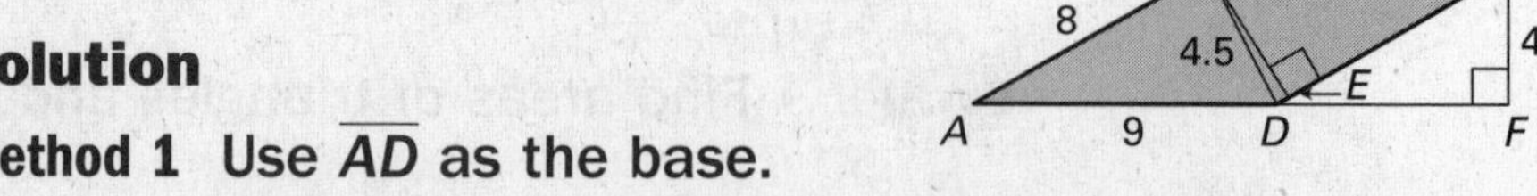

Solution

Method 1 Use $\overline{AD}$ as the base.
The base is extended to measure the height ____. So, b = ___ and h = ____.

Area = bh = ___(___) = ____ square units

Method 2 Use $\overline{AB}$ as the base.
Then the height is ____. So, b = ___ and h = ____.

Area = bh = ___(___) = ____ square units

✔ ***Checkpoint*** **Find the area of the polygon.**

1. 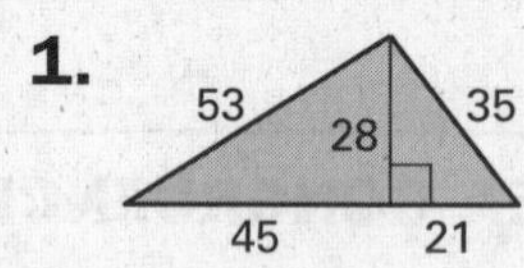	2. 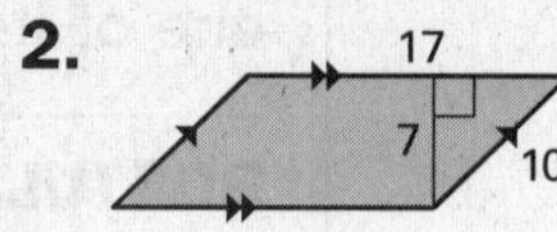

Example 2 *Solve for unknown measures*

The base of a triangle is four times its height. The area of the triangle is 50 square inches. Find the base and height.

Solution

Let h represent the height of the triangle. Then the base is ____.

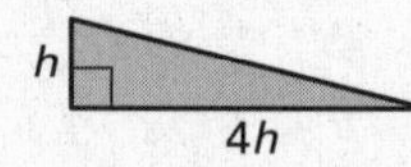

$A = \frac{1}{2}bh$		**Write formula.**
____	$= \frac{1}{2}$(____)(h)	**Substitute ____ for *A* and ____ for *b*.**
	= ___ h^2	**Simplify.**
____	$= h^2$	**Divide each side by ___.**
___	$= h$	**Find positive square root of each side.**

The height of the triangle is ___ inches, and the base is 4 • ___ = ____ inches.

Note that there are other ways you can draw the triangle in Example 2.

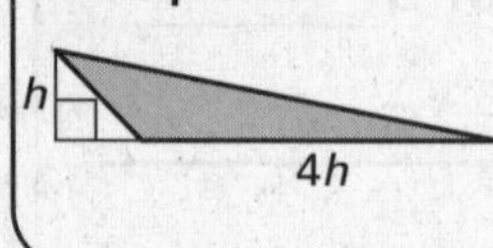

Your Notes

Example 3 ***Solve a multi-step problem***

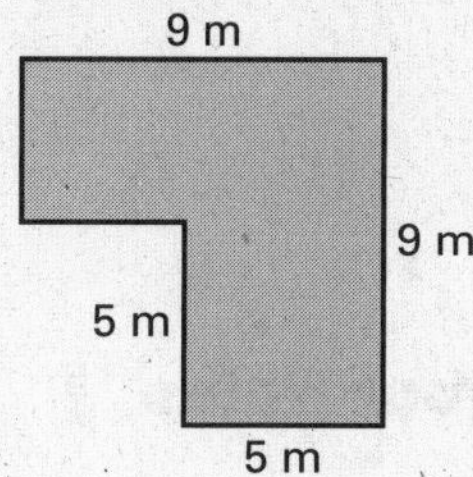

Vacuum A robotic vacuum cleaner can clean 2 square meters of carpet in 8 minutes. About how long does it take for it to clean a carpet covering a room with the dimensions shown at the right?

Solution

Step 1 **Find** the area of the carpet.

Area = Area of rectangle + Area of square

$= 4(\_\_\_) + 5(\_\_\_) = \_\_\_\_ \text{ m}^2$

Step 2 **Determine** how long it takes the robotic vacuum to clean the carpet.

$\_\_\_\_ \cancel{\text{m}^2} \cdot \dfrac{\square \text{ min}}{\square \cancel{\text{m}^2}} = \_\_\_\_\_$ minutes **Use unit analysis.**

It takes _____ minutes, or about ___ hours for the robotic vacuum to clean the carpet.

✔ ***Checkpoint*** **Complete the following exercises.**

3. A parallelogram has an area of 133 square feet and a height of 19 feet. What is the length of the base?

4. In Example 3, suppose there are 4 sections of carpet measuring 1 meter by 2 meters that are covered and cannot be cleaned by the robotic vacuum. About how many hours does it take for the robotic vacuum to clean the carpet?

Homework

11.2 Areas of Trapezoids, Rhombuses, and Kites

Goal • Find areas of other types of quadrilaterals.

Your Notes

VOCABULARY

Height of a trapezoid

THEOREM 11.4: AREA OF A TRAPEZOID

The area of a trapezoid is one half the product of the height and the sum of the lengths of the bases.

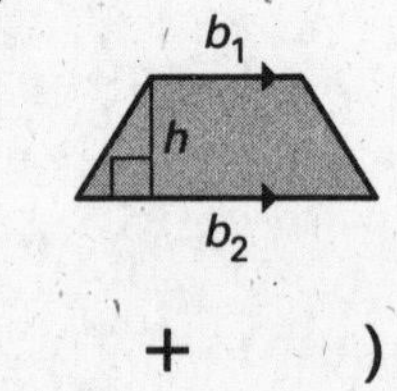

$A = \frac{1}{2}$___(____ + ____)

Example 1 ***Find the area of a trapezoid***

Beavers To prevent beavers from damming a drainage pipe, the trapezoid-shaped fence shown is placed at the pipe. Approximate the area enclosed by the fence.

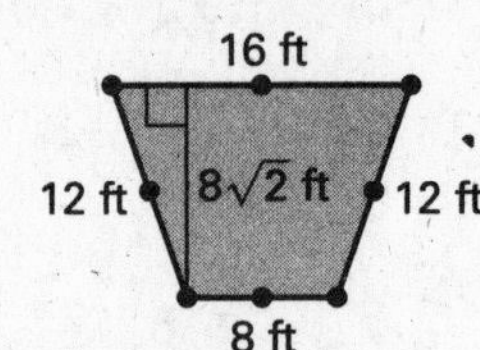

Solution

The height of the trapezoid is _____ feet. The lengths of the bases are ____ feet and ___ feet.

$A = \frac{1}{2}h(b_1 + b_2)$ **Formula for area of a trapezoid**

$= \frac{1}{2}$(______)(____ + ___) **Substitute.**

$\approx$ _____ **Approximate.**

The area enclosed by the fence is about _____ square feet.

Your Notes

THEOREM 11.5: AREA OF A RHOMBUS

The area of a rhombus is one half the product of the lengths of its diagonals.

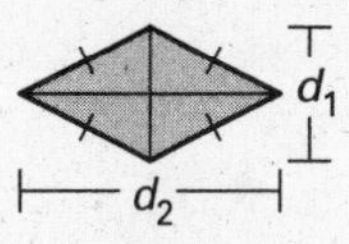

$A = \frac{1}{2}$ ______

THEOREM 11.6: AREA OF A KITE

The area of a kite is one half the product of the lengths of its diagonals.

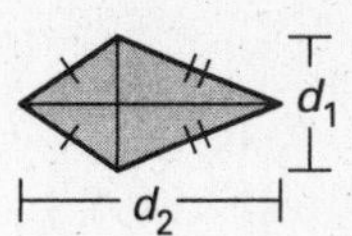

$A = \frac{1}{2}$ ______

Example 2 ***Find the area of a rhombus***

Find the area of the rhombus.

Solution

Step 1 **Find** the length of each diagonal. The diagonals of a rhombus ______ each other, so $QT =$ ______ and $PT =$ ______.

$QS = QT +$ ______ $= 8 +$ ______ $=$ ______ cm

$PR =$ ______ $+ TR =$ ______ $+ 11 =$ ______ cm

Step 2 **Find** the area of the rhombus. Let d_1 represent QS and d_2 represent PR.

$A = \frac{1}{2}d_1d_2$ **Formula for area of a rhombus**

$= \frac{1}{2}$(______)(______) **Substitute.**

$=$ ______ **Simplify.**

The area of the rhombus is ______ square centimeters.

Your Notes

✔ ***Checkpoint*** **Find the area of the figure.**

1.

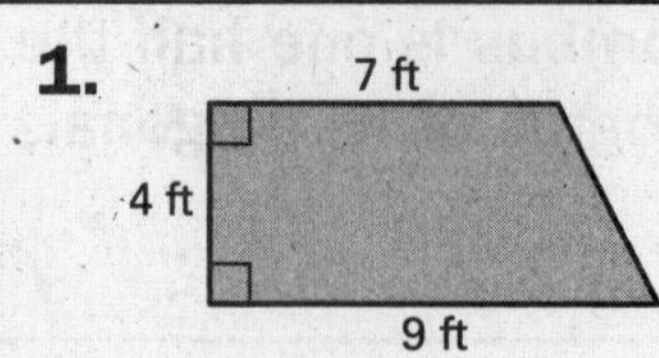

2.

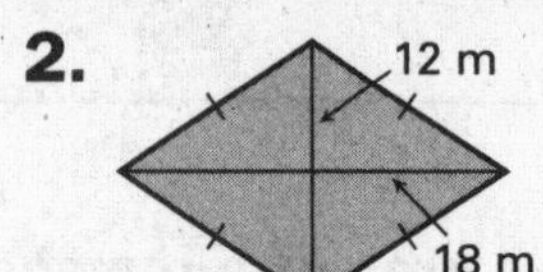

Example 3 ***Solve for unknown measures***

One diagonal of a kite is two times as long as the other diagonal. The area of the kite is 56.25 square inches. What are the lengths of the diagonals?

Solution

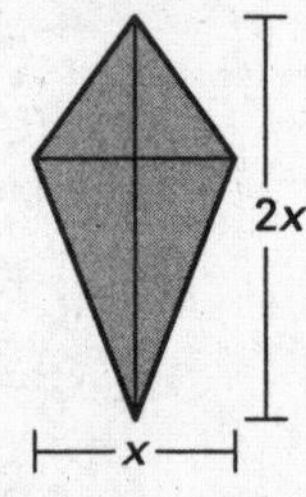

Draw and label a diagram. Let x be the length of one diagonal. The other diagonal is twice as long, so label it ____. Use the formula for the area of a kite to find the value of x.

$A = \frac{1}{2}d_1d_2$	**Formula for area of a kite**
______ $= \frac{1}{2}$(____)(____)	**Substitute.**
______ = ____	**Simplify.**
____ $= x$	**Find positive square root of each side.**

The lengths of the diagonals are ____ inches and 2(____) = ____ inches.

Your Notes

Example 4 Find an area in the coordinate plane

Yard You have a diagram of your backyard. Each square represents a 3 meter by 3 meter square. Find the area of your backyard.

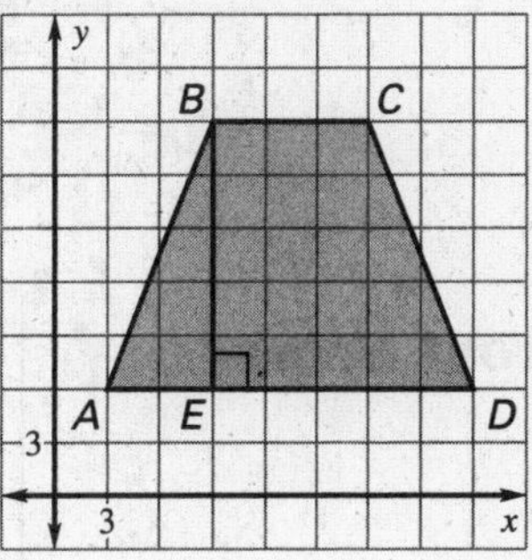

Solution

Step 1 Find the lengths of the bases and the height of trapezoid *ABCD*.

$b_1 = BC = |\_\_\_\_ - \_\_\_\_| = \_\_\_\_$ m

$b_2 = AD = |\_\_\_\_ - \_\_\_\_| = \_\_\_\_$ m

$h = BE = |\_\_\_\_ - \_\_\_\_| = \_\_\_\_$ m

Step 2 Find the area of *ABCD*.

$$A = \frac{1}{2}h(b_1 + b_2) = \frac{1}{2}(\_\_\_\_)(\_\_\_\_ + \_\_\_\_) = \_\_\_\_$$

The area of your backyard is ____ square meters.

Checkpoint Complete the following exercises.

3. One diagonal of a kite is three times as long as the other diagonal. The area of the kite is 73.5 square yards. What are the lengths of the diagonals?

4. Find the area of a rhombus with vertices $M(2, 4)$, $N(5, 6)$, $P(8, 4)$, and $Q(5, 2)$.

Homework

11.3 Perimeter and Area of Similar Figures

Goal • Use ratios to find areas of similar figures.

Your Notes

THEOREM 11.7: AREAS OF SIMILAR POLYGONS

If two polygons are similar with the lengths of corresponding sides in the ratio of $a:b$, then the ratio of their areas is ____ : ____.

$\frac{\text{Side length of Polygon I}}{\text{Side length of Polygon II}} =$ ____

$\frac{\text{Area of Polygon I}}{\text{Area of Polygon II}} =$ ____

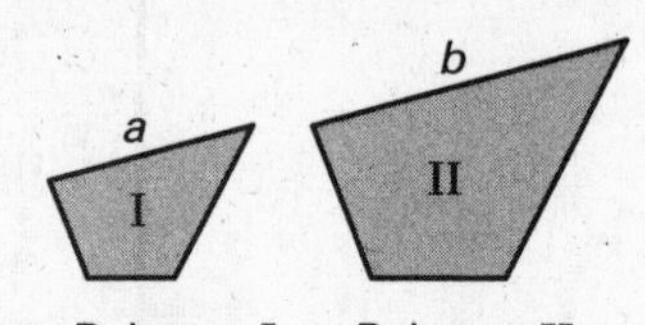

Polygon I ~ Polygon II

Example 1 ***Find ratios of similar polygons***

In the diagram, $\triangle ABC \sim \triangle DEF$. Find the indicated ratio.

a. Ratio (shaded to unshaded) of the perimeters

b. Ratio (shaded to unshaded) of the areas

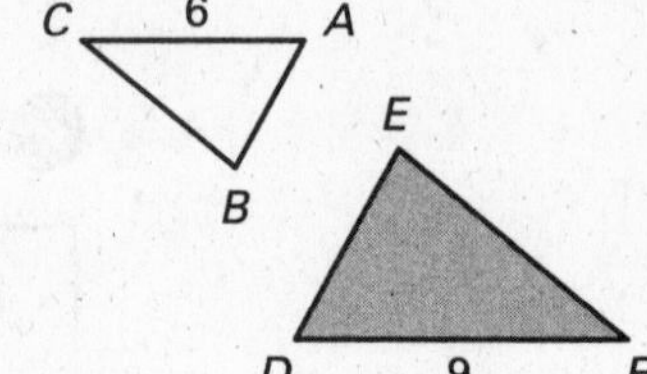

Solution

The ratio of the lengths of corresponding sides is

$\frac{\_\_\_}{\_\_\_} = \frac{\_\_\_}{\_\_\_}$, or ___ : ___.

a. By Theorem 6.1, the ratio of the perimeters is ___ : ___.

b. By Theorem 11.7 above, the ratio of the areas is

____ : ____, or ___ : ___.

You can also compare the measures with fractions. The perimeter of $\triangle DEF$ is three halves the perimeter of $\triangle ABC$. The area of $\triangle DEF$ is nine fourths the area of $\triangle ABC$.

Your Notes

Example 2 *Solve a real-world problem*

Windows You buy two rectangular pieces of aluminum window screening. One is 15 feet long and costs \$135. The other is similar in shape and is 20 feet long. The screen is sold by the square foot. What is the cost of the longer roll?

Solution

The ratio of the length of the longer roll to the shorter roll is ____ : ____, or ___ : ___. So, the ratio of the areas is ____ : ____, or ____ : ___. This ratio is also the ratio of the screen costs. Let x be the cost of the longer roll.

$\frac{\_\_\_}{\_\_\_} = \frac{x}{\square}$ ← **Cost of longer roll** / ← **Cost of shorter roll**

$x =$ _____ **Solve for *x*.**

It costs \$_____ for the longer roll.

Checkpoint Complete the following exercises.

1. Given $\triangle ABC \sim \triangle DEF$, find the ratio (shaded to unshaded) of the perimeters and areas.

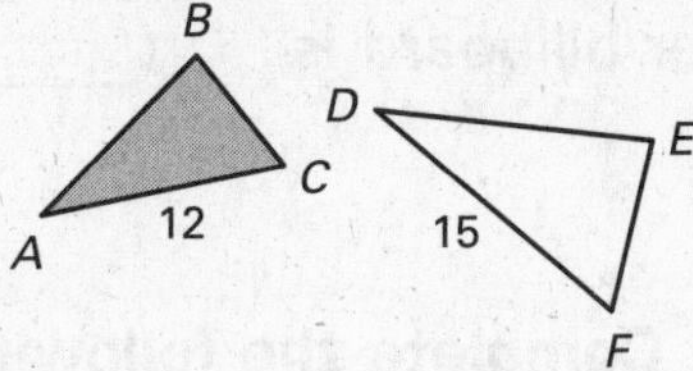

2. In Example 2, suppose you decide to buy a different kind of screening but in the same dimensions. The 20-foot roll of new screening costs \$200. What is the cost of the new 15-foot roll?

Your Notes

Example 3 ***Use a ratio of areas***

Billboards A large rectangular billboard is 12 feet high and 27 feet long. A smaller billboard is similar to the large billboard. The area of the smaller billboard is 144 square feet. Find the height of the smaller billboard.

Solution

First draw a diagram to represent the problem. Label dimensions and areas.

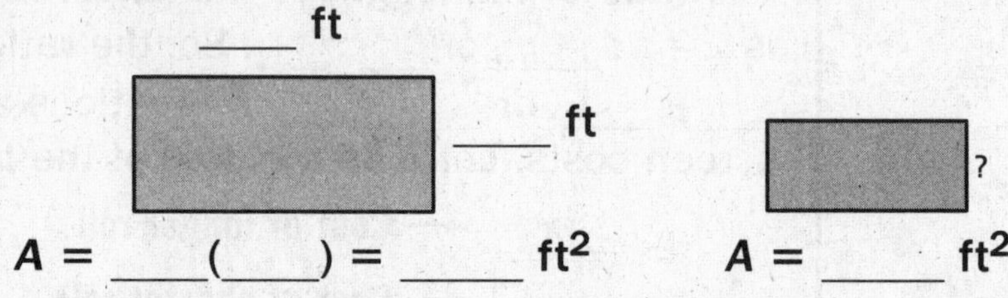

$A =$ ____(____) $=$ ____ ft^2 $\qquad A =$ ____ ft^2

Then use Theorem 11.7. If the area ratio is $a^2 : b^2$, then the length ratio is ___ : ___.

$\frac{\text{area of smaller billboard}}{\text{area of large billboard}} = \frac{\_\_\_}{\_\_\_} = \frac{\_\_\_}{\_\_\_}$

$\frac{\text{length of smaller billboard}}{\text{length of large billboard}} = \frac{\_\_\_}{\_\_\_}$

Any length in the smaller billboard is $\frac{\_\_}{\_\_}$ of the corresponding length in the large billboard. So, the height of the smaller billboard is $\frac{\_\_}{\_\_}$(____ feet) = ___ feet.

Checkpoint Complete the following exercise.

3. In Example 3, suppose the area of the smaller billboard is 225 square feet. Find the height of the smaller billboard.

Your Notes

Example 4 ***Solve a multi-step problem***

Stop sign A stop sign rug is a regular octagon. Each side is 2 feet and the area is about 19.3 square feet. You make a stop sign mat with a perimeter of 72 inches. Find the area of the mat to the nearest tenth of a square inch.

Solution

All regular octagons are similar, so the rug and mat are similar.

Step 1 **Find** the ratio of the lengths of the rug and mat by finding the ratio of the perimeters. Use the same units for both lengths in the ratio.

$$\frac{\text{Perimeter of rug}}{\text{Perimeter of mat}} = \frac{\square}{72 \text{ in.}} = \frac{\square \text{ ft}}{\square \text{ ft}} = \frac{\_\_\_}{\_\_\_}$$

So, the ratio of corresponding lengths (rug to mat) is ___ : ___.

Step 2 **Calculate** the area of the mat. Let x be this area.

$$\frac{(\text{length in rug})^2}{(\text{length in mat})^2} = \frac{\text{area of rug}}{\text{area of mat}}$$

$$\frac{\_\_\_}{\_\_\_} = \frac{\square}{x \text{ ft}^2}$$

$$\_\_\_ x = \_\_\_$$

$$x \approx \_\_\_ \text{ ft}^2$$

Step 3 **Convert** the area to square inches.

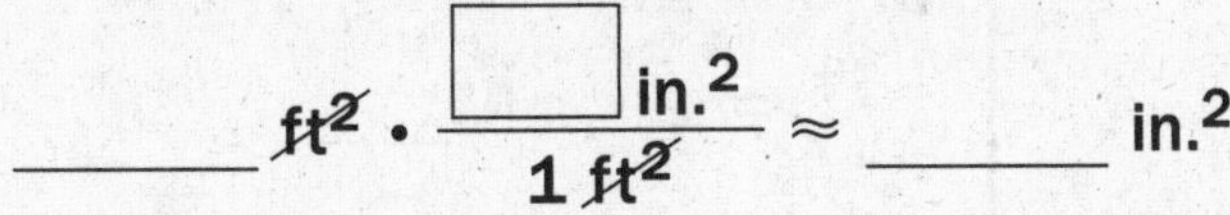

$$\_\_\_ \text{ ft}^2 \cdot \frac{\square \text{ in.}^2}{1 \text{ ft}^2} \approx \_\_\_ \text{ in.}^2$$

The area of the mat is about _____ square inches.

Checkpoint Complete the following exercise.

Homework

4. Rectangles I and II are similar. The perimeter of Rectangle I is 48 inches. Rectangle II is 30 inches by 18 inches. Find the area of Rectangle I.

11.4 Circumference and Arc Length

Goal • Find arc lengths and other measures.

Your Notes

VOCABULARY

Circumference

Arc length

THEOREM 11.8: CIRCUMFERENCE OF A CIRCLE

The circumference C of a circle is $C =$ ____ or $C =$ ____, where d is the diameter of the circle and r is the radius of the circle.

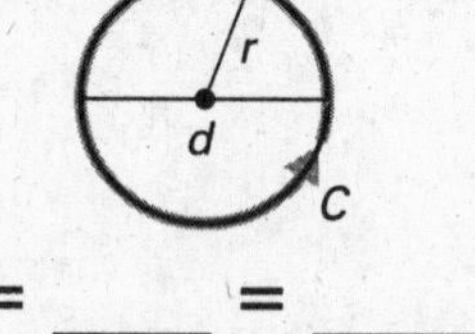

$C =$ ____ $=$ ____

Example 1 ***Use the formula for circumference***

Find the indicated measure.

a. Circumference of a circle with radius 11 meters

b. Radius of a circle with circumference 18 yards

Solution

a. $C = 2\pi r$

$= 2 \cdot \pi \cdot$ ____

$=$ ____ π

$\approx$ ____ m

b. $C = 2\pi r$

____ $= 2\pi r$

$\frac{\_\_\_\_}{\_\_\_\_} = r$

____ yd $\approx r$

Checkpoint Complete the following exercise.

1. Find the circumference of a circle with diameter 23 inches.

Your Notes

Always pay attention to units. As in Example 2, you may need to convert units to get a correct answer.

Example 2 ***Use circumference to find distance traveled***

Skateboarding The dimensions of the skateboard wheel shown at the right are in millimeters. To the nearest meter, how far does the wheel travel when it makes 35 revolutions?

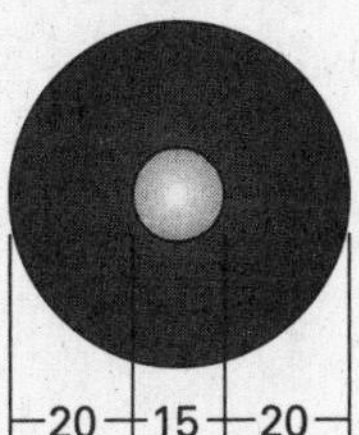

Solution

Step 1 **Find** the diameter of the wheel.

$d =$ ____ + 2(____) = ____ mm

Step 2 **Find** the circumference of the wheel.

$C = \pi d = \pi($____$) \approx$ ______ mm

Step 3 **Find** the distance the wheel travels in 35 revolutions. In one revolution, the wheel travels a distance equal to its ____________. In 35 revolutions, the wheel travels a distance equal to ____ times its circumference.

Distance traveled = Number of revolutions • Circumference

≈ ____ • ______ mm

= ______ mm

Step 4 **Use** unit analysis. Change ______ millimeters to meters.

______ $\cancel{\text{mm}} \cdot \dfrac{1\text{ m}}{1000\ \cancel{\text{mm}}} =$ ______ m

The wheel travels about ___ meters.

✓ ***Checkpoint*** **Complete the following exercise.**

2. A skateboard wheel has a diameter of 56 millimeters. How many revolutions does the wheel make when traveling 3 meters?

Your Notes

ARC LENGTH COROLLARY

In a circle, the ratio of the length of a given arc to the circumference is equal to the ratio of the measure of the arc to 360°.

$\dfrac{\text{Arc length of } \overset{\frown}{AB}}{2\pi r} = \dfrac{m\overset{\frown}{AB}}{360°}$, or

Arc length of $\overset{\frown}{AB} = \dfrac{m\overset{\frown}{AB}}{360°} \cdot 2\pi r$

Example 3 ***Find and use arc lengths***

Find the indicated measure.

a. Arc length of $\overset{\frown}{AB}$

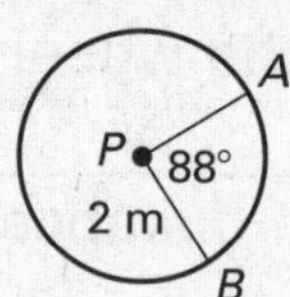

b. $m\overset{\frown}{RS}$

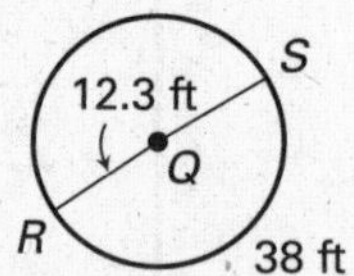

a. Arc length of $\overset{\frown}{AB}$ = ______ • $2\pi($____$)$ ≈ ______ meters

b. $\dfrac{\text{Arc length of } \overset{\frown}{RS}}{2\pi r} = \dfrac{m\overset{\frown}{RS}}{360°}$ **Write equation.**

$\dfrac{\square}{2\pi(\square)} = \dfrac{m\overset{\frown}{RS}}{360°}$ **Substitute.**

______ $\cdot \dfrac{\square}{2\pi(\square)} = m\overset{\frown}{RS}$ **Multiply each side by ______.**

______ $\approx m\overset{\frown}{RS}$ **Use a calculator.**

Checkpoint **Find the indicated measure.**

3. Arc length of $\overset{\frown}{AB}$	4. Circumference of $\odot Z$
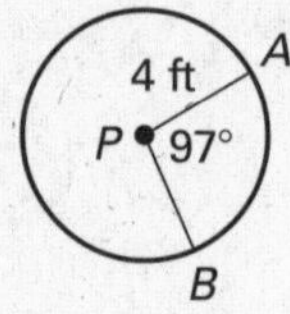	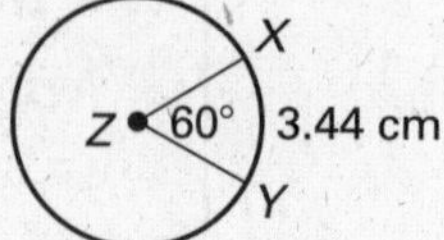

Your Notes

Example 4 *Use arc length to find distances*

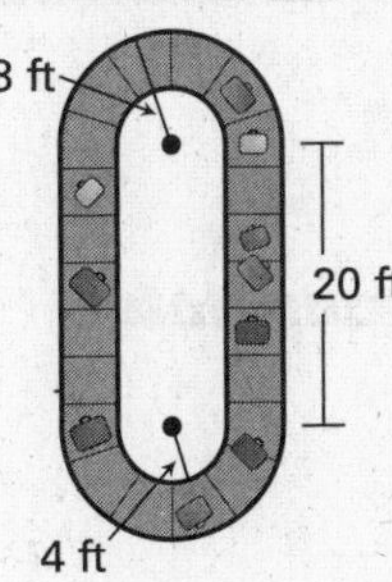

Luggage A conveyor belt for luggage at an airport is shown at the right. The outer part of the belt forms a 180° arc at each end. For each outer arc, the radius is 8 feet. Approximate the distance around the belt for a coin on the outer portion. Round to the nearest foot.

Solution

The outer portion is made of two straight sections and two semicircles. To find the distance around the outer portion, find the sum of the lengths of each part.

Distance = 2 • Length of each straight section + 2 • Length of each semicircle

= 2(_____) + 2 • (__________)

≈ _______ feet

The distance around the outer portion is about _____ feet.

✔ ***Checkpoint*** **Complete the following exercise.**

5. In Example 4, the inner portion of the belt also has 180° arcs on each end. The radius of each inner arc is 4 feet. Find the distance around the belt for a coin on the inner portion. Round to the nearest foot.

Homework

11.5 Areas of Circles and Sectors

Goal • Find the areas of circles and sectors.

Your Notes

VOCABULARY

Sector of a circle

THEOREM 11.9: AREA OF A CIRCLE

The area of a circle is π times the square of the radius.

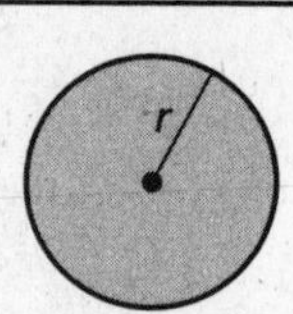

$A =$ ______

Example 1 ***Use the formula for area of a circle***

Find the indicated measure.

a. Area

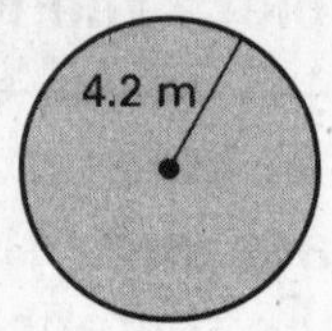

b. Diameter

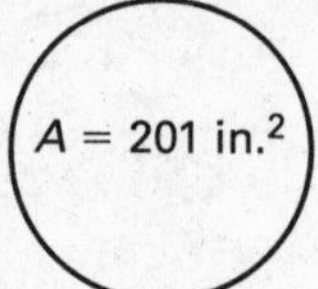

Solution

a. $A = \pi r^2$ **Write formula for the area of a circle.**

$= \pi(\_\_\_\_)^2$ **Substitute ____ for *r*.**

$=$ ______ π **Simplify.**

$\approx$ ______ m^2 **Use a calculator.**

b. $A = \pi r^2$ **Write formula for the area of a circle.**

____ $= \pi r^2$ **Substitute ____ for *A*.**

$\frac{\_\_\_\_}{\_\_\_\_} = r^2$ **Divide each side by ____.**

____ in. $\approx r$ **Find the positive square root of each side.**

The radius is about ___ inches, so the diameter is about ____ inches.

Your Notes

THEOREM 11.10: AREA OF A SECTOR

The ratio of the area of a sector of a circle to the area of the whole circle (πr^2) is equal to the ratio of the measure of the intercepted arc to 360°.

$$\frac{\text{Arc of sector } APB}{\boxed{}} = \frac{\boxed{}}{360^\circ}, \text{ or}$$

$$\text{Area of sector } APB = \frac{\boxed{}}{360^\circ} \cdot \underline{}$$

Example 2 ***Find areas of sectors***

Find the areas of the sectors formed by ∠*RQS*.

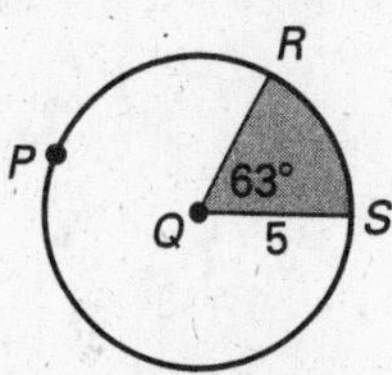

Solution

Step 1 Find the measures of the minor and major arcs.

Because $m\angle RQS =$ _____, $m\overset{\frown}{RS} =$ _____ and $m\overset{\frown}{RPS} = 360^\circ -$ _____ $=$ _____.

Step 2 Find the areas of the small and large sectors.

$$\text{Area of small sector} = \frac{m\overset{\frown}{RS}}{360^\circ} \cdot \pi r^2$$

$$= \frac{\boxed{}}{360^\circ} \cdot \pi \cdot \underline{}^2$$

$$\approx \underline{}$$

$$\text{Area of large sector} = \frac{m\overset{\frown}{RPS}}{360^\circ} \cdot \pi r^2$$

$$= \frac{\boxed{}}{360^\circ} \cdot \pi \cdot \underline{}^2$$

$$\approx \underline{}$$

The areas of the small and large sectors are about ______ square units and ______ square units, respectively.

Your Notes

✔ ***Checkpoint*** **In Exercises 1 and 2, use the diagram to find the indicated measure.**

1. Area

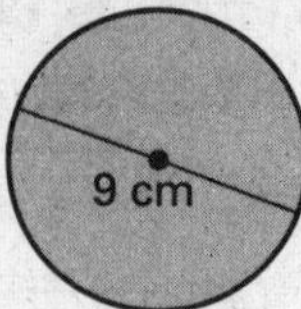

2. Radius

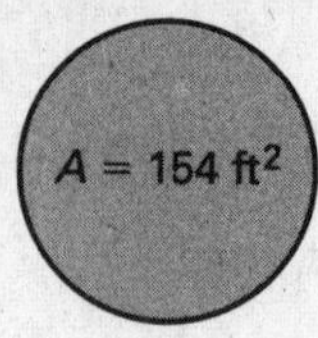

3. Find the areas of the sectors formed by $\angle RQS$.

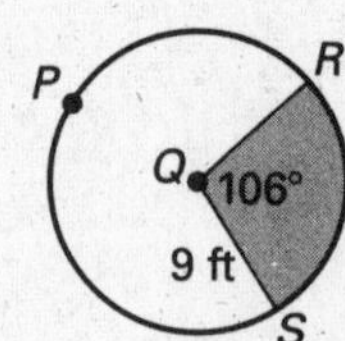

Example 3 *Use the Area of a Sector Theorem*

Use the diagram to find the area of $\odot C$.

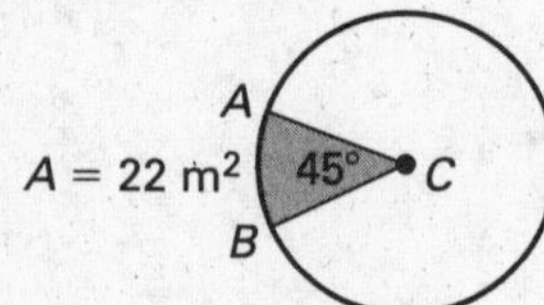

Solution

Area of sector $ACB = \frac{m\overset{\frown}{AB}}{360°} \cdot$ Area of $\odot C$

$\_\_\_\_ = \frac{\square}{360°} \cdot$ Area of $\odot C$

$\_\_\_\_ =$ Area of $\odot C$

The area of $\odot C$ is ____ square meters.

Your Notes

Example 4 ***Find an area***

Construction A contractor needs to cut a section out of a rectangular piece of wood as shown. To the nearest square inch, what is the area of the remaining wood?

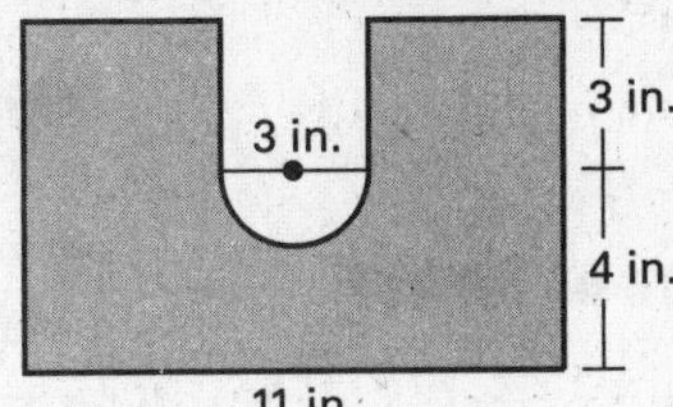

Solution

The area you need to find is the area of the rectangle minus the area of the cut-out section. The cut-out can be divided into a semicircle and a square.

Use the radius (1.5 in.) not the diameter (3 in.) when you calculate the area of the semicircle.

Area of wood

= Area of rectangle − [Area of semicircle + Area of square]

= ____(___) − [____ • (______) + ____]

= ____ − [______ + ___]

≈ ______

The area is about _____ square inches.

Checkpoint Complete the following exercises.

4. Find the area of ⊙G.

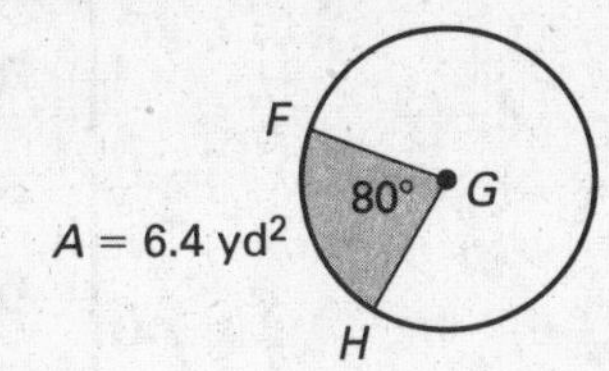

5. Find the area of the figure.

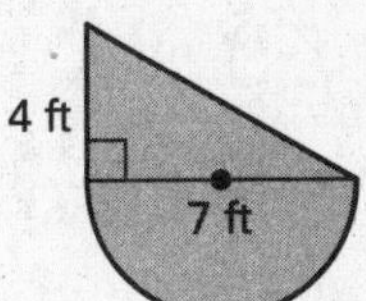

Homework

11.6 Areas of Regular Polygons

Goal • Find areas of regular polygons inscribed in circles.

Your Notes

VOCABULARY

Center of a polygon

Radius of a polygon

Apothem of a polygon

Central angle of a regular polygon

Example 1 ***Find angle measures in a regular polygon***

In the diagram, *ABCDEF* is a regular hexagon inscribed in ⊙*G*. Find each angle measure.

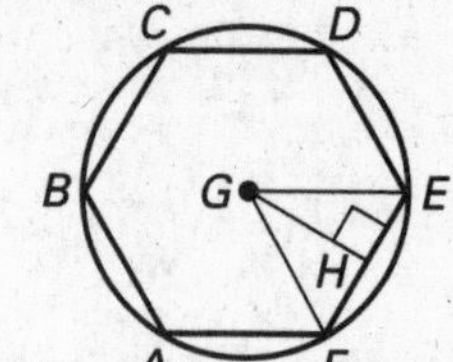

a. $m\angle EGF$

b. $m\angle EGH$

c. $m\angle HEG$

Solution

a. $\angle EGF$ is a central angle, so $m\angle EGF =$ ______, or ______.

b. $\overline{GH}$ is an apothem, which makes it an ________ of isosceles $\triangle EGF$. So, $\overline{GH}$ ________ $\angle EGF$ and

$m\angle EGH = \frac{\quad}{\quad} m\angle EGF =$ ______.

c. The sum of the measures of right $\triangle HEG$ is 180°. So, ______ + ______ + $m\angle HEG = 180°$, and $m\angle HEG =$ ______.

Your Notes

THEOREM 11.11: AREA OF A REGULAR POLYGON

The area of a regular *n*-gon with side length *s* is half the product of the apothem *a* and the perimeter *P*, so

$A = \frac{1}{2}$ _____, or $A = \frac{1}{2}$ ____ • ____.

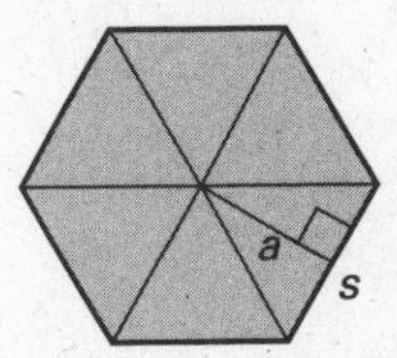

Example 2 ***Find the area of a regular polygon***

Coaster A wooden coaster is a regular octagon with 3 centimeter sides and a radius of about 3.92 centimeters. What is the area of the coaster?

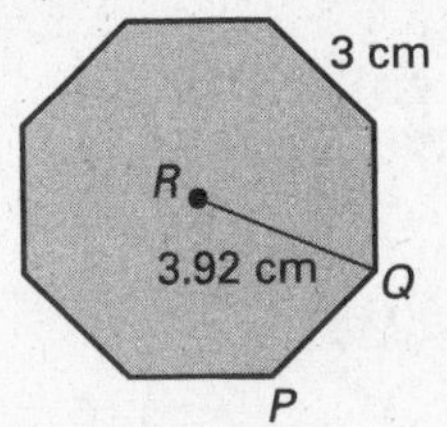

Solution

Step 1 **Find** the perimeter *P* of the coaster. An octagon has ____ sides, so *P* = ____(____) = ____ centimeters.

Step 2 **Find** the apothem *a*. The apothem is height _____ of $\triangle PQR$. Because $\triangle PQR$ is isosceles, altitude $\overline{RS}$ ________ $\overline{QP}$.

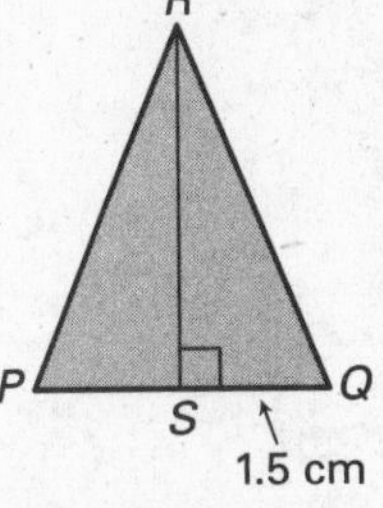

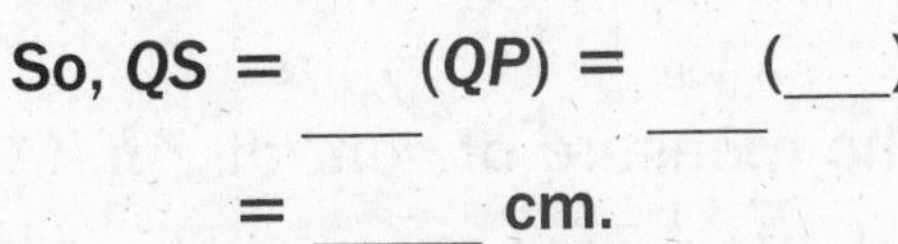

So, *QS* = $\frac{\ \ }{\ \ }$(*QP*) = $\frac{\ \ }{\ \ }$(____)

= _____ cm.

To find *RS*, use the Pythagorean Theorem for $\triangle RQS$.

$a = RS$

$\approx \sqrt{\_\_\_\_^2 - \_\_\_\_^2} = \sqrt{\_\_\_\_\_\_} \approx$ ______

Step 3 **Find** the area *A* of the coaster.

$A = \frac{1}{2}aP$ **Formula for area of regular polygon**

$\approx \frac{1}{2}$(_______)(_____) **Substitute.**

$\approx$ ______ **Simplify.**

The area of the coaster is about ______ square centimeters.

In general, your answer will be more accurate if you avoid rounding until the last step. Round your final answers to the nearest tenth unless you are told otherwise.

Your Notes

✓ *Checkpoint* **Complete the following exercises.**

1. In the diagram, *FGHJ* is a square inscribed in ⊙*K*. Find $m\angle FKJ$ and $m\angle KJF$.

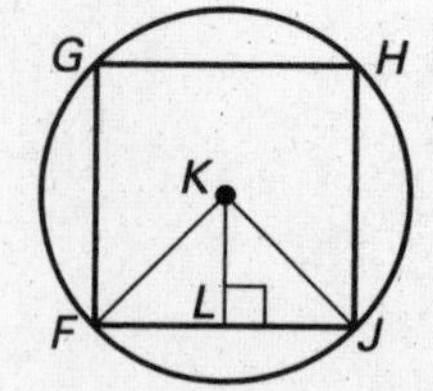

2. The radius of the regular pentagon is about 6.8 inches. Find the area to the nearest square inch.

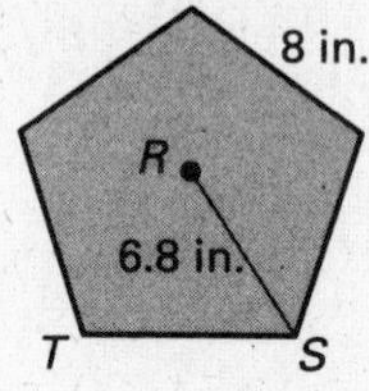

Example 3 ***Find the perimeter and area of a regular polygon***

A regular nonagon is inscribed in a circle with radius 5 units. Find the perimeter *P* and area *A* of the nonagon.

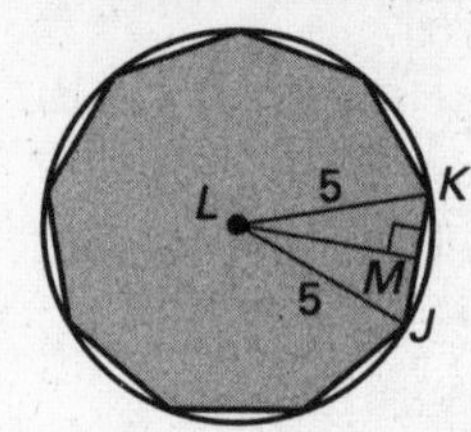

The measure of central $\angle JLK$ is $\frac{\_\_\_}{\_\_\_}$, or _____.

Apothem $\overline{LM}$ bisects the central angle, so $m\angle KLM$ is _____. To find the lengths of the legs, use trigonometric ratios for right $\triangle KLM$.

sin _____ $= \frac{MK}{5}$ cos _____ $= \frac{LM}{5}$

_________ $= MK$ _________ $= LM$

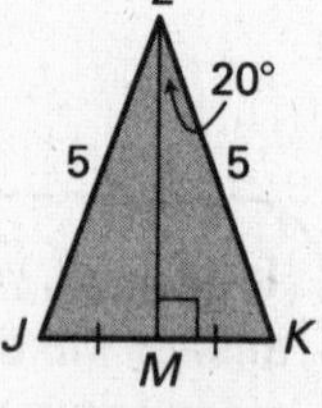

The regular nonagon has side lengths $s = 2MK = 2($_________$) =$ _________ and apothem $a = LM =$ _________.

So,

$P = 9s = 9($_________$) =$ _________ ≈ _____ units,

and

$A = \frac{1}{2}aP$

$= \frac{1}{2}($_________$)($_________$) \approx$ _____ square units.

Your Notes

Checkpoint Complete the following exercise.

3. Find the perimeter and area of the equilateral triangle inscribed in $\odot F$.

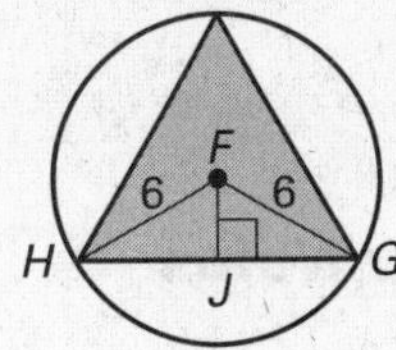

FINDING LENGTHS IN A REGULAR *N*-GON

To find the area of a regular *n*-gon with radius *r*, you may need to first find the apothem *a* or the side length *s*.

You can use . . .	. . . when you know *n* and . . .	. . . as in . . .
Pythagorean Theorem: $\left(\frac{1}{2}s\right)^2 + a^2 = r^2$	Two measures: *r* and *a*, or *r* and *s*	Example 2 and Checkpoint Ex. 2
Special Right Triangles	Any one measure: *r* or *a* or *s* **And** the value of *n* is 3, 4, or 6	Checkpoint Ex. 3
Trigonometry	Any one measure: *r* or *a* or *s*	Example 3 and Checkpoint Ex. 3

Homework

11.7 Use Geometric Probability

Goal • Use lengths and areas to find geometric probabilities.

Your Notes

VOCABULARY

Probability

Geometric probability

PROBABILITY AND LENGTH

Let $\overline{AB}$ be a segment that contains the segment $\overline{CD}$. If a point K on $\overline{AB}$ is chosen at random, then the probability that it is on $\overline{CD}$ is the ratio of the length of $\overline{CD}$ to the length of $\overline{AB}$.

A, C, D, B

$P(K \text{ is on } \overline{CD}) =$ ______

To apply the geometric probability formulas on this page and the next, you need to know that every point on the segment or in the region is *equally likely* to be chosen.

Example 1 ***Use lengths to find a geometric probability***

Find the probability that a point chosen at random on $\overline{FJ}$ is on $\overline{GK}$.

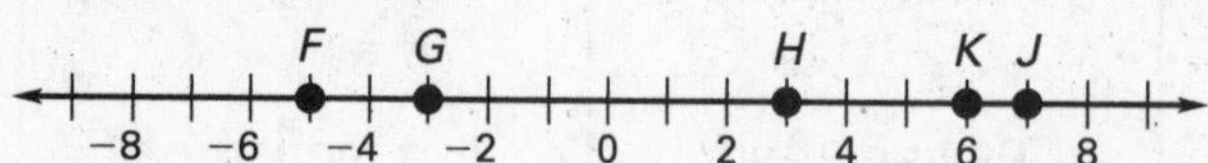

Solution

$P(\text{Point is on } \overline{GK}) = \dfrac{\text{Length of } \square}{\text{Length of } \square}$

$= \dfrac{\square}{\square}$

$=$ ___ $=$ ___ , ______, or _____%

Your Notes

Example 2 *Use a segment to model a real-world probability*

Shuttle A shuttle to town runs every 10 minutes. The ride from your boarding location to town takes 13 minutes. One afternoon, you arrive at the boarding location at 2:41. You want to get to town by 2:57. What is the probability you will get there by 2:57?

Solution

Step 1 **Find** the longest you can wait for the shuttle and still get to town by 2:57. The ride takes 13 minutes, so you need to catch the shuttle no later than 13 minutes before 2:57, or _____. The longest you can wait is ___ minutes (_____ − 2:41 = ___ min).

Step 2 **Model** the situation. The shuttle runs every 10 minutes, so it will arrive in 10 minutes or less. You need it to arrive within ___ minutes.

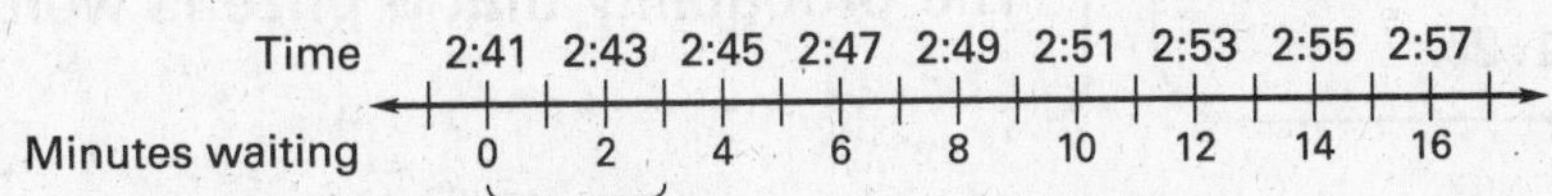

The shuttle needs to arrive within the first ___ minutes.

Step 3 **Find** the probability.

$$P(\text{Get to town by 2:57}) = \frac{\text{Favorable waiting time}}{\text{Maximum waiting time}}$$

$$= \underline{\qquad}$$

The probability that you get to town by 2:57 is _____, or _____%.

PROBABILITY AND AREA

Let *J* be a region that contains region *M*. If a point *K* in *J* is chosen at random, then the probability that it is in region *M* is the ratio of the area of *M* to the area of *J*.

P(*K* is in region *M*) = __________

Your Notes

Example 3 ***Use areas to find a geometric probability***

Golf A golf ball is hit and stops on the green. A prize is won if it stops in the painted circle. The diameters of the green and circle are shown at the right. If the ball is equally likely to stop on any point on the green, what is the probability that a prize is won?

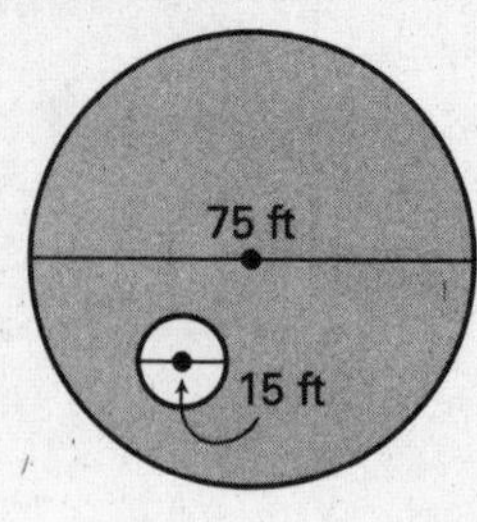

Solution

Find the ratio of the circle's area to the green's area.

$$P(\text{prize is won}) = \frac{\text{Area of painted circle}}{\text{Area of green}}$$

$$= \frac{\pi(\square)^2}{\pi(\square)^2} = \frac{\square\,\pi}{\square\,\pi} = \underline{\quad}$$

The probability that a prize is won is ___, or ___%.

All circles are similar and the Area of Similar Polygons Theorem also applies to circles. The ratio of radii is 7.5:37.5, or 1:5, so the ratio of areas is $1^2:5^2$, or 1:25.

Checkpoint Complete the following exercises.

1. Find the probability that a point chosen at random on $\overline{LP}$ is on $\overline{MN}$.

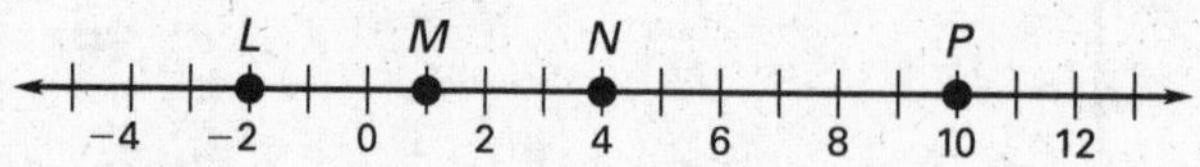

2. In Example 2, suppose you arrive at the pickup location at 2:38. What is the probability that you will get to town by 2:57?

3. On the green in Example 3, the hole is 4.25 inches in diameter. Find the probability that your ball stops in the hole.

Your Notes

Example 4 *Estimate area on a grid to find a probability*

Property A homeowner's property is shown in the scale drawing. If a deer is equally likely to be anywhere on the property, estimate the probability that it is on grass.

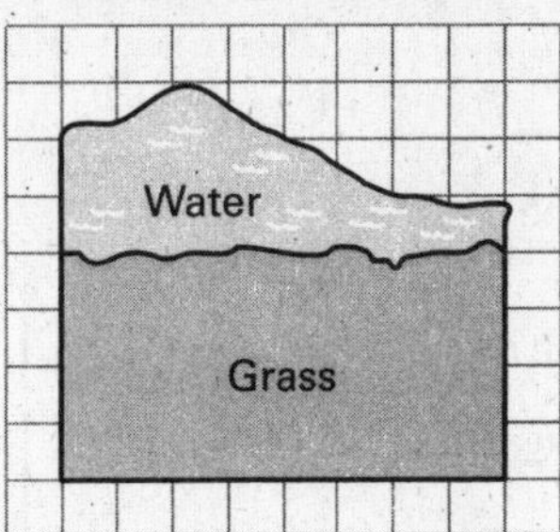

Solution

Step 1 **Find** the grass area. The shape is a rectangle, so the area is bh = ___ • ___ = ____ square units.

Step 2 **Find** the total area of the property.

Count the squares that are fully covered. There are ____ squares in the grass and ____ in the water. So, there are ____ full squares.

Make groups of partial squares so the area of each is about 1 square unit. The total area of partial squares is about ___ square units. So use ____ + ___ = ____ square units for the total area.

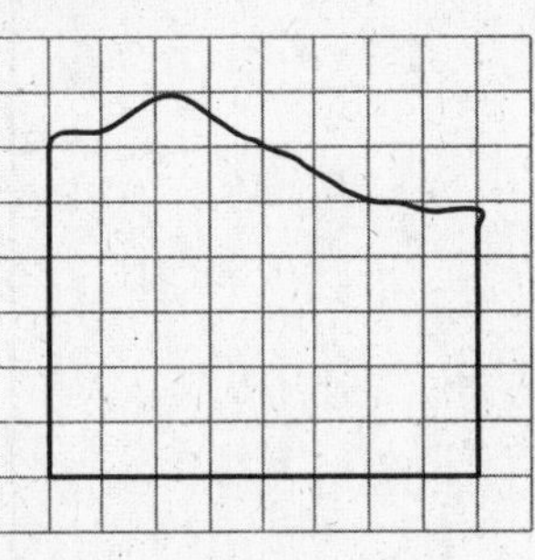

The deer must be in the grass or in the water, so check that the probabilities in Example 4 and Checkpoint Exercise 4 add up to 100%.

Step 3 **Write** a ratio of the areas to find the probability.

$$P(\text{deer on grass}) = \frac{\text{Area of grass}}{\text{Total area of property}} \approx \_\_\_\_$$

The probability that the deer is on grass is about ____, or about ______%.

✔ ***Checkpoint*** **Complete the following exercise.**

4. In Example 4, estimate the probability that the deer is in the water.

Homework

Words to Review

Give an example of the vocabulary word.

Bases, height of a parallelogram	Height of a trapezoid
Circumference	Arc length
Sector of a circle	Center of a polygon, Radius of a polygon
Apothem of a polygon	Central angle of a regular polygon
Probability	Geometric probability

Review your notes and Chapter 11 by using the Chapter Review on pages 780–783 of your textbook.

12.1 Explore Solids

Goal • Identify solids.

Your Notes

VOCABULARY

Polyhedron

Face

Edge

Vertex

Base

Regular polyhedron

Convex polyhedron

Platonic solids

Cross section

Notice that the names of four of the Platonic solids end in "hedron." *Hedron* is Greek for "side" or "face." Sometimes a cube is called a regular *hexahedron*.

Your Notes

TYPES OF SOLIDS

Polyhedra	Not Polyhedra	
Prism	Cylinder	Cone
Pyramid	Sphere	

Example 1 *Identify and name polyhedra*

Tell whether the solid is a polyhedron. If it is, name the polyhedron and find the number of faces, vertices, and edges.

a.

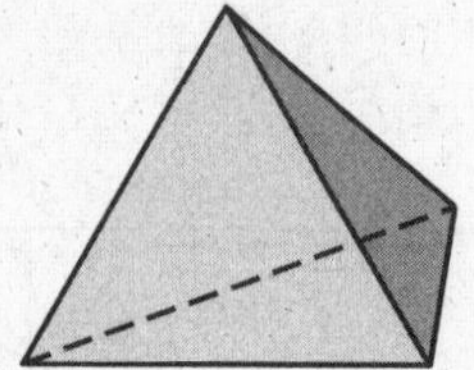

b.

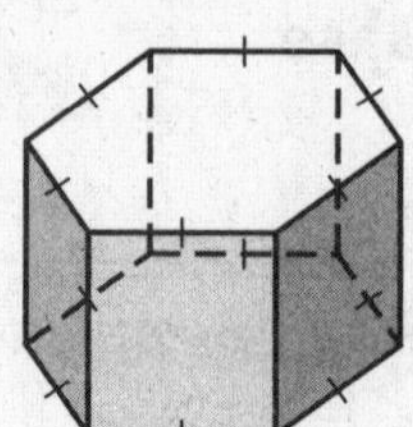

c.

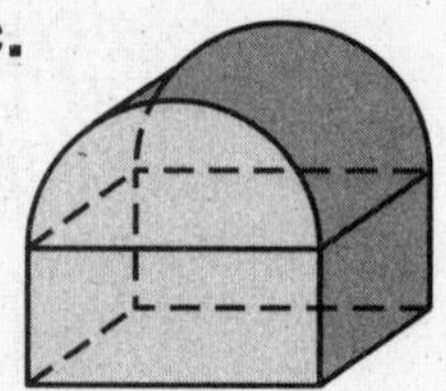

Solution

a. This is a polyhedron. It has ___ faces so it is a _______________. It has ___ vertices and ___ edges.

b. This is a polyhedron. The two bases are congruent hexagons, so it is a __________________. It has ___ faces, ____ vertices, and ____ edges.

c. This is not a polyhedron. The solid has a curved surface.

Your Notes

THEOREM 12.1: EULER'S THEOREM

The number of faces (F), vertices (V), and edges (E) of a polyhedron are related by the formula

$F + V = E +$ ___.

$F = 6$, $V = 8$, $E = 12$
$6 + 8 = 12 + 2$

Example 2 *Use Euler's Theorem*

Find the number of faces, vertices, and edges of the polyhedron shown. Check your answers using Euler's Theorem.

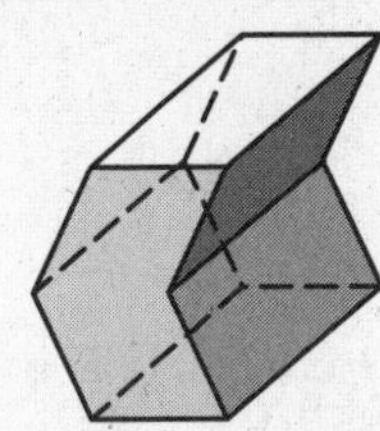

The polyhedron has ___ faces, ____ vertices, and ____ edges.

Use Euler's Theorem to check.

$F + V = E + 2$	**Euler's Theorem**
___ + ____ = ____ + 2	**Substitute.**
____ = ____	**Check.**

Example 3 *Describe cross sections*

Describe the shape formed by the intersection of the plane and the solid.

a.

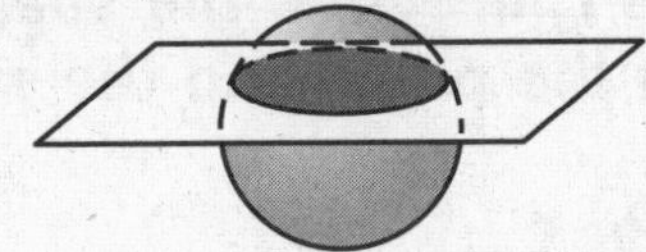

b.

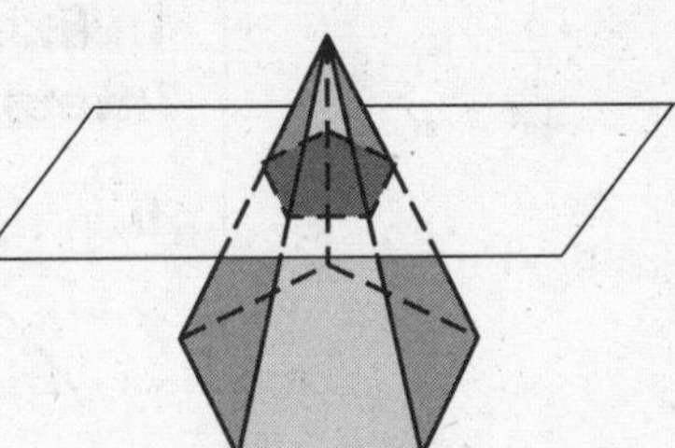

c.

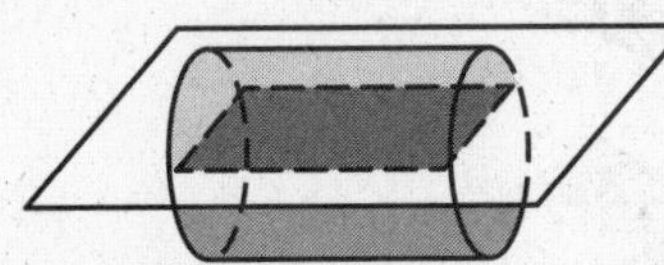

Solution

a. The cross section is a __________.

b. The cross section is a __________.

c. The cross section is a __________.

Your Notes

✓ ***Checkpoint*** **Complete the following exercises.**

In Exercises 1–3, tell whether the solid is a polyhedron. If it is, name the polyhedron and find the number of faces, vertices, and edges.

1.

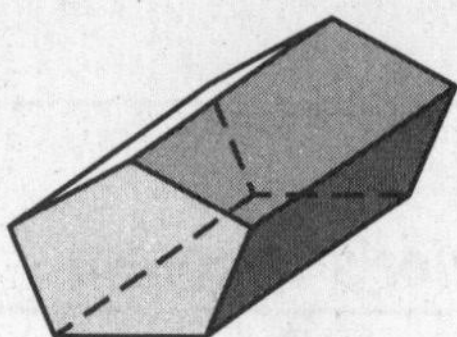

2.

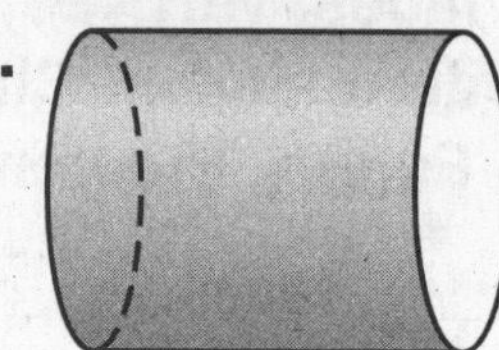

3.

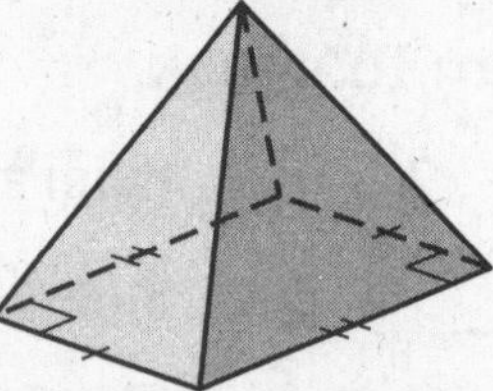

4. **Is it possible for a polyhedron to have 16 faces, 34 vertices, and 50 edges?** ***Explain.***

In Exercises 5–7, ***describe*** **the shape formed by the intersection of the plane and the solid.**

5.

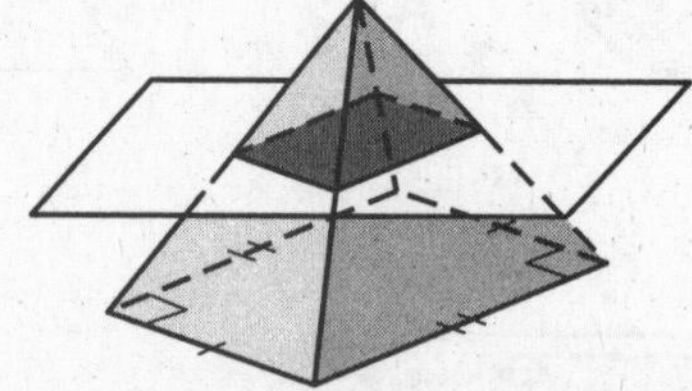

6.

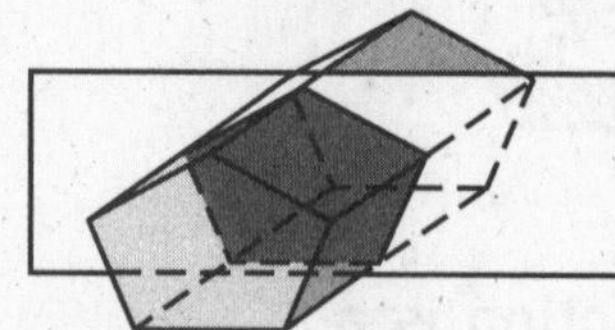

Homework

7.

12.2 Surface Area of Prisms and Cylinders

Goal • Find the surface areas of prisms and cylinders.

Your Notes

VOCABULARY

Prism

Lateral faces

Lateral edges

Surface area

Lateral area

Net

Right prism

Oblique prism

Cylinder

Right cylinder

Your Notes

> Remember, the *apothem* of a polygon is the distance from the center to any side of the polygon.

THEOREM 12.2: SURFACE AREA OF A RIGHT PRISM

The surface area S of a right prism is

$S = 2B +$ _____ $= aP +$ _____,

where a is the apothem of the base, B is the area of a base, P is the perimeter of a base, and h is the height.

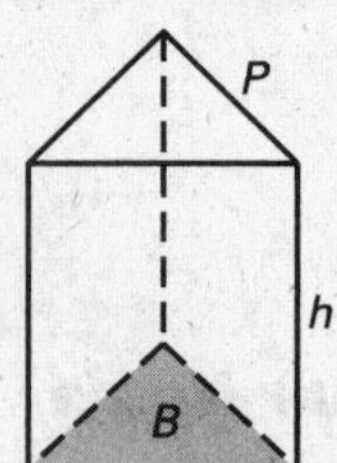

Example 1 ***Find the surface area of a right prism***

Find the surface area of the right prism.

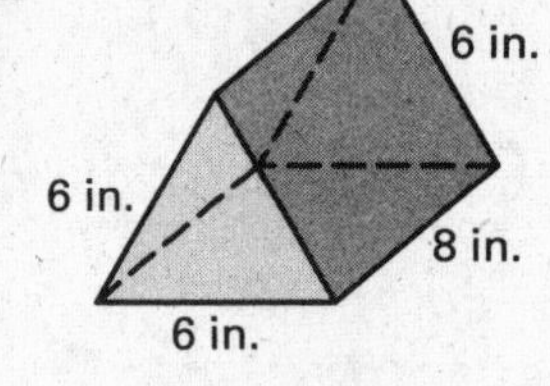

Solution

Each base is an equilateral triangle with a side length s of ___ inches. Using the formula for the area of an equilateral triangle, the area of each base is

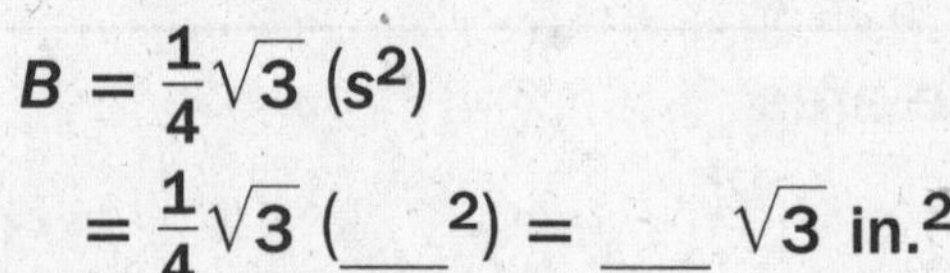

$B = \frac{1}{4}\sqrt{3}\,(s^2)$

$= \frac{1}{4}\sqrt{3}\,(\_\_\_^2) = \_\_\_\sqrt{3}$ in.^{2}

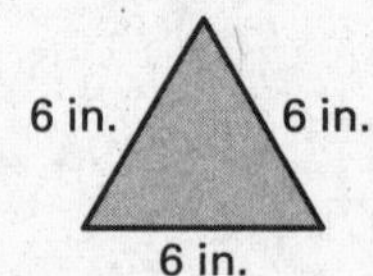

The perimeter of each base is $P =$ _____ in. and the height is $h =$ ____ in.

$S = 2B + Ph$	**Surface area of a right prism**
$= 2(\_\_\_\sqrt{3}) + \_\_\_\_(\_\_\_)$	**Substitute.**
$\approx$ ________	**Simplify.**

The surface area is about ________ square inches.

✔ ***Checkpoint*** **Complete the following exercise.**

1. Find the surface area of a right rectangular prism with height 5 feet, length 11 feet, and width 4 feet.

Your Notes

THEOREM 12.3: SURFACE AREA OF A RIGHT CYLINDER

The surface area S of a right cylinder is

$S = 2B + Ch =$ ________,

where B is the area of a base, C is the circumference of a base, r is the radius of a base, and h is the height.

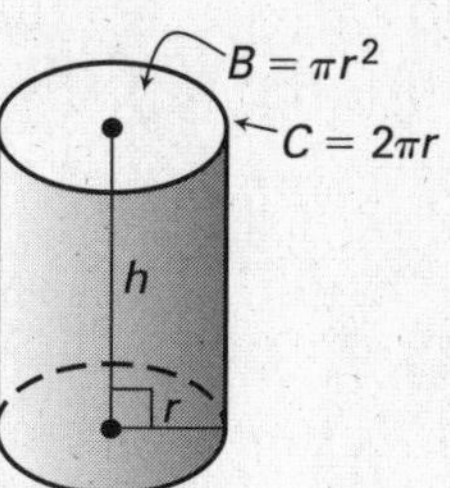

Example 2 ***Find the surface area of a cylinder***

Find the surface area of the right cylinder.

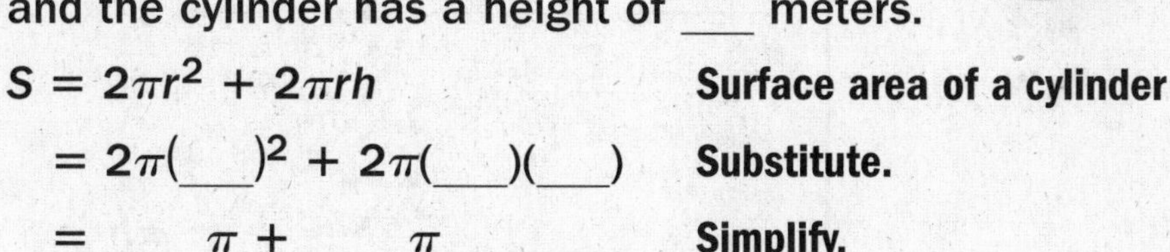

Solution

Each base has a radius of ___ meters, and the cylinder has a height of ___ meters.

$S = 2\pi r^2 + 2\pi rh$	**Surface area of a cylinder**
$= 2\pi(\_\_\_)^2 + 2\pi(\_\_\_)(\_\_\_)$	**Substitute.**
$=$ ____ $\pi +$ ____ π	**Simplify.**
$=$ ____ π	**Add.**
$\approx$ ________	**Use a calculator.**

The surface area is about ________ square meters.

✔ ***Checkpoint*** **Complete the following exercise.**

2. Find the surface area of a right cylinder with height 9 centimeters and radius 6 centimeters. Round your answer to two decimal places.

Your Notes

Example 3 *Find the height of a cylinder*

Find the height of the right cylinder shown, which has a surface area of 198.8 square millimeters.

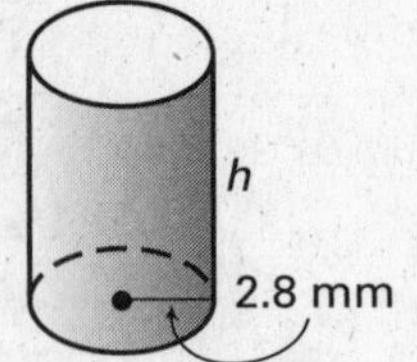

Solution

Substitute known values in the formula for the surface area of a right cylinder and solve for the height *h*.

$S = 2\pi r^2 + 2\pi rh$	**Surface area of a cylinder**
$\_\_\_\_ = 2\pi(\_\_\_\_)^2 + 2\pi(\_\_\_\_)h$	**Substitute.**
$\_\_\_\_ = \_\_\_\_\pi + \_\_\_\_\pi h$	**Simplify.**
$\_\_\_\_ - \_\_\_\_\pi = \_\_\_\_\pi h$	**Subtract $\_\_\_\_\pi$ from each side.**
$\_\_\_\_ \approx \_\_\_\_\pi h$	**Simplify. Use a calculator.**
$\_\_\_\_ \approx h$	**Divide each side by $\_\_\_\_\pi$.**

The height of the cylinder is about ____ millimeters.

✔ ***Checkpoint*** **Complete the following exercise.**

3. **Find the radius of a right cylinder with height 5 inches and surface area 168π square inches.**

Homework

 12.3 Surface Area of Pyramids and Cones

Goal • Find the surface areas of pyramids and cones.

Your Notes

Pyramids are classified by the shapes of their bases.

VOCABULARY

Pyramid

Vertex of a pyramid

Regular pyramid

Slant height

Cone

Vertex of a cone

Right cone

Lateral surface

Your Notes

Example 1 *Find the area of a lateral face of a pyramid*

Find the area of each lateral face of the regular square pyramid.

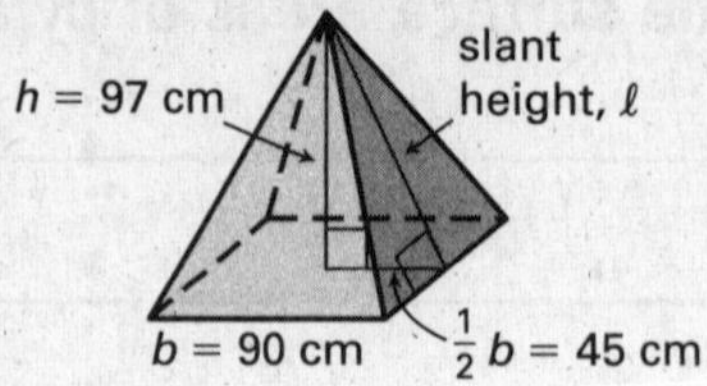

Solution

Use the Pythagorean Theorem to find the slant height ℓ.

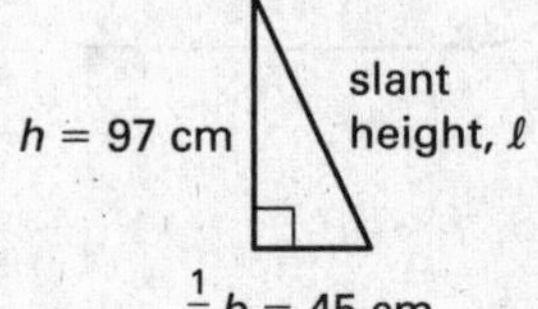

$\ell^2 = h^2 + \left(\frac{1}{2}b\right)^2$ **Write formula.**

$\ell^2 =$ ____^{2} + ____^{2} **Substitute for h and $\frac{1}{2}b$.**

$\ell^2 =$ ________ **Simplify.**

$\ell =$ ____________ **Take the square root of each side.**

$\ell \approx$ ________ **Find the positive square root.**

Find the area of each triangular face.

$A = \frac{1}{2}b\ell$ **Write formula.**

$\approx \frac{1}{2}$(____)(________) **Substitute for b and ℓ.**

$\approx$ ________ **Simplify.**

The area of each lateral face is about ________ square centimeters.

THEOREM 12.4: SURFACE AREA OF A REGULAR PYRAMID

The surface area S of a regular pyramid is

$S = B +$ ______,

where B is the area of the base, P is the perimeter of the base, and ℓ is the slant height.

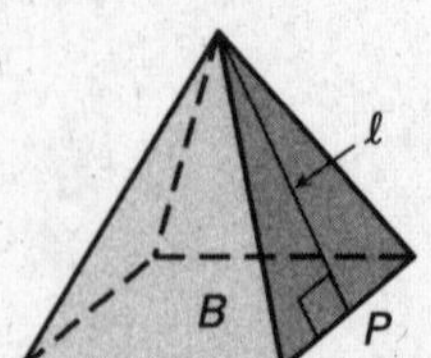

Your Notes

Example 2 *Find the surface area of a pyramid*

Find the surface area of the regular hexagonal pyramid.

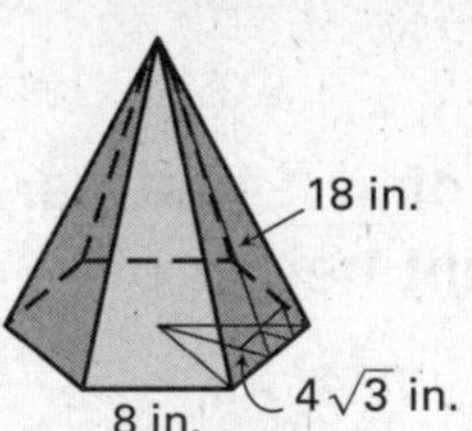

Solution

> Remember, the *apothem* of a polygon is the distance from the center to any side of the polygon.

First, find the area of the base using the formula for the area of a regular polygon, $\frac{1}{2}aP$. The apothem a of the hexagon is ______ inches and the perimeter P is 6 • ____ = ____ inches.

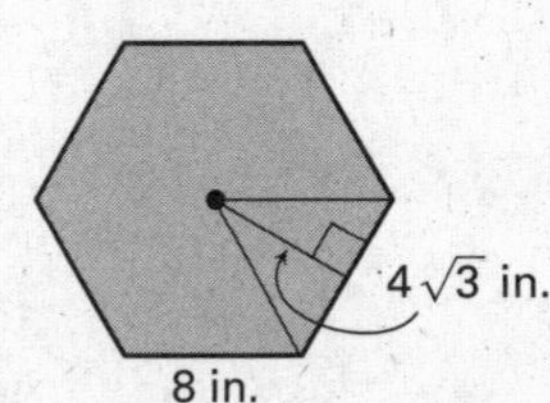

So, the area of the base B is $\frac{1}{2}$(______)(_____) = ______ square inches. Then, find the surface area.

$S = B + \frac{1}{2}P\ell$	Surface area of regular pyramid
= ______ + $\frac{1}{2}$(_____)(_____)	Substitute.
= ______ + _____	Simplify.
≈ ______	Use a calculator.

The surface area of the regular hexagonal pyramid is about ______ square inches.

THEOREM 12.5: SURFACE AREA OF A RIGHT CONE

The surface area S of a right cone is

$S = B + \frac{1}{2}C\ell$ = __________,

where B is area of the base, C is the circumference of the base, r is the radius of the base, and ℓ is the slant height.

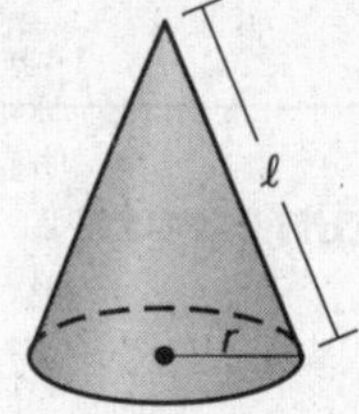

Your Notes

Example 3 ***Find the surface area of a right cone***

Find the surface area of the right cone.

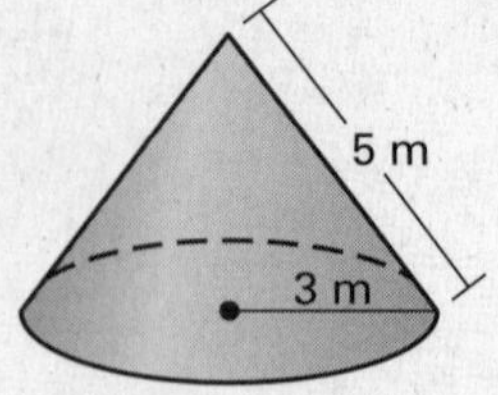

Solution

The base has a radius of ___ meters, and the cone has a slant height of ___ meters.

$S = \pi r^2 + \pi r\ell$	**Surface area of right cone**
$= \pi(\_\_\_)^2 + \pi(\_\_\_)(\_\_\_)$	**Substitute.**
$= \_\_\_\pi + \_\_\_\pi$	**Simplify.**
$= \_\_\_\pi$	**Add.**
$\approx \_\_\_$	**Use a calculator.**

The surface area of the right cone is about ___ square meters.

Checkpoint **Complete the following exercises.**

1. Find (a) the area of each lateral face and (b) the surface area of the regular square pyramid.

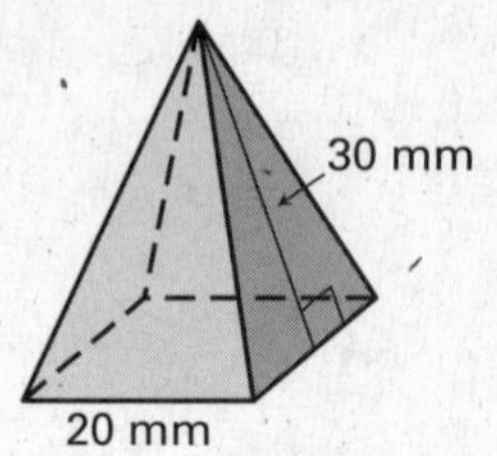

2. Find the surface area of the right cone. Round your answer to two decimal places.

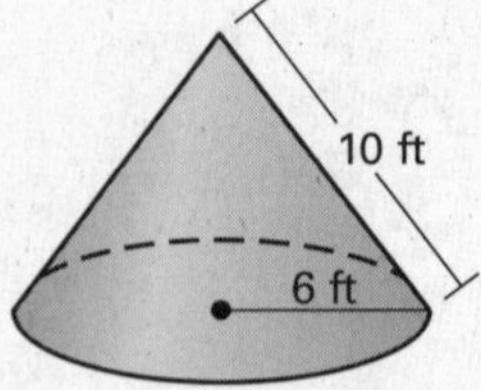

Homework

12.4 Volume of Prisms and Cylinders

Goal • Find volumes of prisms and cylinders.

Your Notes

VOCABULARY

Volume

POSTULATE 27: VOLUME OF A CUBE POSTULATE

The volume of a cube is the cube of the length of its side.

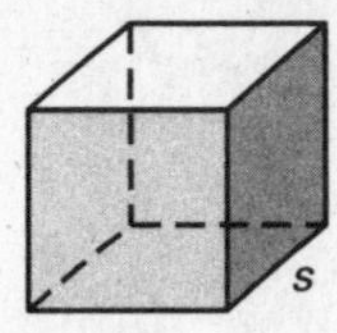

$V =$ ____

POSTULATE 28: VOLUME CONGRUENCE POSTULATE

If two polyhedra are congruent, then ____________ ____________.

POSTULATE 29: VOLUME ADDITION POSTULATE

The volume of a solid is the ______ of the volumes of all its nonoverlapping parts.

THEOREM 12.6: VOLUME OF A PRISM

The volume V of a prism is $V =$ ____, where B is the area of the base and h is the height.

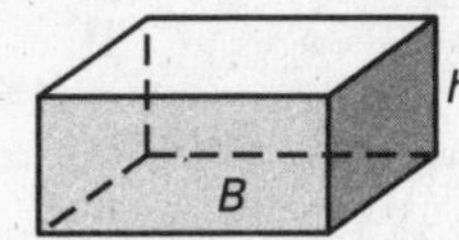

THEOREM 12.7: VOLUME OF A CYLINDER

The volume V of a cylinder is $V = Bh =$ ______, where B is the area of a base, h is the height, and r is the radius of a base.

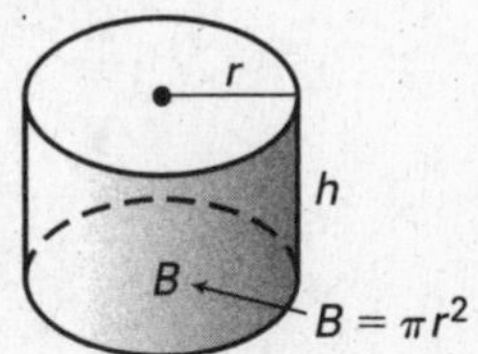

Your Notes

Example 1 *Find volumes of prisms and cylinders*

Find the volume of the solid.

a. Right triangular prism

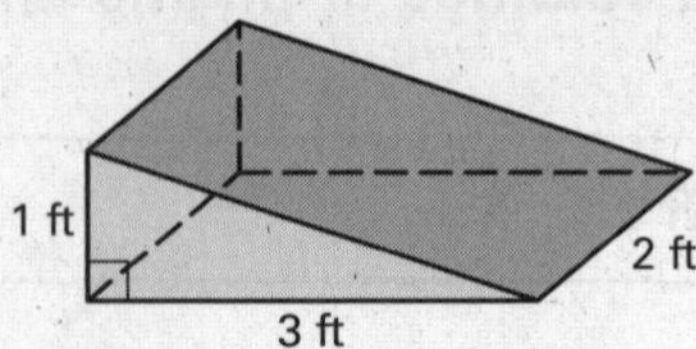

b. Right cylinder

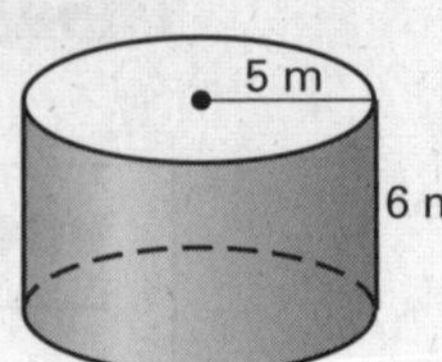

Solution

a. The area of the base is $\frac{1}{2}$(___)(___) = ___ ft^2 and $h = 2$ ft.

$V = Bh =$ ___ • ___ = ___ ft^3

b. The area of the base is $\pi \cdot$ ___^{2}, or ___ π m^2. Use $h = 6$ to find the volume.

$V = Bh =$ ___π(___) = ___$\pi \approx$ ___ m^3

Example 2 *Use volume of a right cylinder*

The volume of the right cylinder shown is 1253 cubic centimeters. Find the value of *x*.

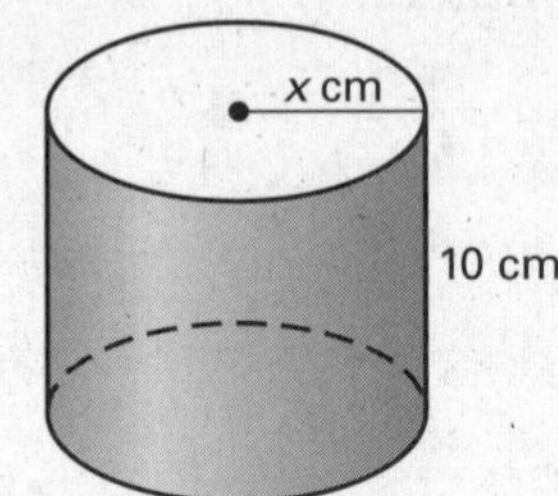

Solution

The area of the base is πx^2 square centimeters.

$V = Bh$	**Formula for volume of a cylinder**
___ $= \pi x^2$(___)	**Substitute.**
___ = ___πx^2	**Rewrite.**
$\frac{\square}{\square\,\pi} = x^2$	**Divide each side by** ___π**.**
___ $\approx x^2$	**Simplify.**
___ $\approx x$	**Find the positive square root.**

The radius of the cylinder is about ___ centimeters.

Your Notes

THEOREM 12.8: CAVALIERI'S PRINCIPLE

If two solids have the same height and the same cross-sectional area at every level, then they have the same ________.

Example 3 ***Find the volume of an oblique cylinder***

Find the volume of the oblique cylinder.

Solution

> Cavalieri's Principle tells you that the volume formulas work for oblique prisms and cylinders.

Cavalieri's Principle allows you to use Theorem 12.7 to find the volume of the oblique cylinder.

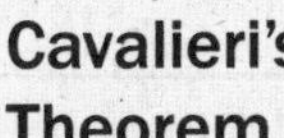

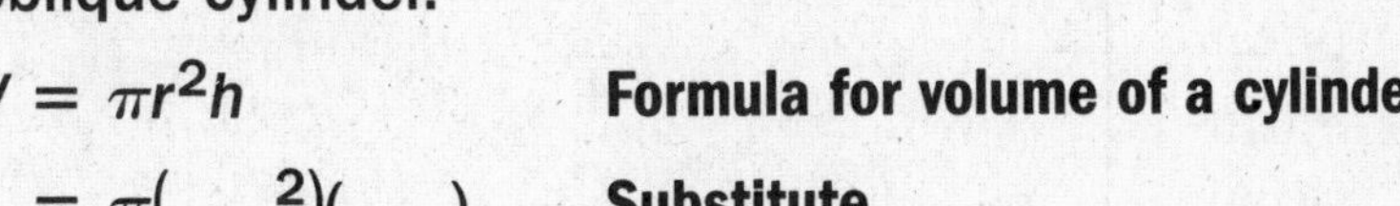

$V = \pi r^2 h$	**Formula for volume of a cylinder**
$= \pi(\_\_\_^2)(\_\_\_)$	**Substitute.**
$= \_\_\_\_\_\pi$	**Simplify.**
$\approx \_\_\_\_\_\_$	**Use a calculator.**

The volume of the oblique cylinder is about ________ in.^{3}

Example 4 ***Find the volume of a composite solid***

Find the volume of the solid.

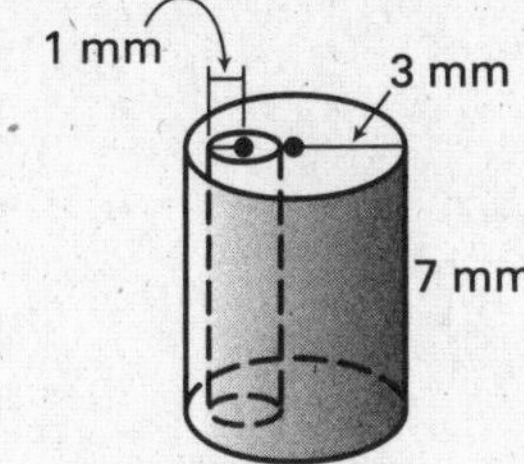

Solution

The area of the base B can be found by subtracting the area of the small circle from the area of the large circle.

B = Area of large circle − Area of small circle

$= \pi(\_\_\_^2) - \pi(\_\_\_^2) = \_\_\_\pi \approx \_\_\_\_\_\_$ mm^2

Use the formula for volume of a cylinder.

$V = Bh$	**Formula for volume of a cylinder**
$= (\_\_\_\_\_\_)(\_\_\_)$	**Substitute.**
$= \_\_\_\_\_\_$	**Use a calculator.**

The volume of the solid is about ________ cubic millimeters.

Your Notes

Checkpoint Complete the following exercises.

In Exercises 1 and 2, find the volume of the solid. Round your answer to two decimal places, if necessary.

1. Right rectangular prism

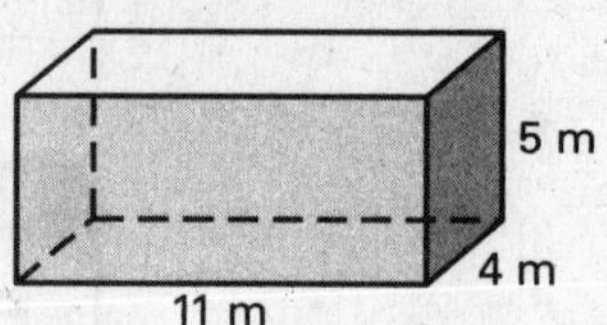

2. Right cylinder

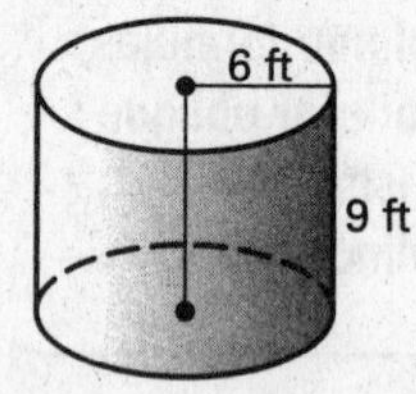

3. The volume of the right cylinder is 200π cubic centimeters. Find the value of x.

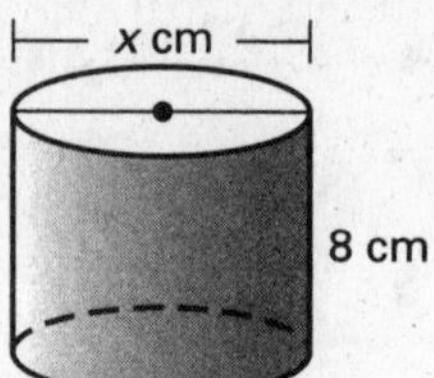

In Exercises 4 and 5, find the volume of the solid. Round your answer to two decimal places.

4. Oblique cylinder

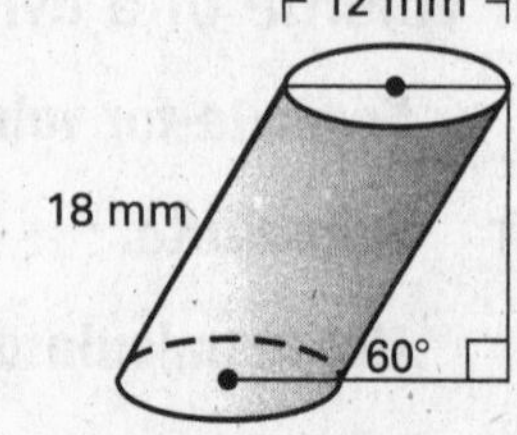

5. Composite solid

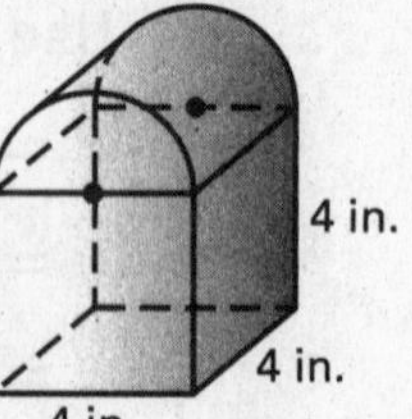

Homework

12.5 Volume of Pyramids and Cones

Goal • Find volumes of pyramids and cones.

Your Notes

THEOREM 12.9: VOLUME OF A PYRAMID

The volume V of a pyramid is

$V = \underline{\qquad\qquad}$,

where B is the area of the base and h is the height.

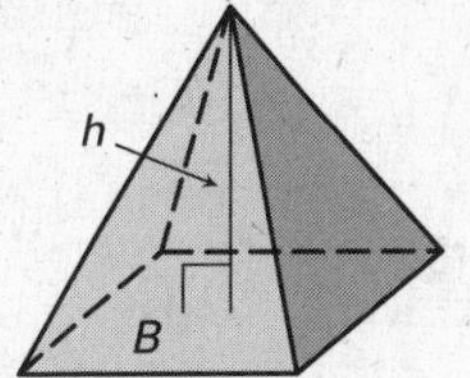

Example 1 ***Find the volume of a pyramid***

Find the volume of the pyramid with the regular base.

Solution

First, find the area of the base using the formula for the area of a regular polygon, $\frac{1}{2}aP$. The apothem a of the hexagon is $\underline{\qquad\quad}$ inches and the perimeter P is $6 \cdot \underline{\qquad} = \underline{\qquad\quad}$ inches.

So, the area of the base B is $\frac{1}{2}(\underline{\qquad\quad})(\underline{\qquad\quad}) = \underline{\qquad\qquad}$ in.^{2}.

Then, find the volume.

> The formula given in Theorem 12.9 applies to both right and oblique pyramids. This follows from Cavalieri's Principle.

$V = \frac{1}{3}Bh$ **Formula for volume of a pyramid**

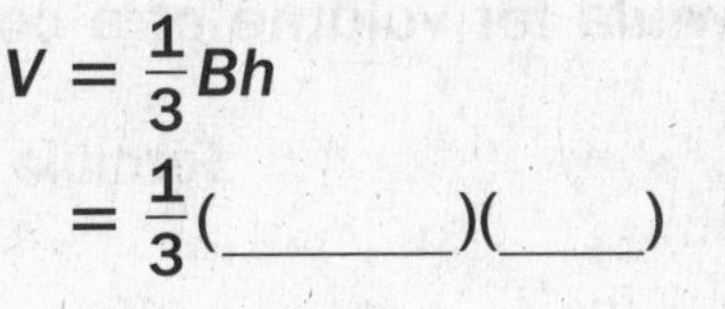

$= \frac{1}{3}(\underline{\qquad\qquad})(\underline{\qquad\quad})$ **Substitute.**

$= \underline{\qquad\qquad}$ **Simplify.**

$\approx \underline{\qquad\qquad}$ **Use a calculator.**

The volume of the pyramid is about $\underline{\qquad\qquad}$ cubic inches.

Your Notes

THEOREM 12.10: VOLUME OF A CONE

The volume V of a cone is

$V = \_\_\_\_\_ = \_\_\_\_\_\_\_$,

where B is area of the base, h is the height, and r is the radius of the base.

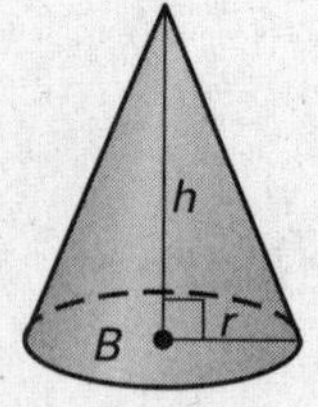

Example 2 ***Find volumes of cones***

Find the volume of the cone.

a. Right cone

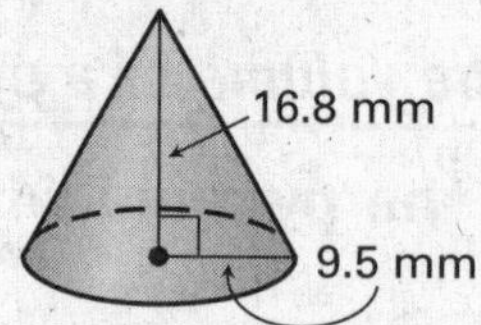

b. Oblique cone

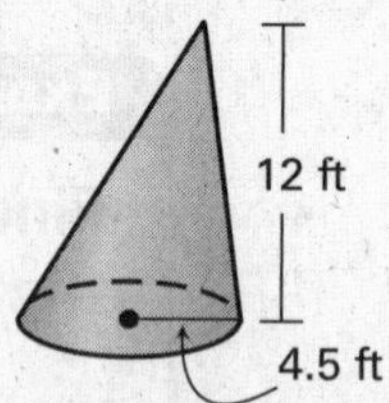

Solution

a. Use the formula for volume of a cone.

$V = \frac{1}{3}\pi r^2 h$ **Formula for volume of a cone**

$= \frac{1}{3}\pi(\_\_\_\_)^2(\_\_\_\_\_)$ **Substitute.**

$= \_\_\_\_\_\_\pi$ **Simplify.**

$\approx \_\_\_\_\_\_$ **Use a calculator.**

The volume of the right cone is about ______ mm^3.

b. Use the formula for volume of a cone.

$V = \frac{1}{3}\pi r^2 h$ **Formula for volume of a cone**

$= \frac{1}{3}\pi(\_\_\_\_)^2(\_\_\_\_)$ **Substitute.**

$= \_\_\_\_\pi$ **Simplify.**

$\approx \_\_\_\_\_\_$ **Use a calculator.**

The volume of the oblique cone is about ______ ft^3.

The formula given in Theorem 12.10 applies to both right and oblique cones. This follows from Cavalieri's Principle.

Your Notes

Example 3 ***Use trigonometry to find the volume of a cone***

Find the volume of the right cone.

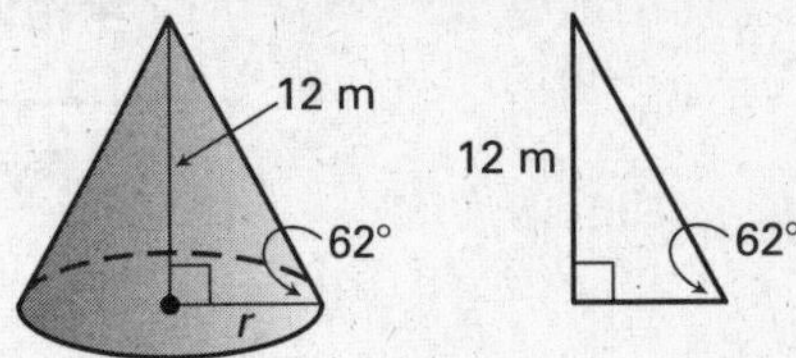

Solution

To find the radius r of the base, use trigonometry.

$\_\_\_\_ \ 62° = \frac{\text{opp.}}{\text{adj.}}$ **Write ratio.**

$\tan 62° = \frac{}{\_\_\_\_}$ **Substitute.**

$r = \frac{\boxed{}}{\boxed{}} \approx \_\_\_\_$ **Solve for *r*.**

Use the formula for the volume of a cone.

$V = \frac{1}{3}(\pi r^2)h \approx \frac{1}{3}\pi(\_\_\_\_)^2(\_\_\_\_) \approx \_\_\_\_$

The volume of the cone is about ______ cubic meters.

Example 4 ***Find volume of a composite solid***

Find the volume of the solid shown. The cone and the cylinder are right.

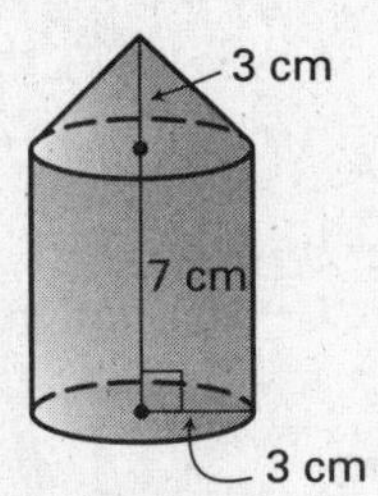

Solution

Volume of solid $=$ Volume of ______ $+$ Volume of ______

$= \pi r^2 h + \frac{1}{3}\pi r^2 h$

$= \pi(\_\_)^2(\_\_) + \frac{1}{3}\pi(\_\_)^2(\_\_)$ **Substitute.**

$= \_\_\pi + \_\_\pi$ **Simplify.**

$= \_\_\_\_$ **Use a calculator.**

The volume of the solid is about ______ cubic centimeters.

Your Notes

Checkpoint Find the volume of the solid. Round your answer to two decimal places.

1. Pyramid with regular base

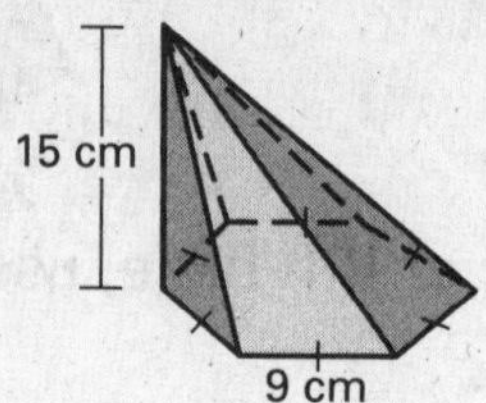

2. Right cone

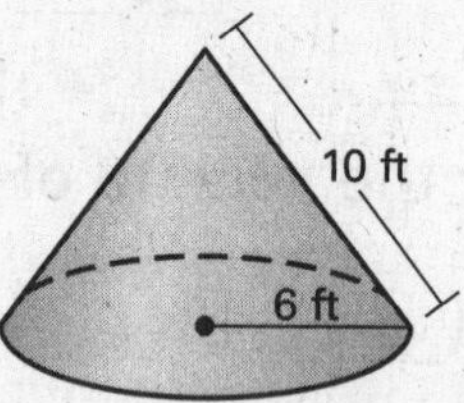

3. Right cone

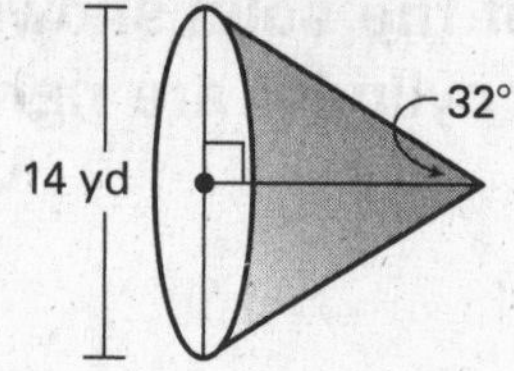

4. Composite solid

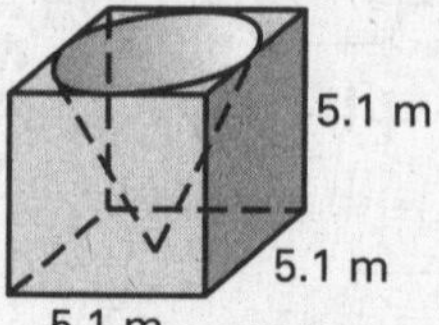

Homework

12.6 Surface Area and Volume of Spheres

Goal • Find surface areas and volumes of spheres.

Your Notes

VOCABULARY

Sphere

Center of a sphere

Radius of a sphere

Chord of a sphere

Diameter of a sphere

Great circle

Hemisphere

THEOREM 12.11: SURFACE AREA OF A SPHERE

The surface area S of a sphere is

$S =$ ______,

where r is the radius of the sphere.

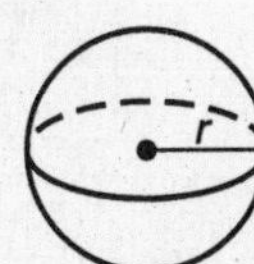

Your Notes

Example 1 *Find the surface area of a sphere*

Find the surface area of the sphere.

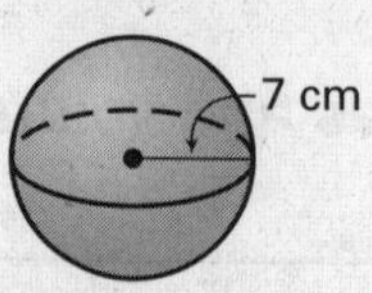

Solution

$S = 4\pi r^2$ — **Formula for surface area of a sphere**

$= 4\pi(\_\_\_)^2$ — **Substitute ___ for *r*.**

$= \_\_\_\_\_\pi$ — **Simplify.**

$\approx \_\_\_\_\_\_$ — **Use a calculator.**

The surface area of the sphere is about ______ cm^2.

Example 2 *Find the diameter of a sphere*

The surface area of a sphere is 110.25π square feet. Find the diameter of the sphere.

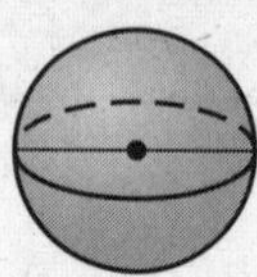

Solution

$S = 4\pi r^2$ — **Formula for surface area of a sphere**

$\_\_\_\_\_\_ = 4\pi r^2$ — **Substitute ______ for *S*.**

$\_\_\_\_\_\_ = r^2$ — **Divide each side by ____.**

$\_\_\_\_ = r$ — **Find the positive square root.**

The diameter of the sphere is

$2r = 2 \cdot \_\_\_\_ = \_\_\_\_$ feet.

Be sure to multiply the value of *r* by 2 to find the diameter.

Your Notes

THEOREM 12.12: VOLUME OF A SPHERE

The volume V of a sphere is

$V =$ ______,

where r is the radius of the sphere.

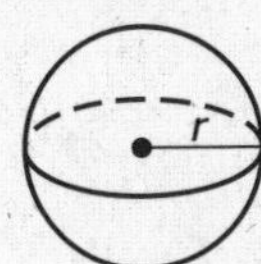

Example 3 ***Find the volume of a sphere***

Find the volume of the sphere.

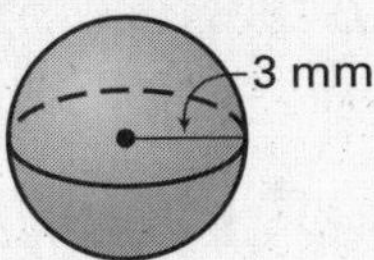

Solution

$V = \frac{4}{3}\pi r^3$	**Formula for volume of a sphere**
$= \frac{4}{3}\pi(\_\_\_)^3$	**Substitute ___ for *r*.**
$\approx$ ______	**Use a calculator.**

The volume of the sphere is about ______ cubic millimeters.

Example 4 ***Find the volume of a composite solid***

Find the volume of the composite solid.

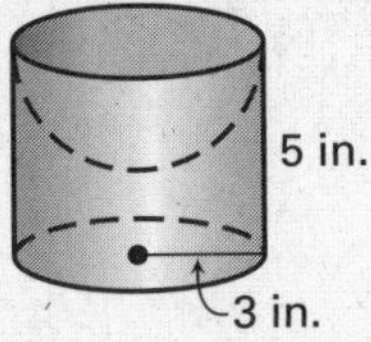

Solution

Volume of solid $=$ Volume of ______ $-$ Volume of ______

$= \pi r^2 h - \frac{1}{2}\left(\frac{4}{3}\pi r^3\right)$	**Volume formulas**
$= \pi(\_\_\_)^2(\_\_\_) - \frac{1}{2}\left(\frac{4}{3}\pi(\_\_\_)^3\right)$	**Substitute.**
$= \_\_\_\_\pi - \_\_\_\_\pi$	**Simplify.**
$\approx$ ______	**Use a calculator.**

The volume of the solid is about ______ cubic inches.

Your Notes

Checkpoint Complete the following exercises.

1. The diameter of a sphere is $\frac{1}{\sqrt{\pi}}$ meter. Find the surface area of the sphere.

2. The surface area of a sphere is 169π square inches. Find the radius of the sphere.

3. The radius of a sphere is 2.4 cm. Find the volume of the sphere. Round your answer to two decimal places.

4. Find the volume of the composite solid. Round your answer to two decimal places.

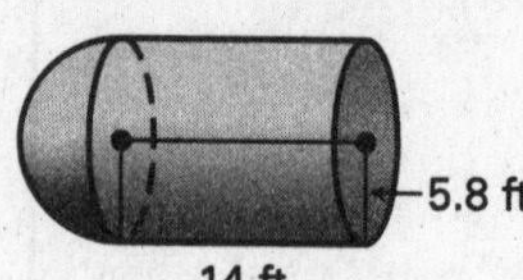

Homework

12.7 Explore Similar Solids

Goal • Use properties of similar solids.

Your Notes

VOCABULARY

Similar solids

Example 1 ***Identify similar solids***

Tell whether the given right rectangular prism is similar to the right rectangular prism shown at the right.

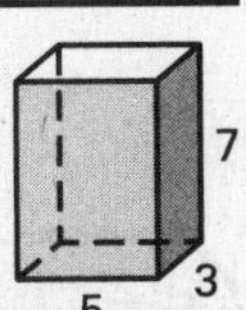

a.

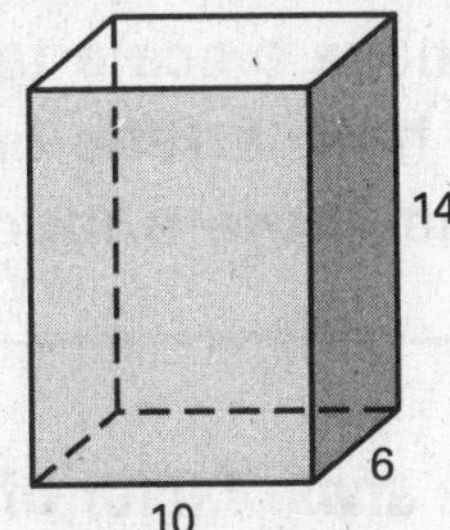

b.

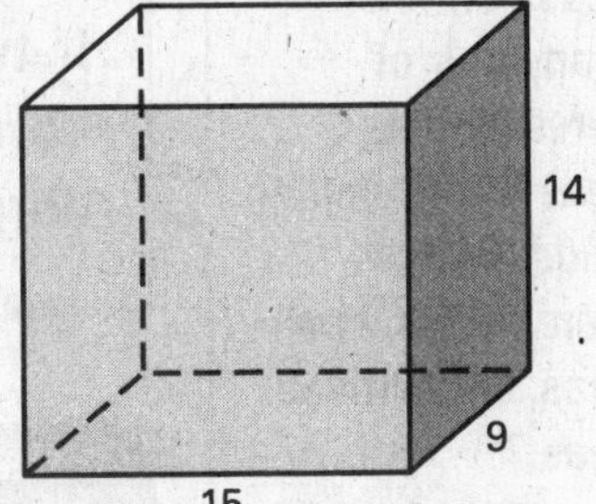

Solution

To compare the ratios of corresponding side lengths, write the ratios as fractions in simplest form.

a. The prisms are similar because the ratios of corresponding linear measures are equal, as shown. The solids have a scale factor of ___ : ___.

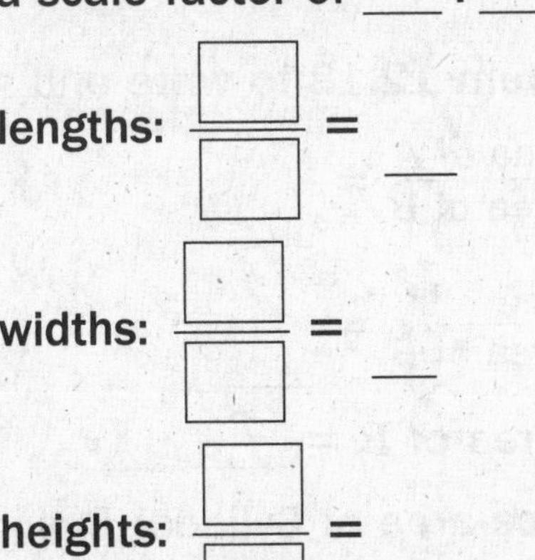

b. The prisms are not similar because the ratios of corresponding linear measures are not equal, as shown.

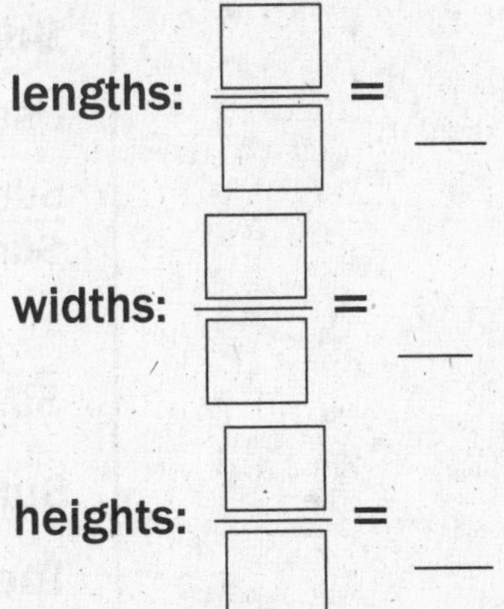

Your Notes

✔ ***Checkpoint*** **Tell whether the pair of solids is similar. *Explain* your reasoning.**

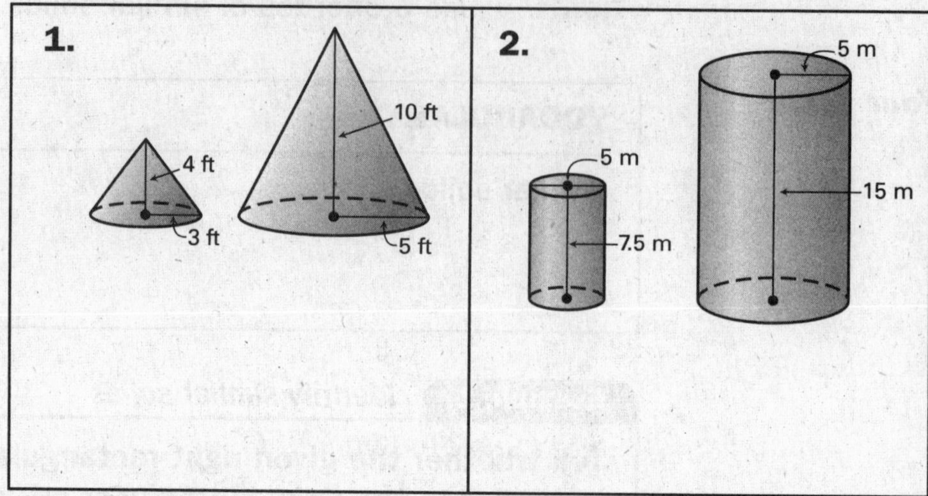

In Theorem 12.13, areas can refer to any pair of corresponding areas in the similar solids, such as lateral areas, base areas, and surface areas.

THEOREM 12.13: SIMILAR SOLIDS THEOREM

If two similar solids have a scale factor of $a:b$, then corresponding areas have a ratio of ____ : ____, and corresponding volumes have a ratio of ____ : ____.

Example 2 ***Use the scale factor of similar solids***

Cylinders *A* and *B* are similar with a scale factor of 2 : 5. Find the surface area and volume of Cylinder *B* given that the surface area of Cylinder *A* is 96π square feet and the volume of Cylinder *A* is 128π cubic feet.

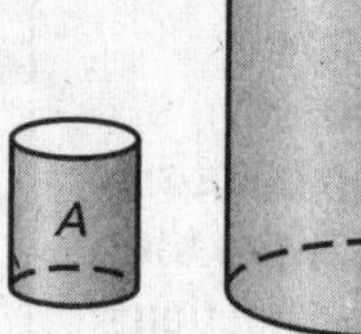

Solution

Use Theorem 12.13 to write and solve two proportions.

$\frac{\text{Surface area of } A}{\text{Surface area of } B} = \_\_\_\_$ $\qquad$ $\frac{\text{Volume of } A}{\text{Volume of } B} = \_\_\_\_$

$\frac{96\pi}{\text{Surface area of } B} = \_\_\_\_$ $\qquad$ $\frac{128\pi}{\text{Volume of } B} = \_\_\_\_$

Surface area of B = ________ $\qquad$ Volume of B = ________

The surface area of Cylinder *B* is ________ square feet, and the volume of Cylinder *B* is ________ cubic feet.

Your Notes

Example 3 ***Find the scale factor***

The two cones are similar. Find the scale factor.

$V = 108\pi$ cm^3

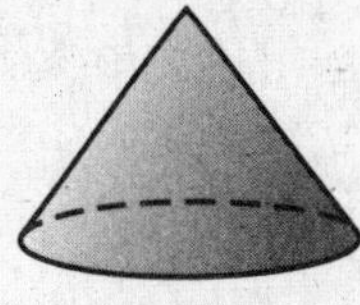

$V = 256\pi$ cm^3

Use Theorem 12.13 to find the ratio of the two volumes.

$\frac{a^3}{b^3} = \frac{108\pi}{256\pi}$ **Write ratio of volumes.**

$\frac{a^3}{b^3} =$ ______ **Simplify.**

$\frac{a}{b} =$ ______ **Find cube roots.**

The two cones have a scale factor of ___ : ___.

Checkpoint Complete the following exercises.

3. Cones A and B are similar with a scale factor of 5 : 2. Find the surface area and volume of Cone B given that the surface area of Cone A is 2356.2 square centimeters and the volume of Cone A is 7450.9 cubic centimeters. Round your answers to two decimal places.

4. The two cylinders are similar. Find the scale factor of Cylinder I to Cylinder II.

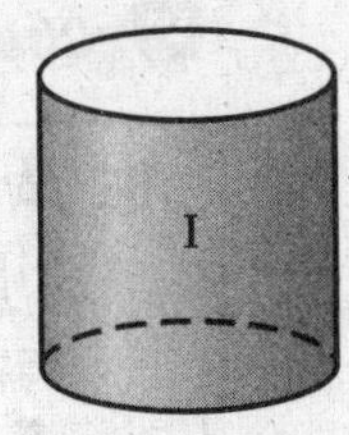

$S = 288$ in.^{2}

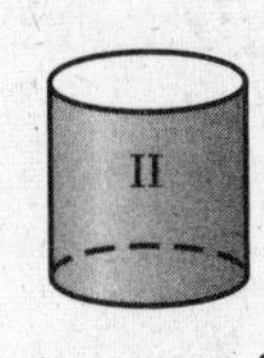

$S = 128$ in.^{2}

Your Notes

Example 4 ***Compare similar solids***

A store sells balls of string in two different sizes. The diameter of the larger ball is 1.5 times the diameter of the smaller ball. If the balls of string cost $4.99 and $1.49, respectively, which ball of string is the better buy?

Step 1 **Compute** the ratio of volumes using the diameters.

$$\frac{\text{Volume of large ball}}{\text{Volume of small ball}} = \frac{\boxed{}^3}{\boxed{}^3} \approx \frac{\boxed{}}{\boxed{}},$$

or about ______ : ___

Step 2 **Find** the ratio of costs.

$$\frac{\text{Price of large ball}}{\text{Price of small ball}} = \frac{\boxed{}}{\boxed{}} \approx \frac{\boxed{}}{\boxed{}},$$

or about ______ : ___

Step 3 **Compare** the ratios in Steps 1 and 2.

If the ratios were the same, neither ball would be a better buy. Comparing the smaller ball to the larger one, the price increase is less than the volume increase. So, you get more string for your dollar if you buy the ______ ball of string.

The ______ ball of string is the better buy.

Checkpoint **Complete the following exercise.**

5. A store sells birdseed in two sizes of cube-shaped blocks. The smaller block measures 3 in. on an edge and sells for $1.99. The larger block measures 5 in. on an edge and sells for $5.99. Which block of birdseed is the better buy?

Homework

Words to Review

Give an example of the vocabulary word.

Polyhedron, face, edge, vertex, base	Regular, convex polyhedron
Platonic solids	Tetrahedron
Cube	Octahedron
Dodecahedron	Icosahedron
Cross section	Prism, lateral faces, lateral edges

Surface area	Lateral area
Net	Right prism
Oblique prism	Cylinder
Right cylinder	Pyramid
Vertex of a pyramid	Regular pyramid

Slant height	Cone
Vertex of a cone	Right cone
Lateral surface	Volume
Sphere, center, radius, chord, diameter	Great circle
Hemisphere	Similar solids

Review your notes and Chapter 12 by using the Chapter Review on pages 857–860 of your textbook.